MIYAKE ISSEY 展：三宅一生の仕事
2016年3月16日（水）— 6月13日（月）
国立新美術館
主催：国立新美術館
共催：公益財団法人 三宅一生デザイン文化財団、株式会社 三宅デザイン事務所、株式会社 イッセイ ミヤケ
協賛：株式会社 資生堂、株式会社 マリ・アート、三井不動産株式会社
協力：Artemide S.p.A.、株式会社 NTTドコモ、キヤノンプロダクションプリンティングシステムズ 株式会社、
セーレン株式会社、株式会社 丹青ディスプレイ、東リ株式会社、株式会社 七彩、吉忠マネキン株式会社

MIYAKE ISSEY EXHIBITION: The Work of Miyake Issey
March 16–June 13, 2016
The National Art Center, Tokyo
Organized by The National Art Center, Tokyo
Co-organized by The Miyake Issey Foundation, Miyake Design Studio, Issey Miyake Inc.
With the sponsorship of Shiseido Co.,Ltd., MARI・ART Co.,Ltd., Mitsui Fudosan Co.,Ltd.
With the cooperation of Artemide S.p.A., NTT DOCOMO, Inc., Canon Production Printing Systems Inc.
SEIREN CO.,LTD., Tansei Display Co.,Ltd., TOLI Corporation, NANASAI CO.,LTD., Yoshichu Mannequin Co.,Ltd.

# MIYAKE ISSEY 展 EXHIBITION

## 三宅一生の仕事
The Work of Miyake Issey

撮影：岩崎寛
Photographed by Hiroshi Iwasaki

求龍堂
KYURYUDO

## 目次

pp.018—035　　_展覧会場 A

pp.036—061　　_展覧会場 B

pp.062—191　　_展覧会場 C

p.006　　青木保　　_「驚きと親しみ」
　　　　国立新美術館長

p.008　　三宅一生　　_「出発、そして次の時代へ」

p.010　　本橋弥生　　_「三宅一生の仕事」
　　　　国立新美術館主任研究員

p.193　　ディディエ・グランバック　　_「はじめて国を越えたデザイナー」
　　　　フランス国立近代美術館友の会会長
　　　　フランス・プレタポルテ連盟名誉会長
　　　　オートクチュール組合名誉会長

p.196　　アンジェロ・フラッカヴェント　　_「未来を見つめる、人間主義、自伝的な……」
　　　　インディペンデント・ファッション評論家、キュレーター

p.203　　ティエン　　_「イッセイ氏のこと」
　　　　クリエイティヴ・ディレクター、フォトグラファー

p.206　　蔡國強　　_「写意的な衣服と情感」
　　　　美術家

p.210　　森山明子　　_「ホップ・ステップ・三宅一生」
　　　　デザイン・ジャーナリスト、武蔵野美術大学教授

p.218　　小林康夫　　_「プリーツ」
　　　　哲学者

p.222　　リー・エデルコート　　_「132 5. ISSEY MIYAKE」の数秘術
　　　　トレンド・フォーキャスター

p.228　　_寄稿者プロフィール
p.230　　_三宅一生 主な活動
p.234　　_作品リスト

## CONTENTS

pp.018—035 —section A

pp.036—061 —section B

pp.062—191 —section C

p.007     Tamotsu Aoki     _SURPRISE AND GOOD FEELING
Director General, The National Art Center, Tokyo

p.009     Issey Miyake     _DEPARTURE… TOWARD A NEW ERA

p.014     Yayoi Motohashi     _THE WORK OF MIYAKE ISSEY
Curator, The National Art Center, Tokyo

p.195     Didier Grumbach     _THE FIRST INTERNATIONAL FASHION DESIGNER
President of the Société des Amis du Musée national d'Art Moderne Centre Pompidou
Honorary President of Fédération Française de la Couture, Chambre Syndicale de la Haute Couture

p.200     Angelo Flaccavento     _FUTURISM, HUMANISM, AUTOBIOGRAPHY
Independent Fashion Critic, Curator

p.203     TYEN     _ISSEY BY TYEN
Creative Director, Photographer

p.208     Cai Guo-Qiang     _FREEHAND CLOTHING AND AFFECTION
Artist

p.214     Akiko Moriyama     _HOP-STEP-JUMPING ISSEY MIYAKE
Design Journalist
Professor at Musashino Art University

p.220     Yasuo Kobayashi     _PLEATS
Philosopher

p.226     Lidewij Edelkoort     _THE NUMEROLOGY OF 132 5. ISSEY MIYAKE
Trend Forecaster

p.229     _PROFILES OF CONTRIBUTING AUTHORS

p.232     _MIYAKE ISSEY SELECTED CHRONOLOGY

p.234     _LIST OF WORKS

## 驚きと親しみ

青木 保　国立新美術館長

「MIYAKE ISSEY展：三宅一生の仕事」の開催を心から嬉しく名誉に感じています。国立新美術館として開館以来の念願でした。

　三宅さんといえば、私にとってはまさに驚きと親しみの存在です。1986年の秋のこと、北インドのジョードプールで大掛かりなシンポジウムがあり、招待されて1週間ほど滞在したことがあります。そのある夜、旧王城で晩餐会があるというので出かけると、20人ほどの参加者の中に素敵なマントを着ている背の高いインド人がいたのです。思わず近寄って、このマントどこで手に入れたのか、と訊くと、にやりと笑って、昨日パリから戻ったばかり、これはパリで、「ISSEY MIYAKE」というではありませんか。おしゃれなインド人、デリーの大学の教授だったかと思いますが、驚くと同時に急に親しみがわいてきて、食事の間中話が弾みました。新世紀が明けたころ、春節の時期の香港にいたことがあります。中国正月ですが、昼ごろホテルのラウンジに行くと、地元の若者たちが大勢いてテーブルを占拠していました。みんなおめかしをしていて、これが「ISSEY MIYAKE」を身に着けている。驚きそして親しみを覚えたのです。パリやニューヨークでなら驚かないのですが、北インドと香港、新鮮な感動でいまでも鮮やかに想い出します。

　実は素敵なマントは求めそこないましたが、いま遅ればせながら、「HOMME PLISSÉ ISSEY MIYAKE」(オム プリッセ)のジャケットを着て、これが着心地もすばらしく、おしゃれな感覚に身を包まれたようで、しかも楽しい。

　三宅さんに「ジーンズやTシャツのように多くの人が自由に着られる服をつくりたい」という言葉がありますが、これは本当にすばらしいことだと思います。日本の「ものづくり」の伝統を継承し、「服づくり」、三宅さんのお仕事に接していつも驚きを覚えると同時に親しみを感じるのは、その「日常の哲学」が基盤に確固として存在するからなのでしょうか。それにしても、このような展覧会が開催できるとは。三宅一生さん、公益財団法人 三宅一生デザイン文化財団、株式会社 三宅デザイン事務所、株式会社 イッセイ ミヤケの皆様のご指導とご協力に心から感謝いたします。

　この展覧会をきっかけに、三宅一生さんのさらなる驚きと親しみの作品にこれまで以上に接する機会が増えることを期待します。

# SURPRISE AND GOOD FEELING

**Dr. Tamotsu Aoki**  Director General, The National Art Center, Tokyo

It is with a feeling of great honor and joy that The National Art Center, Tokyo presents *MIYAKE ISSEY EXHIBITION: The Work of Miyake Issey*. This is a project that we have pursued with great intensity ever since the Center opened in 2007.

　Mr. Issey Miyake has long been an invaluable source of surprise and good feeling for me. In the autumn of 1986 I was invited to a large symposium in Jodhpur, northern India, and stayed there for a week. One evening, I attended an official dinner at what once had been a royal palace. Among some twenty guests I took notice of a tall Indian wearing an attractive coat. I could not help but approach him and ask where he had gotten the coat. He answered, grinning, "In Paris, it's an ISSEY MIYAKE. I just returned yesterday." Right away, and feeling a bit surprised, I saw something charming in this Indian gentleman with good taste, and who, I believe, was a university professor in Delhi. We spent the rest of the evening in conversation together, and I had a feeling of deep intimacy with him.

　Years later, around the turn of the century I happened to be in Hong Kong. During the celebrations of the Chinese New Year, I happened to be in the lounge of a hotel; I found groups of Chinese youth occupying the many tables — all of them, it seemed, in their best outfits, and most of those by ISSEY MIYAKE! Surprise and a sense of feeling good struck me once again. My reaction would probably have been different had I been in New York or Paris, but in northern India and Hong Kong — at that time these were fresh sensations and I still recall those occasions vividly.

　I confess that I failed to buy that nice coat for myself, but now, I am happy (though belatedly) to say, I am wearing an HOMME PLISSÉ ISSEY MIYAKE jacket; it's really a good feeling.

　Mr. Miyake once said that his wish was to make "clothes like t-shirts and jeans, clothes anyone would feel easy in." I find this a truly wonderful statement. Mr. Miyake works in the Japanese tradition of *mono-zukuri* (making things) while creating clothing from out of his own inspiration. Whenever I come across his work, I have surprise and good feeling. Why? Because, at the base of his work is this philosophy of "everyday life."

　Dreams come true. It's really fantastic. I would like to express our gratitude for the kind cooperation of Mr. Issey Miyake and the staffs of The Miyake Issey Foundation, Miyake Design Studio, and Issey Miyake Inc..

## 出発、そして次の時代へ

三宅一生

　出発にはいつも期待と不安がある。美術大学を卒業し、パリへと旅立った。オートクチュールを学び、五月革命が起こった。そのパリで、モードは継続のうちにすでに完成されていて、自分がやることはそこにはないと思った。身体、言語、国籍のハンディも感じた。けれど、デザインとは発見なのだから、一般の人たちのために自分ができることを見つけていこうとものづくりを始めた。

　その途上で、たくさんのすばらしい人たちとの出会いがあった。イサム・ノグチさん、アーヴィング・ペンさん、いつも身近で仕事を見て力をくれた田中一光さん……。他にも、数えきれないたくさんの人たちと出会い、感動を受けてきた。

　いま思うのは、日本に生まれて服づくりを志したのは、実はハンディではなかったのだということ。仕事をなかなか理解してもらえず辛いこともあったが、人と違うということを逆にバネにし、努力し、克服する。そうすれば、思いがけない出会いがあり、ものづくりをしながら生きていける。そう、若い人たちへ伝えたい。日本では文化が語られることがあまりない。難しいものと思われている。服のデザインは着る人をワクワクさせるだけでなく、着る人を取り巻く社会もよくできると信じている。

　この展覧会はデザイン文化を近未来に伝えようと、さまざまな分野の方々と力を合わせて企画した。デザインは生き物であって、常に追い求め行動を起こさないと人を惹きつけることも次の時代に引き継ぐこともできない。引き継ぐ先に、デザインミュージアムがあればと願う。この二十年来、安藤忠雄さんや青柳正規さんはじめ、共鳴してくれるたくさんの人々とデザインミュージアムの設立を呼びかけているのは、人づくりと、世界各都市と連携するためだ。今回の出品作にはバルセロナ五輪にソ連崩壊後、独立国として初参加したリトアニア選手団の公式ユニフォーム以来の、未発表作を含む各国ユニフォームがある。躍動するアスリートには未来への希望の架け橋となってほしい。

　日々発想し、それまでにないものをつくり、新しい現実をつくる。making THINK、making THINGS、making REALITY。これらが私の仕事の里程標（りていひょう）であることに変わりはない。

# DEPARTURE… TOWARD A NEW ERA

## Issey Miyake

Departures are often accompanied by certain expectations and anxieties. I left Tokyo for Paris after graduating from an art university. I studied fashion, until after the May Revolution of 1968. Haute couture had already reached a certain peak in its long history and tradition, and so I concluded that there was nothing for me to do there. I also felt that, as a Japanese, I had certain handicaps in terms of physique, language and nationality. Nevertheless I said to myself, "designing is an act of discovery," and so I tried to find out what I could discover and create that would touch the lives of the many and not just those of the few. I set out to make things, or *mono-zukuri*.

Since that time, I have encountered many wonderful people, along my path. Isamu Noguchi, Irving Penn, Ikko Tanaka, who watched my progress and gave me energy. But they were but a few. There have been innumerable others who have moved me deeply.

As I look back now, it was not such a "handicap" to have been born in Japan and yet aspire to design clothing. There were certainly tough times when my work was barely understood, but I tried to take advantage of my difference to get past the roadblocks that I encountered. This in fact led to many chance encounters with a wide variety of people. And, I have managed to survive by making things. I hope that today's youth will understand what I mean here. We Japanese rarely allow ourselves to talk about our culture. This sort of topic is considered to be too difficult. But I believe that clothing design is a tool that not only excites its wearers but can also improve the society in which they dwell.

This exhibition was planned together with specialists from diverse variety of fields as an opportunity to pass along the culture of design to the next generation. Designing is like a living organism in that it pursues what matters for its well-being and continuity. I have hoped for some time now that we can create a dedicated museum, that is, a design museum. Together with architect Tadao Ando, art historian Masanori Aoyagi, and many other like-minded people, I have worked for over 20 years toward the establishment of a design museum in Japan. Such a site would serve both to nurture young designers as well as to serve as Japan's vehicle through which to communicate with people in major cities around the world. For example, in the current exhibition the uniforms of athletes from a variety of countries are shown. Several are being shown here for the first time. This "uniform project" started in 1992 when the Lithuanian team participated in the Olympics in Barcelona for the first time as an independent country after collapse of the Soviet Union. I see athletes as figures who cross bridges of hope and connect us all to the future.

In my daily work I try to make things that are completely new and different, which in turn inform our new realities. My work's touchstone phrases are: Making Think, Making Things and Making Reality.

# 三宅一生の仕事

本橋弥生 　国立新美術館主任研究員

　未知なもの、新しいもの、胸が躍りだすほど楽しく、着心地の良い服を生み出すデザイナー、三宅一生。「一枚の布」の追求によって生み出された、着る人誰からも受け入れられ、幸せな気持ちにさせる魔法のような服に、私たちはいつも驚かされ続けてきた。それは、人々の日常生活を快適にし、ワクワクする気持ちや躍動感を与えるだけでなく、年齢や国籍、性別を問わず、着る人を輝かせてきた。

　パリやニューヨークのみならず、インドや中近東、アジア、アフリカに至るまで、服に無関心な人でさえその名を知っている、そのようなデザイナーは他にはいないだろう。三宅一生はこれまでになかった新しい衣服を次々と「発明」し、それによって、私たちの装いを確実に進化させてきた。それは、「ウォークマン」やスマートフォンなど私たちの生活を向上させた発明品に匹敵する。着る喜びを感じながら、日常生活を快適に営むことを可能にする服。着ることにより、むしろ身体が解放され、自由を享受することのできる服。折りたたまれているときのたたずまいの美しさ。身体が包まれたときのこの上ない幸福感——私たち自身が生きる彫刻(アート)に変身し、自分の新たな力が引き出される驚き。それは、パワードスーツを着用し、万能の力を得てヒーローになったような高揚感にも似ているのかもしれない。特にプリーツに至っては、パーティー会場で見かけないことはないほど、世界中に浸透している。三宅一生の服は、日常生活を豊かにするものであると同時に、公式の場でフォーマルとしても着られている、従来の「衣服」の概念を超えたものなのだ。

　「MIYAKE ISSEY展：三宅一生の仕事」は世界的デザイナー、三宅一生の服づくりに対する考え方やデザインへのアプローチについて、初期から現在進行形のプロジェクトまでを通して紹介する初めての展覧会である。

　戦後の高度経済成長期、既成の制度に異議を唱えた若者たちによって新しい価値観が提示され、社会が振り子のように大きく揺れ動いていた時代——1964年の東京オリンピック開催後、人々がより良い生活を目指して社会に熱気が満ちていた1970年、三宅一生は東京にデザイン事務所を立ち上げた。それは日本万国博覧会（大阪万博）が開催され、ウーマン・リブ運動が盛んであった年でもある。以来、46年間にわたり、三宅一生は革新的な服づくりを続けている。

　本展はまた、国立新美術館における初めてのデザイナーの個展であり、2007年の開館前からの構想が約10年かけて結実した一大プロジェクトでもある。三宅一生氏ご本人および三宅デザイン事務所、三宅一生デザイン文化財団の多大なご協力や並々ならぬ熱意と惜しみないご尽力があったからこそ、本展の

開催が可能となった。

　さらに言えば、三宅一生の仕事を紹介する展覧会を日本で構成し、開催することは日本の美術館にとっても大変重要なことである。1988年にパリ装飾美術館で開催された「ISSEY MIYAKE A-ŪN」展や1998年にカルティエ現代美術財団（パリ）からニューヨーク、東京へ巡回した「ISSEY MIYAKE MAKING THINGS」展（2000年に東京都現代美術館で「三宅一生展 ISSEY MIYAKE Making Things」として開催）など、三宅の仕事を紹介する大きな展覧会は海外で構成されることが多かった。本展は、日本で企画構成され日本から発信する初めての大規模な「三宅一生展」である。

　そして何より、本展は三宅一生から私たちへの、そして未来の若者たちへの愛のこめられた贈物なのだと思う。幸せに生きるために、今、私たちは何をすべきなのか——本展の主役はまぎれもなく三宅一生であると同時に、その仕事を見て考える私たちでもあるのだ。

＊

　展覧会では、三宅一生の仕事を大きく3つに分けて紹介する。

　戦後に洋装が一般化した日本において、三宅は衣服デザイナーという新しい道を切り拓いてきた先駆者である。1960年、多摩美術大学在学中であった三宅は、日本での世界デザイン会議の開催を知り、衣服デザインが含まれないことに疑問を持ち質問状を送っている[※1]。大学を卒業後、1964年に海外渡航が自由化されたことに伴い翌1965年にはパリに渡り、オートクチュール（高級仕立服）の学校へ留学。ギィ・ラロッシュやジヴァンシィのメゾンで働き、1969年まで計4年間滞仏した。1968年に目撃した五月革命は大きな転機となる。若者たちによる既存の体制に反対する抗議運動の熱気は、三宅を既製服（プレタポルテ）へと方向づけた。その時の心境を、三宅はこう語っている。「僕が作りたいのは、限られたお金持ちに向けた服ではない。ジーンズやTシャツのように多くの人に身近で、洗えて、使いやすいものと確信しました。」[※2] その後、ニューヨークを経て、一旦、日本へ帰国。そして1970年、三宅デザイン事務所を東京に立ち上げた。

◎ セクション［A］

　既成の価値観が崩され、女性が社会に進出しジーンズやパンツ（パンタロン）を当然のごとく履くようになった70年代に、装いは生き方の表明であり、自己表現でもあることを三宅は女性たちに伝えている。当時の三宅の女神（ミューズ）が、女性参政権運動を主導していた政治家の市川房枝であったように、三宅は信念を持って社会に出て働く女性に美を見出した。

　三宅の服づくりには、活動当初から現在に至るまで一貫している特徴が大きく3つある。まず、三宅一生の代名詞でもある「一枚の布」と身体の間（ま）の追求。身体の輪郭に沿って布を裁断縫製する従来の洋服のつくり方とは異なり、一枚の布をできるだけそのままに、いかにして身体の動きに呼応する衣服をつくるのかという問いを探求してきた。そして、三宅の自由な発想と刺し子やプリーツなど古来から伝わる服づくりの技法と最先端の技術の融合。これこそが三宅の服づくりを進化させてきた。最後に、独自の素材の開発

と専門家とのコラボレーション。活動初期からの繊維メーカーとの素材開発やテキスタイル・デザイナー、様々な分野の専門家、アーティストとの協働が、三宅の比類ない活動を支えてきた。

《タトゥ》(1970年/1971春夏 p.22)は、ニューヨークで開催した最初の単独ショウで発表されたジャンプスーツである。ジミ・ヘンドリックスとジャニス・ジョプリンへのオマージュが刺青の技法で描かれたプリントは皆川魔鬼子の手によるもので、三宅が「ISSEY MIYAKE」のコレクションを率いた1999年まで、皆川がテキスタイル・ディレクターを務めた。このプリントは単なる装飾ではない。皮膚をカンヴァスに見立て精神世界を表現する刺青同様、ここには三宅の個人的なメッセージがこめられている。皮膚と一体化し身体の動きを束縛することのないこのボディウエアは、刺青というモティーフも相まって、まさに衣服が「第二の皮膚」であることを強く意識させる。

またこの時代から、刺し子や丹前など庶民の生活の中で継承されてきた衣服や手仕事を新しい技術と融合させ、三宅独自の作品世界をつくり出してきた。西洋文化崇拝の風潮が強かった当時の日本では、地方の農村に伝わる作業着に美を見出し取り入れることは、まさに革新的であった。

◎ セクション［Ｂ］

身体の動きとフォルムをさらに突き詰めた三宅は、1980年代には「ボディ」と呼ばれる胴体部を覆うシリーズの服を展開した。繊維強化プラスティックや合成樹脂、ラタンなど従来の衣服には用いられてこなかった硬い素材による服である。型に流し込んでつくるため大量生産の可能な《プラスティック・ボディ》(1980年/1980秋冬 pp.41-45)やアメリカの美術雑誌『ARTFORUM』(1982年2月号)の表紙を初めて服が飾った《ラタン・ボディ》(1981年/1982春夏 pp.46-49)など、彫刻のような衣服は、三宅のあくなき探求心とそれを可能にするテクノロジーや伝統技術との融合から生み出された。

◎ セクション［Ｃ］

あらゆる素材から服をつくる三宅は、多様な服を生み出してきたが、その中のひとつに《コロンブ》(1990年/1991春夏 pp.68-69)がある。モノフィラメントのポリエステルの布地をヒートカットで裁断し、布に取り付けられたスナップを留めることによって「一枚の布」から生み出されるドレス——事実上、鋏(ハサミ)や針、糸が一切使われていない。

1989年春夏コレクション(1988年発表)では初めて「製品プリーツ」が登場した。生地を服の形に裁断縫製してから熱を加えてプリーツ加工を施すという独自の発想に基づく画期的な方法により、服づくりの概念を根本から覆す全く新しい衣服が開発されたのである。布に(時にはさらに折りを加え)プリーツを施すことによって生み出される生命力に満ちた立体的な美しいフォルム——身体の動きに合わせ空気を孕み、美しく軽やかに躍動的な表情を見せる三宅のプリーツは、1991年にはウィリアム・フォーサイス率いるフランクフルト・バレエ団のためのニット素材によるプリーツへと進化する。さらに素材や技術に改良が加え

られ1993年には「PLEATS PLEASE ISSEY MIYAKE」(プリーツ プリーズ)が誕生した。熱処理が可能なポリエステルの布地を用いて、三宅が成し遂げたこと——それは、人類が古代から受け継いできた、布を身体に寄り添わせる最古の方法のひとつである襞(ひだ)を、美的な要素だけでなく手入れが簡単で着心地の良い実用性も備えた衣服に変貌させたことである。

その後、藤原大と共に開発した「A-POC」(エイ・ポック)(1998年〜)もプリーツのさらなる進化形である。服のデザインがプログラミングされた編み機から服やバッグ、靴下などが編みこまれた筒状のニットが編み出される——これは、従来の服づくりの発想を根本から覆し、さらなる可能性を押し広げた。

現在進行形の最新プロジェクト「132 5. ISSEY MIYAKE」(2010年〜)は、ペットボトルなどポリエステルの再生繊維を素材に、一枚の布を複雑な折り構造によって立体化した衣服である。その複雑な工学アルゴリズムの幾何学的形態は、スカートにもジャケットにも、バッグにもランプシェードにもなる驚くべきデザイン性とサスティナビリティを持ち合わせている。

半世紀にわたり、私たちを刺激し、私たちのライフスタイルまでをも軽やかで楽しいものへと変化させてきた三宅一生。本展は、三宅一生が現在を生きる私たちへ、デザインすること、ひいては生きることの喜びを伝えるものであり、未来の若者たちへの愛に溢れたメッセージなのだと思う。

※1:「モードから都市計画を結ぶ／世界デザイン会議」『装苑』1960年5月号163頁に三宅が抗議文を委員長であった建築家・坂倉準三に郵送し、それが事務局の機関紙に発表され委員総会でも議論されたことが記載されている。最終的に同会議において服飾デザインもテーマとして取り上げられた。
※2:小坂佳子、谷本陽子「被爆体験 今だから語る 戦後70年」『読売新聞』2015年12月6日朝刊1、7面

# THE WORK OF MIYAKE ISSEY

**Yayoi Motohashi**  Curator, The National Art Center, Tokyo

Things unknown, things new and things exhilaratingly pleasurable—not to mention being quite comfortable to wear—this is what Issey Miyake creates. His work is born out of his fundamental belief in "a piece of cloth"; a belief that is accepted by anyone who happily wears a piece of clothing designed by Issey Miyake. Magical clothing, which has constantly surprised us, that has made our everyday lives pleasant, our inner selves excited, as well as adding a touch of brilliant flair to the person wearing it, regardless of her or his nationality, age or gender.

His name is known to people in Paris and in New York, certainly, but also in India, the Far and the Middle East, South East Asia and on to Africa, and even among those not particularly interested in clothes – no other designer in the world enjoys such borderless popularity. Issey Miyake has "invented" unprecedented styles of clothing, one after another, and thanks to these, our dress life has undergone a constant evolution. The result is comparable to the effects that such products as the *Walkman* and the smart phone have had upon our lives. His clothing allows us to genuinely rejoice in what we wear for the comfort of everyday life. It liberates the body and we enjoy its freedom. There is beauty when it is still and folded; and infinite happiness when we are wrapped in it. It transforms us into living art, while we ourselves are surprised by how it crystalizes a new kind of power from within our own bodies—like wearing "super gear" feeling like a hero. The pleated pieces, in particular, are so omnipresent that one inevitably finds someone wearing them at almost every party one attends. Whether in everyday life or the most formal occasion, Issey Miyake-designed clothes transcend any older concept of "clothing."

*MIYAKE ISSEY EXHIBITION: The Work of Miyake Issey* is the first full-scale exhibition—from his earliest activities to current projects—to showcase the many varied ideas concerning clothes-making and designing of the globally important designer Issey Miyake.

During the post-war period of high-rate economic growth, and following the 1964 Tokyo Olympics, Japanese society was boiling with hopes for a better life; society swayed dramatically like a pendulum, while counter-cultural youth sought a new set of values, and the women's liberation movement had come to take root here. It was in this context, that in 1970 the Miyake Design Studio (MDS) was launched in Tokyo. (In the same year, Expo'70 was held in Osaka, a manifesto of Japan's rapid economic growth.) During the 46 years since then, Issey Miyake has been making innovative clothing with an unwavering passion.

It should also be mentioned that this is the first ever solo exhibition organized by the National Art Center, Tokyo (NACT) exclusively dedicated to a designer, and, as such, it is truly a major project for us. In fact, it represents the fruit of a decade's effort since it was first conceived—that is, even before NACT opened in 2007. Realization of the exhibition has been made possible thanks to the generous cooperation, rare passion and dedicated efforts of Mr. Issey Miyake himself, Miyake Design Studio and The Miyake Issey Foundation.

Further, that this exhibition has been curated in Japan and is being presented to the world for the first time is of the utmost importance for Japanese art centers and museums as a whole. Until now, major exhibitions of Miyake's work have been conceived abroad more often than in Japan — to name just two: *ISSEY MIYAKE A-ŪN* at the Musée des Arts Décoratifs in Paris, 1988; *ISSEY MIYAKE MAKING THINGS,* at the Fondation Cartier pour l'art contemporain, again in Paris, 1998, and that subsequently toured to New York and Tokyo where it was shown at the Museum of Contemporary Art Tokyo, in 2000. The current exhibition is the first major Issey Miyake show fully conceived from the beginning in Japan and to subsequently tour the world.

Above all, one is inclined to believe it is a gift, filled with love, from Issey Miyake to us, and, in particular, to the young people of today and to those to come. What can we do — now — if we hope to live with strength and happiness? The protagonist of this show is obviously Issey Miyake, but, at the same time, we too are at the center — minds and spirits invited to speculate and to be inspired by this work.

✳

The works is being shown in three sections.

In post-war Japan, as Western clothing became more generally worn than traditional Japanese clothing, Miyake was a forerunner in the role of clothing designer. In 1960, while still a student at Tama Art University, he learned that the World Design Conference would be held in Japan, but that any discussion of fashion design was not on the agenda. He sent an open letter of protest to the Conference organizer.[*1] Restrictions on overseas travel were lifted for the Japanese in 1964. So, following his graduation, Miyake arrived in Paris in 1965, enrolled in a school for haute couture ; he also worked at the Guy Laroche and Givenchy maisons. He stayed in Paris for four years, including witnessing the 1968 May Revolution, which inspired him to make a drastic change. Influenced by the heat of youth and protest, he redirected himself towards ready-to-wear clothing *prêt-à-porter*. Decades later, he recalled his thinking then: "I was determined. I wanted to make clothes not for a limited group of rich people, but to make things like jeans and t-shirts, clothes that everyone knows and can easily wash and wear."[*2]

He first moved to New York, then subsequently returned home to Japan, where he launched the Miyake Design Studio in Tokyo in 1970.

◎ section–A

During the 1970's, as women became more visibly active in society, they also matter-of-factly came to wear jeans and pants, Miyake declared that their appearance and clothing was a manifesto of their own self-expression, of the way they chose to live their lives. His muse then was Fusae Ichikawa, a politician who led the women's suffrage movement, but he was equally inspired by the beauty of working women who determinedly chose to enter society at large.

There are three major characteristics that were coherent from early in his career and up to this point. First, examining the space between the body and "a piece of cloth", this idiosyncratic concept of his. His approach was different from the conventional one; that is, instead of cutting material by adapting it to the body's shape, he wanted to make clothing that maintained the cloth as it initially is, while at the same time allowing the clothes to respond to the body's movements. His unbounded imagination merged with his interests in time-honored clothes-making skills such as pleats and *sashiko* (quilting), combined with state-of-the-art technologies. All of these factors have continued to be behind the evolution of Miyake's way of clothes making. The last part of this section is dedicated to his development of original materials, and his collaborations with highly specialized experts. Since early on, Miyake's unique activities have been supported by his collaboration with textile manufacturers for new materials development, as well as by those with textile designers and specialists with a diversity of expertise, as well as working with a variety of artists.

TATTOO (1970/SS1971, p.22) is a jumpsuit that was initially introduced in his first solo show in New York. The printed pattern was created by Makiko Minagawa, who used traditional tattooing techniques, and was in homage to Jimi Hendrix and Janis Joplin. Makiko Minagawa was the textile director up to 1999, when Miyake departed from the direction of the ISSEY MIYAKE collections. The tattoo print shown in New York is not simply decorative. As in the actual tattoo tradition, where spiritual elements are expressed on the skin—as—canvas, here, too, Miyake's personal message is felt. Combined with its tattoo motif, this bodywear, which does not restrict the body's movement, and in fact is felt in union with the underlying skin, makes us even more aware that clothing is indeed our "second skin."

Also, at around this time Miyake began to create further original work that merged traditional clothing and hand-made items. These were drawn from quotidian life, such as *sashiko* fabric and the *tanzen* informal gown. This was done at a time when Japan was so enamored of Western culture; thus, it was quite an innovative attitude to see beauty in the working clothes worn in provincial agrarian villages, not to mention incorporating them into one's own creative work.

◎ section-B
Miyake continued delving further into the form and movement of the body, and in the 1980s he launched "Body", a series of clothes to cover the torso and that were made of hard materials that had never been used for clothing before: fiber-reinforced plastic, synthetic resins, rattan, and other materials. PLASTIC BODY (1980/AW1980, pp.41-45) was easily mass-produced because it was manufactured with a pouring-in method; and RATTAN BODY (1981/SS1982, pp.46-49) was chosen as the very first item of clothing to appear on the cover of the art magazine *ARTFORUM*, from the United States. These sculptural clothes–clothing for militant women, we might say– were created out of both Miyake's unrestrained and ever-searching mind as well as his efforts in support of new technologies and traditional skills.

◎ section-C
Miyake uses any and every material so as to create a wide variety of styles of clothing. One is called COLOMBE (dove,1990/SS1991, pp.68-69). Clothing of this line is made with a piece of monofilament polyester cloth cut by a heating method, and the dress is shaped by fastening snap-buttons. The astonishing fact is that there are no threads, needles nor scissors used at all in the manufacturing process.

A wholly new breed of clothes, PLEATS, was announced in 1988 as a part of the Spring/Summer 1989 collection. PLEATS items are first cut and sewn into their finished forms, and then they are pleated by a heating method. PLEATS are simply the brilliant combination of a unique idea and a new method that fundamentally overturned conventional norms of clothes-making. By pleating cloth (or in some cases, by making more folds on a piece of cloth), Miyake brought about a truly three-dimensional aesthetic form, one that is abundant with the life force. PLEATS incorporate the very air around it, and possess infinitely beautiful features of light and supple movement. Miyake's pleated items further evolved and gave birth to pleated clothing made with knit materials; these were first used in 1991 by William Forsyth & the Ballet Frankfurt. Even further fabric and technology improvements were pursued and resulted in the launch of PLEATS PLEASE ISSEY MIYAKE in 1993. What did Issey Miyake achieve in this use of thermally processed polyester fabrics? Pleating is one of humanity's most ancient methods of making clothes that adapt to the body, and Miyake achieved a modern metamorphosis of pleats by making them both aesthetically valuable as well as being comfortable and practical (not to mention easy to care for).

PLEATS was followed by A-POC (announced in 1998), developed by Miyake together with Dai Fujiwara, and may be regarded as an extension of the PLEATS enterprise. This line uses knitting machines furnished with computer programs to make clothing designs. What "pops out" from them are tubular fabrics with knitted-in designed materials ready for producing dresses, bags, socks and other items. A-POC, like PLEATS before it, is an operation that fundamentally inverted conventional ways of thinking about the manufacture of clothing, and has continued to develop further possibilities.

The current and most recent project, 132 5. ISSEY MIYAKE (announced in 2010) uses textiles derived from PET bottles and other polyester-based recycled materials to make clothing items. In this case, their 3-D forms—comprised of a mere "a piece of cloth"—were made possible thanks to technologies used for realizing complicated folded structures. The fabrics' geometrical forms are shaped by intricate engineering algorithms designed to result in very high levels of design quality and sustainability; they can be applied to skirts, jackets and bags, as well as even to lamp shades.

Issey Miyake has been stimulating us for almost half a century; he has added immeasurable comfort and pleasure to our lives. In this exhibition he shares with us—immersed as we are in our day-to-day lives—the joy of designing and, more importantly, that of living. This exhibition is a message from Miyake to us all—all of us young -at- heart.

＊1. "Make Urban Plans from the Mode ; World Design Conference", an article in the *So-en* magazine, May issue, 1960, p.163, reported that Miyake had sent a letter of protest to the conference committee chairperson and architect, Junzo Sakakura, and that it was published in the conference secretariat's papers and discussed by the committee members' general assembly.
The final result was that the conference added the theme of clothing design to its agenda.
＊2. "Seventy Years after the End of WWII: Now We Tell You about Being A-bombed", a dialogue by Yoshiko Kosaka and Yoko Tanimoto, *The Yomiuri Shimbun* daily, 6 Dec., 2015 morning issue, p.1 and p.7.

# A

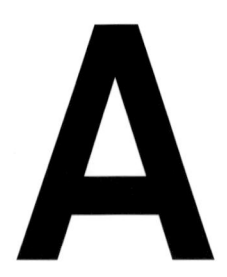

**展覧会場 A／section A**

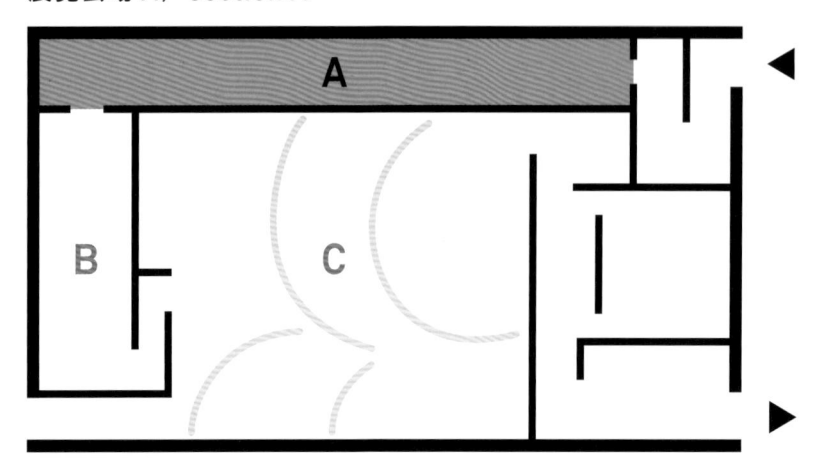

基礎となる問いがある——三次元である身体を二次元の布でいかにして包むか。
ここには身体の「動き」が変数として含まれる。身体を布で包む——という問い
に対して、進化する有機的で明解な答えを際限なく出していく。
はてしない好奇心と実験、それが三宅一生の仕事を推進させる原動力だ。
革新的な解決策に向かって驚くべき一貫性と熱意を貫いている。


Since man began to wear clothing, a basic question has existed: how to wrap
the body which is three dimensional, with fabric which is two dimensional.
Added to this question is the movement of the body as the defining variable.
Miyake offers answers with ever-evolving solutions from his organic
and articulated repertoire. The work of Issey Miyake is fueled by a boundless
curiosity and love of experimentation. He is constant in his pursuit of innovative
solutions that seem to resonate with striking coherence and enthusiasm.

**展覧会場 A**

　初期のデザインにおける試みを探る。1970年、三宅一生は自らの表現の拠点としてデザイン事務所を設立する。それはのちの比類なき足跡を刻む原点となる。大学でグラフィック・デザインを専攻した三宅は、衣服のかたちや風合いなど直接服づくりに関わることだけではなく、デザインのためのイメージづくりやコミュニケーションにおける服のあり方についても独創的な見解を抱いていた。その後パリに学びクチュールメゾンで研鑽を積んでいた1968年、権威主義に抗議するパリの若者たちの動きを目の当たりにし、三宅は「民主的な言語としての服」を根底から模索し始める。精神と身体の自由をめぐる既成の枠にとらわれない発想は、心底にあった日本の伝統的文化への敬意と重なり、他に類を見ない固有の創造性を発揮する。

　タトゥの柄をプリントしたショート丈のボディウエア（1970年）は第二の皮膚となり、身体とひとつになる。「衣服は着ることではじめてかたちをなす。そのとき布と身体との空間もまた活かされる」。一枚の布で造形された服にはこのことが如実に表れている。「一枚の布」は三宅が繰り返し立ち戻る試金石なのだ。

　たとえば、一枚の布からつくる《コクーン・コート》（1977年）、あるいは三枚の正方形の布をバイアスの地の目で組み合わせた《ハンカチーフ・ドレス》（1970年）。かたちに生命を吹き込むのは人である。三宅の服はそれまでの束縛から着る人を解放する。着ることにより人は自由を謳歌するのだ。一見するとかたちの大胆さに驚かされるが、実際の着やすさは明らかだ。これは革新的な素材開発の賜物である。また、伝統的な素材や技術を新たなかたちで活かす例として、男性の着物の裏地として使用されてきた《正花木綿》（1976年）や、柔道着や野良着に使われてきた木綿地の《刺し子》（1972年）を用いることなどがあげられる。絹を素材とする服では、美術家、横尾忠則とのコラボレーションによる《パラダイス・ロスト（失楽園）》（1976年）がある。横尾のデザインをプリントした「一枚の布」を象徴する一着である。

　人にもっとも身近な衣服の分野において、身体を解放し心を自由にする可能性にみちたデザインを提示し続けることこそ、世界を繋ぎ、次の時代を開くことに直結する。——三宅一生の服づくりには、はじまりから現在まで、一貫した思想とものづくりの姿勢が見られる。

## section A

Issey Miyake founded the Miyake Design Studio in 1970. Almost immediately he emerged as a clothing designer whose unique and personal point of view was the driving force toward the path ahead. After graduating from Tama Art University with a degree in graphic design, he went on to Paris, where he was trained in the haute couture tradition. His design background gave him not only a different outlook on the development of shapes and textures, but also a different medium in which to express forms of communication and image-making. Moreover, his vivid memories of the 1968 Parisian protests, and the sense that what people wanted was not in the old tradition, led him on a quest for a radically new, democratic language for clothing. These different elements coalesced into a personal idea of freedom— of both mind and body—that combined with a deep respect and love for Japanese traditions, and resulted in singular creations. Miyake quickly developed a unique grammar of forms, addressing the body as the entity that makes design come alive through movement, gesture and posture.

The tattooed body wear from 1970, for instance, is literally a second skin that clings to the body. In other words, a shape is created only when clothing is worn, as the space between cloth and body becomes active. His fascination with the idea of clothing the body from a single piece of cloth, which quickly became a touchstone for all his work, is visible in the sweeping COCOON COAT from 1977, for instance, or the HANDKERCHIEF DRESS from 1970, made using three different squares of fabric joined on the bias. These free forms are activated only by the wearer, and heralded an unprecedented freedom from traditional constraints. This was the result of Miyake's focus on innovative development. His exploration and development of materials, and particularly new synthetic textiles, led to work such as SHOHANA-MOMEN (1976), a cotton broadcloth that was used for the lining of men's kimono, and SASHIKO (1972), a traditional workman's garment, made soft and comfortable through the use of innovative weaving techniques. PARADISE LOST (1976), a collaboration with graphic artist Tadanori Yokoo, is the most symbolic of his early experiments using "a piece of cloth."

For Issey Miyake, clothing is a tool by which to liberate the body as well as human spirit since it is the area of design that is most intimately associated with the human body. It is the medium that connects to the world as well as to the future. Miyake's belief in clothes-making has been, is, and continues to be constant.

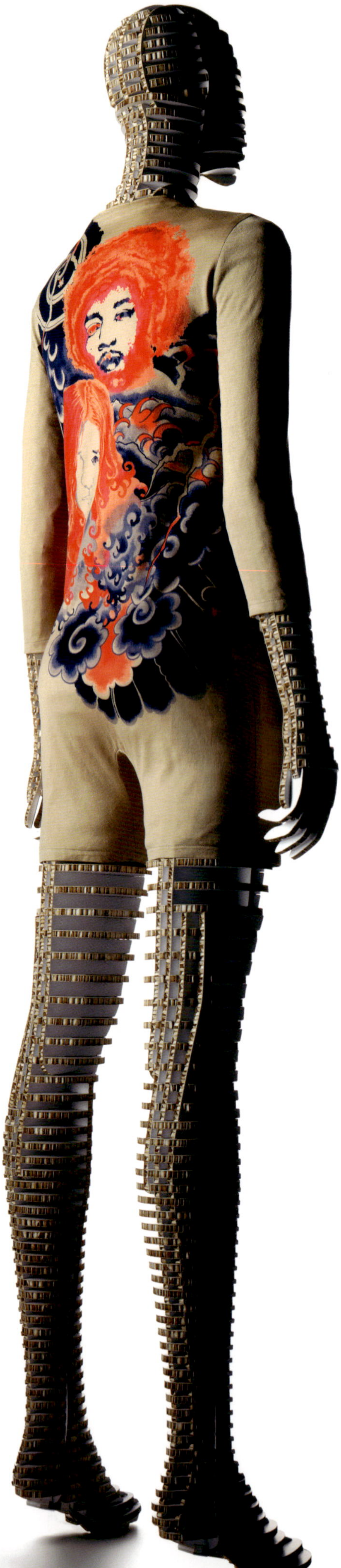

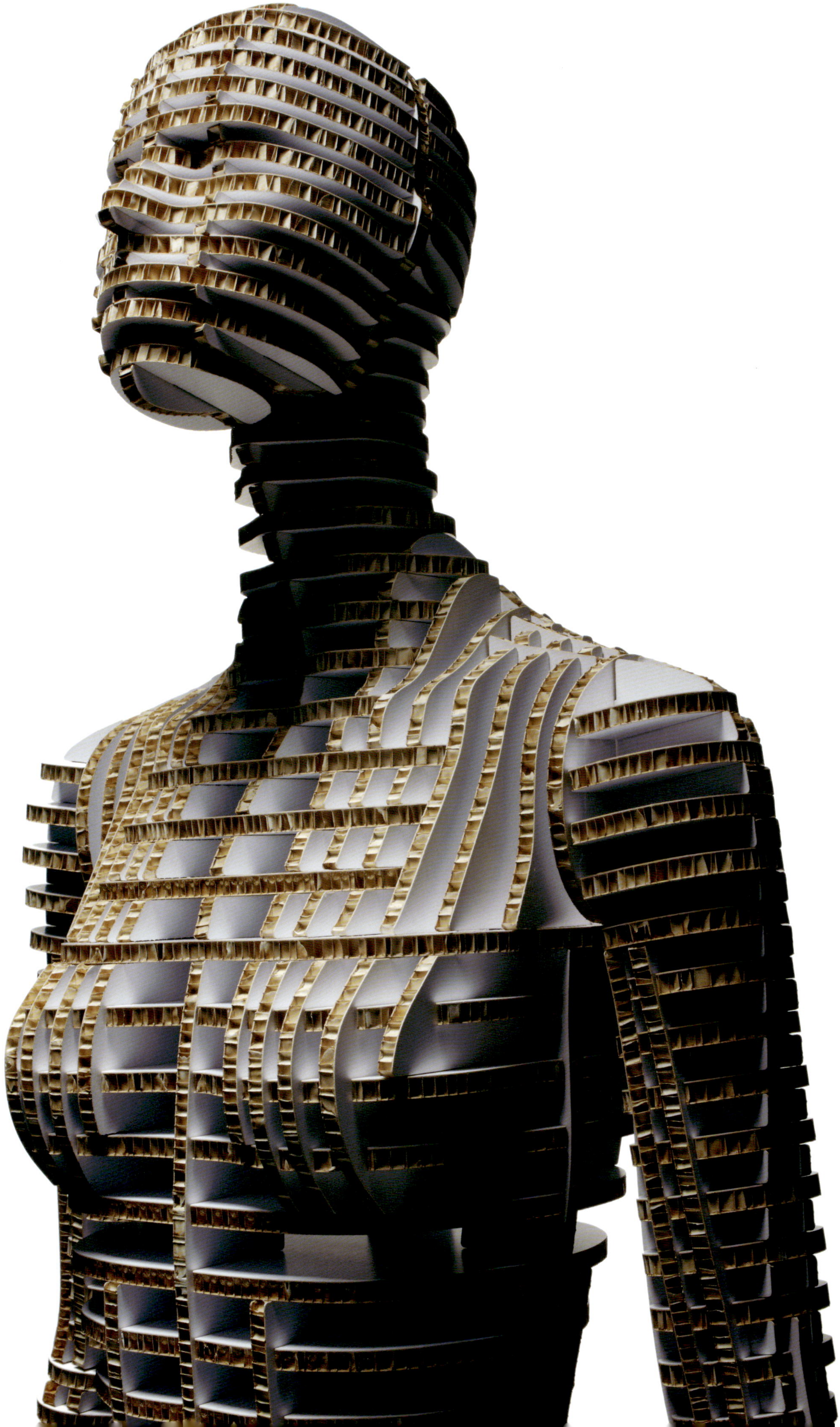

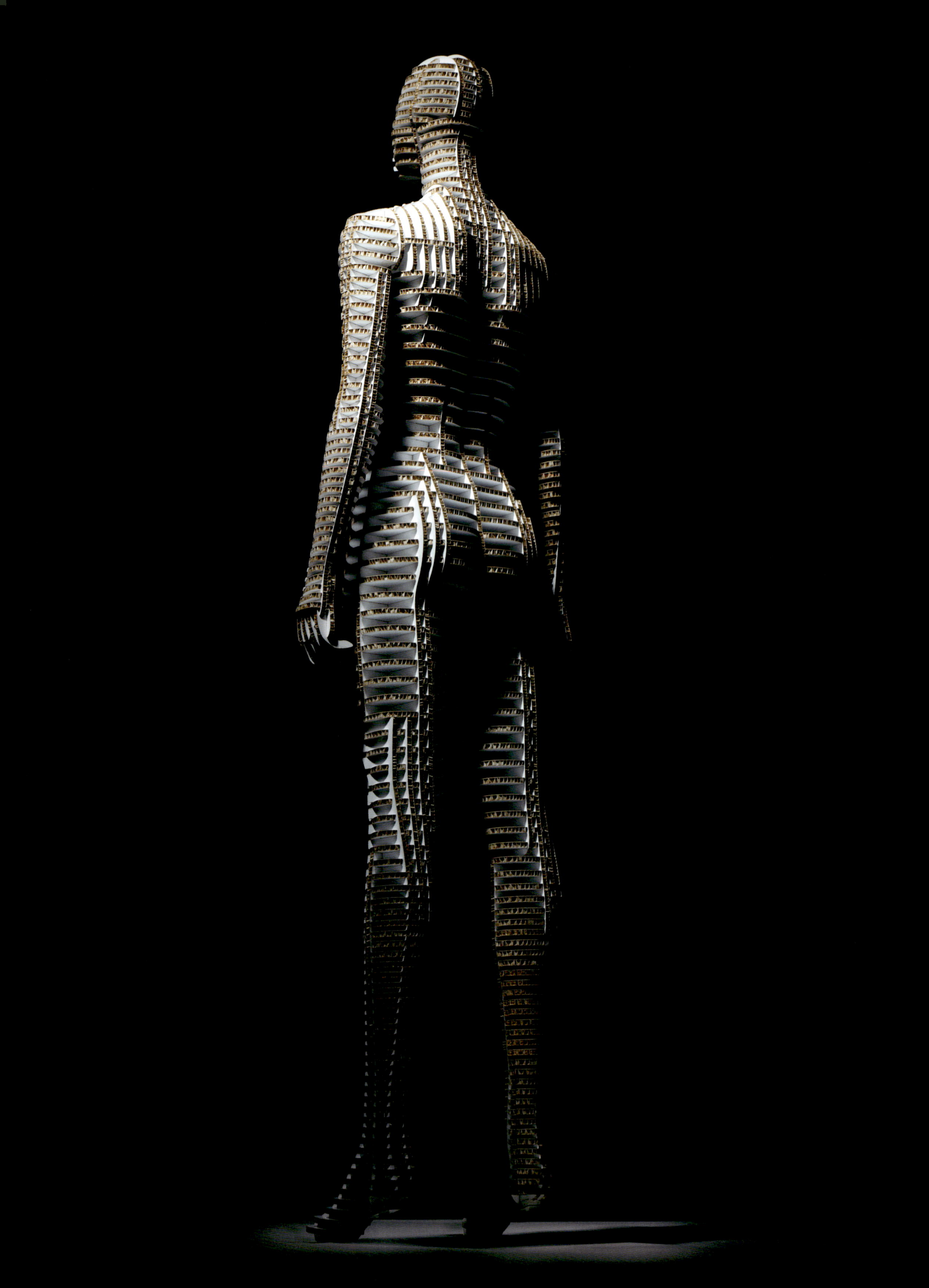

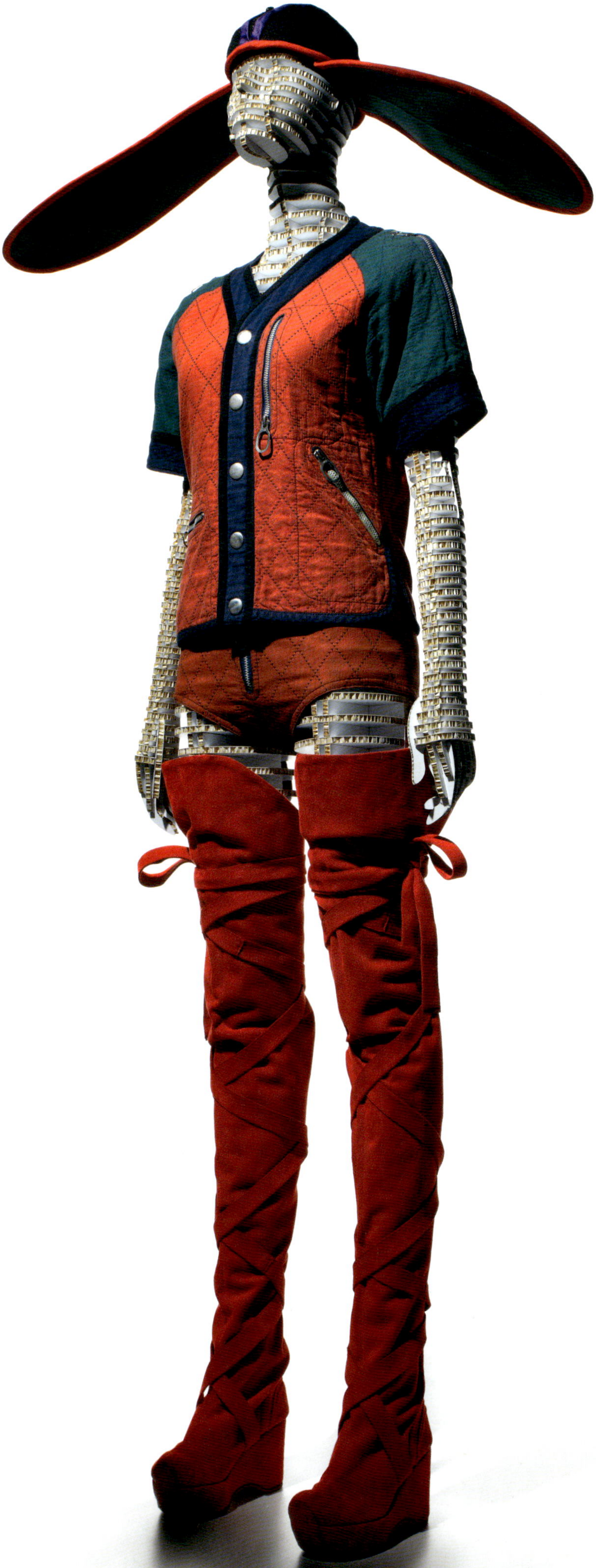

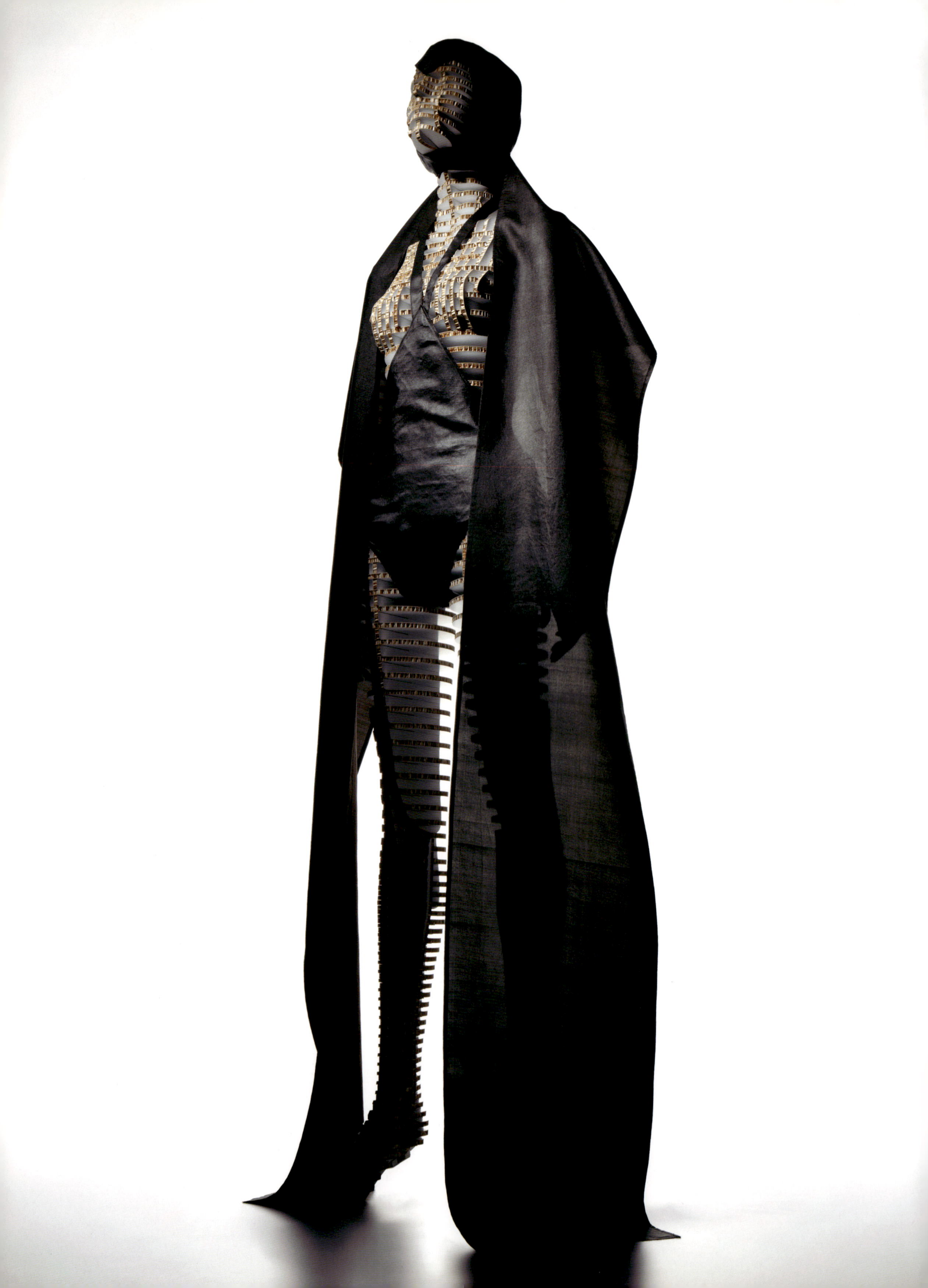

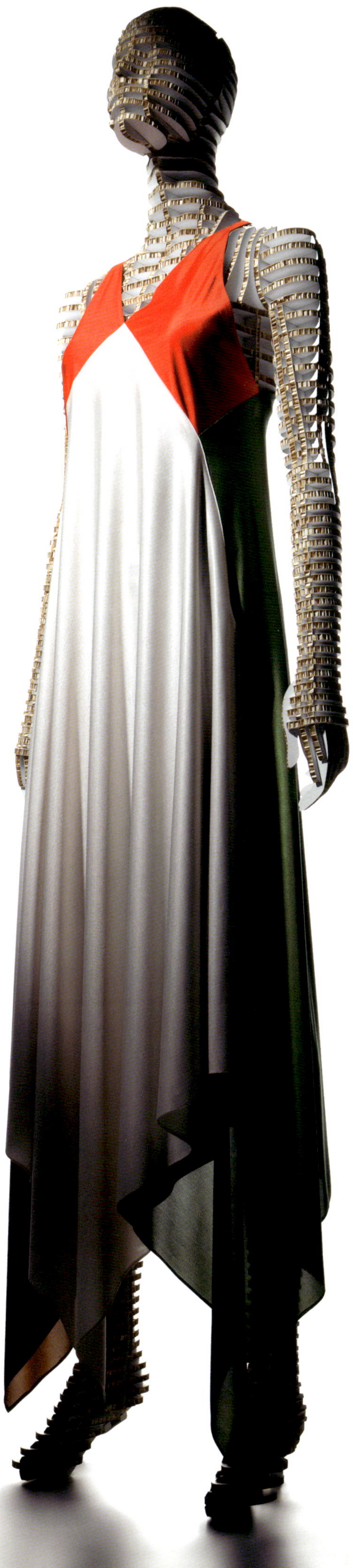

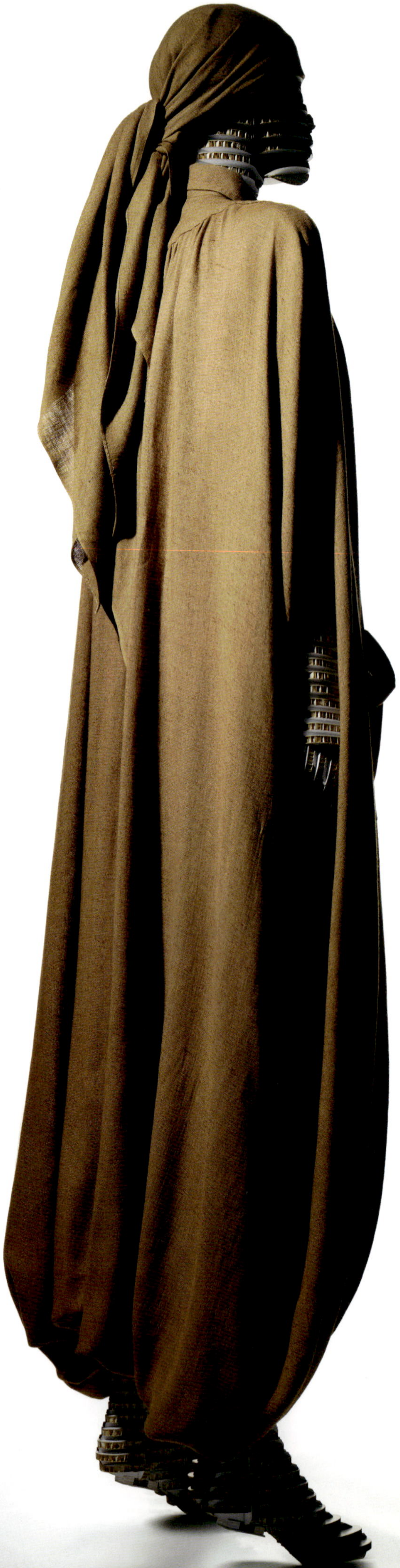

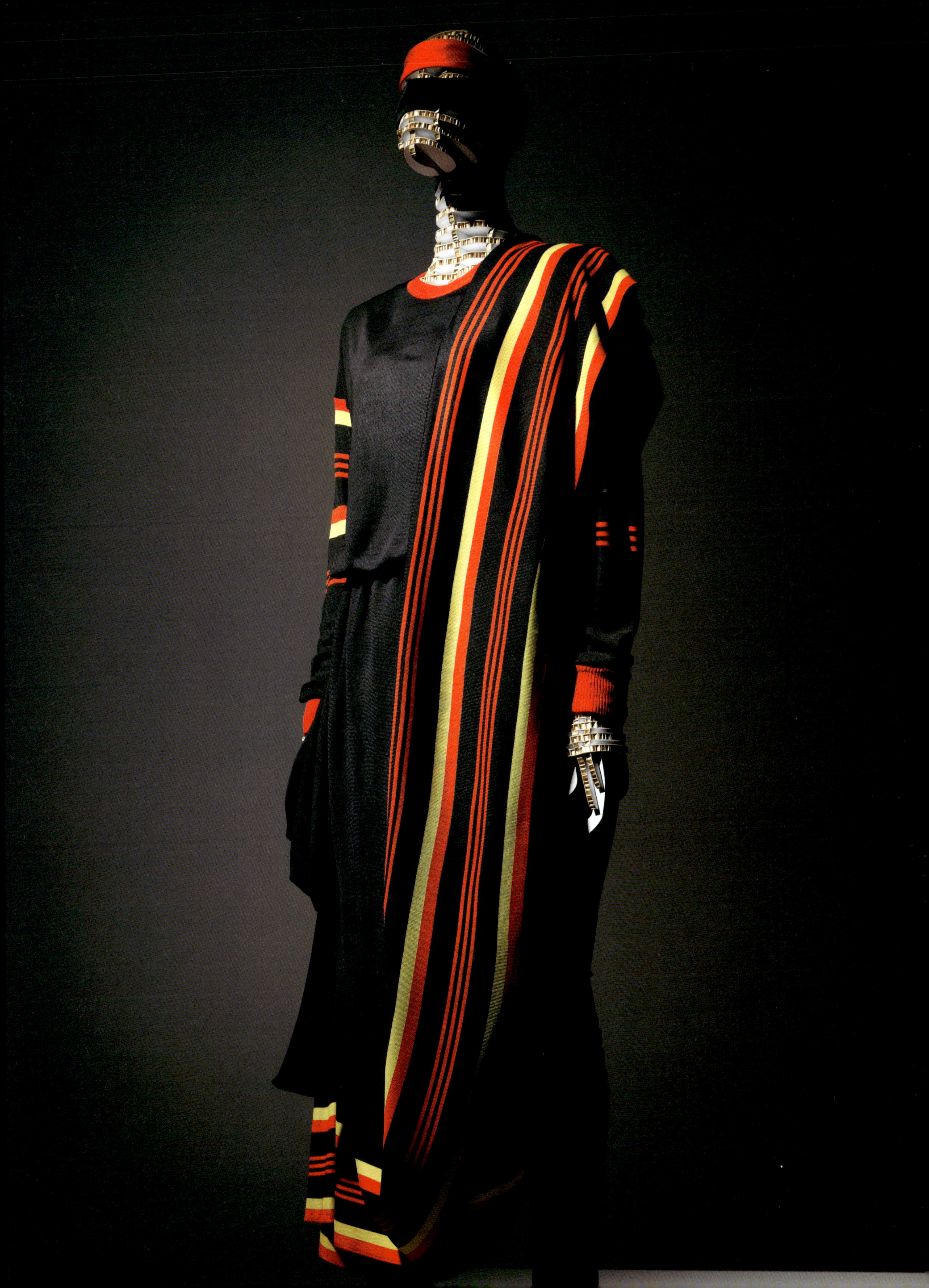

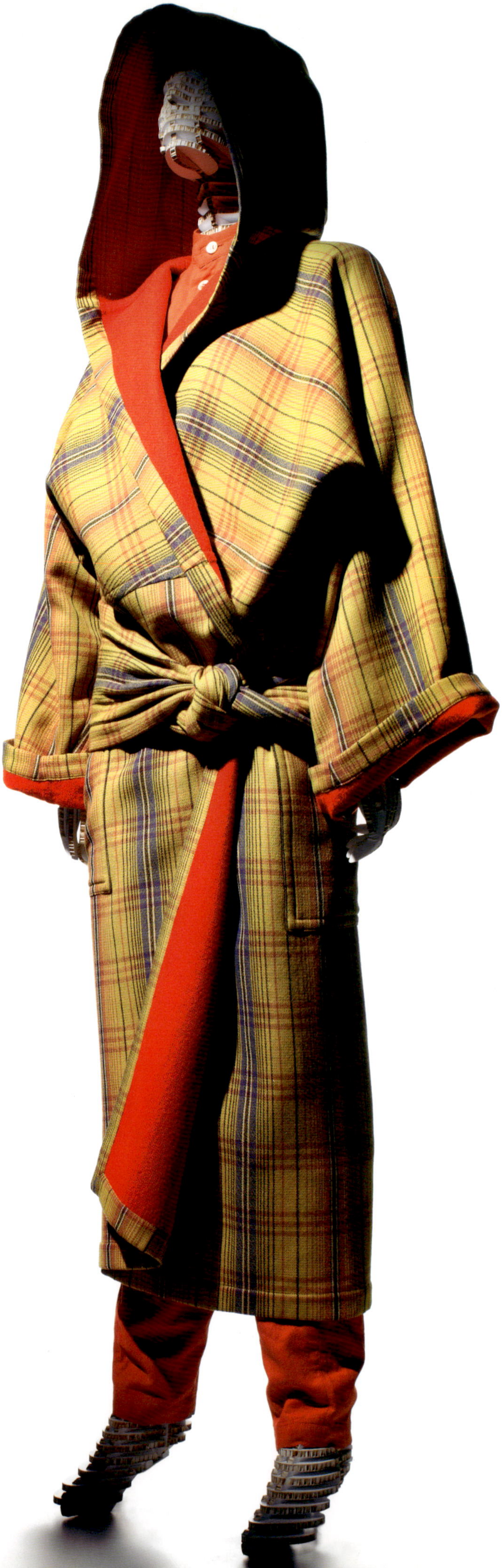

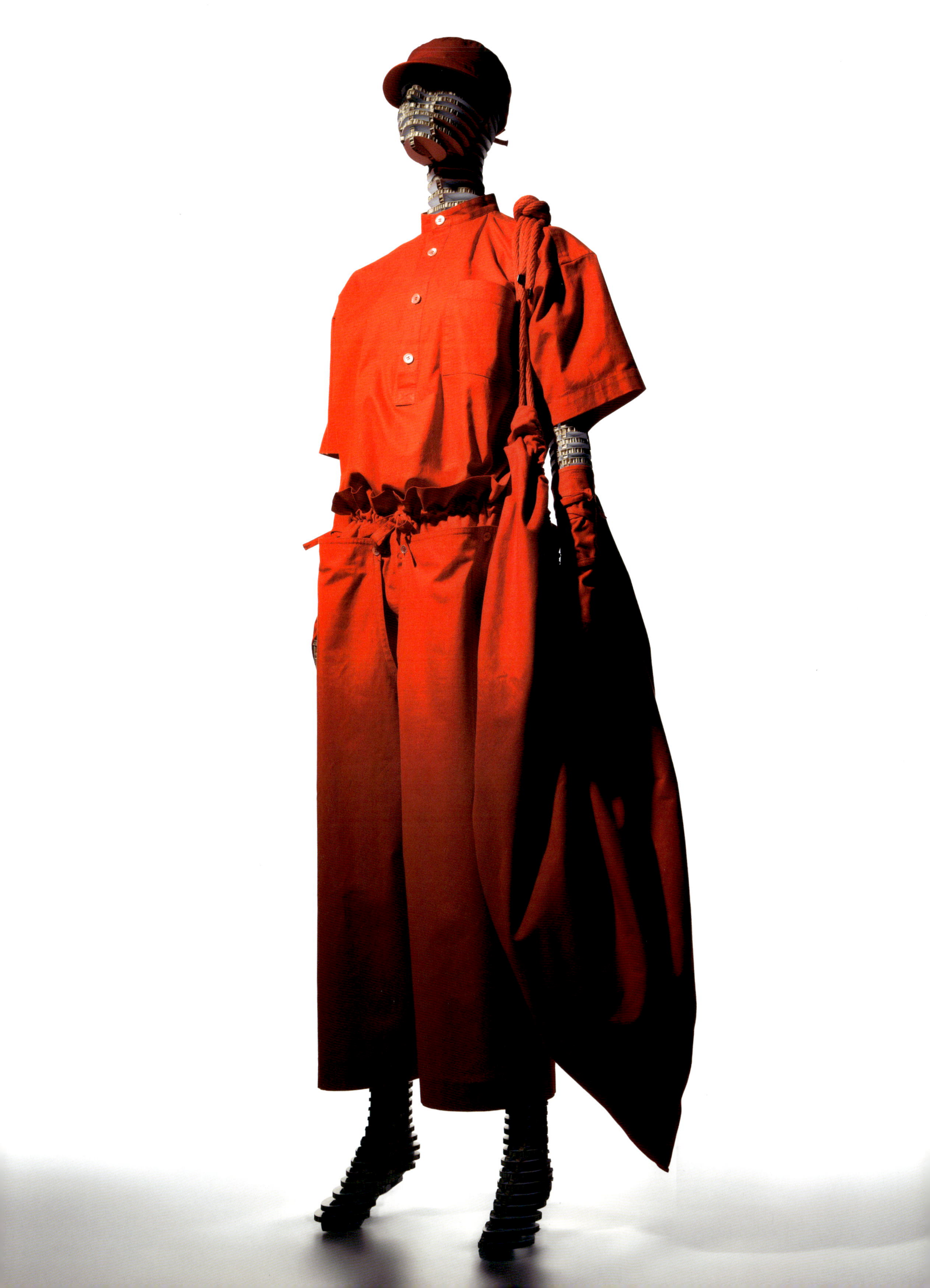

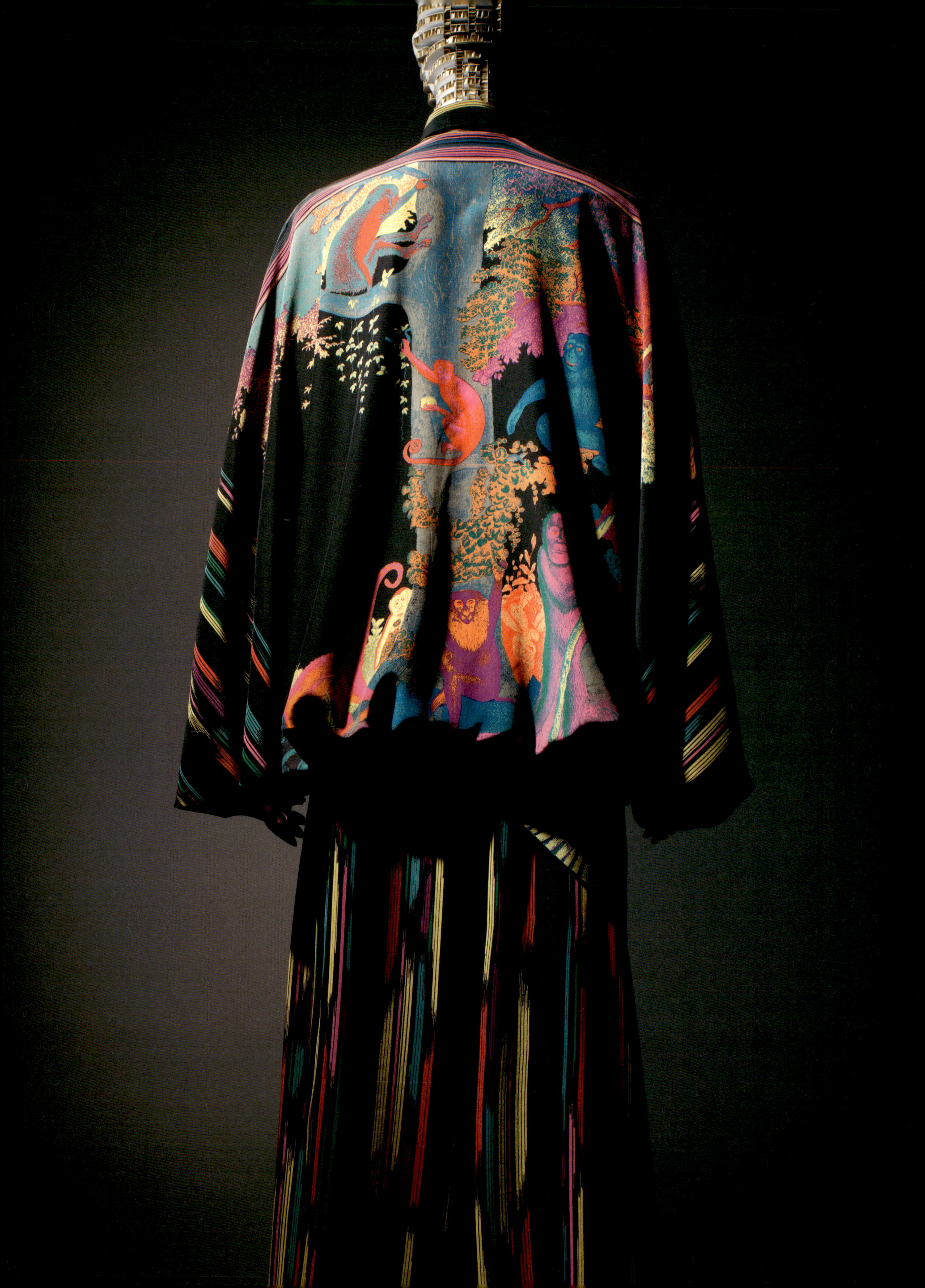

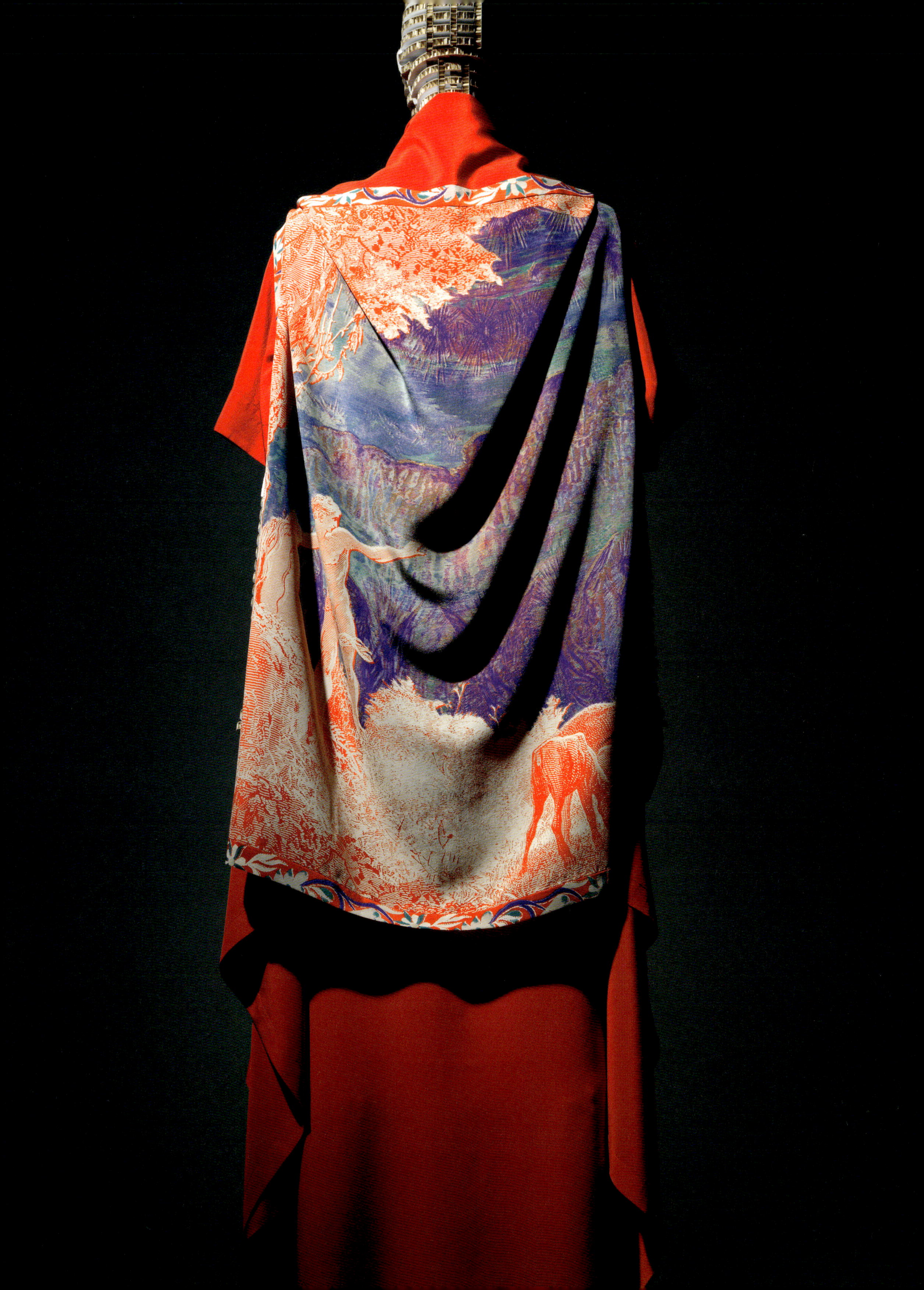

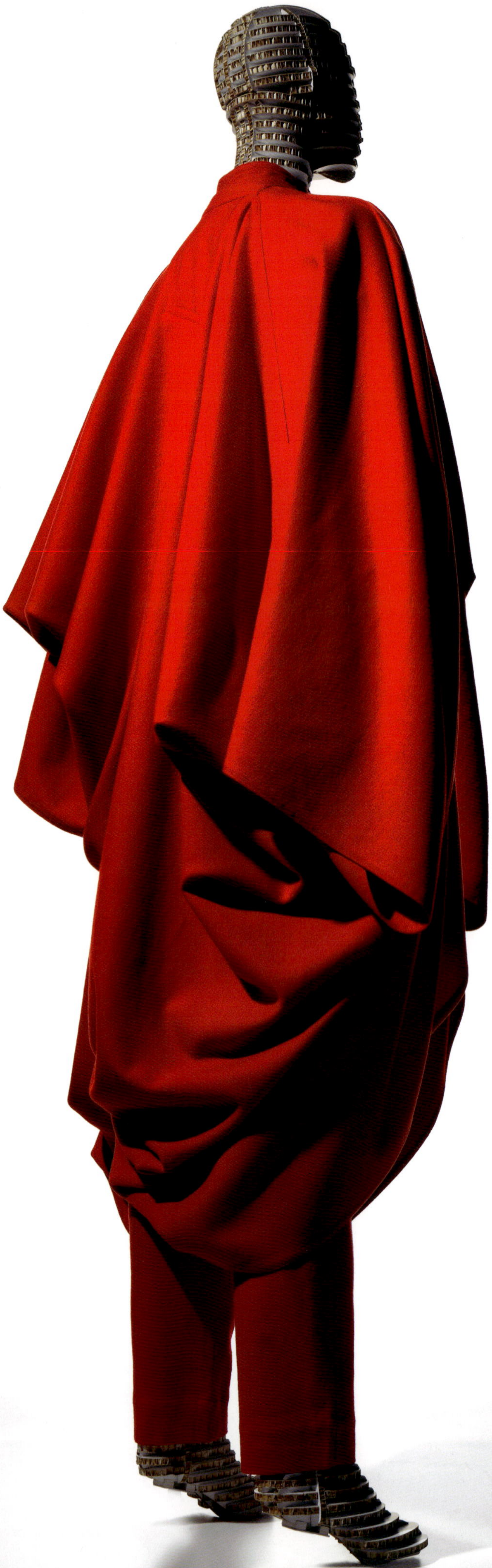

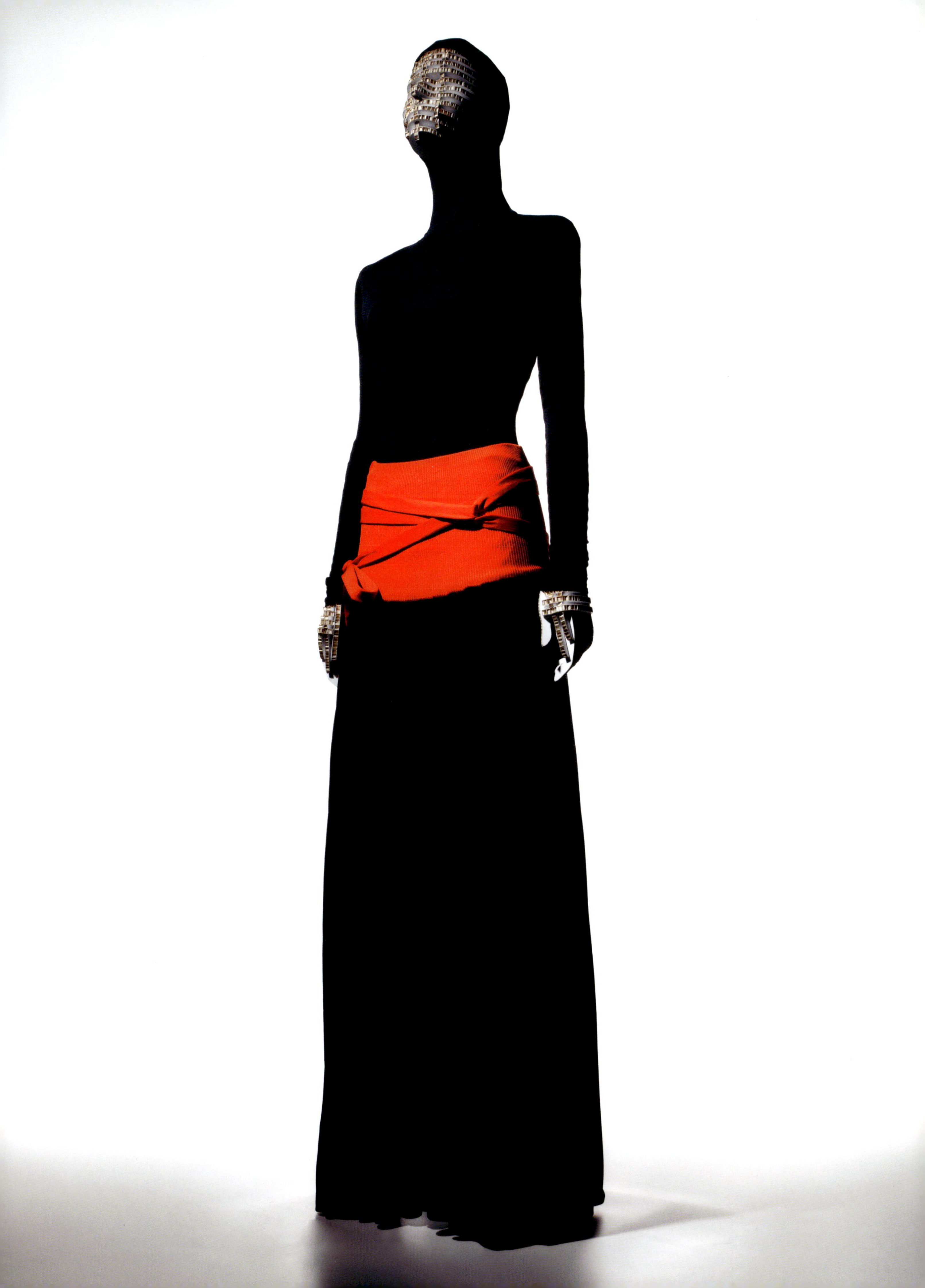

# B

**展覧会場 B ／ section B**

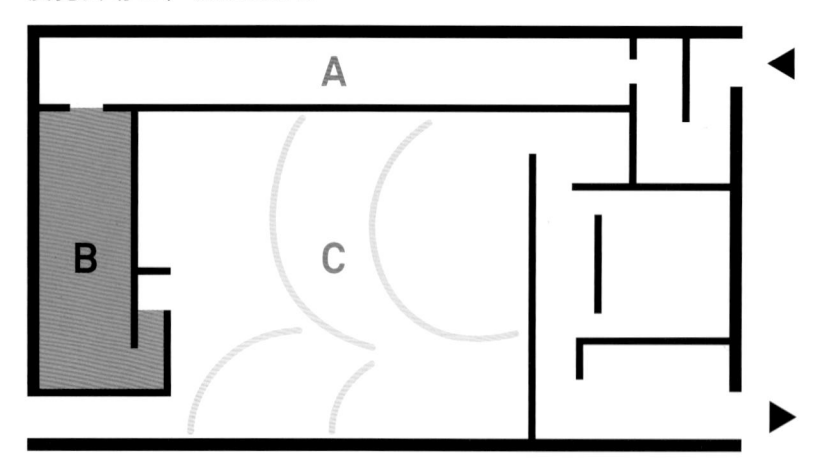

section B

36

主役は身体である。身体は衣服に動きと生命をあたえる。三宅一生の服を
介して身体は際立ち、線を描き、デザインされる。素材を試し、伝統の技に託し、
先端技術を用いる。「ボディ」は芸術作品を意図してはいない。工業的に生産
されるものとしてつくられながら、自己を表象する鋭い発言力をたずさえ、
さらには東洋と西洋の対話を生み出している。


The body is the protagonist. The body not only gives life and motion,
but also enhances, streamlines and adds dimension to the clothing of Issey Miyake.
He experiments with materials, employing traditional handcrafts alongside
the latest technologies. The "Body" series was not intended as an artwork; each was
created as an industrial product that conveyed a clear message of self-expression.
This series also served to engage Western and Eastern values in a dialogue.

**展覧会場 B**

　1980年、「ボディ」と呼ぶ胴体部を覆う衣服の制作を始め、以降1985年まで継続的に制作している。この制作では、三宅は従来の衣服には使われることのなかった素材や手法に挑戦し、工学的なアプローチも試みている。

　最初に制作されたのが《プラスティック・ボディ》(1980年)である。オブジェのように見えるが、芸術作品を意図したものではない。工学的な要素を媒介として、繊維強化プラスチックを素材に用い、型を使い、多数生産も可能な製法でつくられている。それにも関わらず、身体の上に着るフィクションとしての「ボディ」は、さまざまなマスクの効果を発揮し、自己を表象する鋭い発信作用を衣服に付与しているといえるだろう。《ラタン・ボディ》(1981年)は、籐と竹を素材とし、工芸作家・小菅小竹堂による伝統の匠の手技で制作された。「過去と未来、西洋と東洋、硬さと柔らかさ、自然と人工の交差点におけるモダニズムのアイコンである」と記された巻頭文とともに、『ARTFORUM』誌(1982年2月号)の表紙に取り上げられた。これはアート誌に掲載された最初の衣服デザインである。

　ボディ・ブレスレットとして衣服の上につける金属製の《ワイヤー・ボディ》(1983年)やジップアップで着用する、バストやヒップが抽象化された《シリコン・ボディ》(1985年)も発表された。

　一枚の布を用いながら、彫刻的な身体を表現する新たな方法で制作されたのが《ウォーターフォール・ボディ》(1984年)だ。部分的にシリコンを染み込ませたしなやかなピューロン・ジャージーをトルソーの上に置き、水の流れをイメージし、手でドレープを寄せて固めている。手仕事と科学的な作用が融合し完成した「ボディ」は、時代を超えた優雅ささえ醸し出しているようだ。

　触覚と対照的である一連の「ボディ」の流れるような曲線的フォルムは、「一枚の布」がつくり出すかたちへの飽くなき探求と、それを可能にするテクノロジーや伝統工芸の技から生み出されている。

## section B

In this phase of Issey Miyake's work the "Body" becomes an entity to enhance, streamline and design, using clothes as a sculptural medium. He experimented with body-centric creations in 1980 and continued to develop manufacturing techniques to create them until 1985. Technology is Miyake's key to not only creating modern solutions to reviving dying traditional handcrafts using materials never before adapted to clothesmaking, as well as to explore the possibilities of new techniques by which to make clothing.

His first creation, PLASTIC BODY (1980), may look like an object, but was not intended as a work of art. It is made of FRP (fiber reinforced plastic) that is applied to a mold, in effect making them industrially-produced multiples. Nonetheless, by allowing a fictitious "Body" to be worn over a real one, coming across as a mask of sorts, these pieces made an astute commentary on clothes as objects of self-representation.

For RATTAN BODY (1981), Miyake used rattan and bamboo materials, collaborating with artisan Shochikudo Kosuge to apply traditional processes in its production. It was featured on the cover of *ARTFORUM* (February 1982), where it was described as "An icon of modernism at the intersection between past and future, East and West, hardness and softness, nature and artifice." It was the first time that an art journal had accepted clothing design an its cover page.

Other creations included WIRE BODY (1983), a metallic "body bracelet" worn over the clothing, and SILICON BODY (1985), a zippered bodysuit that abstracts the bust and hips.

He also explored new ways of working in a sculptural manner using a single piece of cloth: the WATERFALL BODY (1984), made of Pewlon jersey partially soaked with silicone was placed on the torso and draped as though it were flowing water, mixing handwork and science with lyrical, timeless elegance.

The "Body" series is notable for its flowing curves and smooth forms, in direct contrast to the tactile feel of the materials. It is a tenacious exploration of the forms created by "piece of cloth," and the technologies and traditional craftsmanship that make them possible.

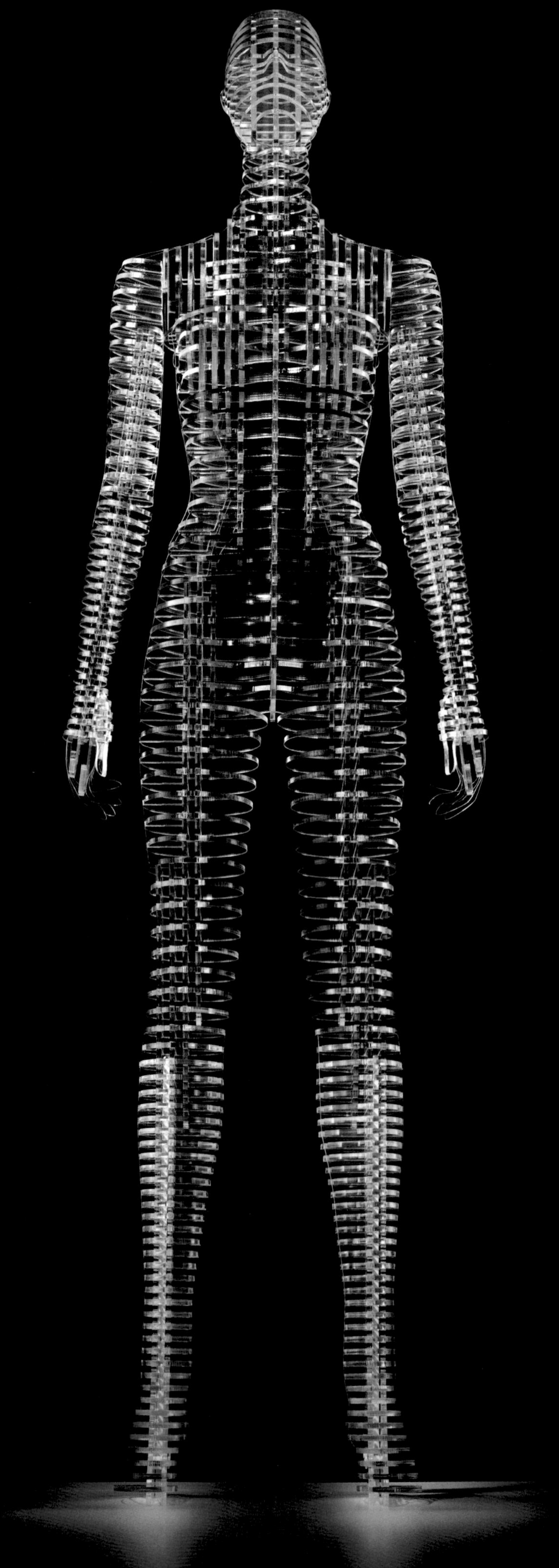

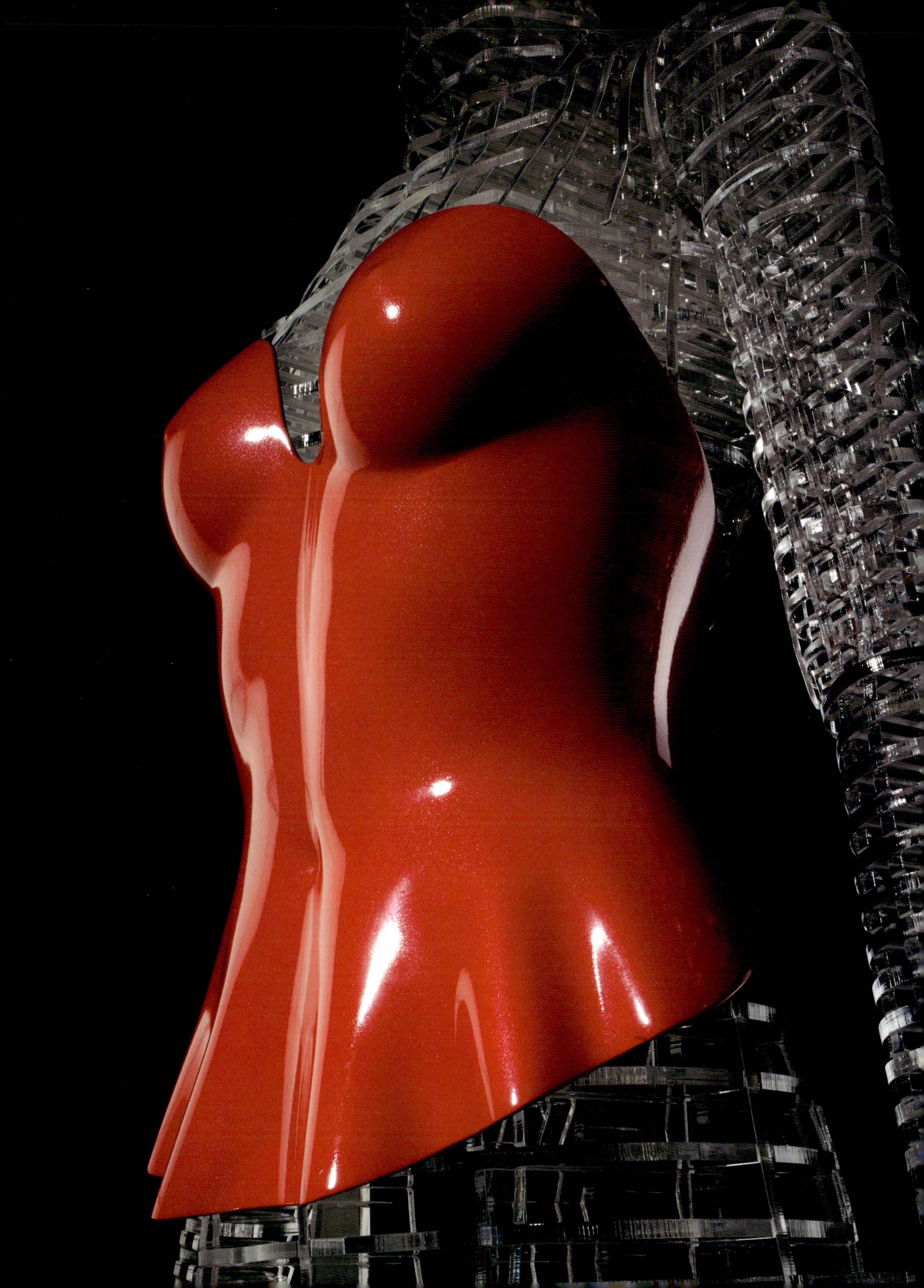

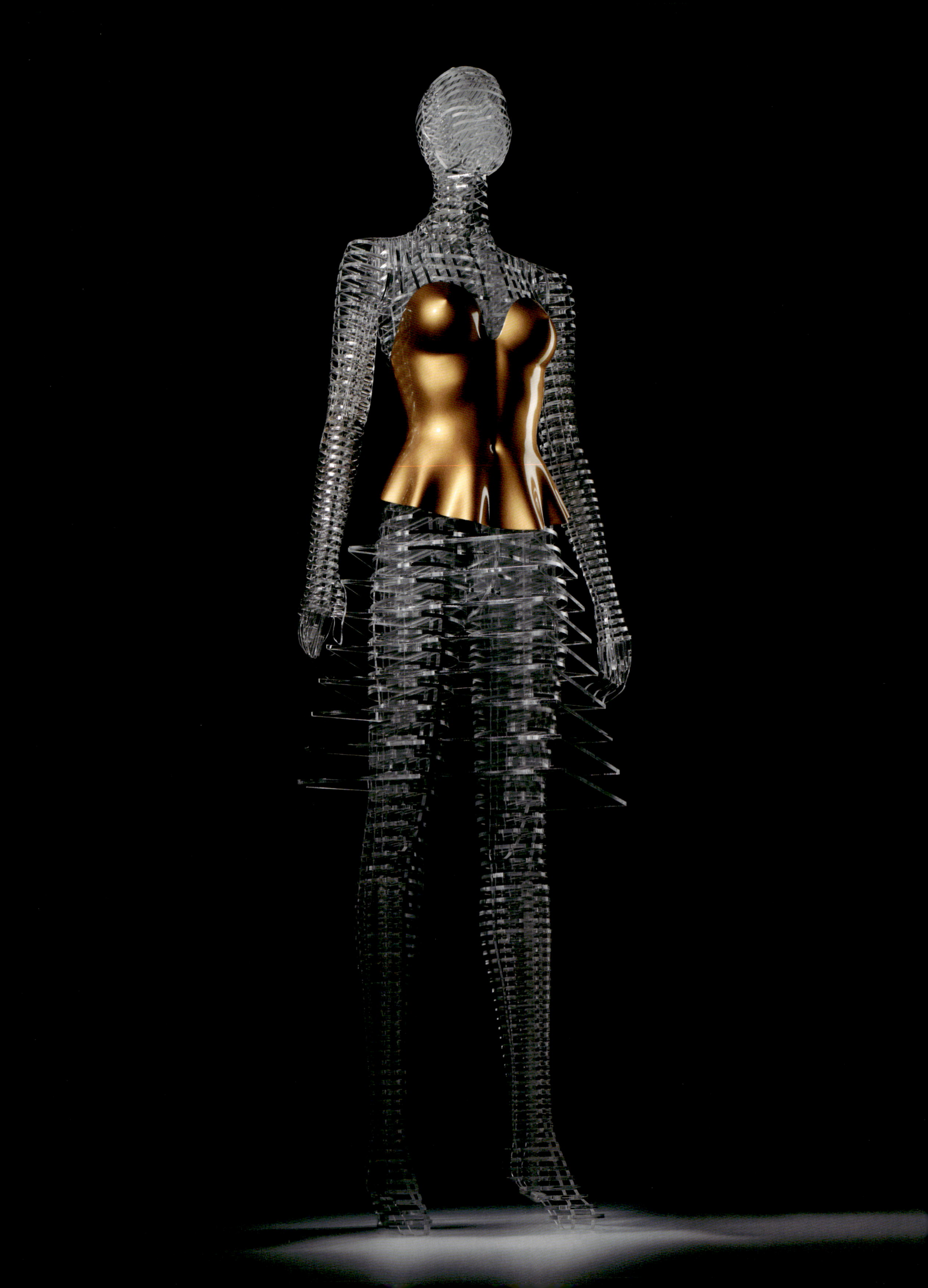

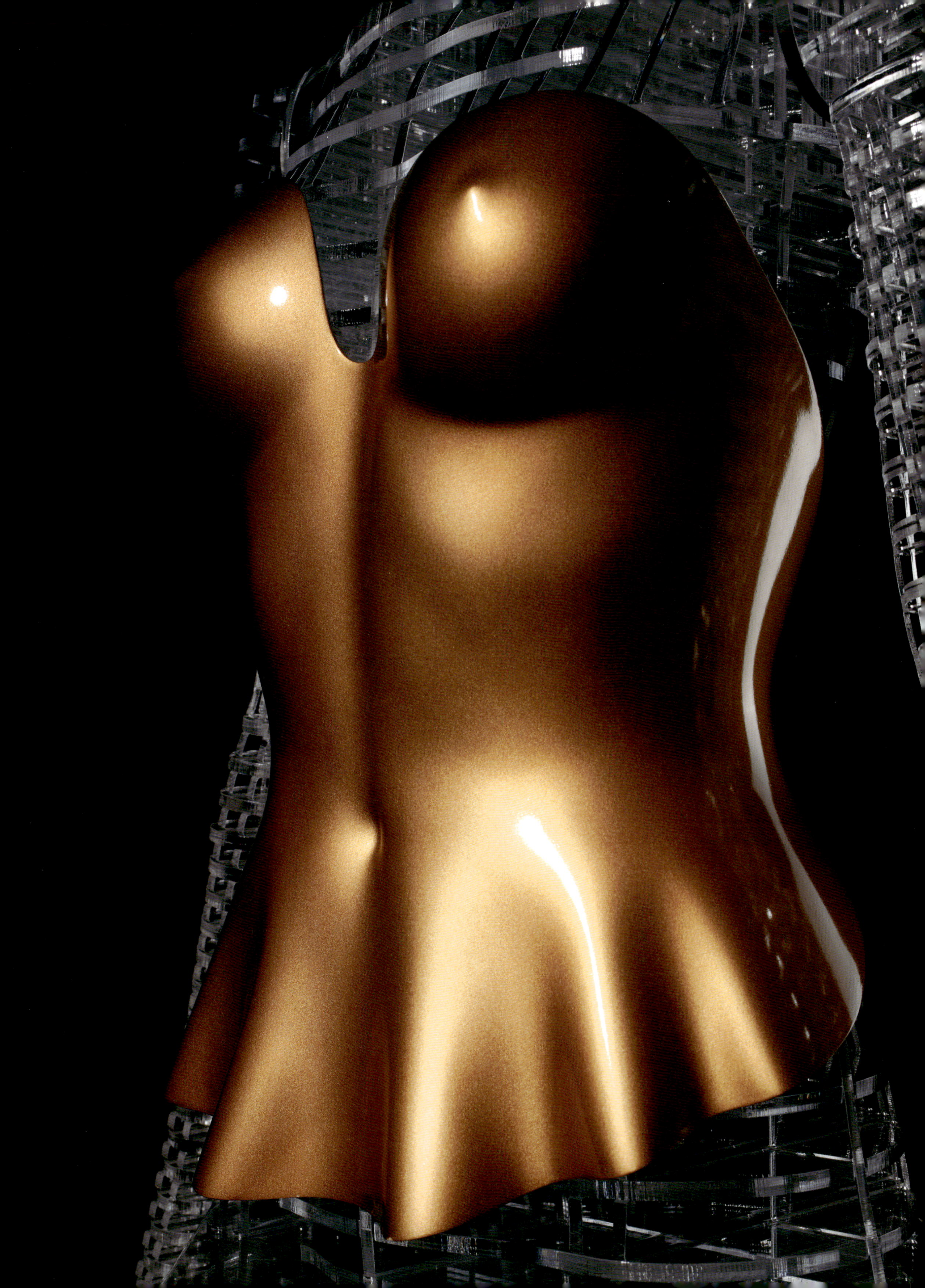

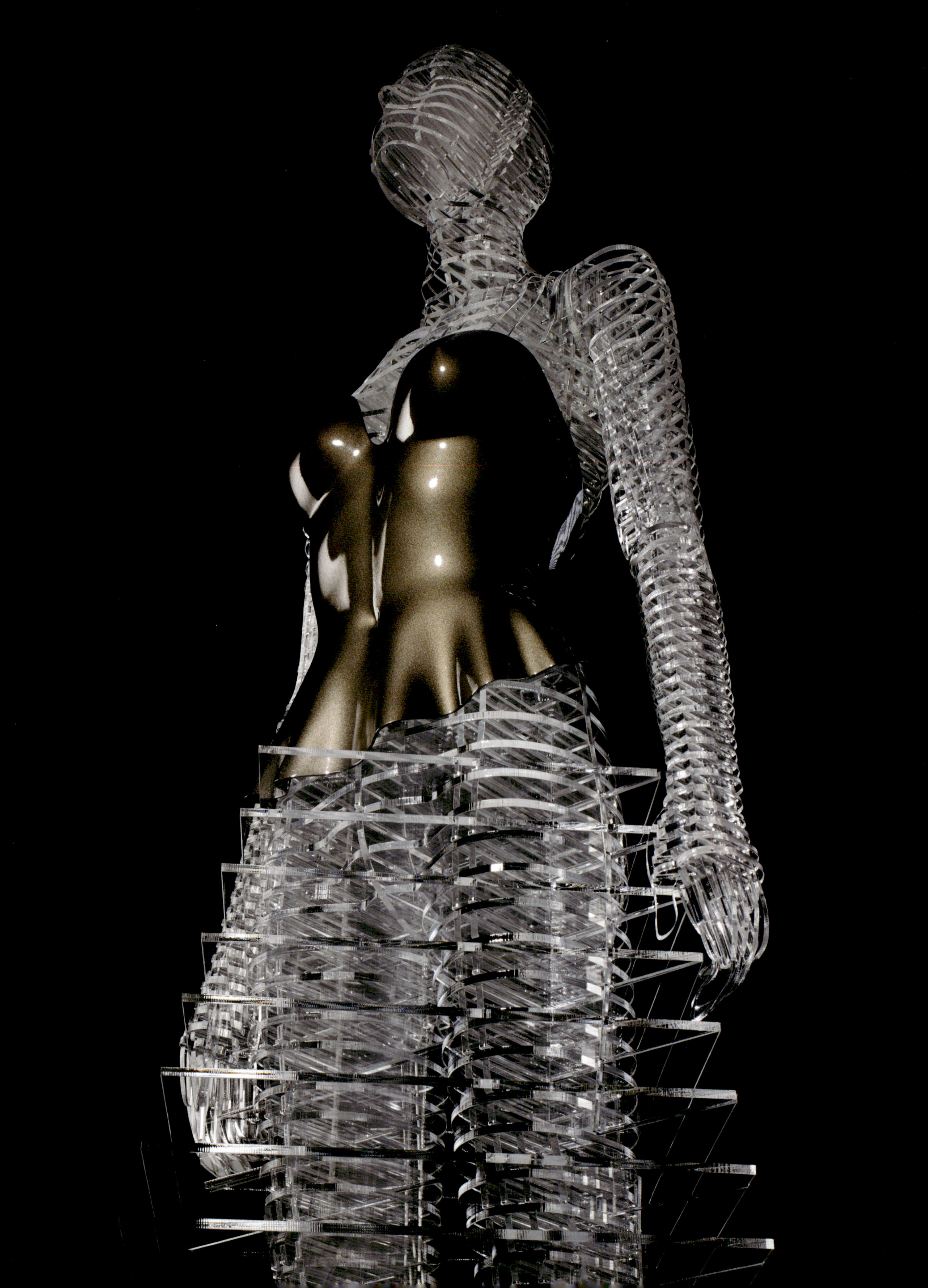

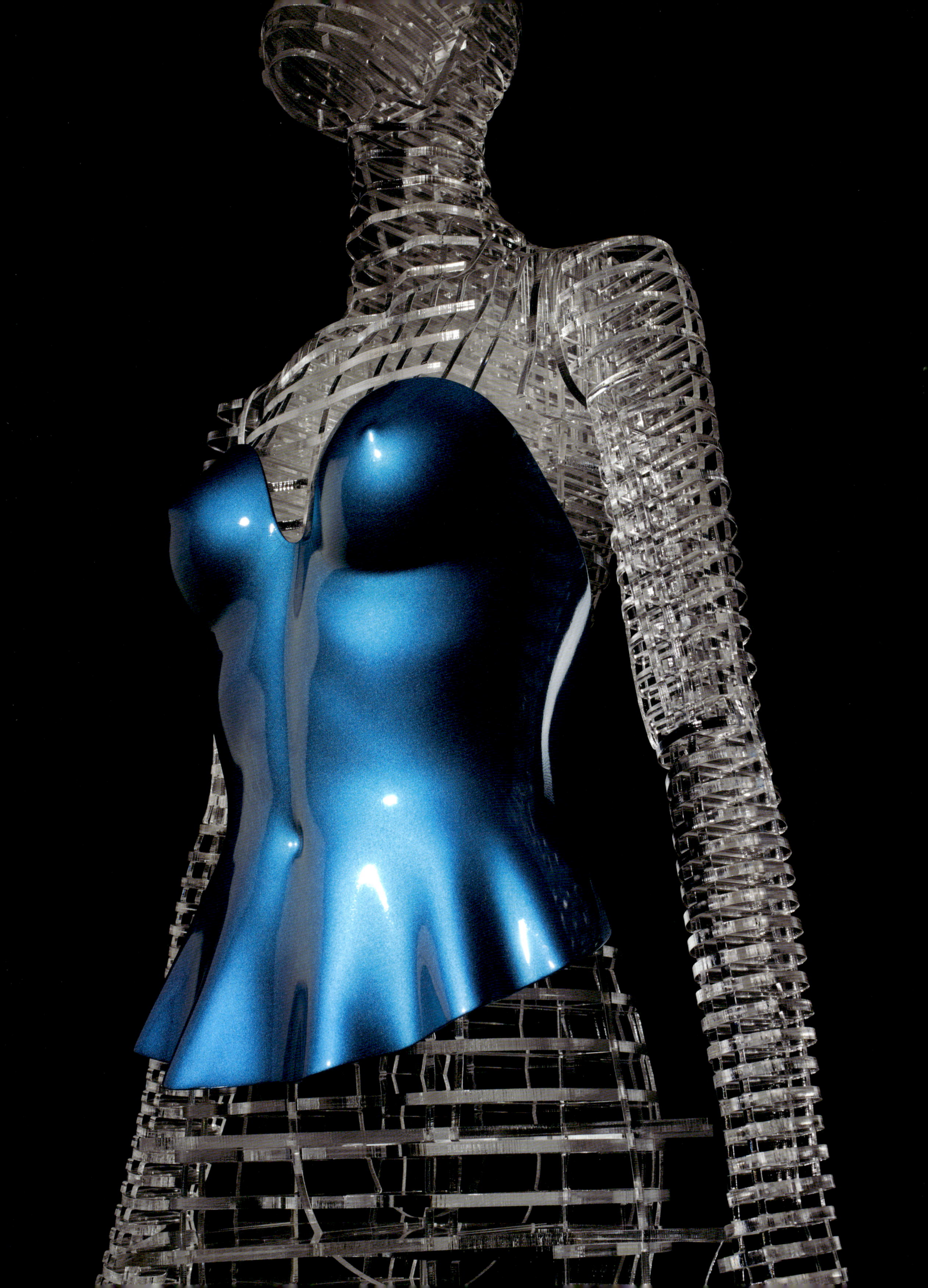

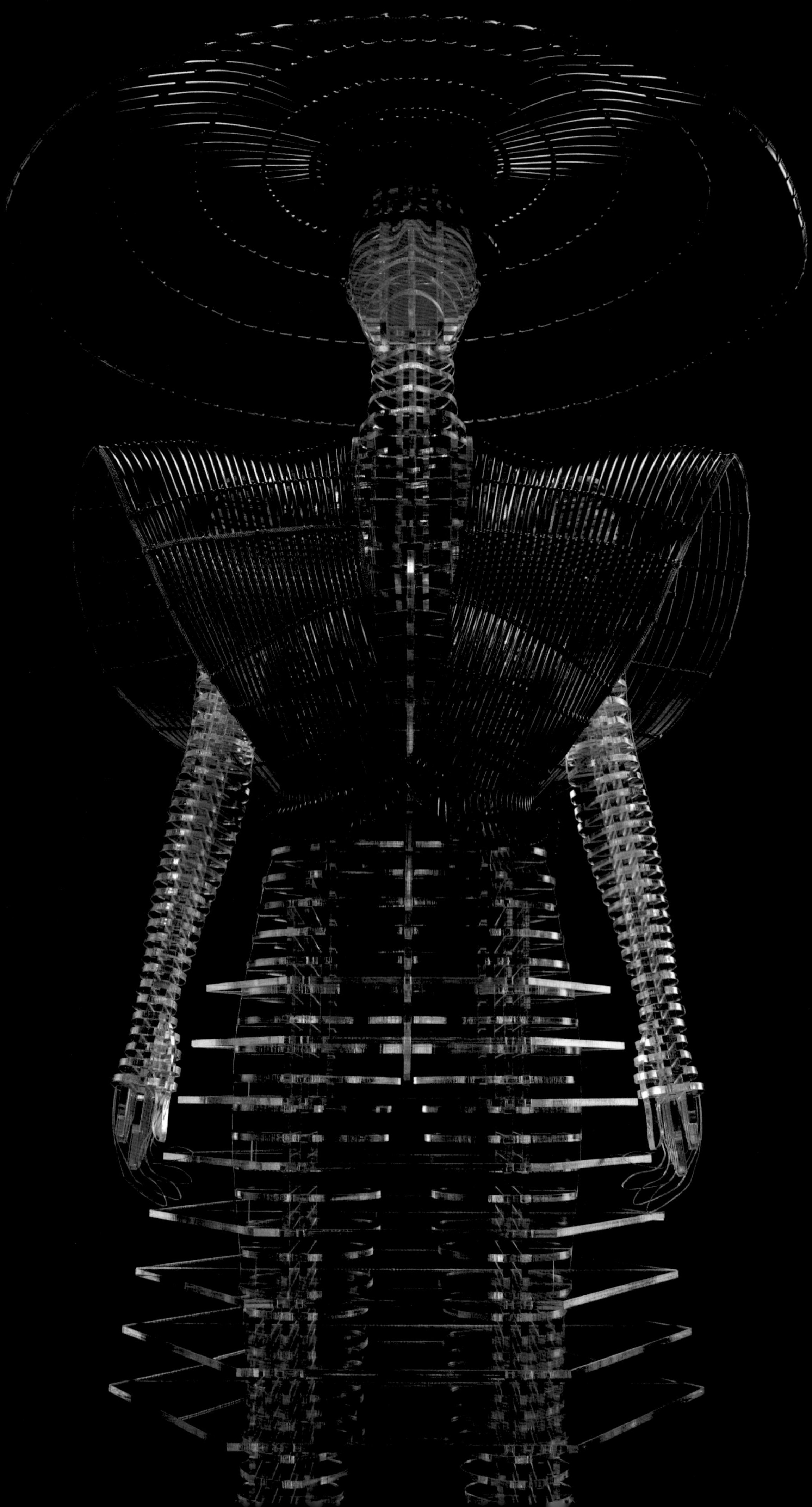

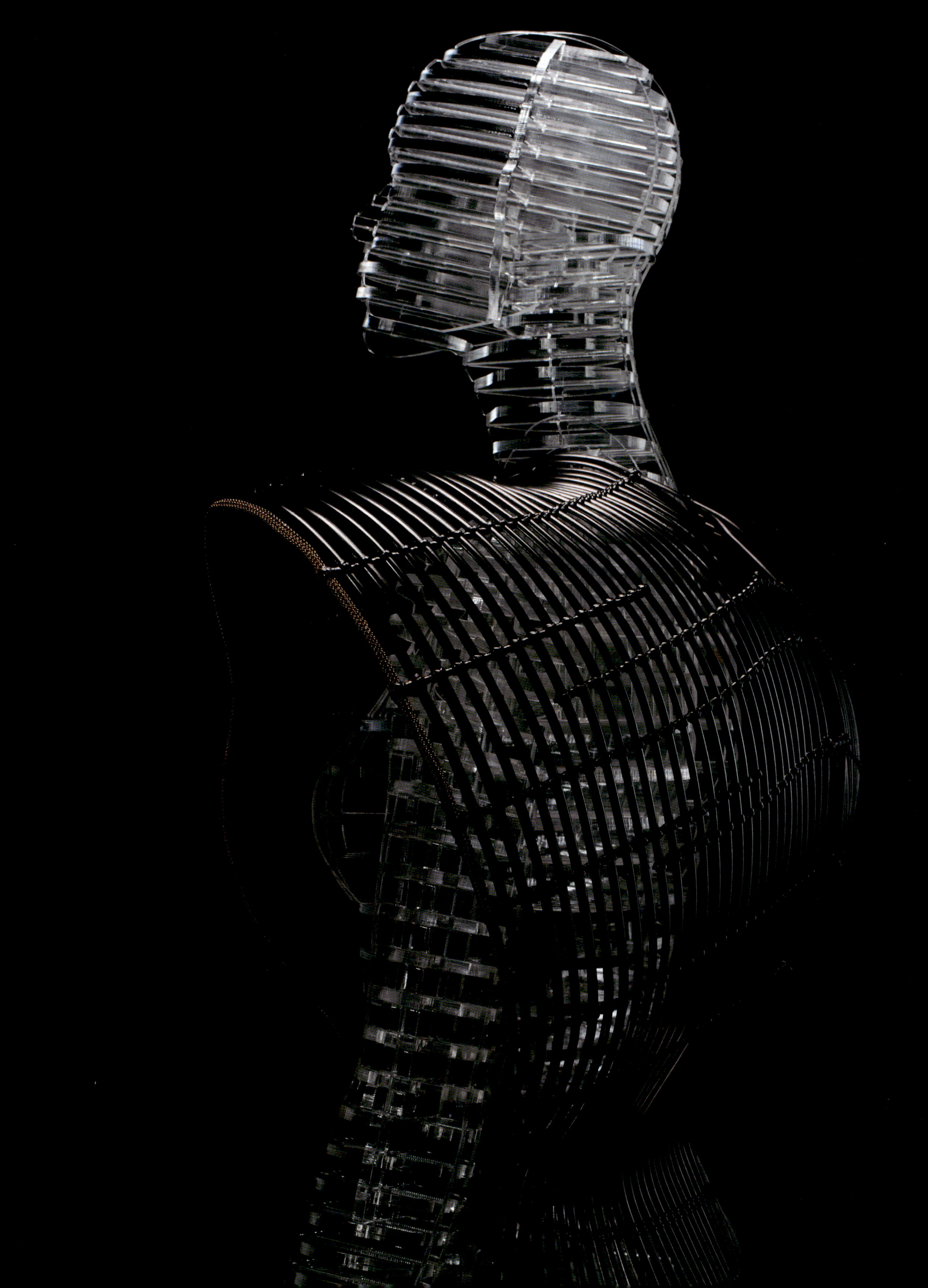

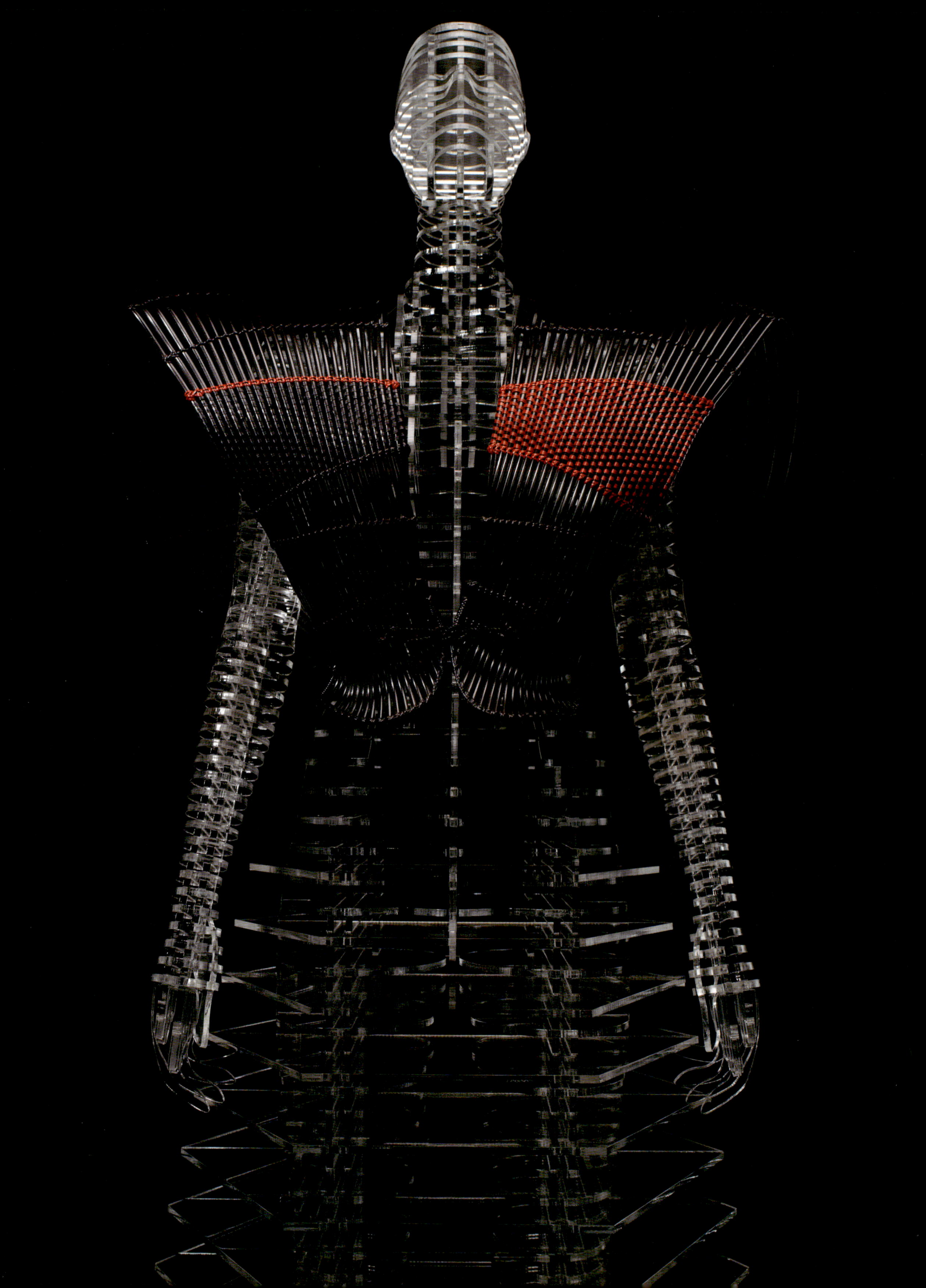

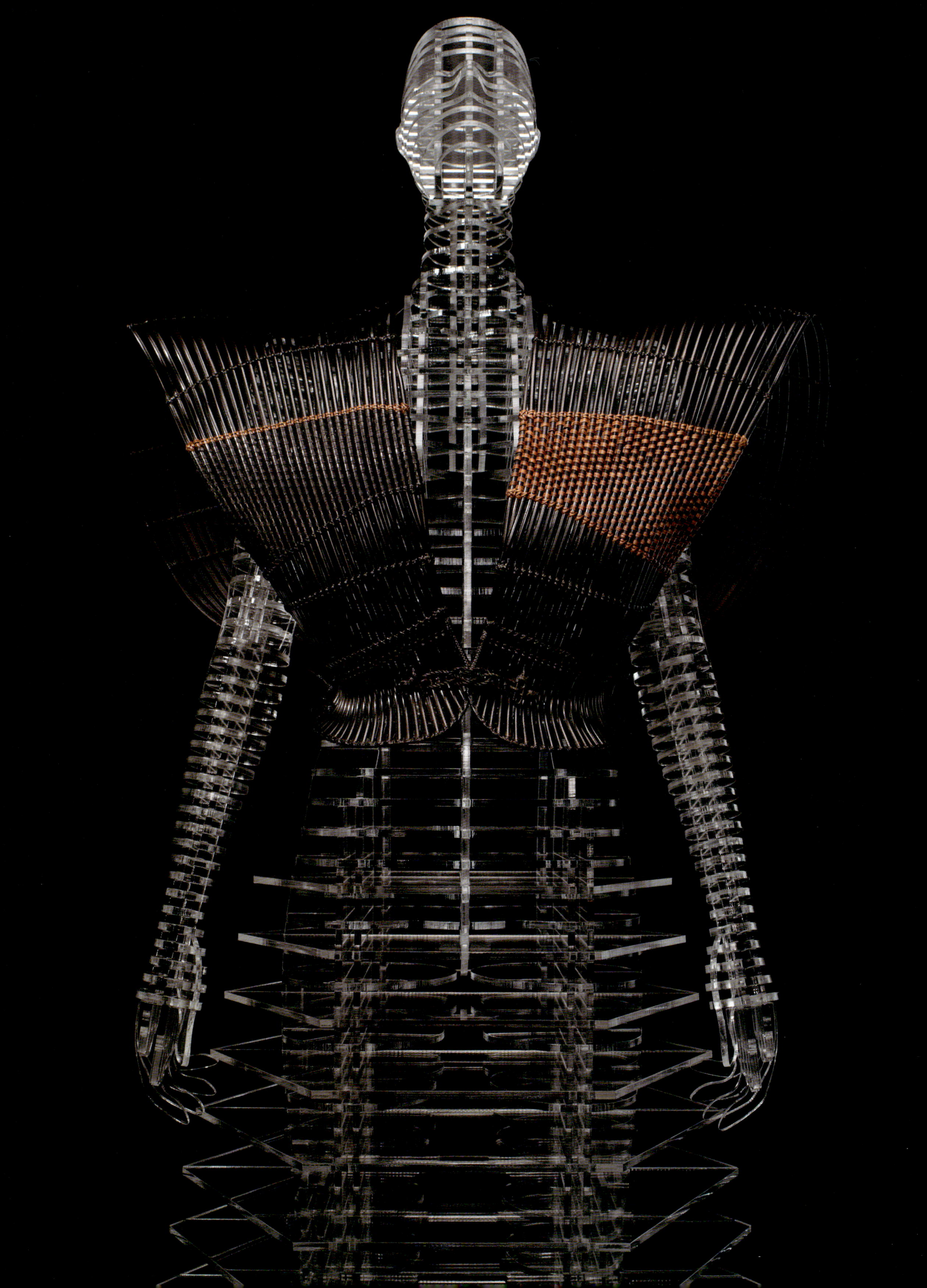

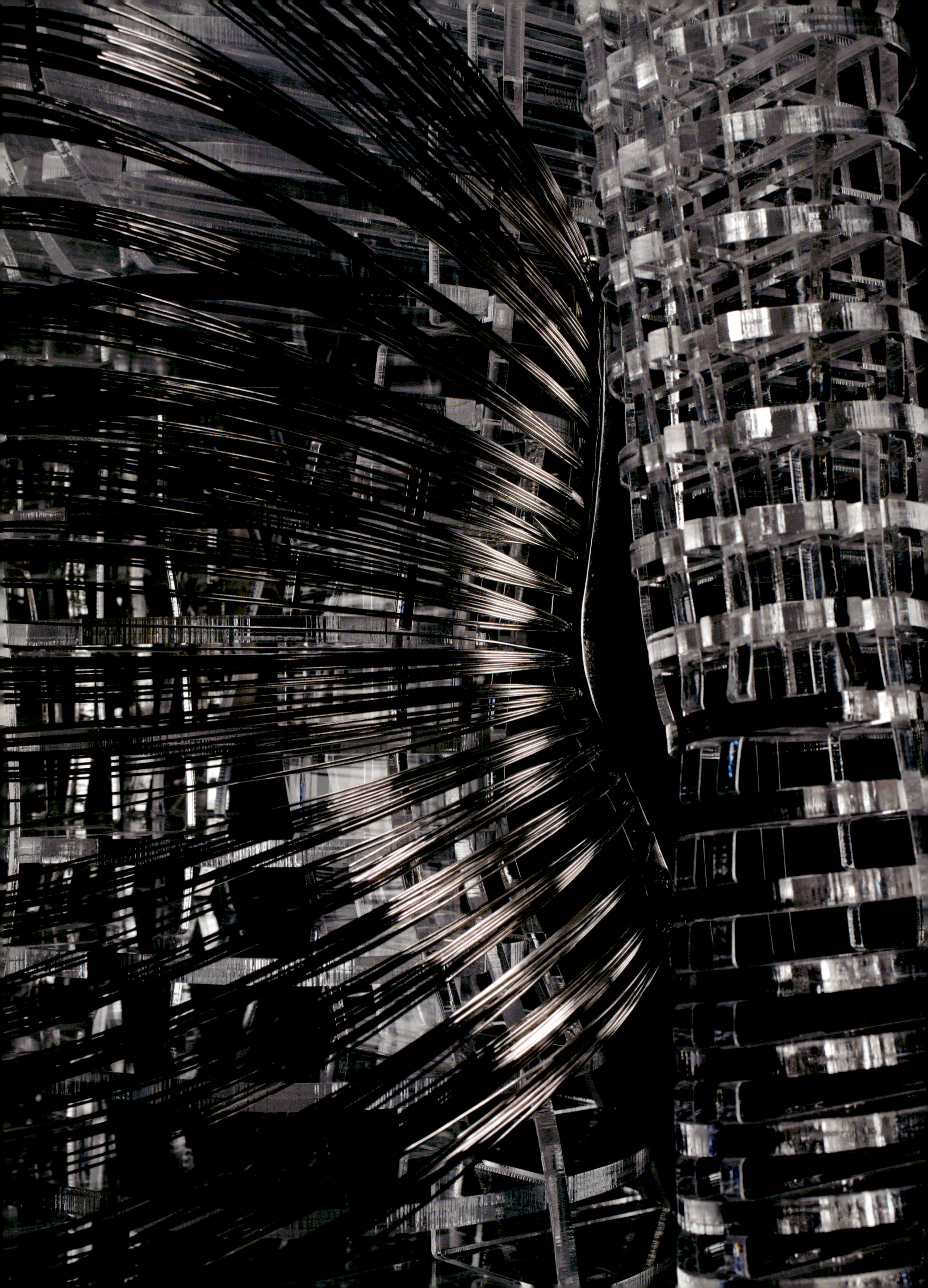

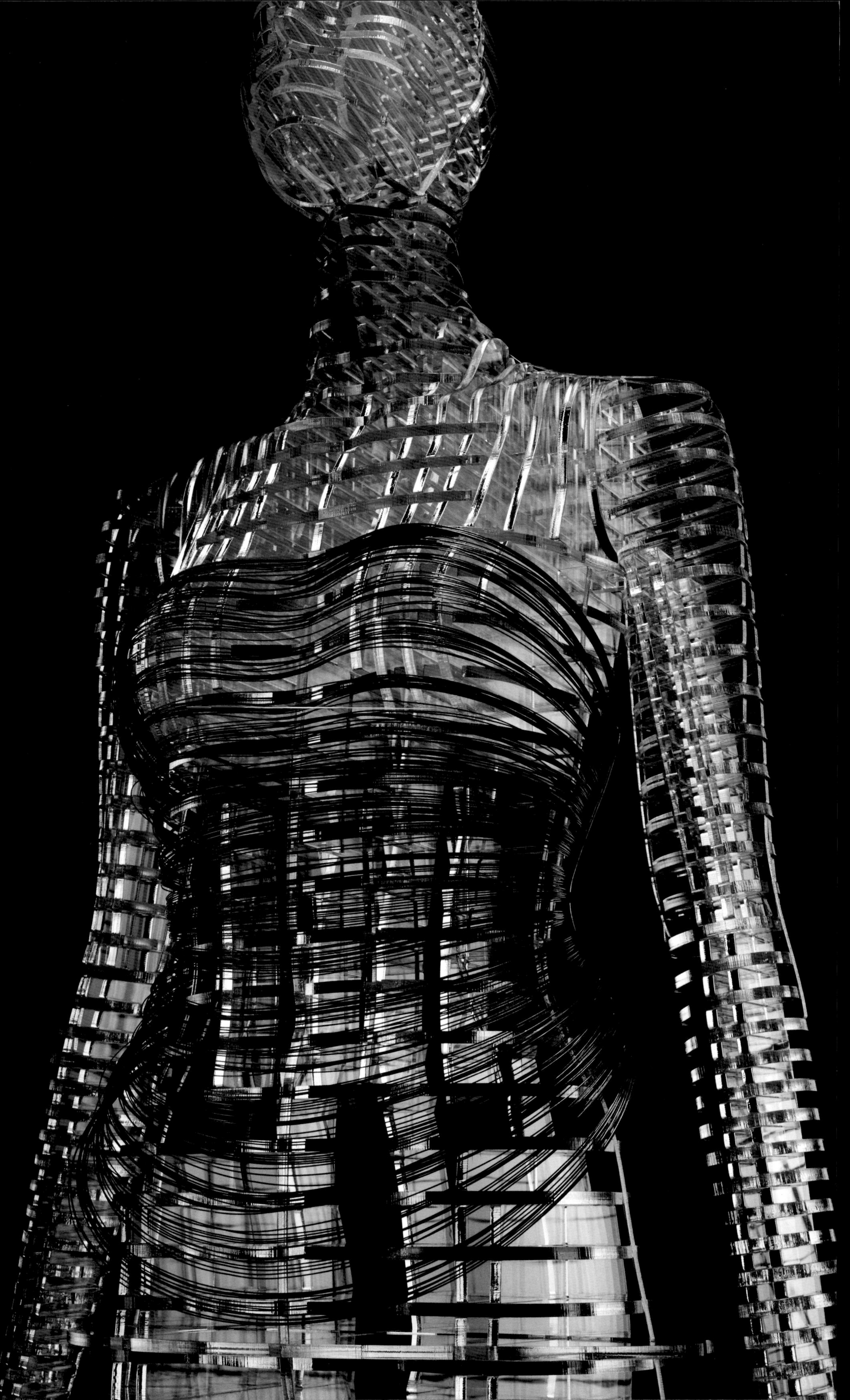

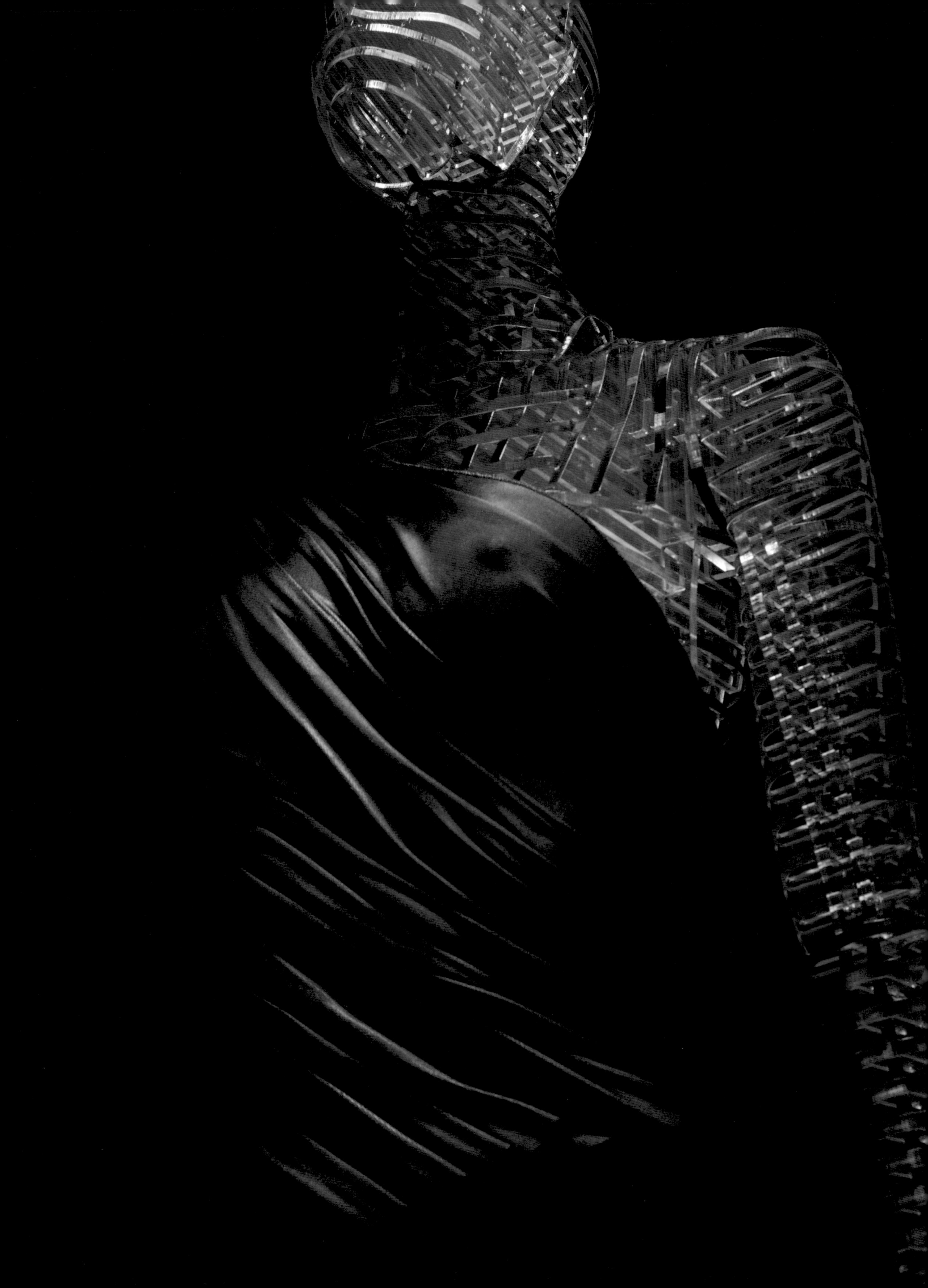

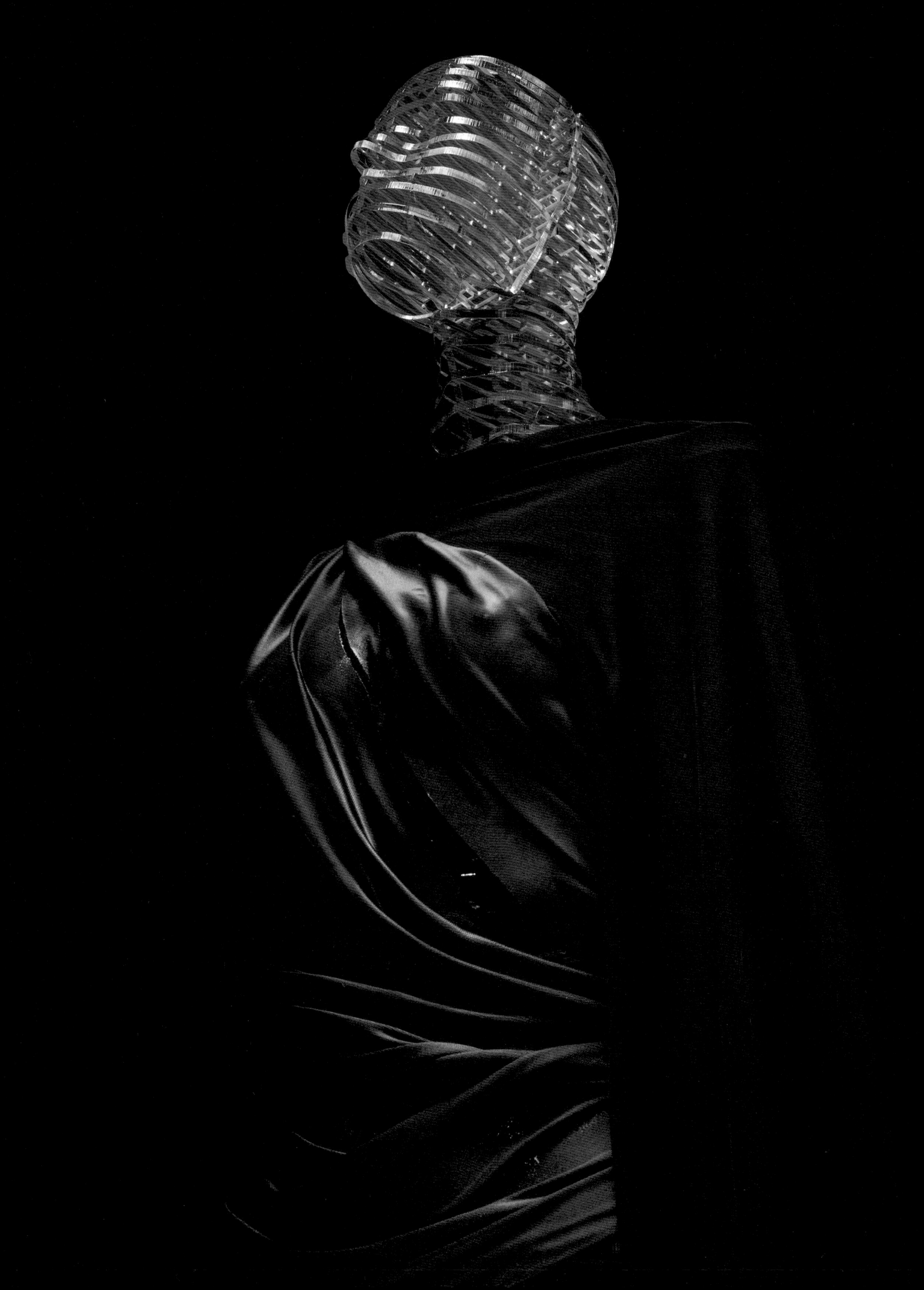

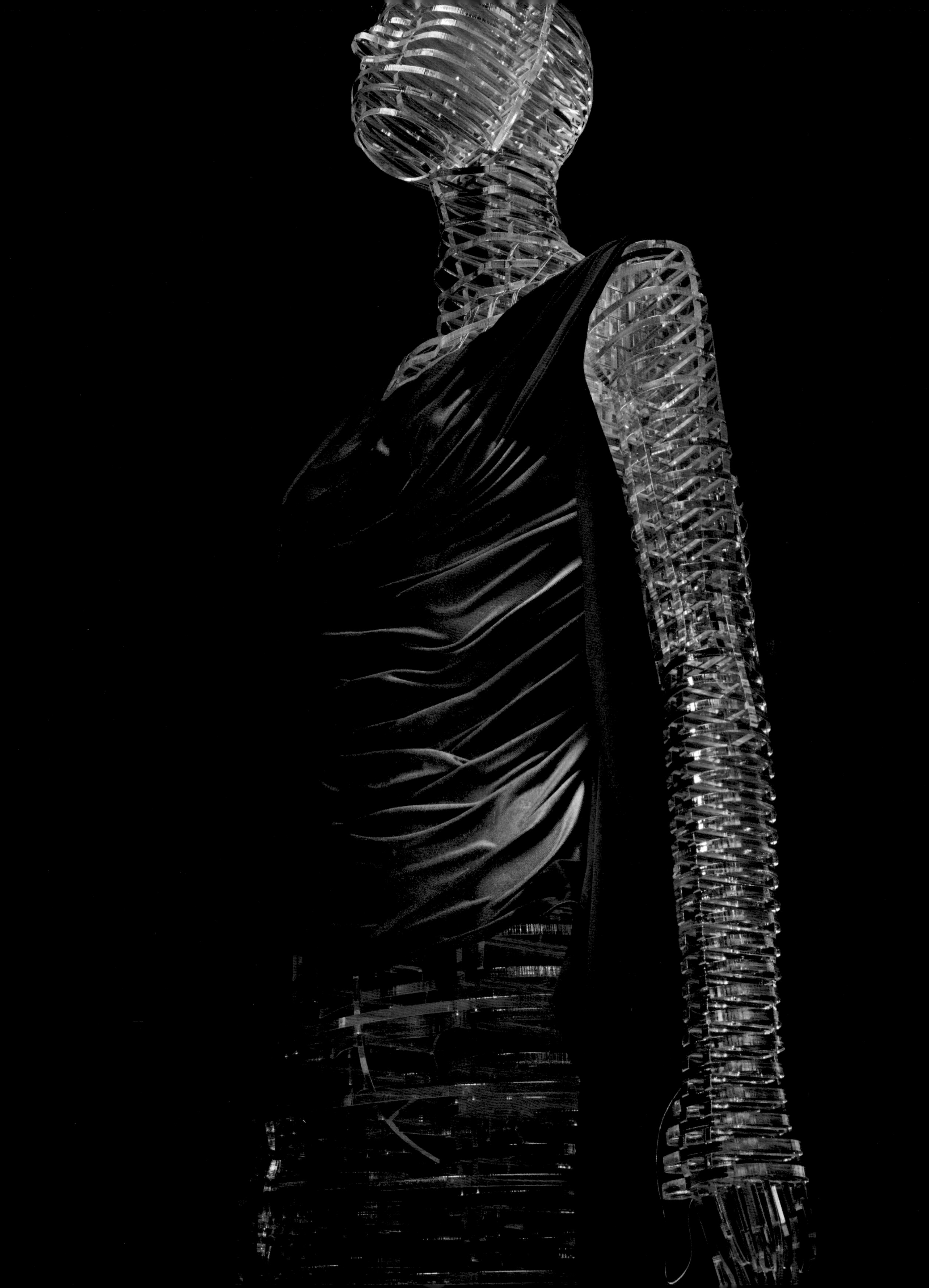

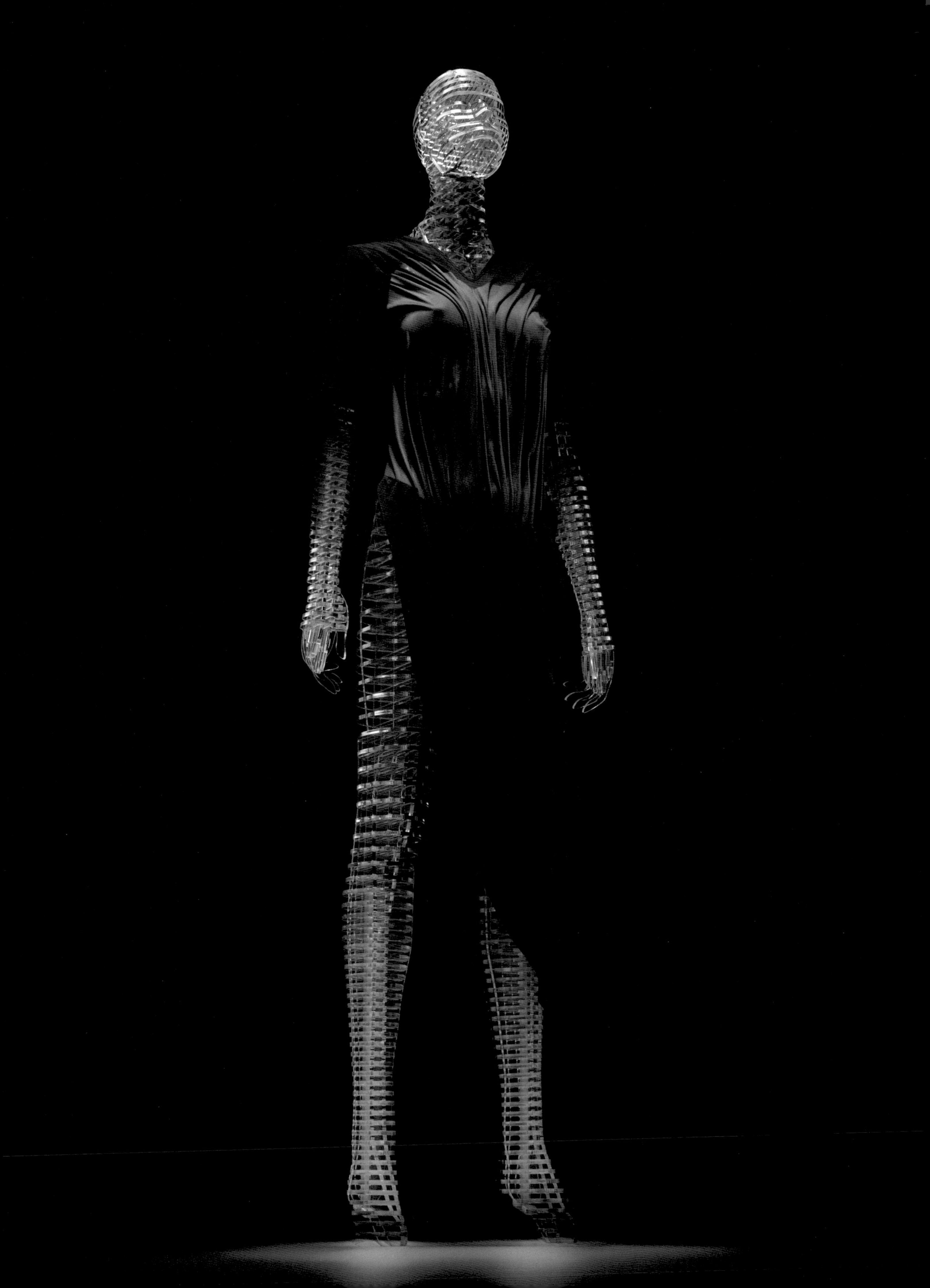

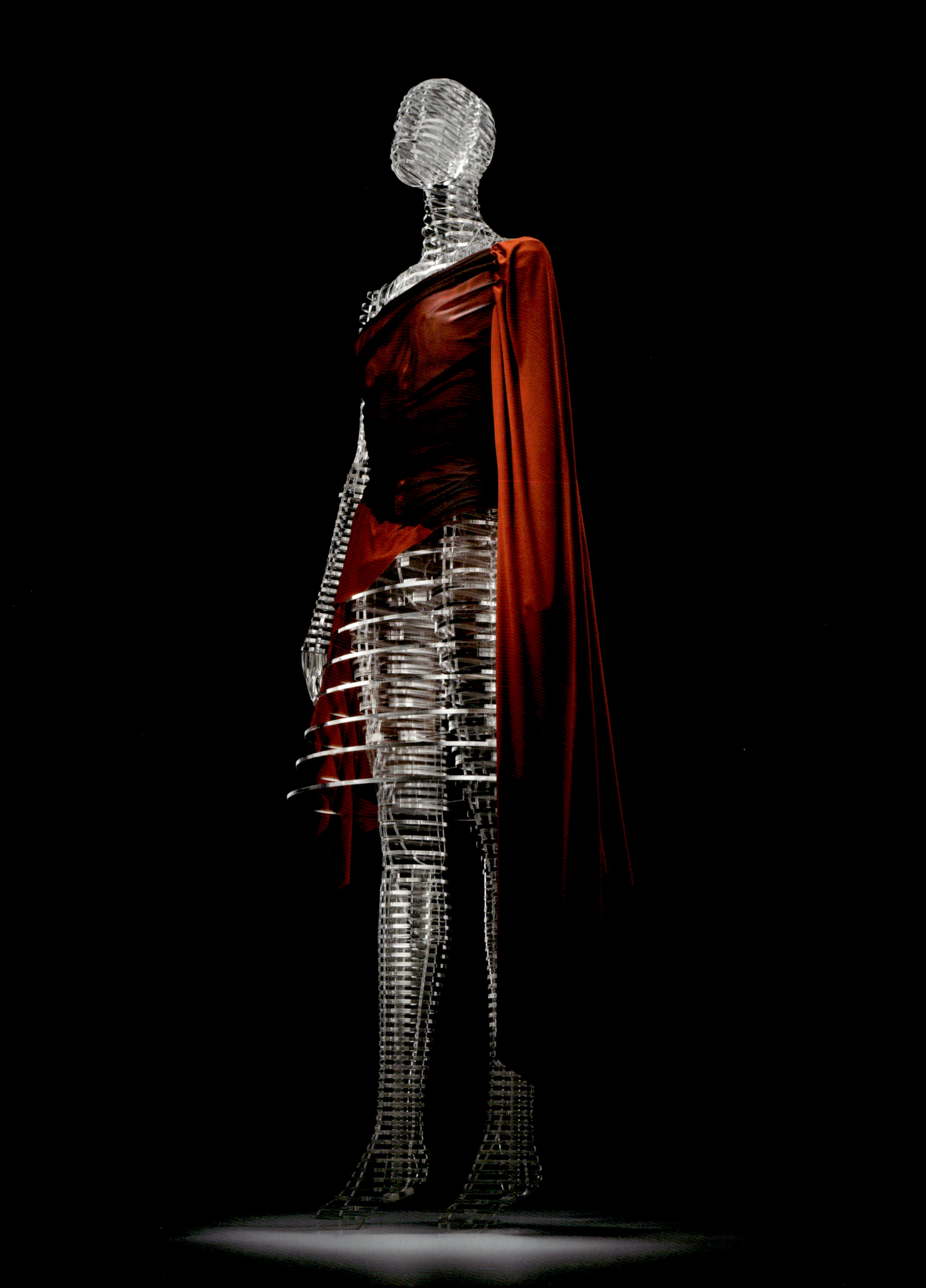

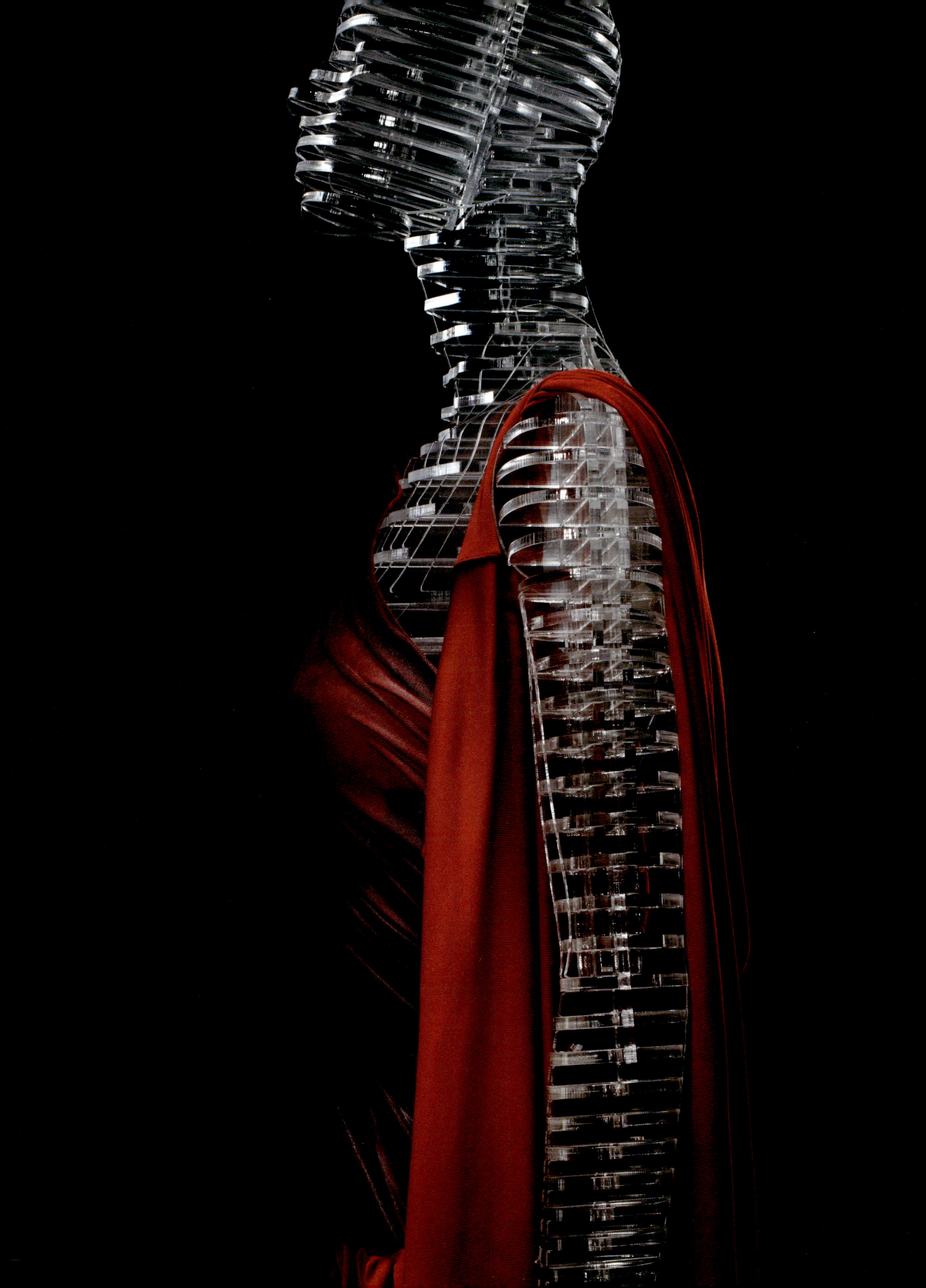

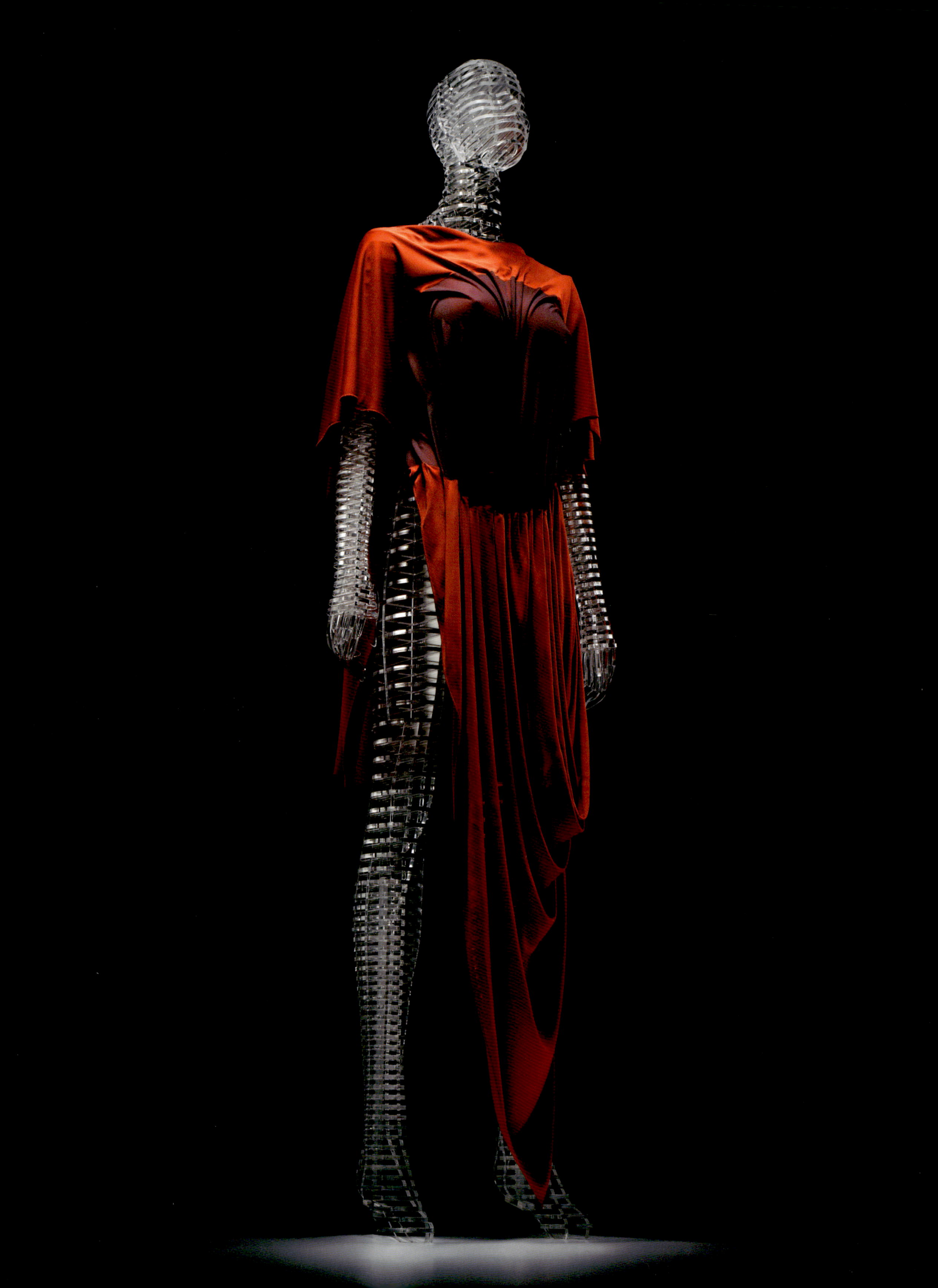

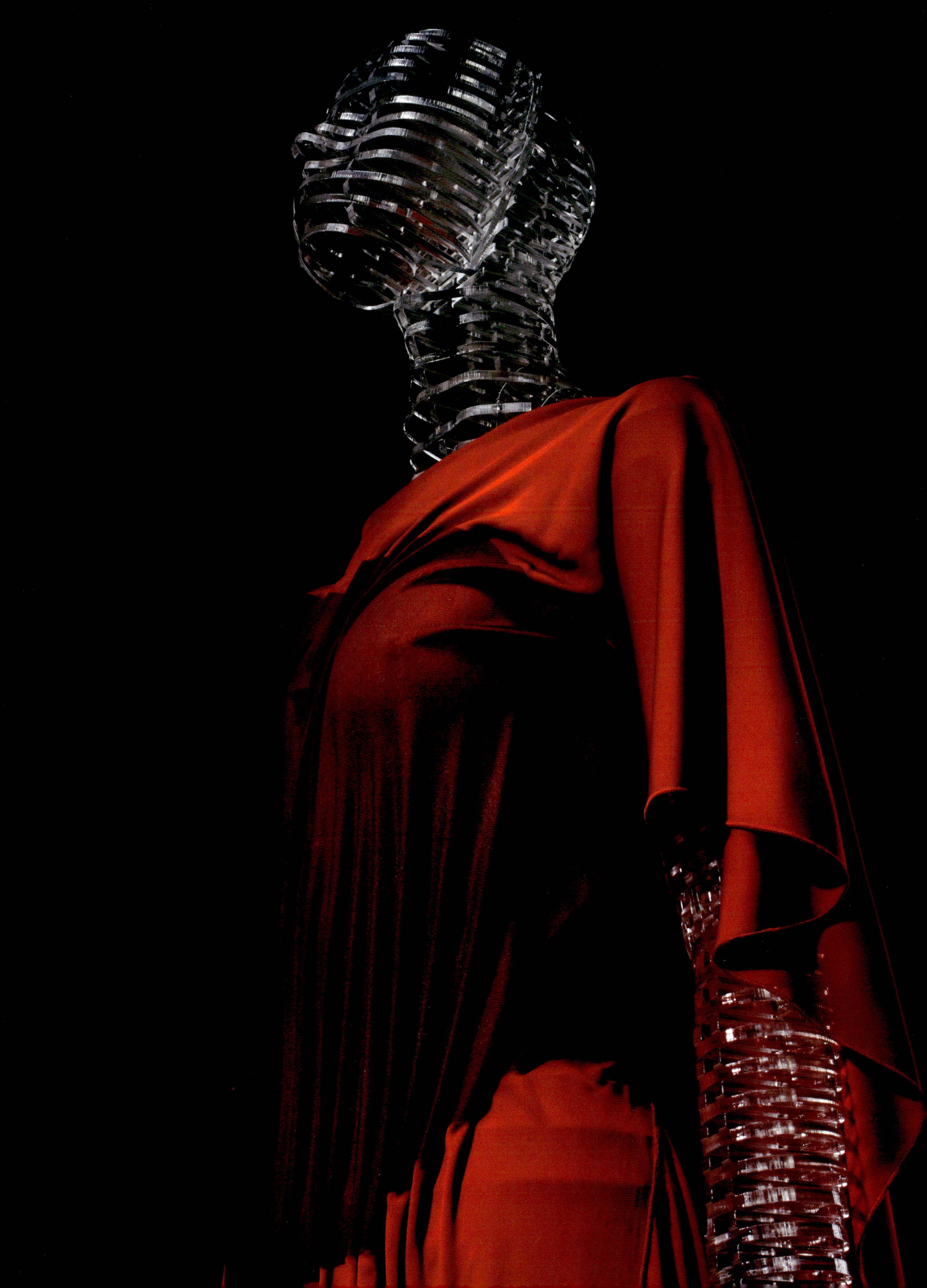

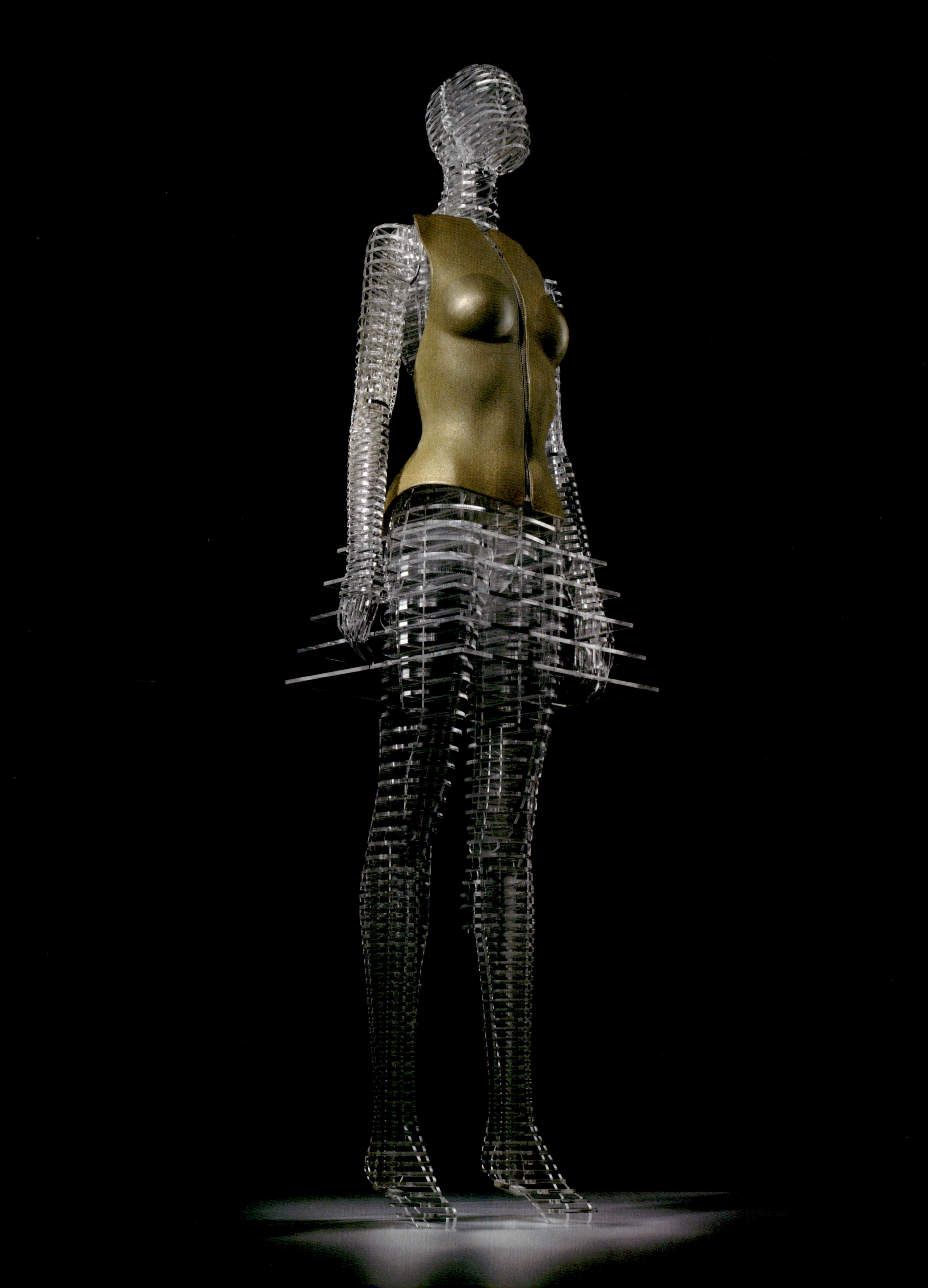

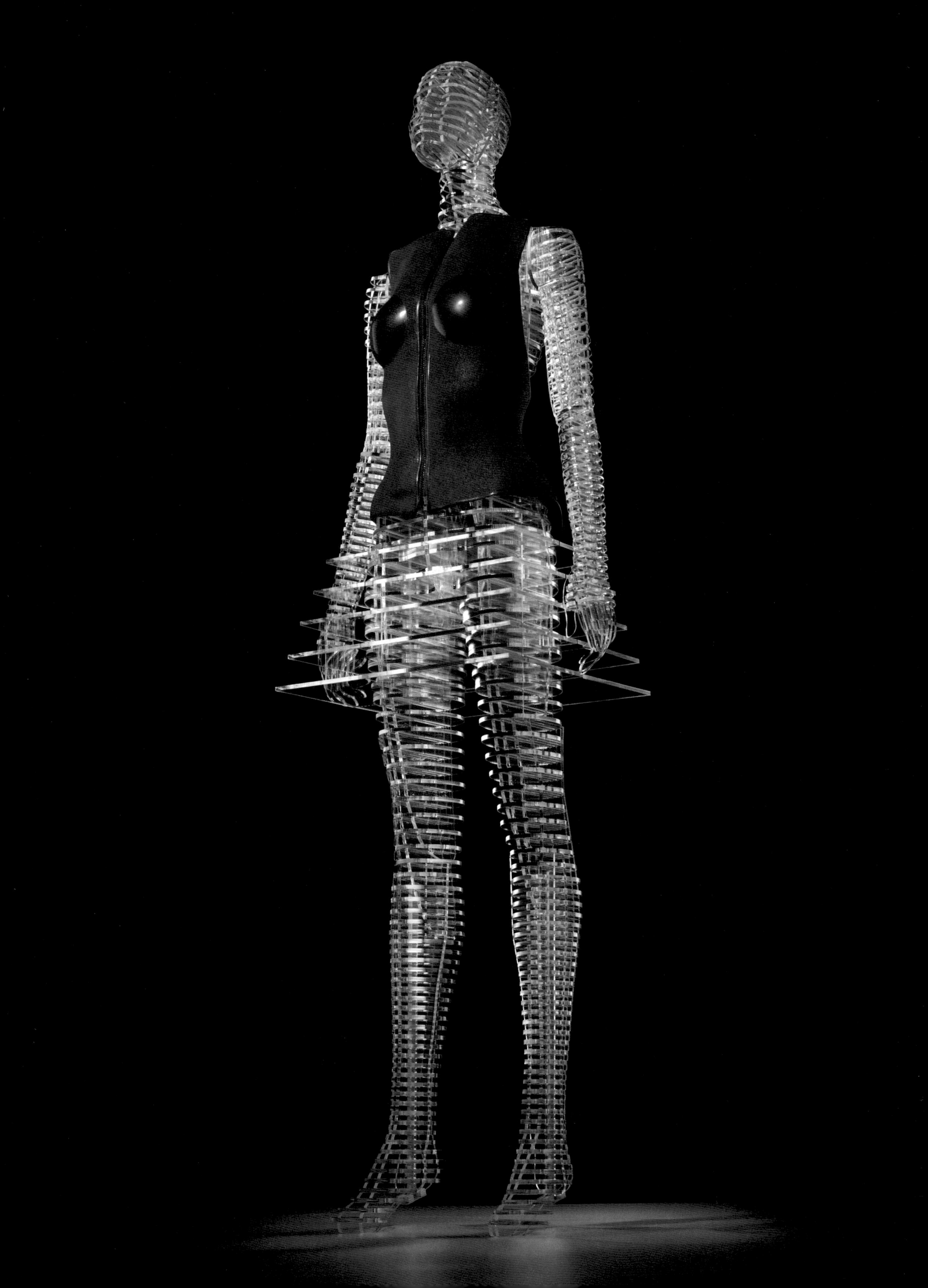

# C

**展覧会場 C ／ section C**

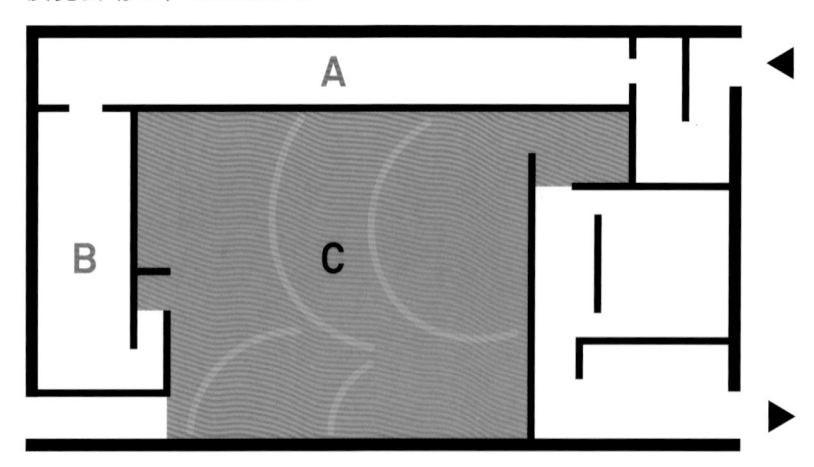

三宅一生の出す解答の幅は驚くほどに広い。かたちの創出、実用主義、人間の要素に向かう鋭いまなざしが、デザインとなって融合している。歩みは止まらない。ひとつの段階の成果は同時に新たなる段階の始まりとなる。無限の可能性を秘めて進行する曲線のようだ────とする三宅一生のデザイン観そのままに、次世代へと向かう積極的な展望を提示する。

This section explores the main themes of Issey Miyake's innovative drive and groups them into thematic clusters. The span of solutions Miyake has developed is strikingly broad in range, combining the creation of forms, pragmatism and above all a keen attention to the human factor. Intrinsically faithful to Miyake's view of design as an evolutionary curve with infinite possibilities, the exhibition follows a trajectory, marking the conclusion of phase and the beginning of a new one.

## 展覧会場 C

　革新への絶え間ない探求──このセクションでは、三宅一生の原動力となるいくつかのテーマを探る。
　「チーム精神」を尊重して仕事をする──デザインチームをはじめ、アイデアを具現化する技術をもった企業とも実りある豊かな共同作業に発展させる。そのアプローチには多面性があり、デザイン的であり、工学的でもあり、純粋に発明的ともいえる。あらゆる境界を押し拡げる三宅は未来志向でありながら、機能性や実用性に富み、なおかつ詩的なものをつくり続けている。
　三宅のデザインにおいて、素材とかたちは一体のものである。素材に視点をおいたデザインの厳選は、特徴ある造形と一致する。発想の具現化には、手の仕事と開発されるテクノロジーの活用、そして両者が融合して、服づくりの新たな方法が生まれる。特に、1988年に発表されたオリジナルの製法によるプリーツ、「製品プリーツ」の開発以降、視覚的、触覚的なデザインにとどまらず、従来の服づくりの工程をも変える。その仕事の発展に、プロダクトとして語られる衣服「PLEATS PLEASE ISSEY MIYAKE（プリーツ プリーズ）」が誕生する。三宅は日常で人々が潜在的に人々の求めるものを掘り起こし、答えとなるデザインを生み出す。それがもっとも顕著に見てとれるのが、「PLEATS PLEASE ISSEY MIYAKE」であり、その意味で彼はファッション・デザイナーではなく、デザイナーとよぶに相応しい。この「服の段階でプリーツをつける」方法を産業としてもたらしたことで、創意に溢れ、きわめて実用的で至便な服の新たな一大分野を開拓した。
　また、デザインには人間と環境への敬いが必要だ、と三宅は行動する。三宅が藤原大とともに開発した革命的な製造工程で生まれる「A-POC（エイ・ポック）」は、精密な技術の水準に達している。一本の糸がコンピュータ・プログラミングされた編機にかけられ、完成形までたどりつく服づくりのプロセスからは、廃棄される布はごくわずかだ。また、サイエンティストとの協働から発した折りの構造を追求する「132 5. ISSEY MIYAKE」では、再生繊維の研究と開発が続く。三宅の仕事は、深く社会と関わっているのだ。三宅の出す解答の幅は驚くほど広い。それでいて、その多様性に通底する要素がある。何度も繰り返してきた作業のなかで、三宅一生にとって、一枚の布から服をつくるということが、第一の創造的な挑戦であり、その核心は揺るぎない。それは単に創造上の要素に限らず、倫理的な要素にも深く配慮が注がれている。
　大きなプロジェクトは、およそ8年から10年をかけて取り組まれ、ある成果が生まれるとその先に課題が浮かび、また新たな動きが始まる。いずれの仕事も一過性ではなく、進化し次なる現実がつくり出される。

## section C

A constant quest for innovation is the driving force behind Issey Miyake's approach to clothing design.

Other constants include a love of collaboration and always working with and respecting a team spirit. Miyake has also made efforts throughout his career to foster good working relationships with outside companies. His approach to making things is part engineering, part design and part pure invention, all of which combine toward a practical use in everyday life. Issey Miyake has always pushed beyond all boundaries and has reached unprecedented levels of formal abstraction in his futuristic, pragmatic and poetic creations.

In Miyake's designs, there is a fusion of material and form; the materials-oriented designs match the distinctive forms of the clothing. A combination of craftsmanship and new technology turn the ideas into reality, and it is the fusion of these that creates new methods by which to make clothing. In 1988, Miyake developed his distinctive pleats using a new process called garment pleating. Since that time he has not only continued to innovate in the visual and tactile design of clothing, but also in the processes by which the clothing itself is made. Issey Miyake creates solutions to everyday needs, a design characteristic that is most clearly visible in his PLEATS PLEASE ISSEY MIYAKE. By creating products, things that not only enhance the lives of the wearers with beauty but that are also practical solutions to their needs, he is a designer, not a fashion designer. He has been able to provide inventive solutions to busy, traveling women whose needs combine practicality, versatility as well as aesthetic beauty.

He believes that any form of design should respect both the human being and the environment. A-POC, the revolutionary process that Miyake developed in 1998 with Dai Fujiwara, expresses this idea, bringing it to groundbreaking levels of technical finesse. By feeding a single thread into an industrial knitting machine programmed by a computer, he was able to create form and texture as well as fully-finished garments in a single process, thus eliminating waste. 132 5. ISSEY MIYAKE started from the collaboration with a scientist whose research was in the structure of folds; today his Reality Lab team continues its research and development of recycled fibers to make future 132 5. designs from sustainable materials. Miyake's work is deeply linked with society. The span of solutions Miyake has developed is striking. Yet, in their diversity, they are bound by a single unifying element. Anytime Miyake is faced with the need for a new creative challenge he returns to his original touchstone: making clothing from a single piece of cloth.

Issey Miyake's larger projects usually require between eight and ten years to develop, and at the end, they always raise new questions and challenges, and inspire movement in new directions. None of these designs are transient; each is an evolutionary step toward a new reality.

素材

　素材は無限。どんな素材でも服にすることが可能だと三宅一生は考える。テキスタイル・ディレクターの皆川魔鬼子がコレクション・チームに加わり、布を研究することからコレクション制作を始めた70年代の仕事を基礎に、80年代は、より実験的な素材づくりに向かう。従来服には使われない材質にも挑戦し衣服デザインの可能性をさらに広げた。未知の生地を求める三宅の抽象的な発信をうけて、研究と開発を繰り返し試作を重ね、解答を出していく素材づくりは、さまざまな布地を生み、服としてかたちづくられコレクションで発表されていった。工場の片隅に置き去りにされた布端も、使われなくなった機械も、三宅とチームにとっては魅力ある存在として輝いて見えた。そしてまた、新しい技術を駆使して手工芸を現代の生活に生かし、伝統に新しい生命を吹き込み、ものづくりにテクノロジーと人の手のぬくもりを融合していく。常に社会に目をむけ、その先の服づくりを目指す三宅は、早くからくらしの環境に配慮し、限られた資源を使うものづくりにおいて、既存のものも生かす「再利用」を提案している。

## MATERIAL

Materials are infinite, and Issey Miyake has always been confident that any material can be used for clothing. Makiko Minagawa joined the Miyake Design Studio as a Textile Director in the early 70s with a strong background in textile design. Minagawa and Miyake immediately embarked upon a journey that has lasted over 40 years and resulted in a more experimental exploration of materials and a collaborative approach with textile manufacturers. Facing and overcoming the challenges presented by materials not normally used in clothing, Miyake expanded the possibilities for clothing design. Miyake's material developments are, in the abstract, a search for the unknown, an experimentation and research with new textiles that is repeated over and over again. It is a constant process of prototyping new kinds of fabric, which he then brings to the world in new collections. A piece of cloth discarded in some corner of a factory, a machine that has fallen into disuse: these are irresistible objects for the Miyake team. New technologies are used to bring traditional handicrafts new life and adapt them to modern requirements. The result is a fusion of manufacturing and the warmth of human hands. Miyake is both attuned to his society and constantly seeking out the next stage of design. Manufacturing is, in some senses, a question of how to best use limited resources, and Miyake was one of the first to recognize environmental concerns and propose concrete solutions to the reuse of pre-existing materials.

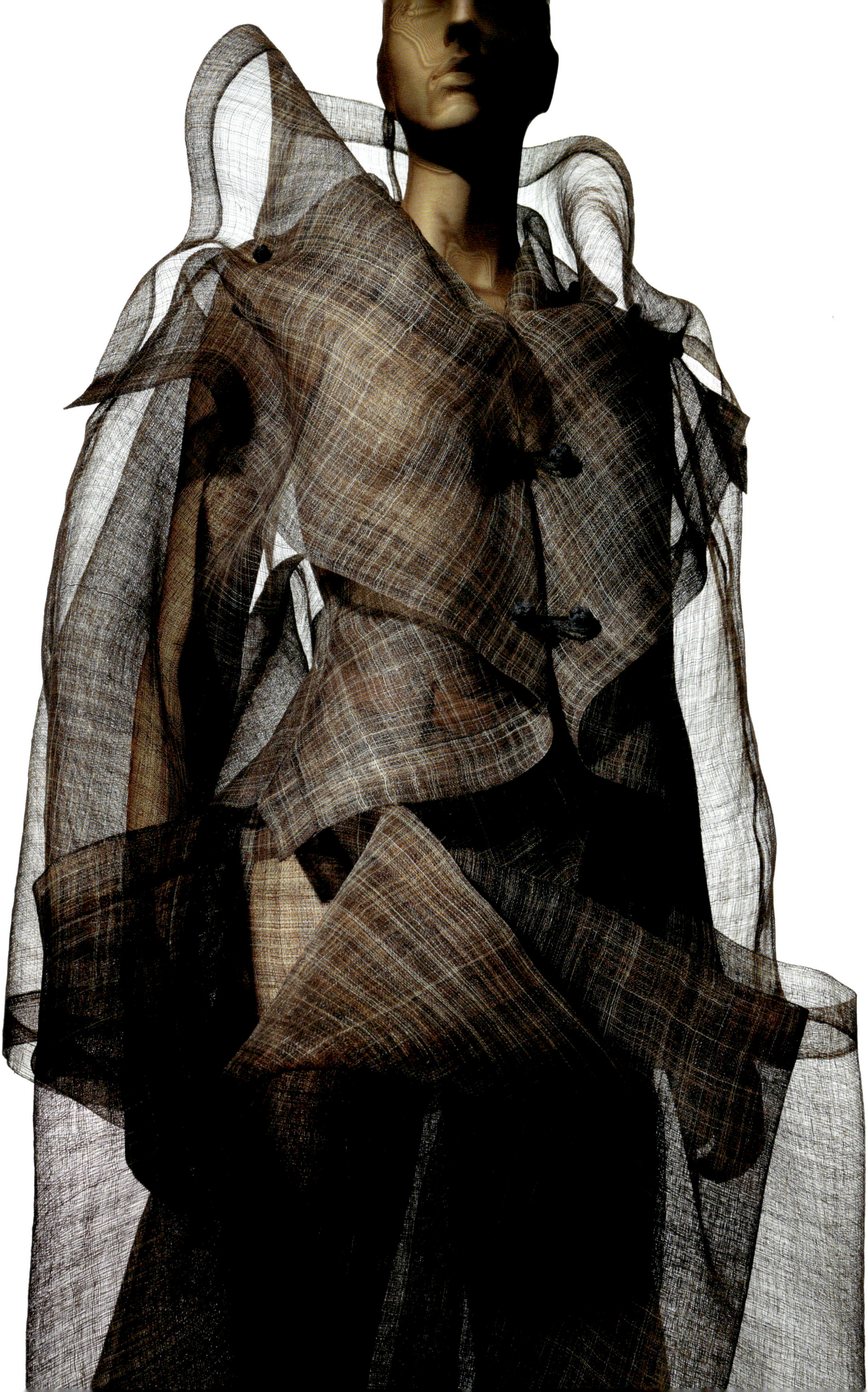

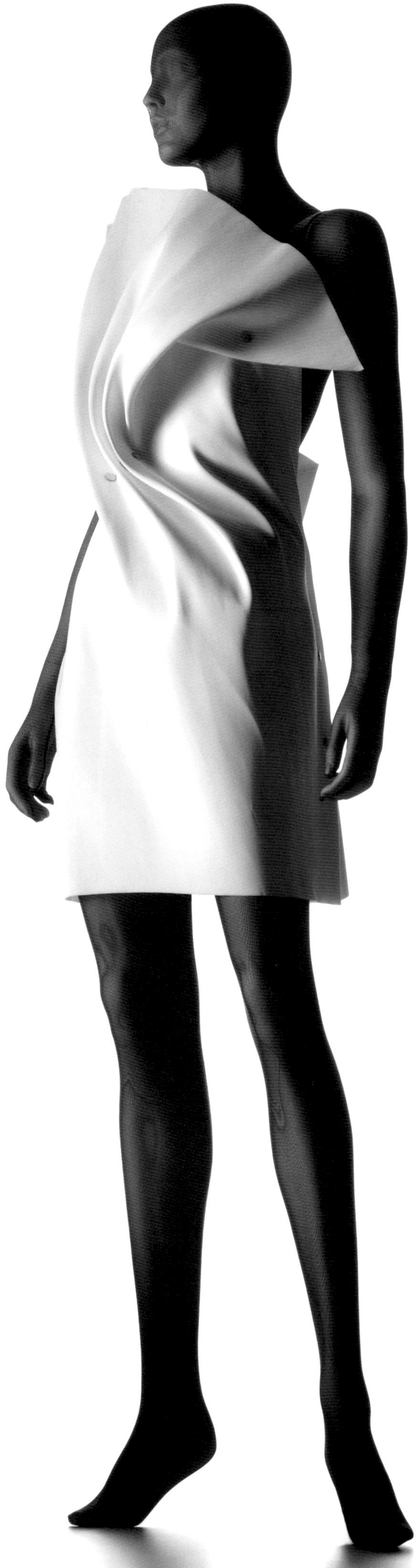

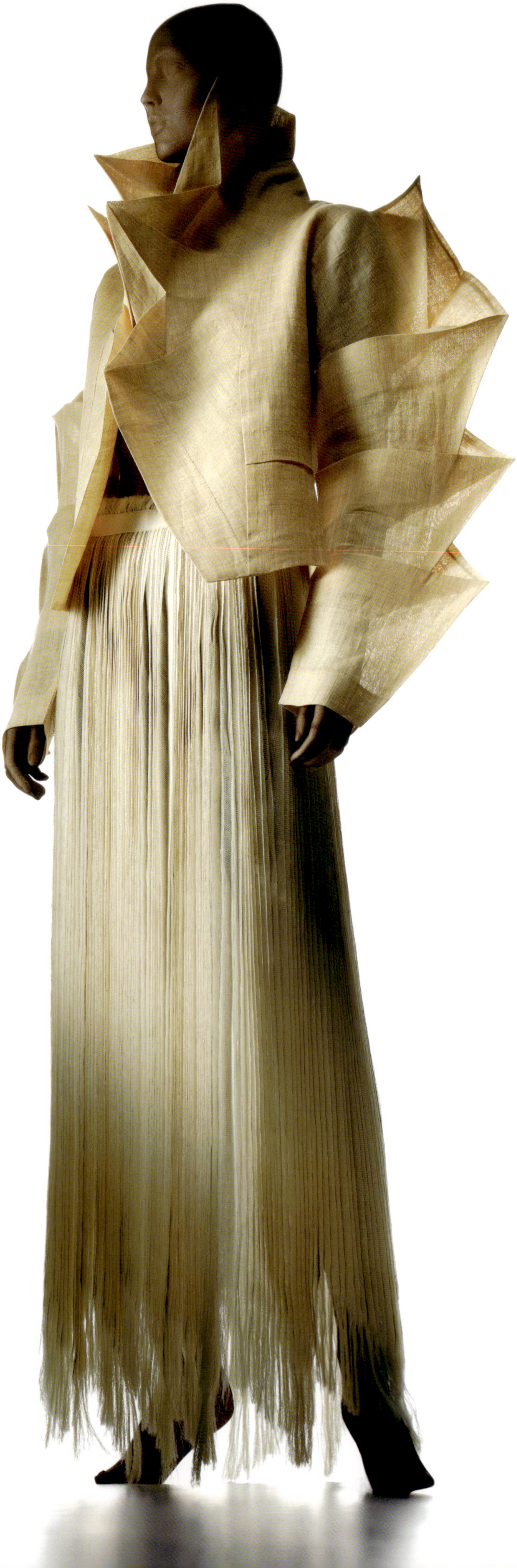

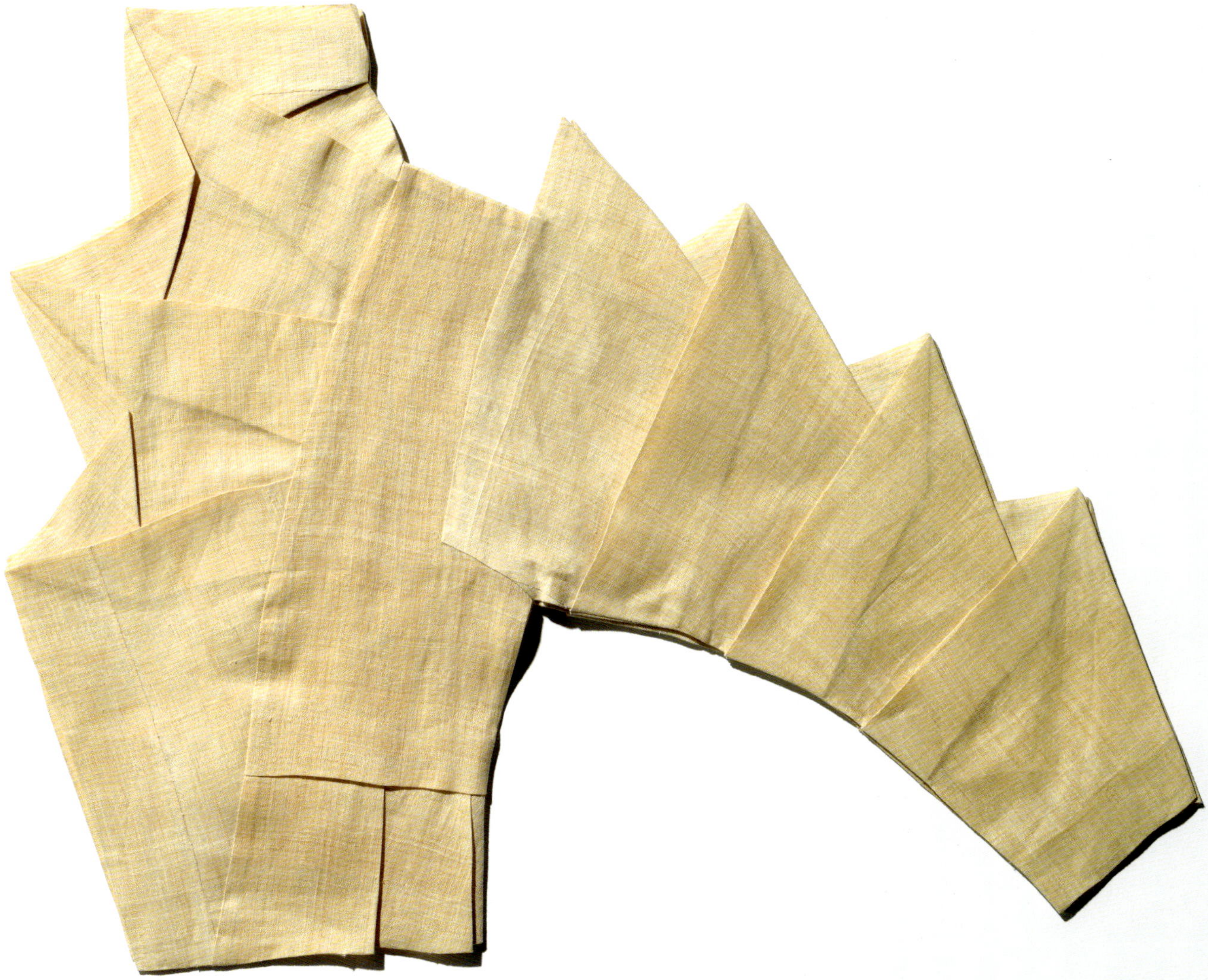

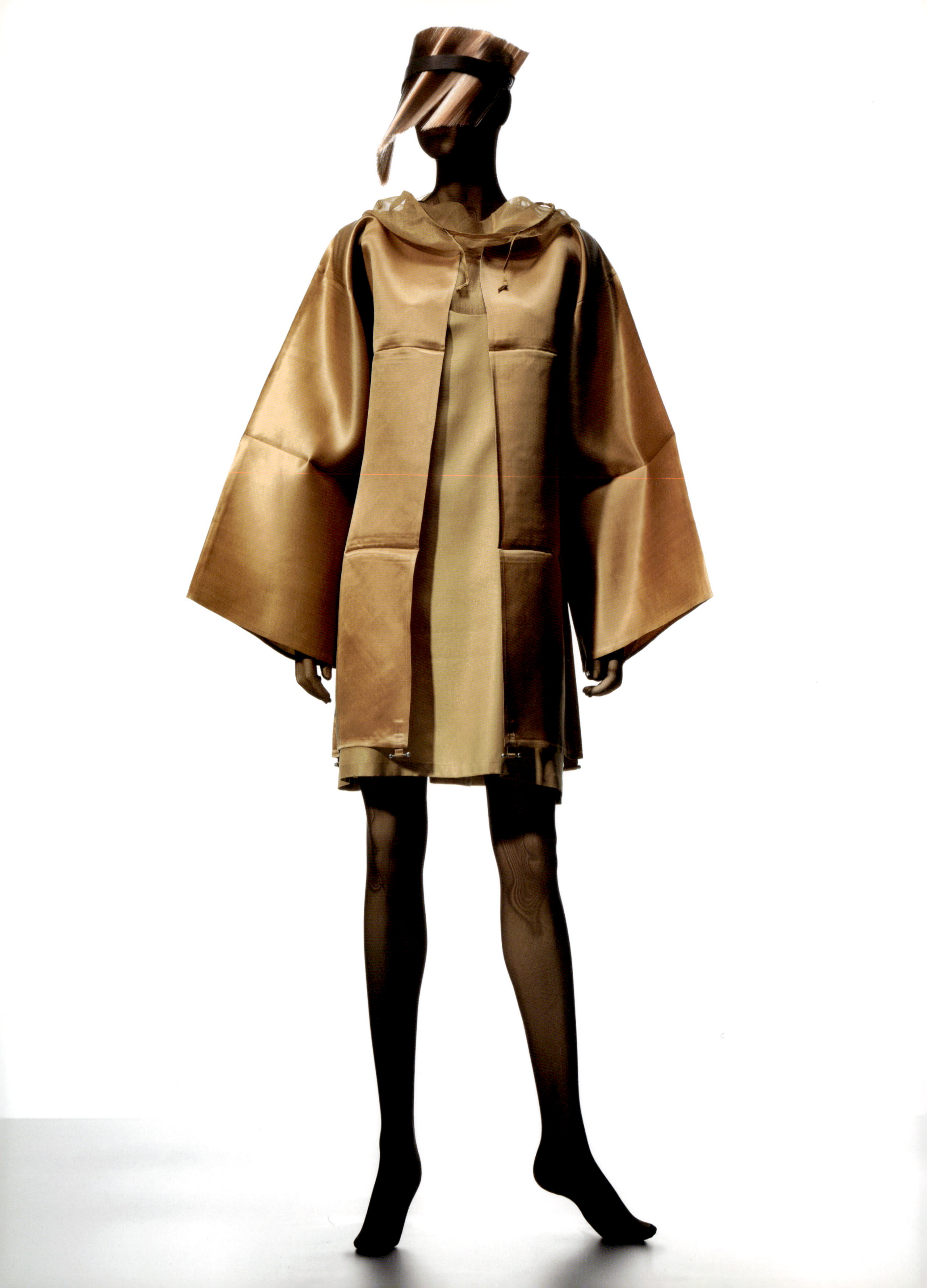

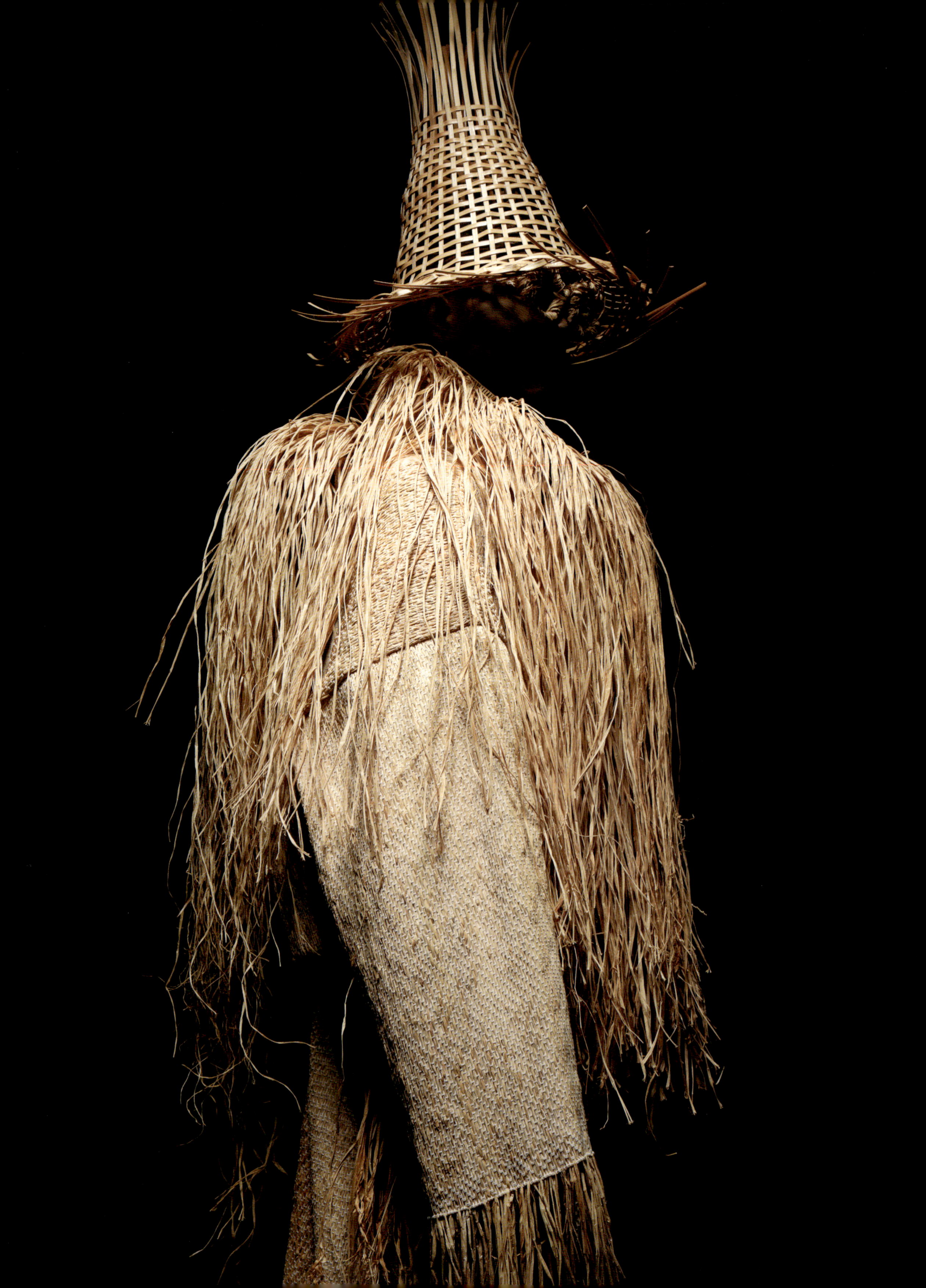

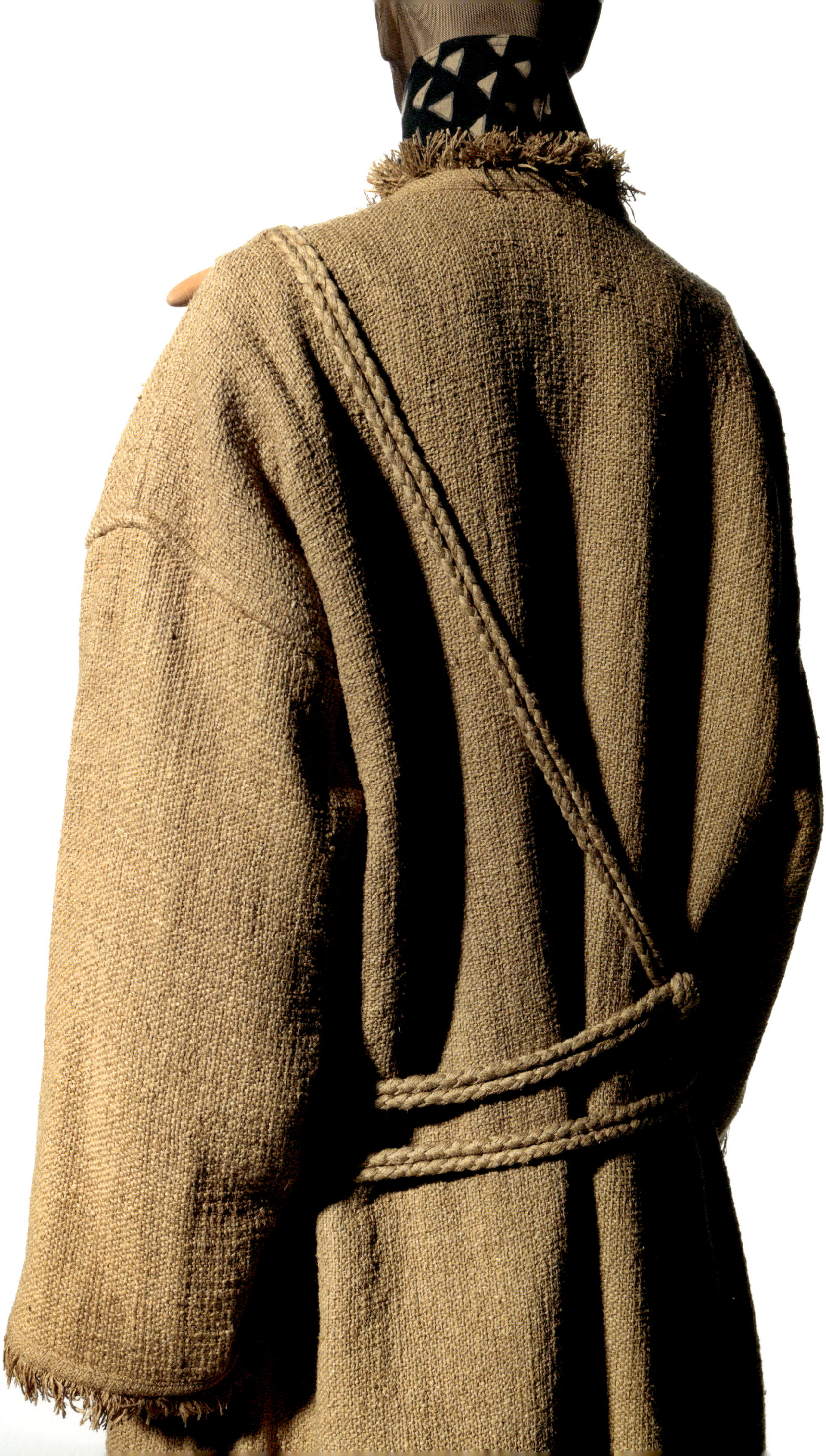

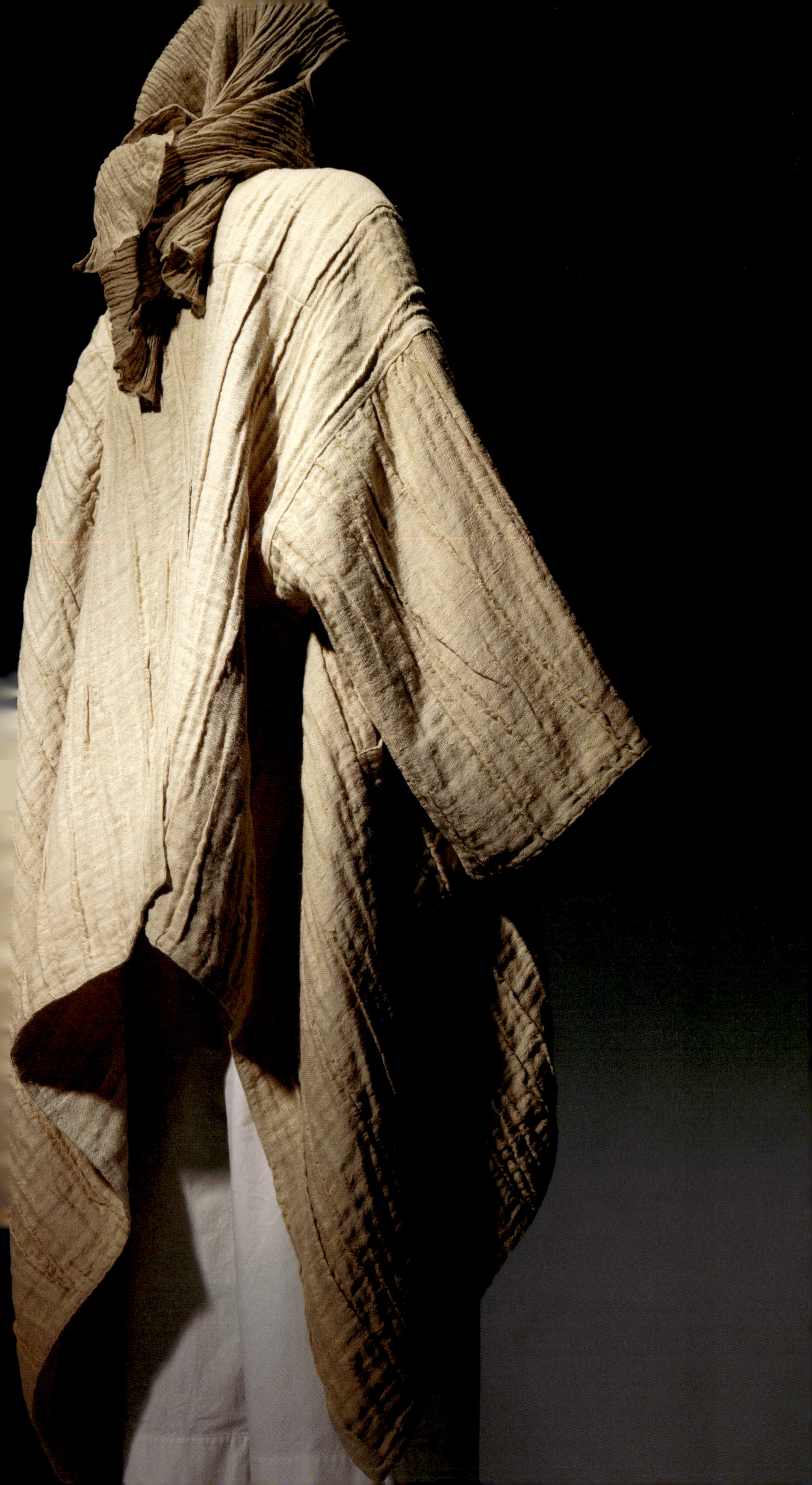

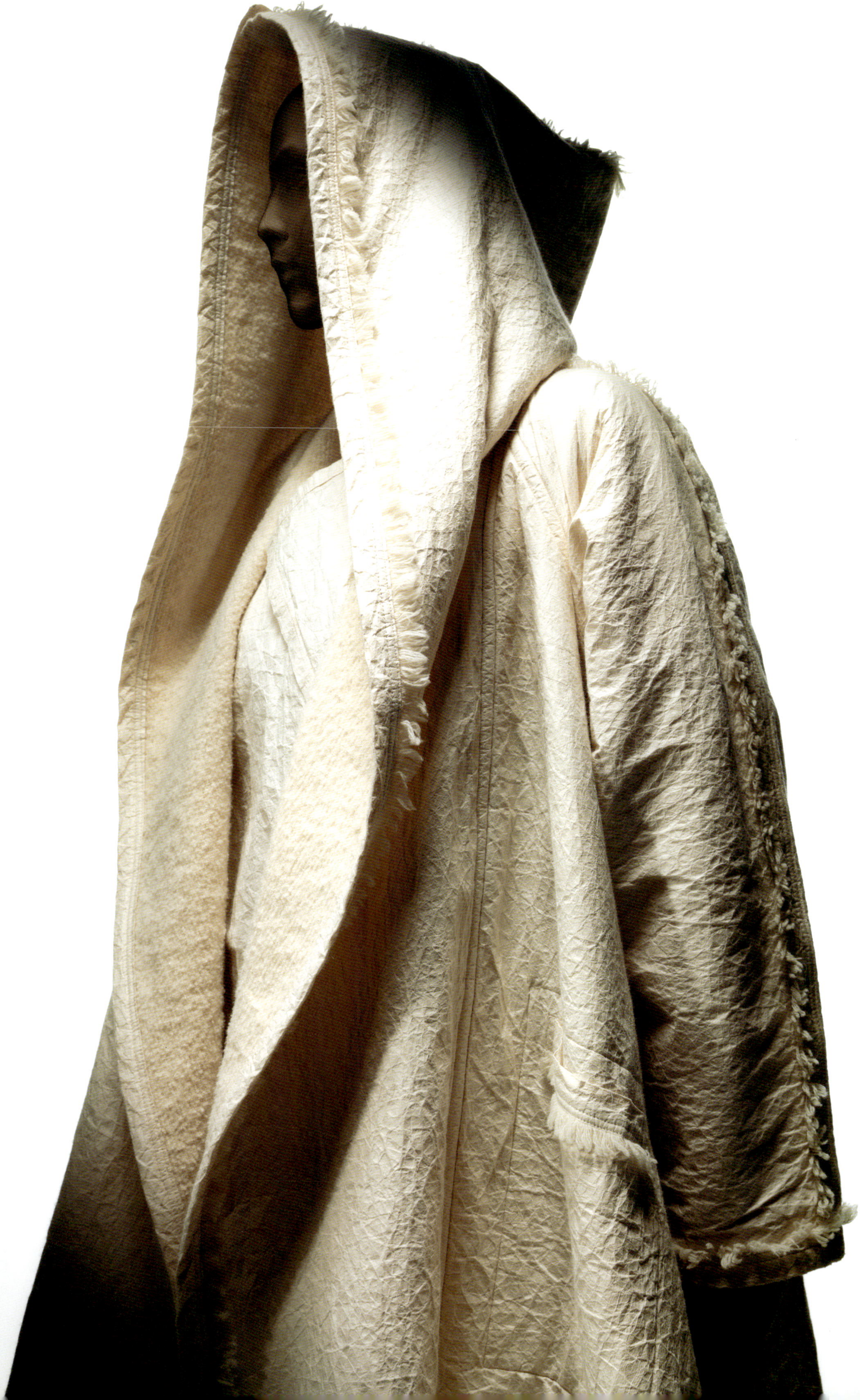

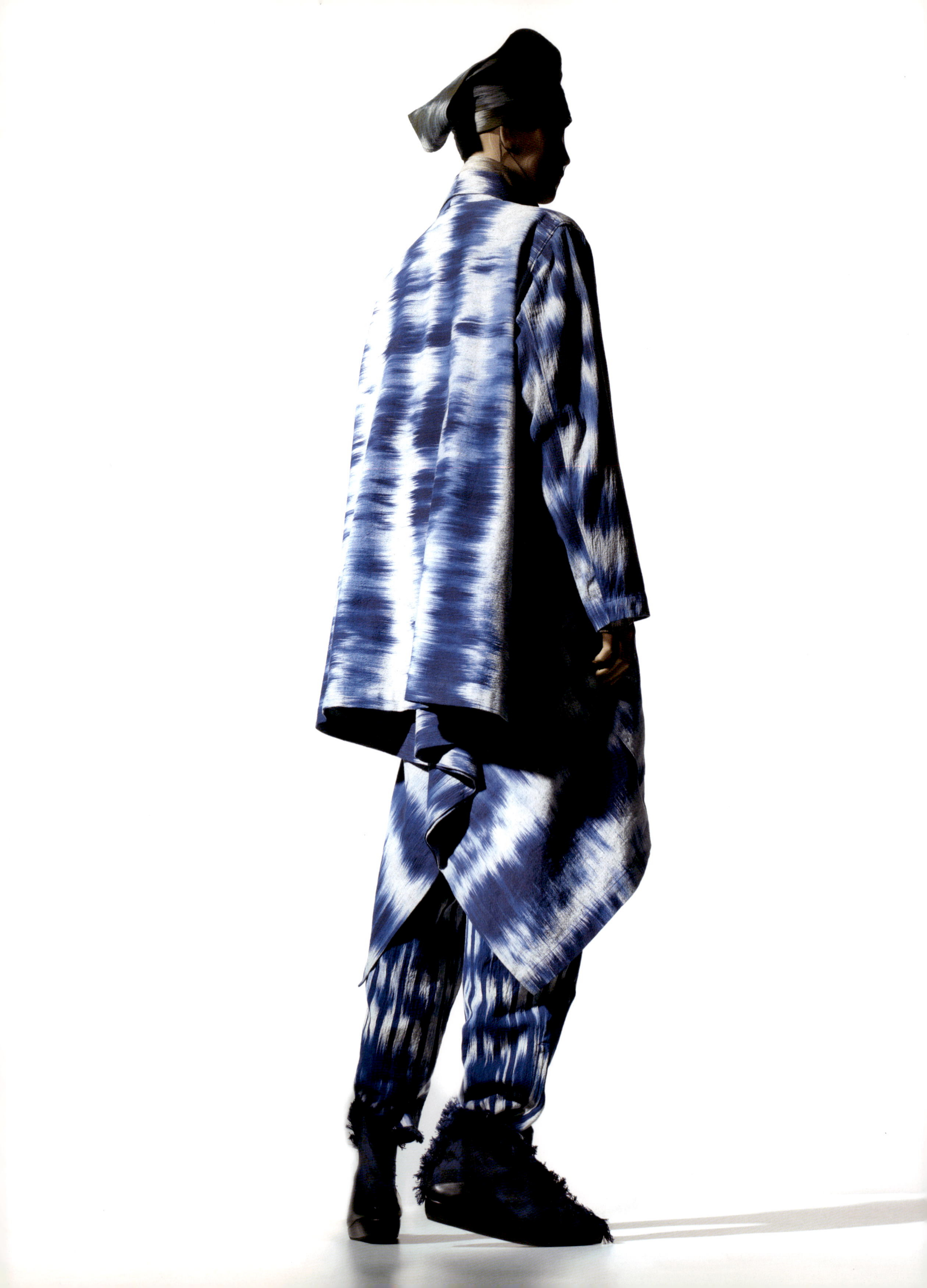

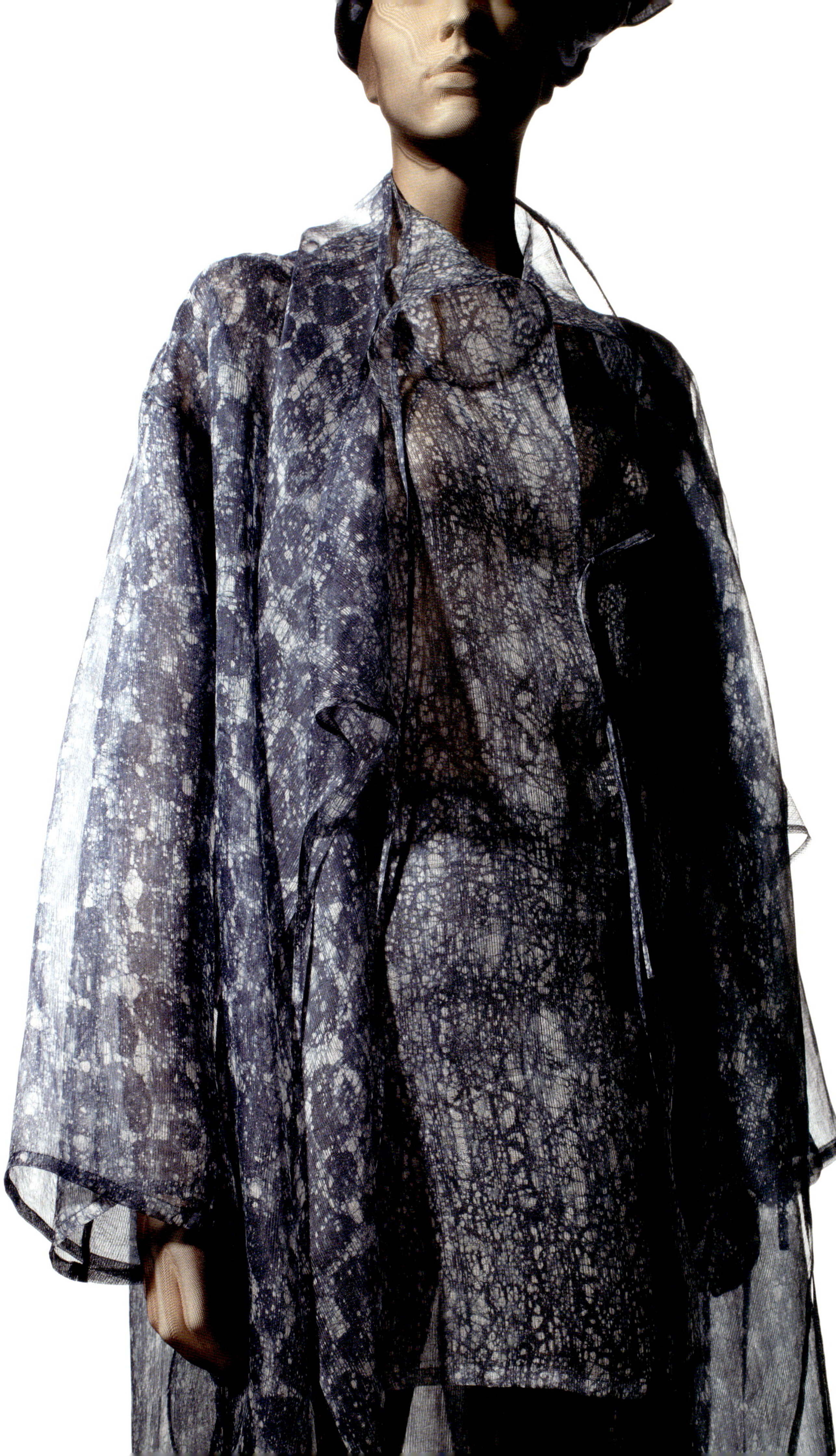

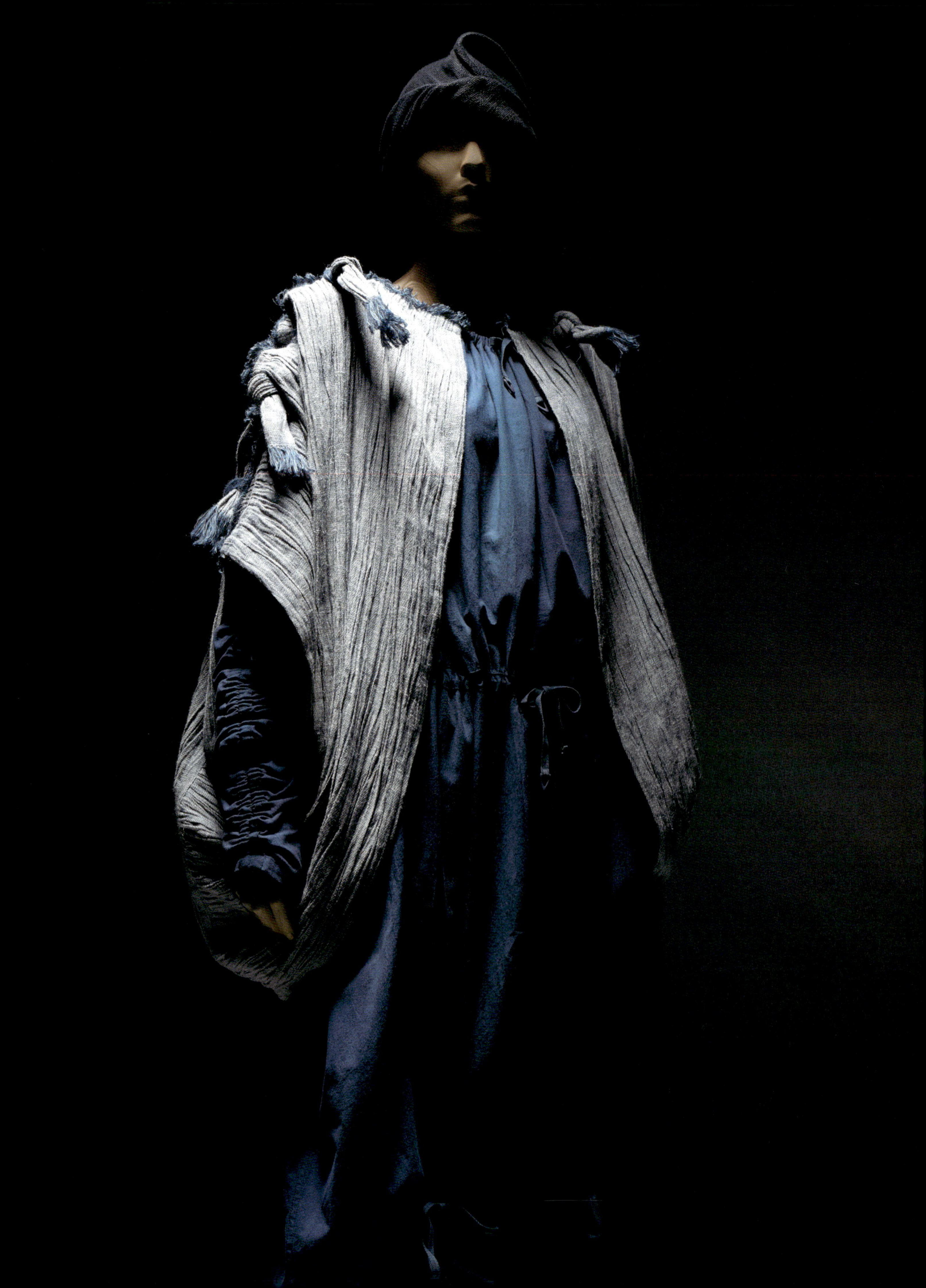

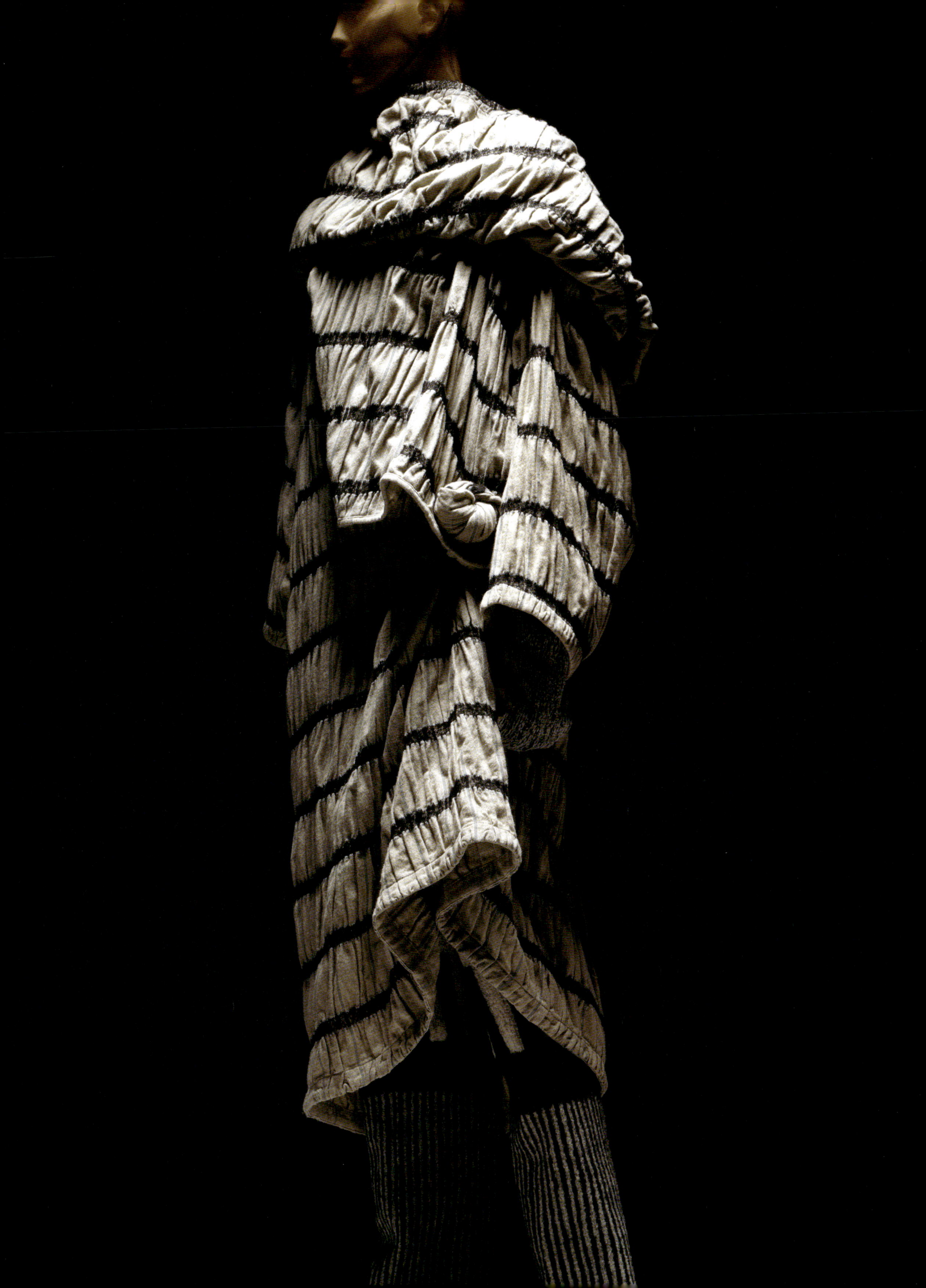

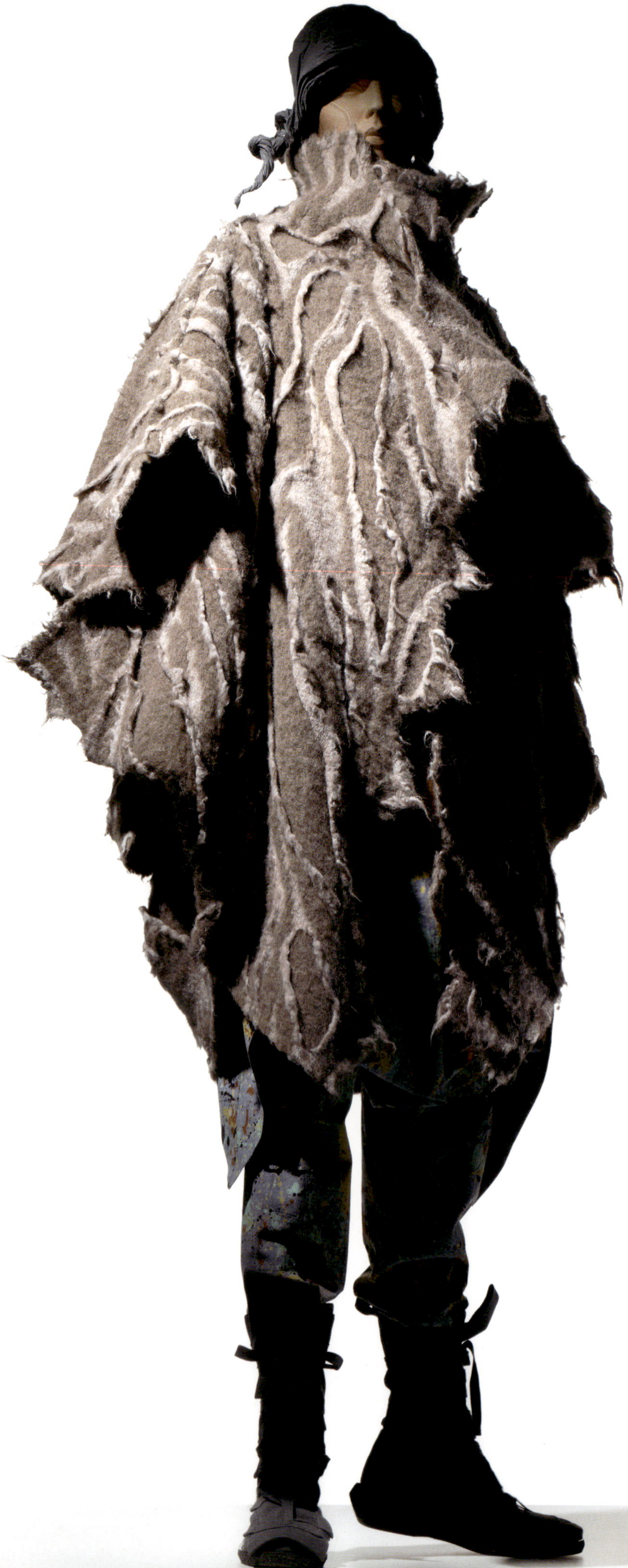

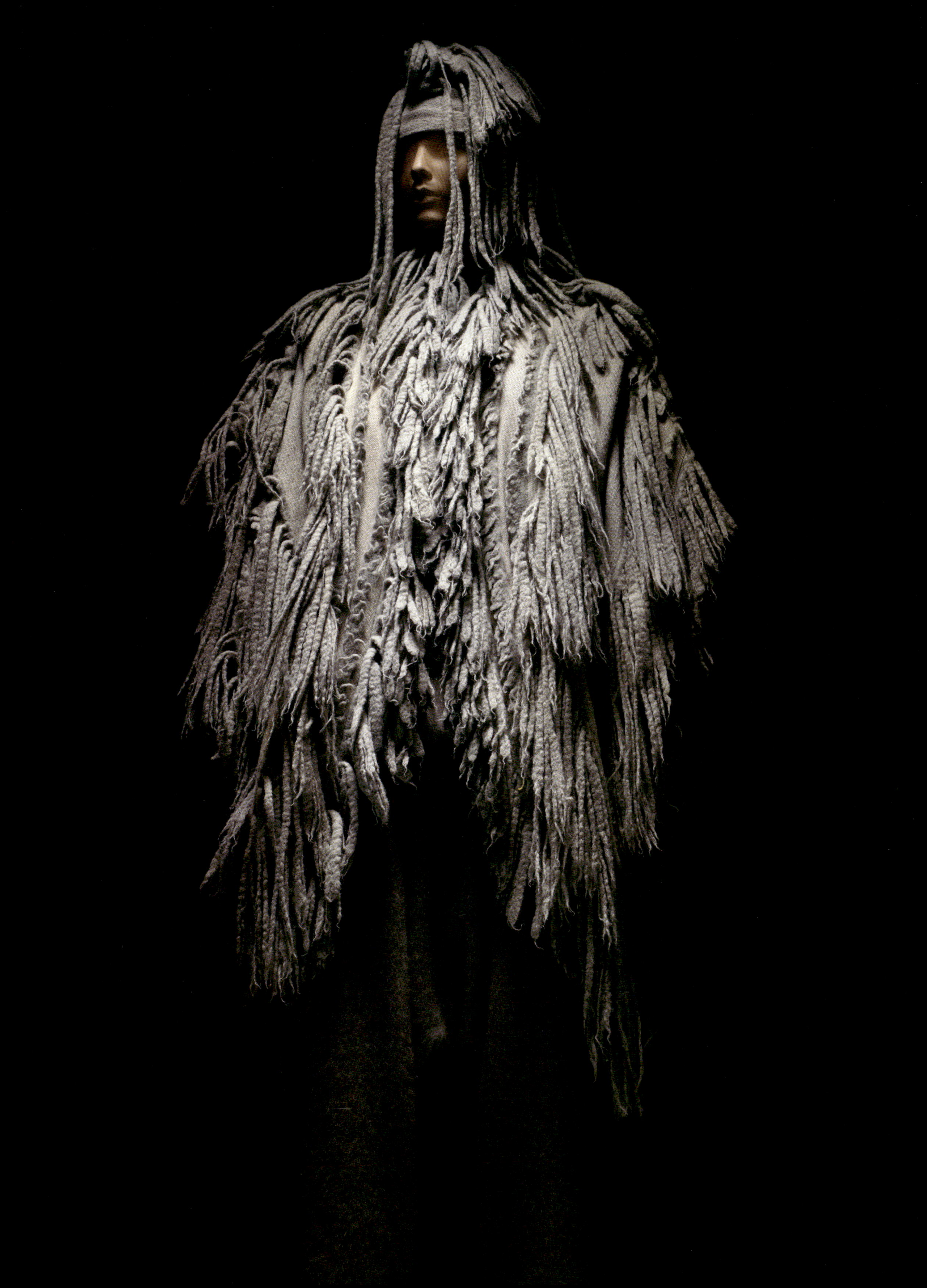

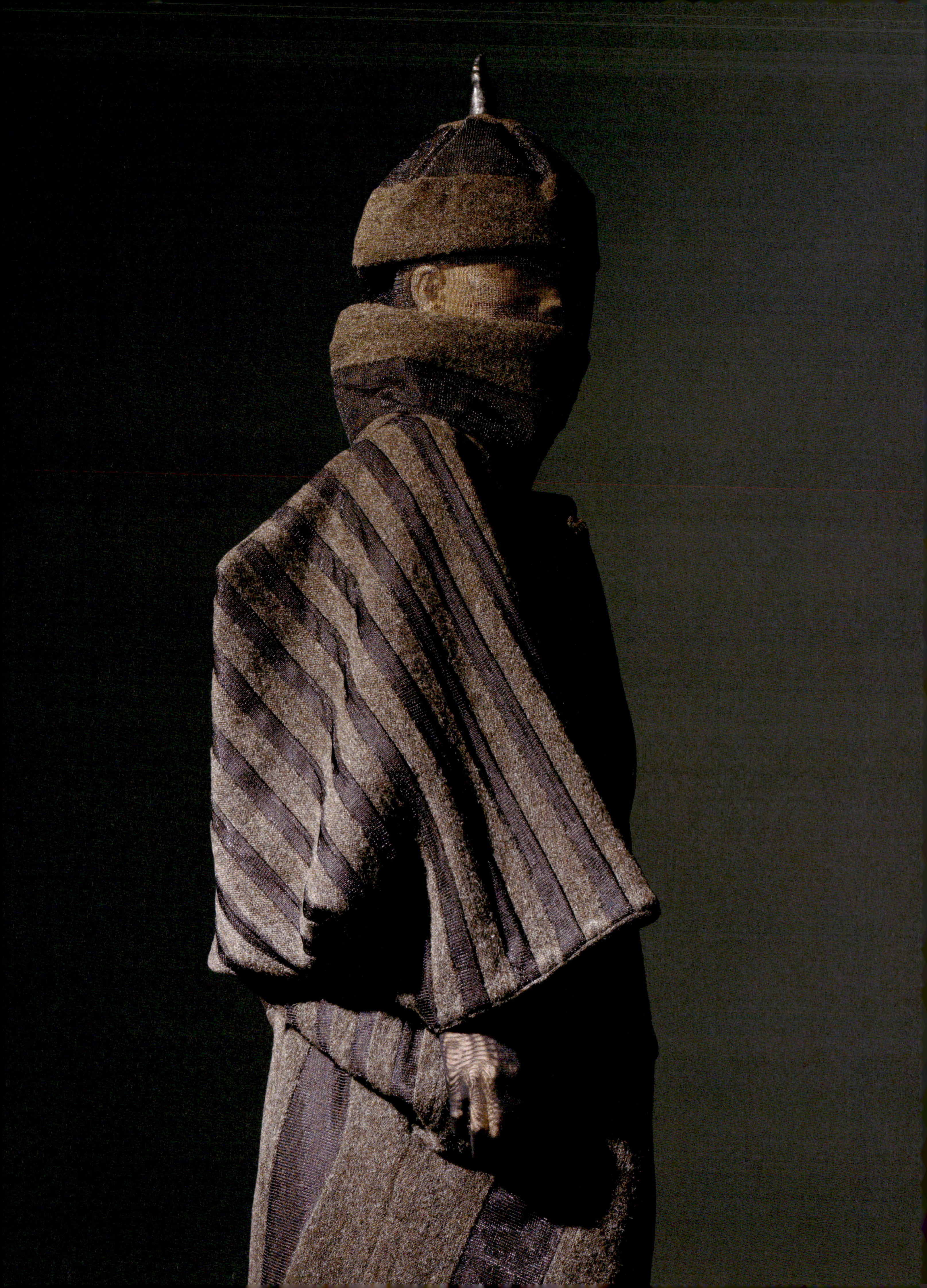

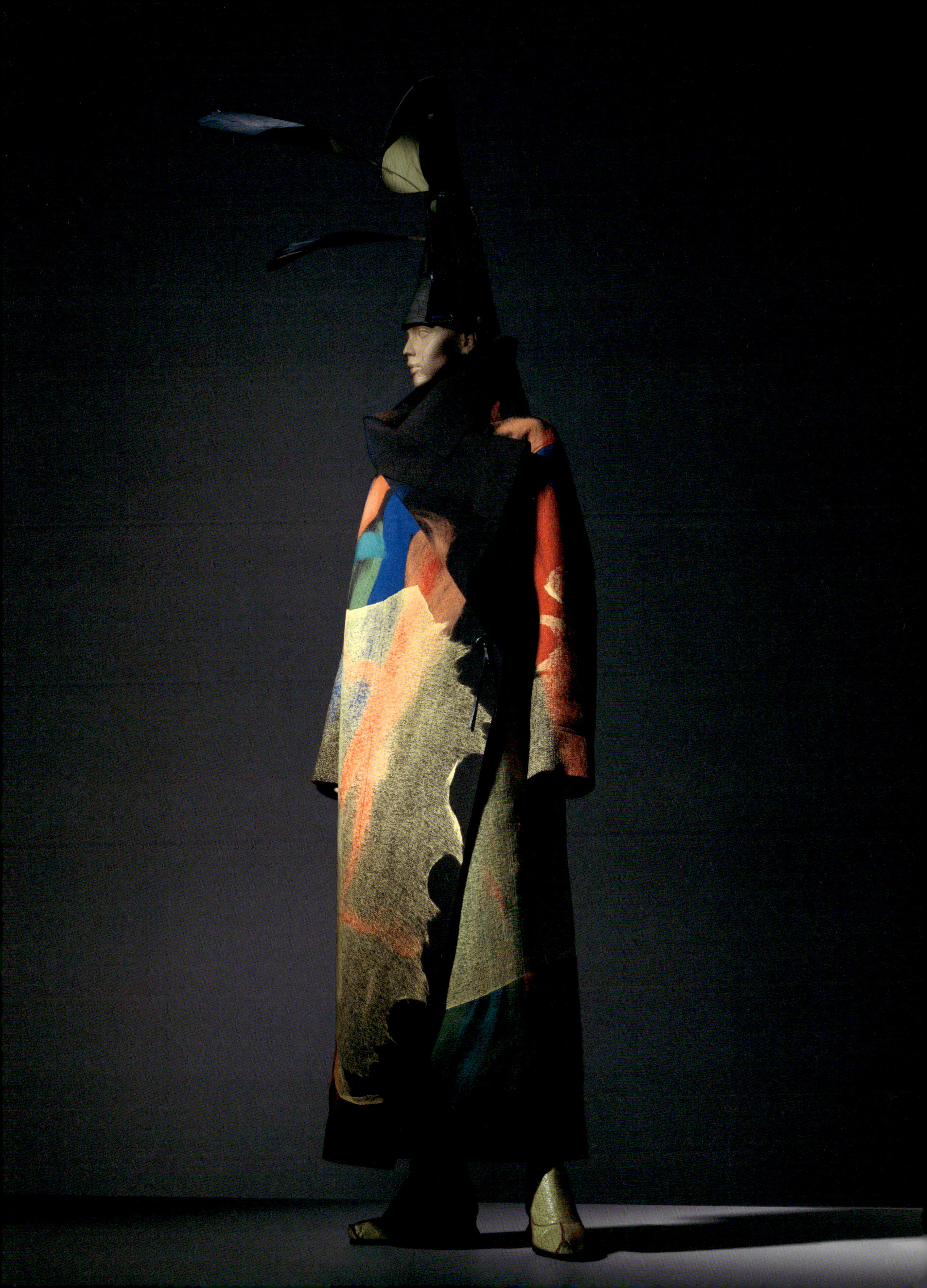

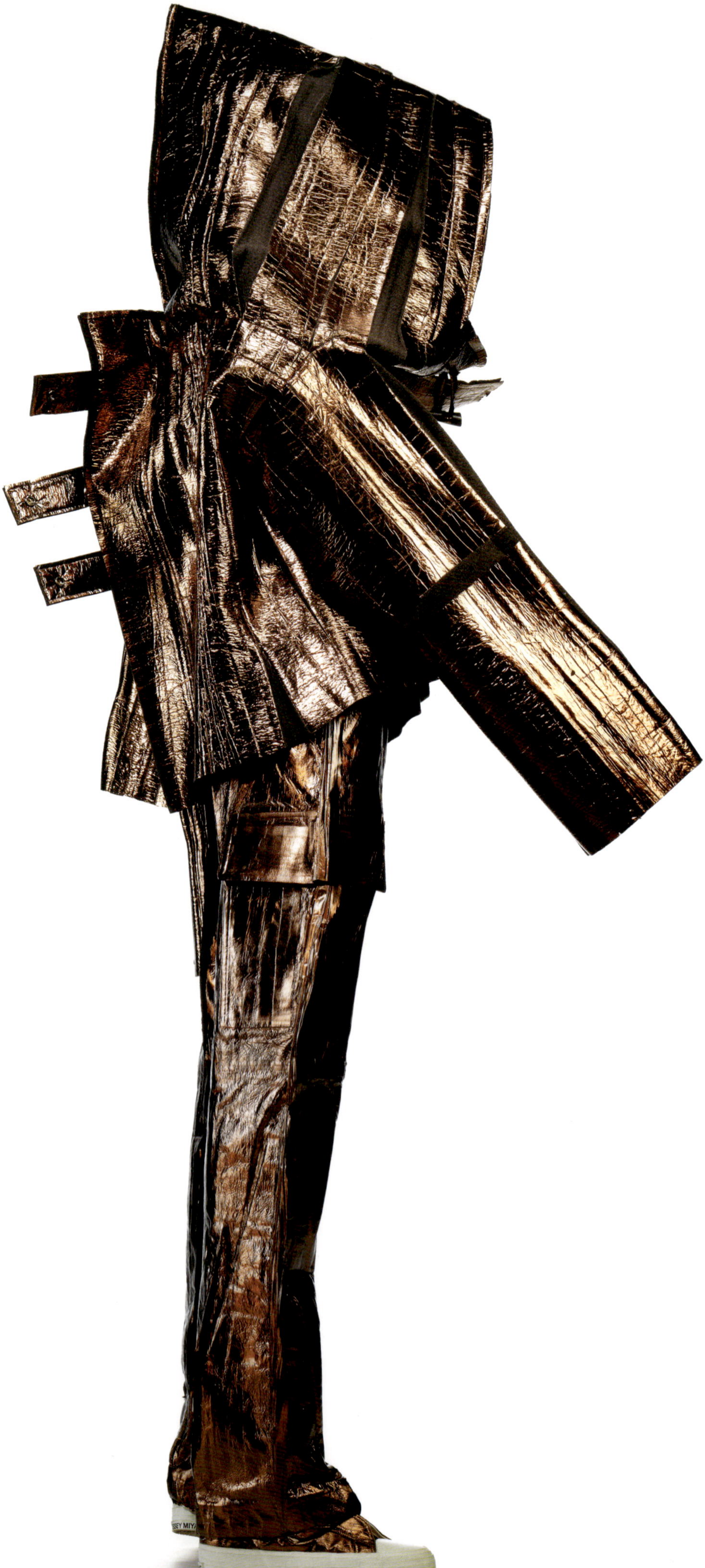

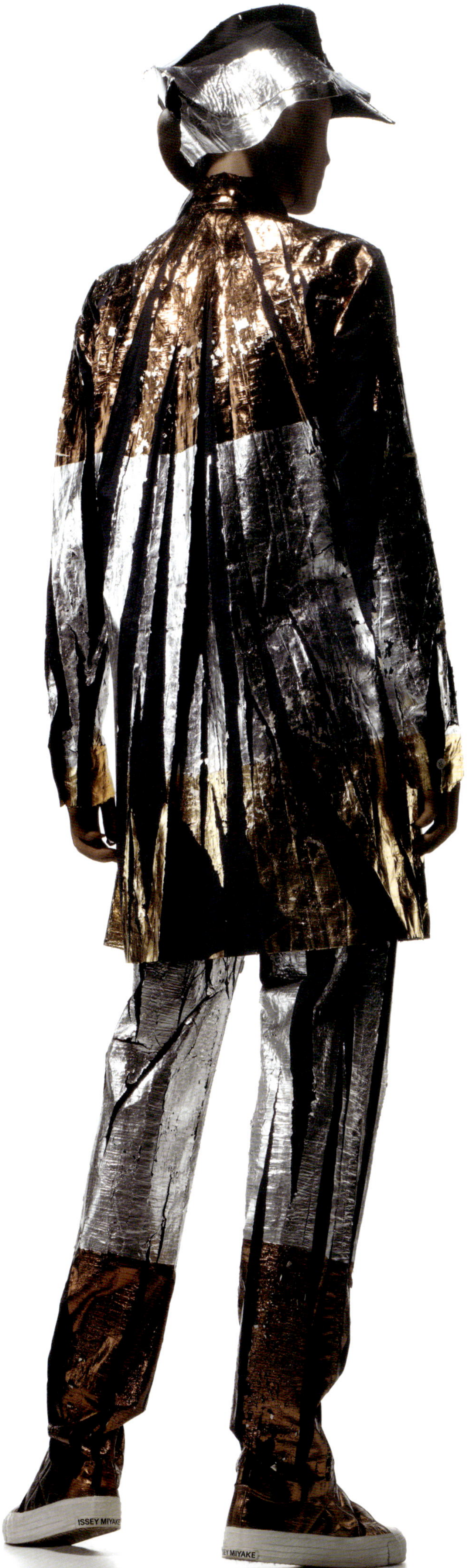
ISSEY MIYAKE
SEY MIYAKE

プリーツ

　熱処理で折り目が長期間保たれるポリエステル素材を使って、三宅一生は何を成し遂げたのか。布を身体に寄り添わせる最古の方法のひとつである襞を、服のかたちに縫製し折りを加えてから施す独自の工程によって、実用性とともに審美的な普遍性を兼ね備えるものに変貌させたのだ。1989年春夏コレクションで発表されたこの製法による「製品プリーツ」のシャープで優美な襞と造形に、誰もが目を見張った。三宅は以前にもプリーツの布を使ったデザインをしているが、一枚のスカーフを四角く折りたたんで斜めにプリーツをかけたことをきっかけに、テクノロジーを取り入れた服づくりが始まった。服の形が仕上がると同時に、襞の陰影が平坦な布の表情と風合いを変化させる。できあがった平面の服は、身体の上でうねり有機的なかたちに変容するが、プリーツの目にそってくるくると巻いて簡単に収納することができる。パーツごとに折りを加えてプリーツ加工したのちに組み立てると、さらに変化に富んだ多様な服が生まれた。さらに直線的なプリーツに加え、人が手を使って服を捻り皺づけする《ツイスト》（1991年）、縫い縮めて寄せた襞を定着させる《ギャザー・プレス》（1991年）など手仕事が加わると、その加工のバリエーションと表現は無限に広がっていく。

## PLEATS

Issey Miyake started with a polyester thread that could be heat-processed to seal pleats in permanently. Through its use, he was able to turn pleat, one of the most ancient ways to adapt fabric to the body, into an expression of aesthetic pureness with a pragmatic aim. He developed a radically new process called garment pleating, which means that a piece of clothing is pleated after it is cut and sewn and then pleated. When examples that used the garment pleating technique came out on the runway in the 1989 Spring-Summer Collection, everyone was stunned by their simple elegance. As the worked on a pleated scarf, folded several times and pleased diagonally, Miyake began to apply the technology to different form of cloth. Pleats do more than just add the finishing touches to a garment. The shadows that they create can transform flat fabric, giving it both expression and texture. The new clothing that resulted shifts and undulates organically as it is worn on the body, but can still be stored away just by rolling it up. Processing the position of each pleat on its own prior to assembly gives even greater variety to the forms. The pleats are added using a heat press machine; and Miyake took the idea even further by adding hand processing, to create limitless permutations. Examples include TWIST (1991) and GATHER PRESS (1991).

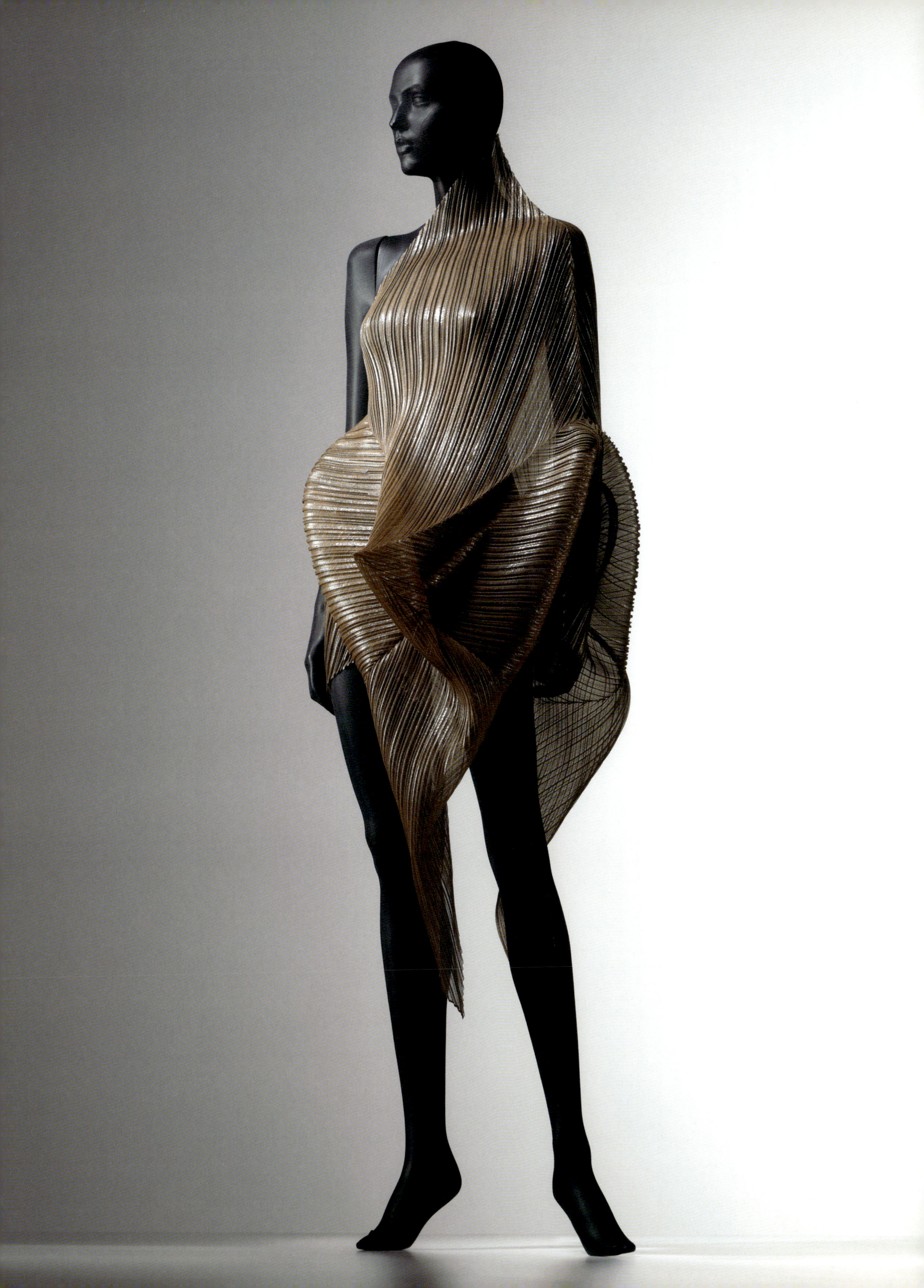

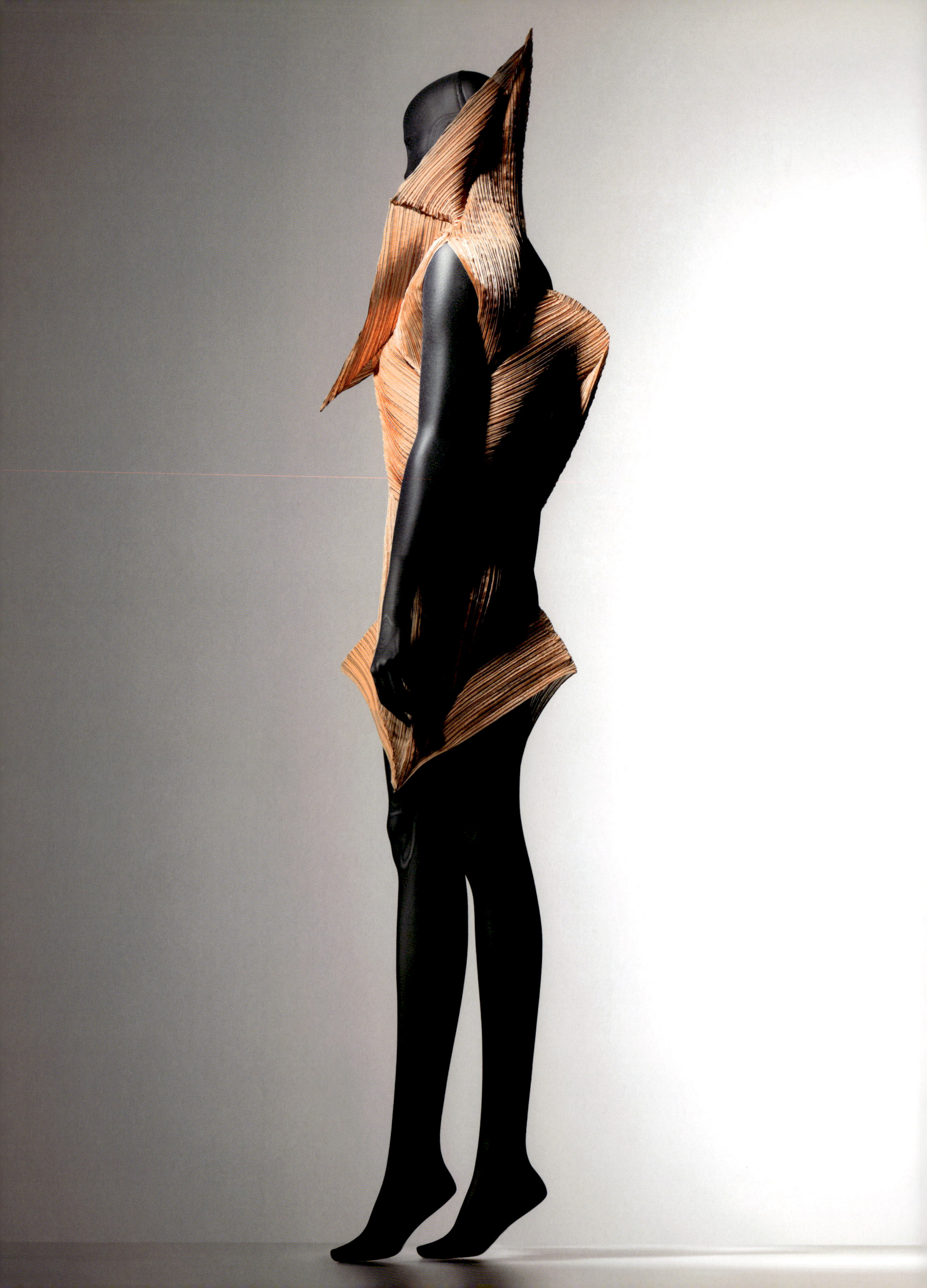

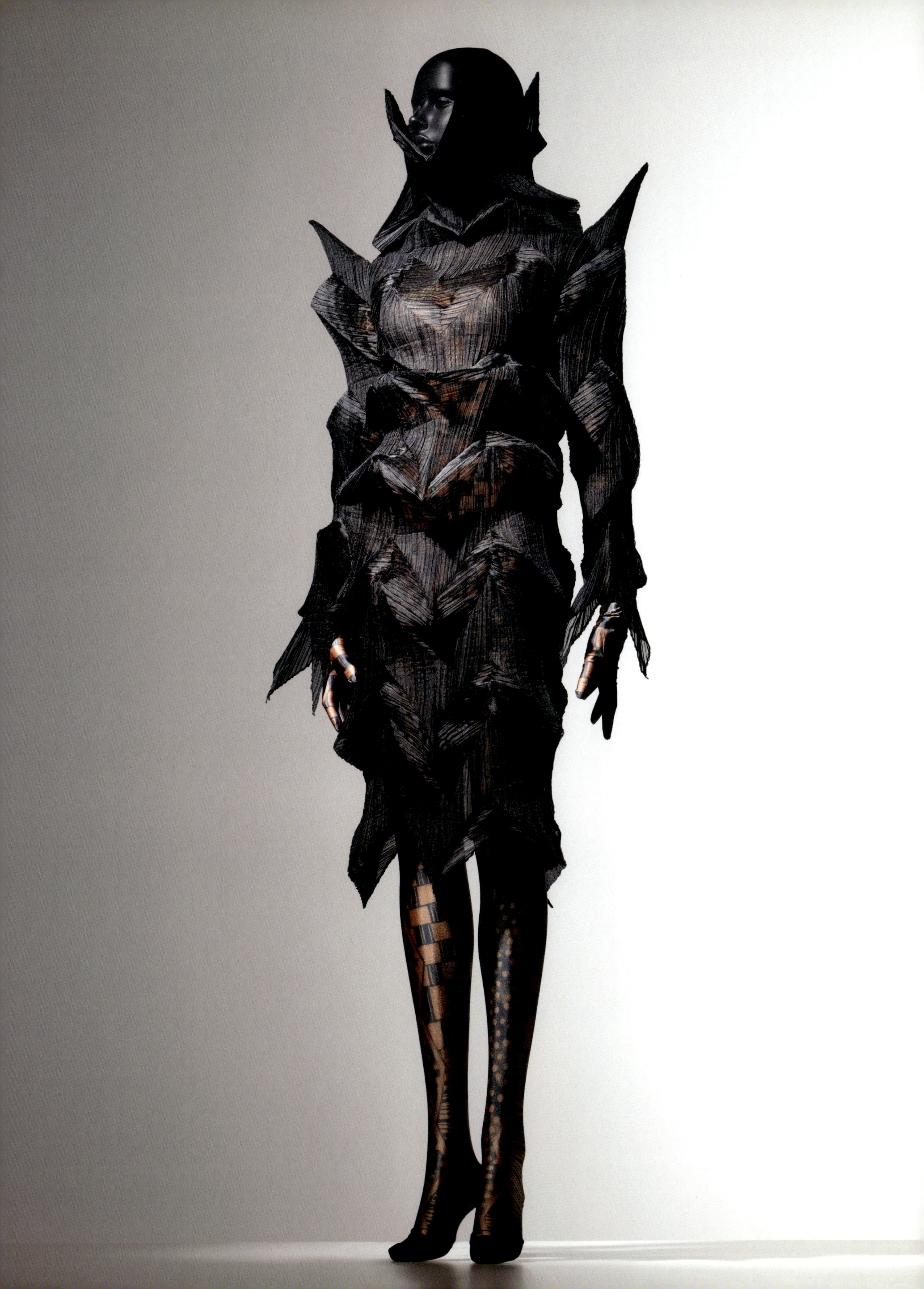

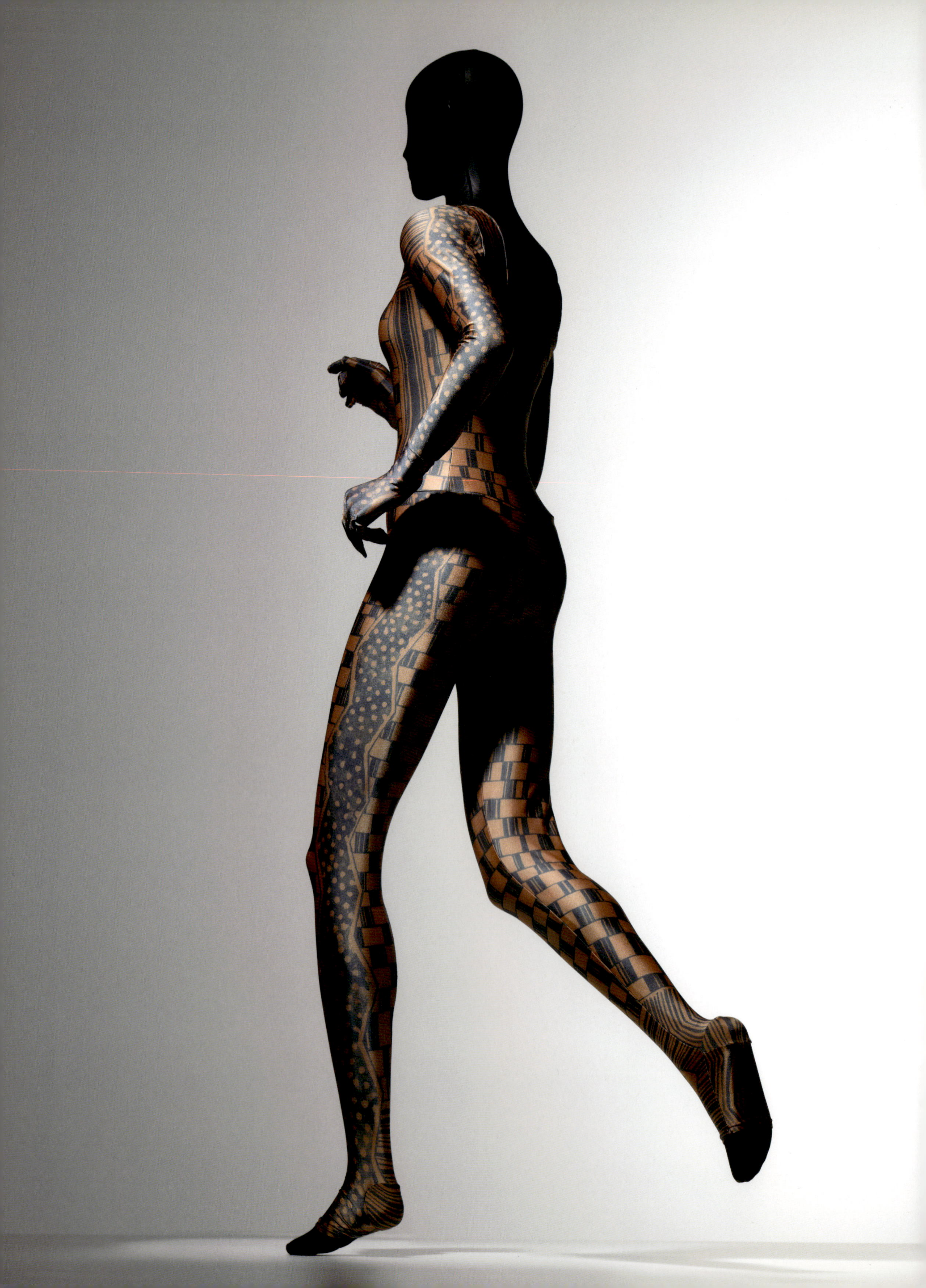

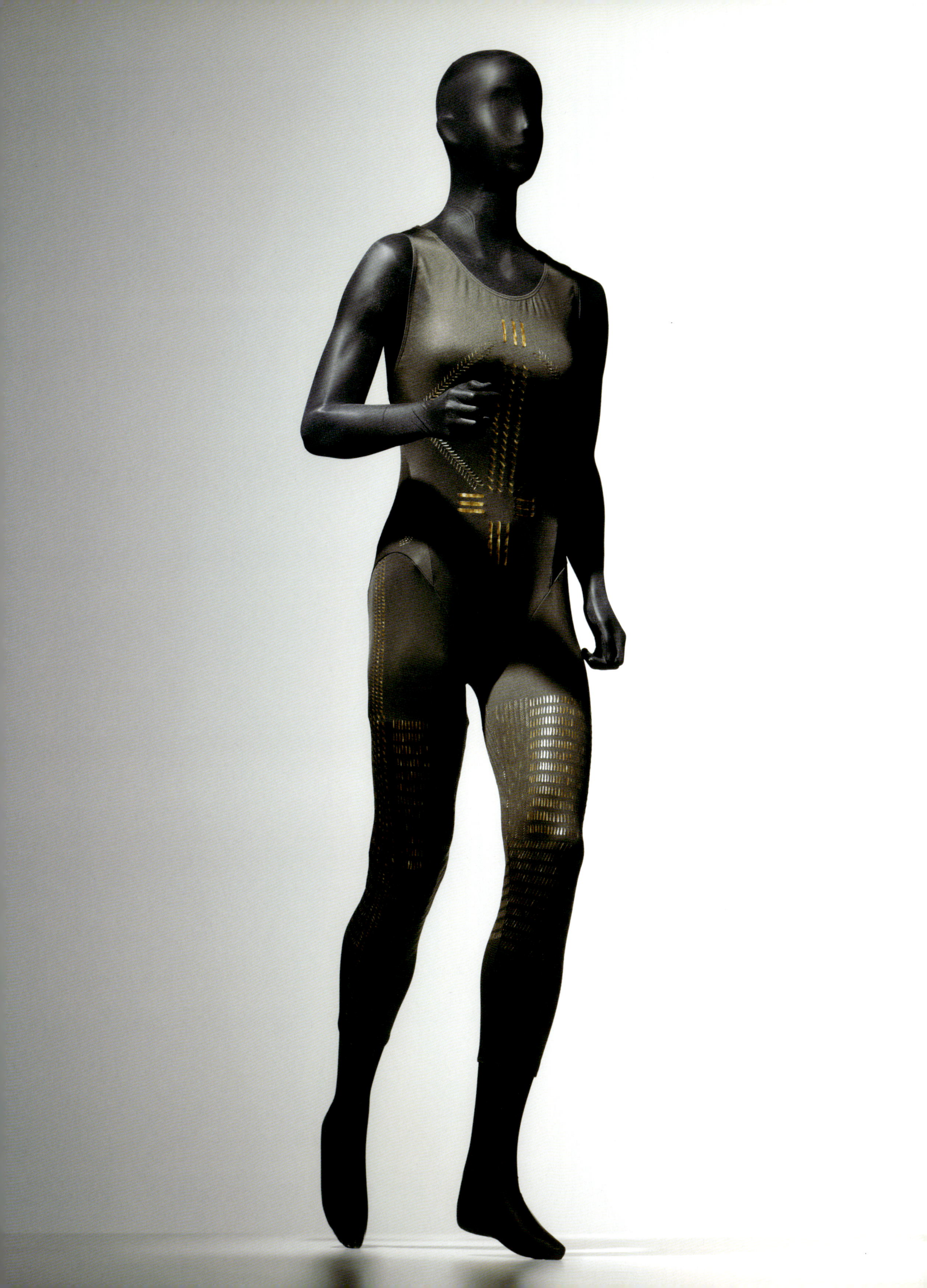

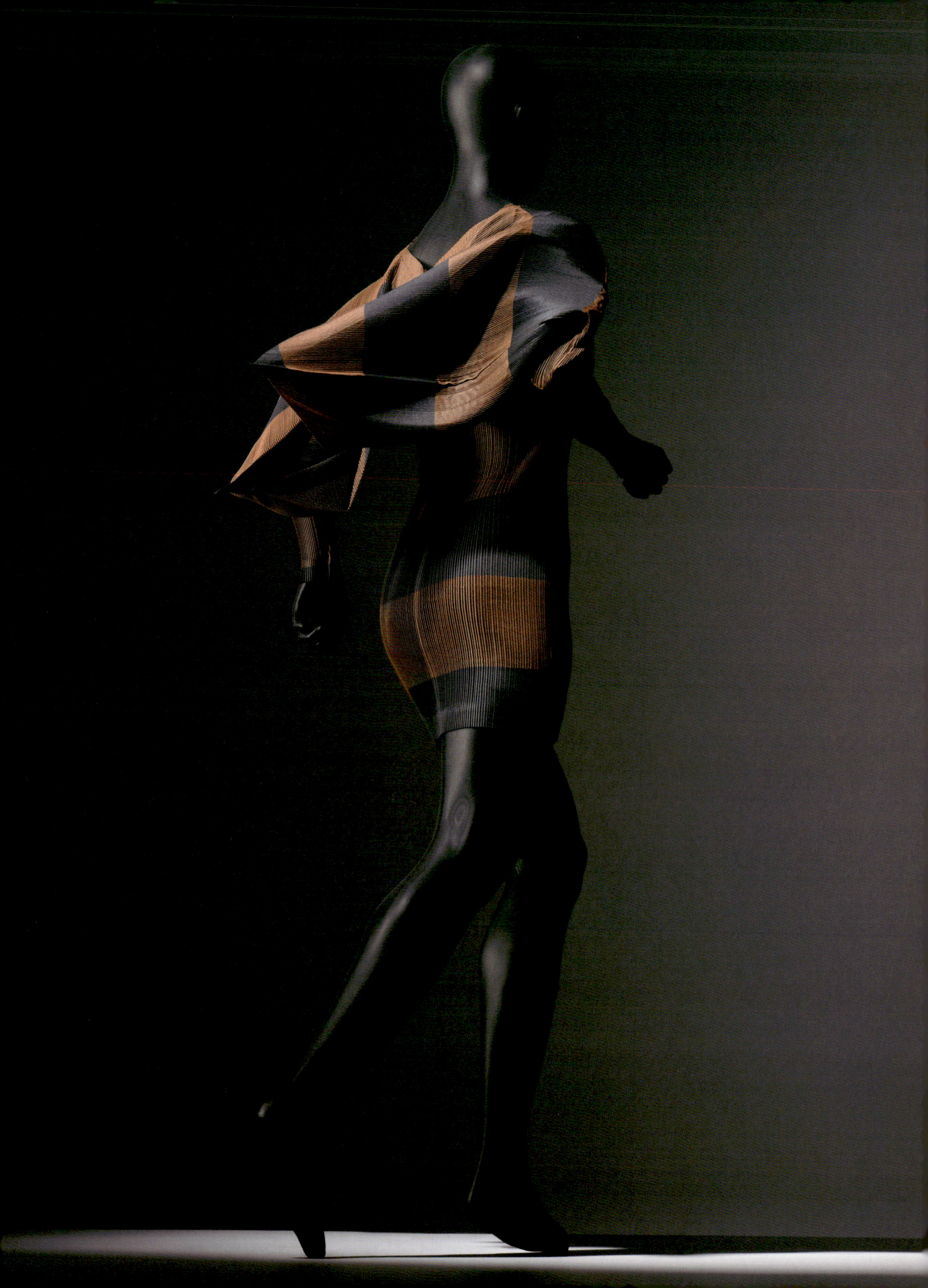

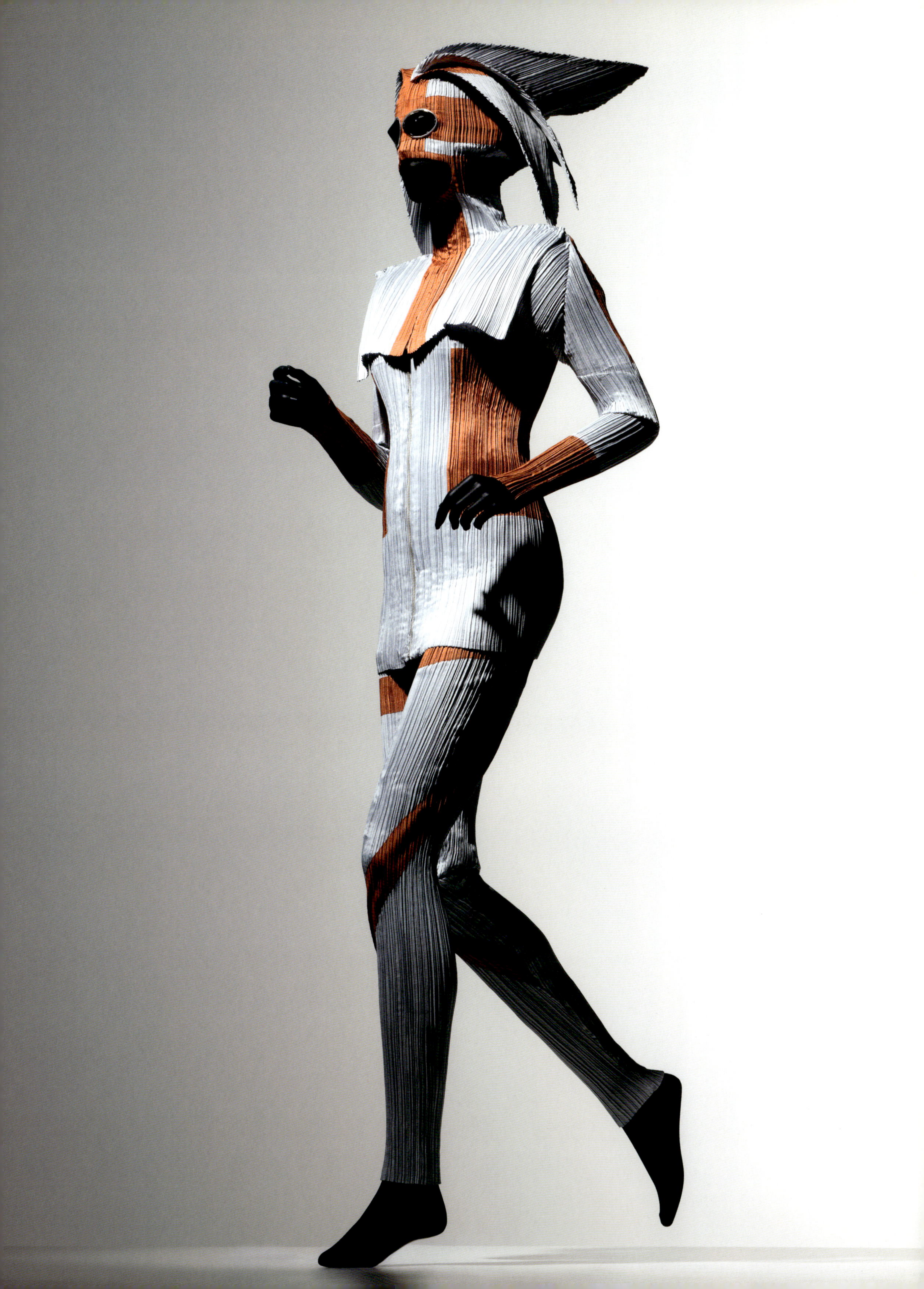

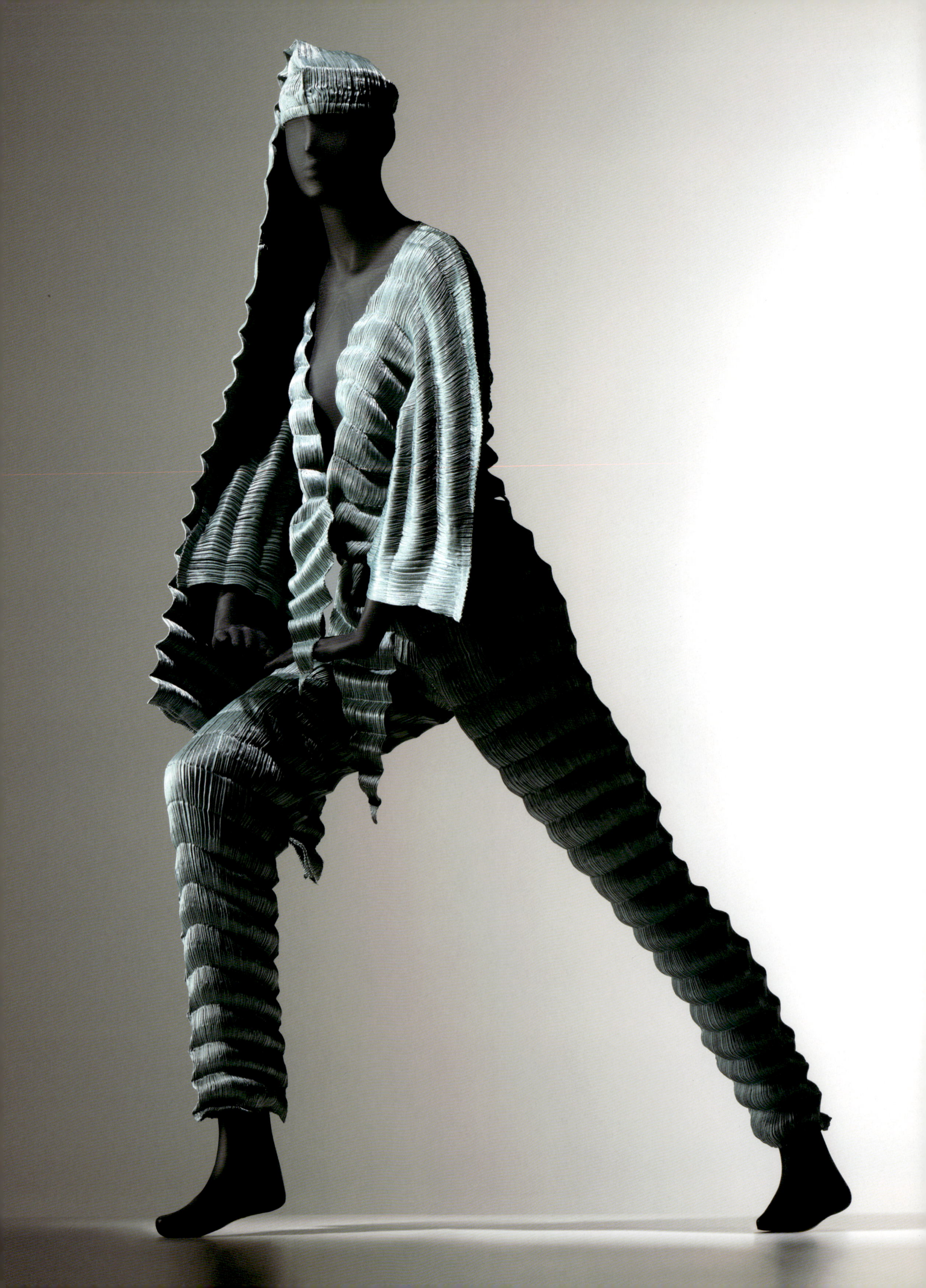

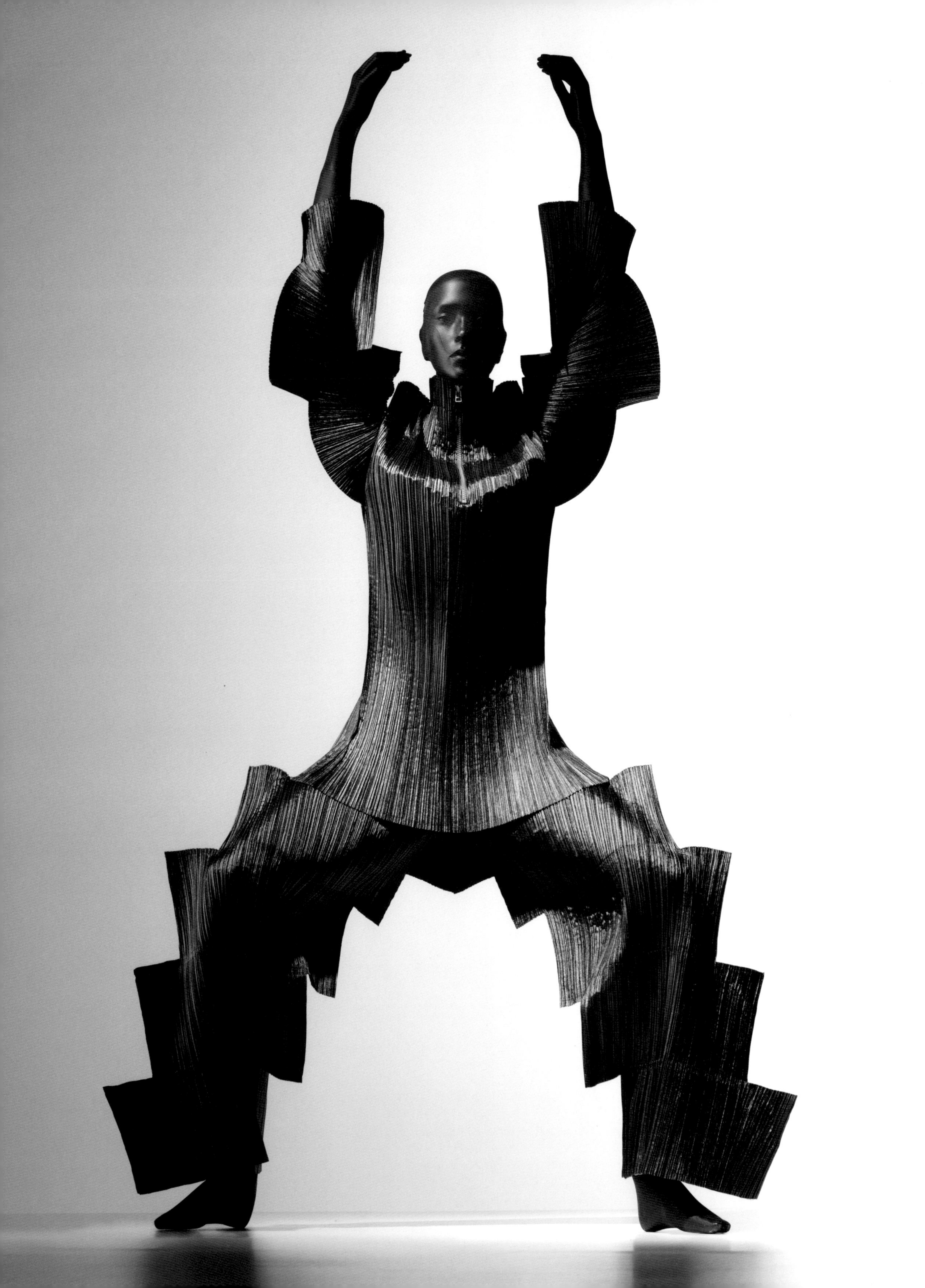

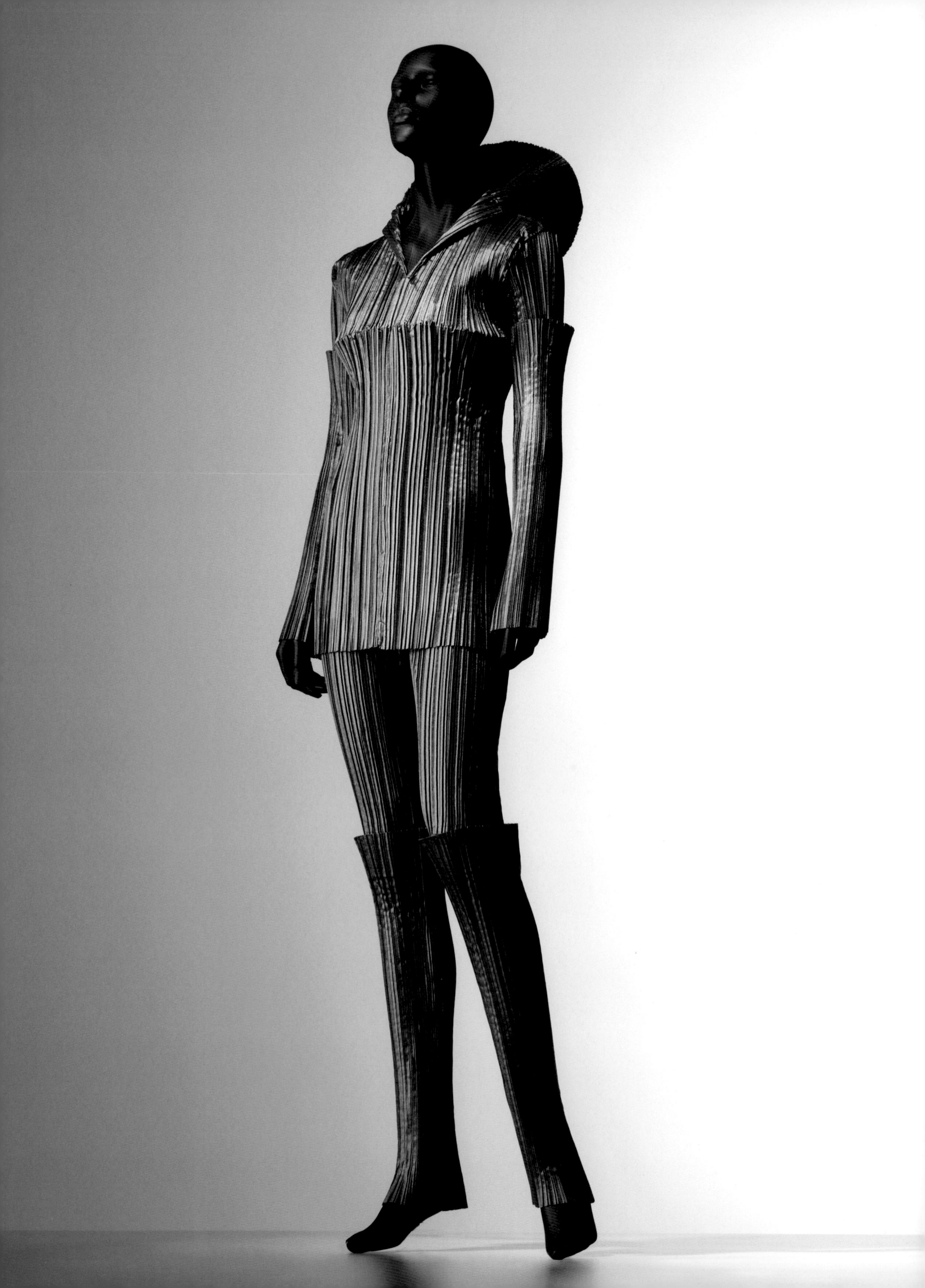

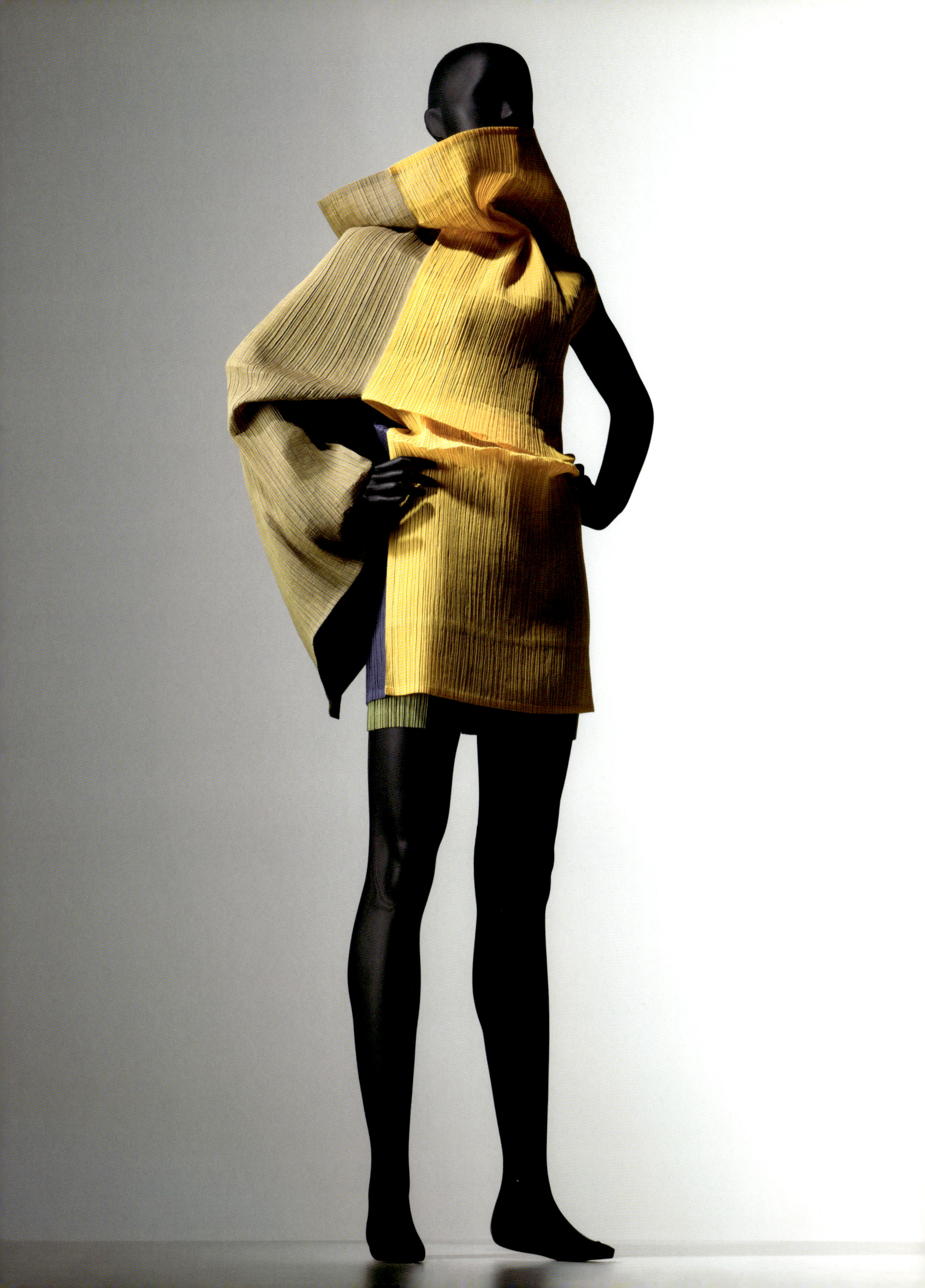

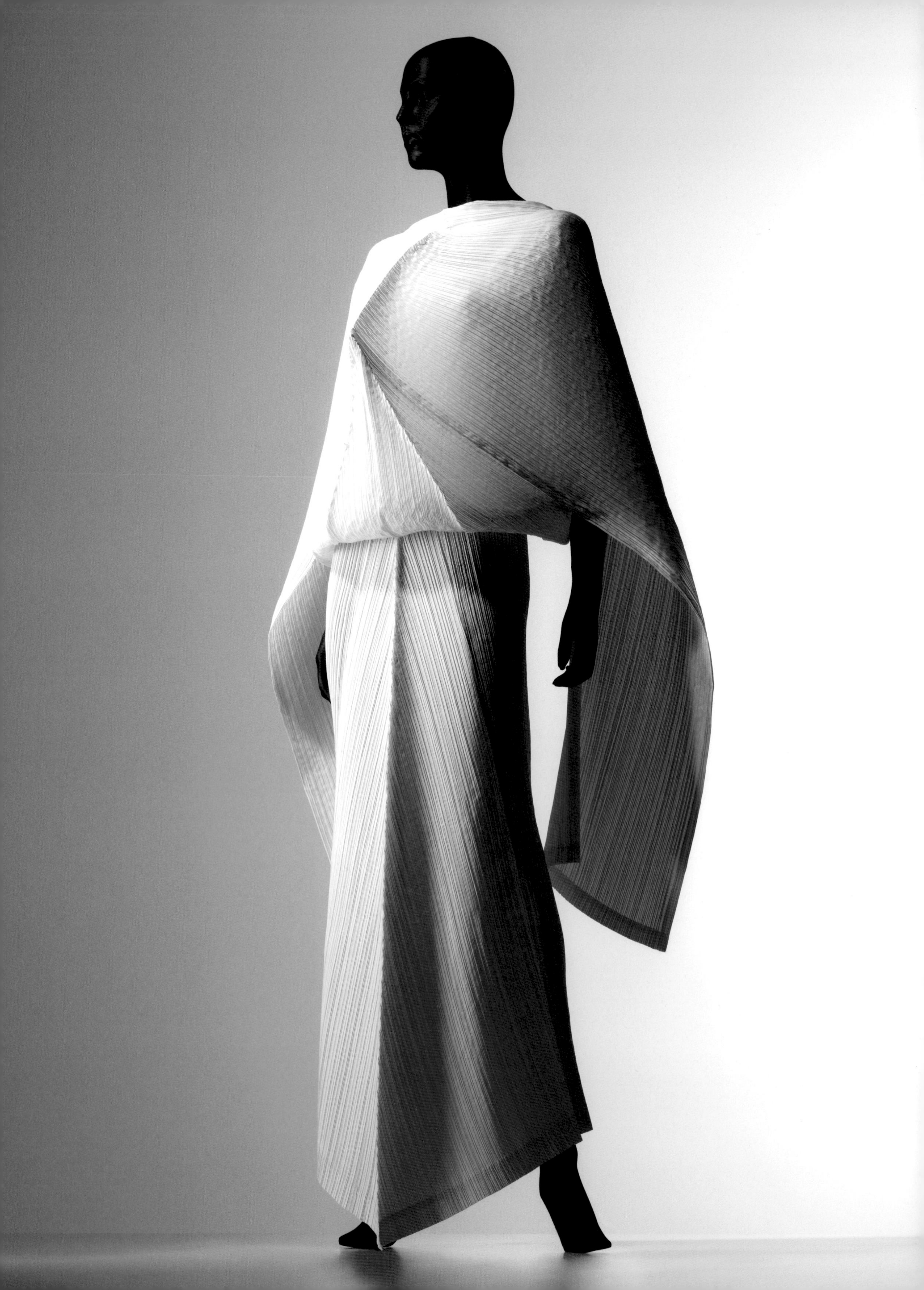

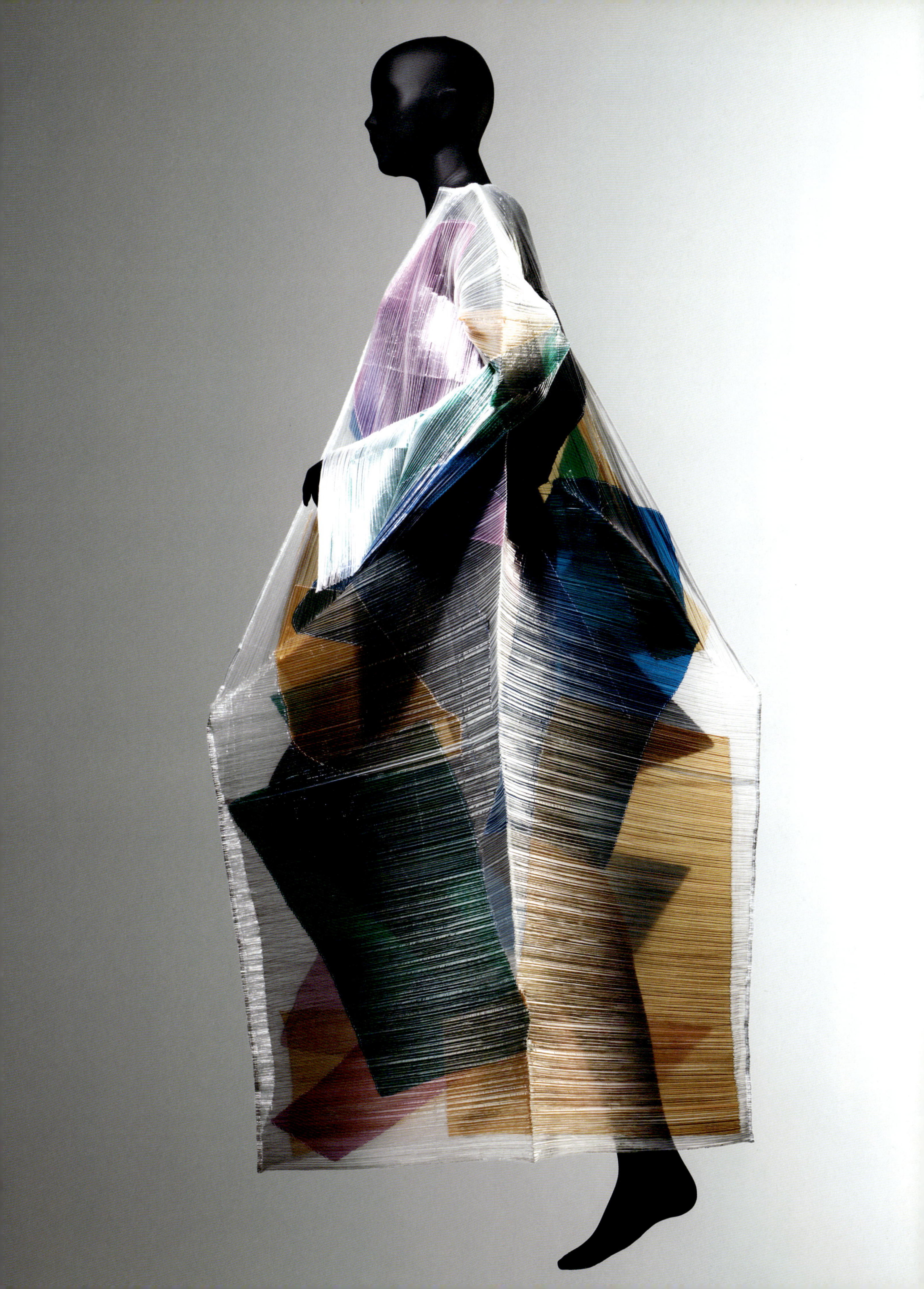

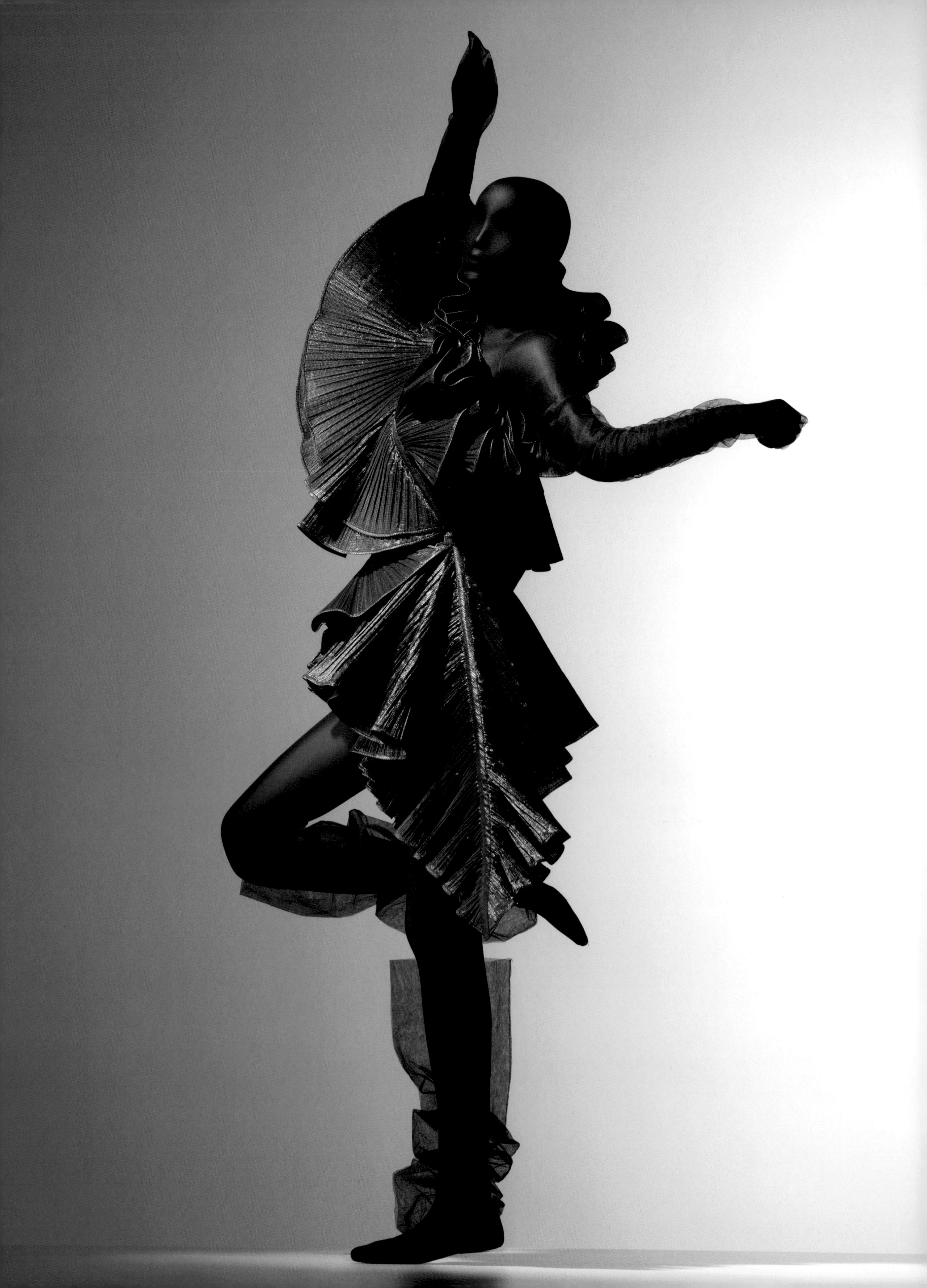

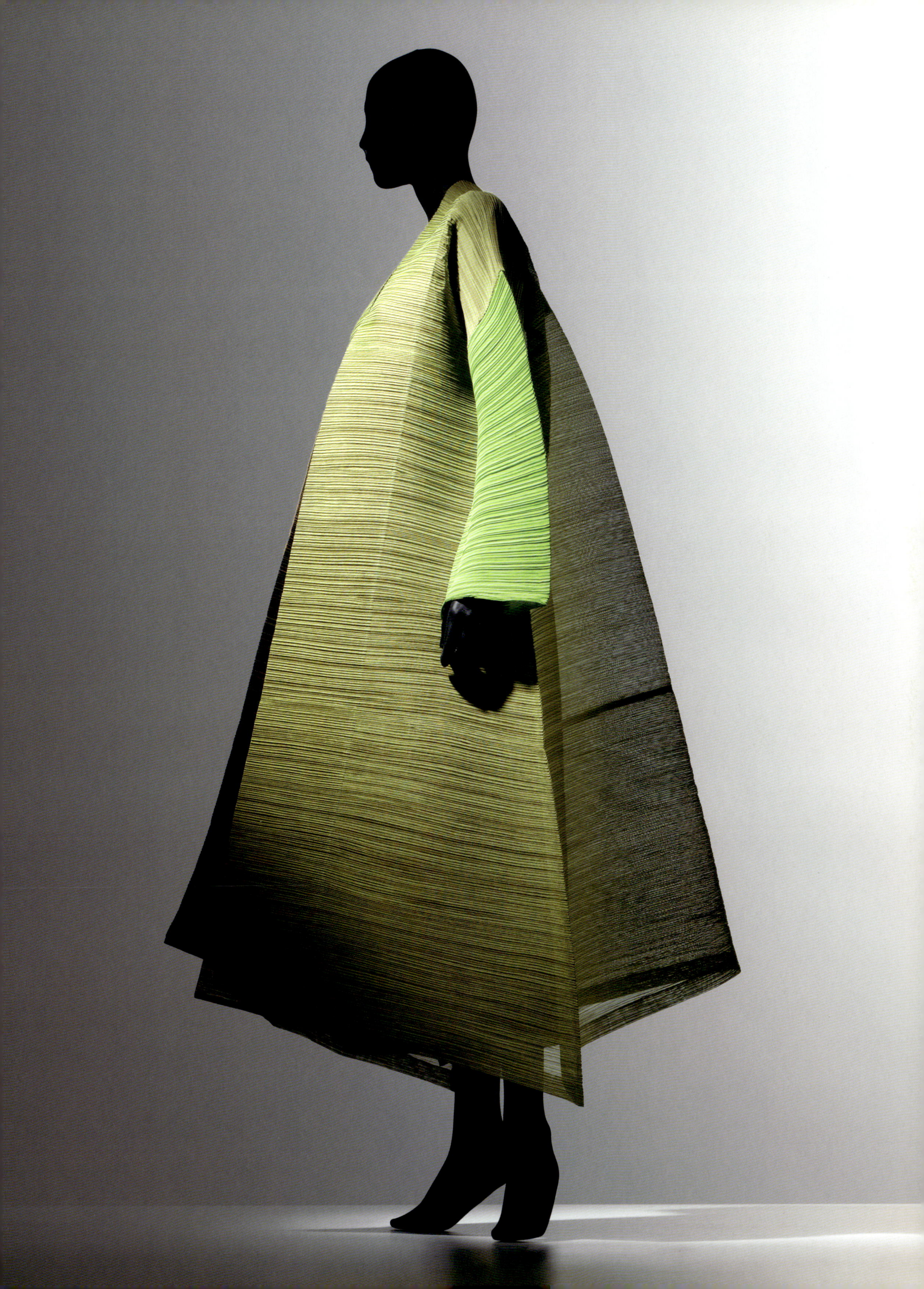

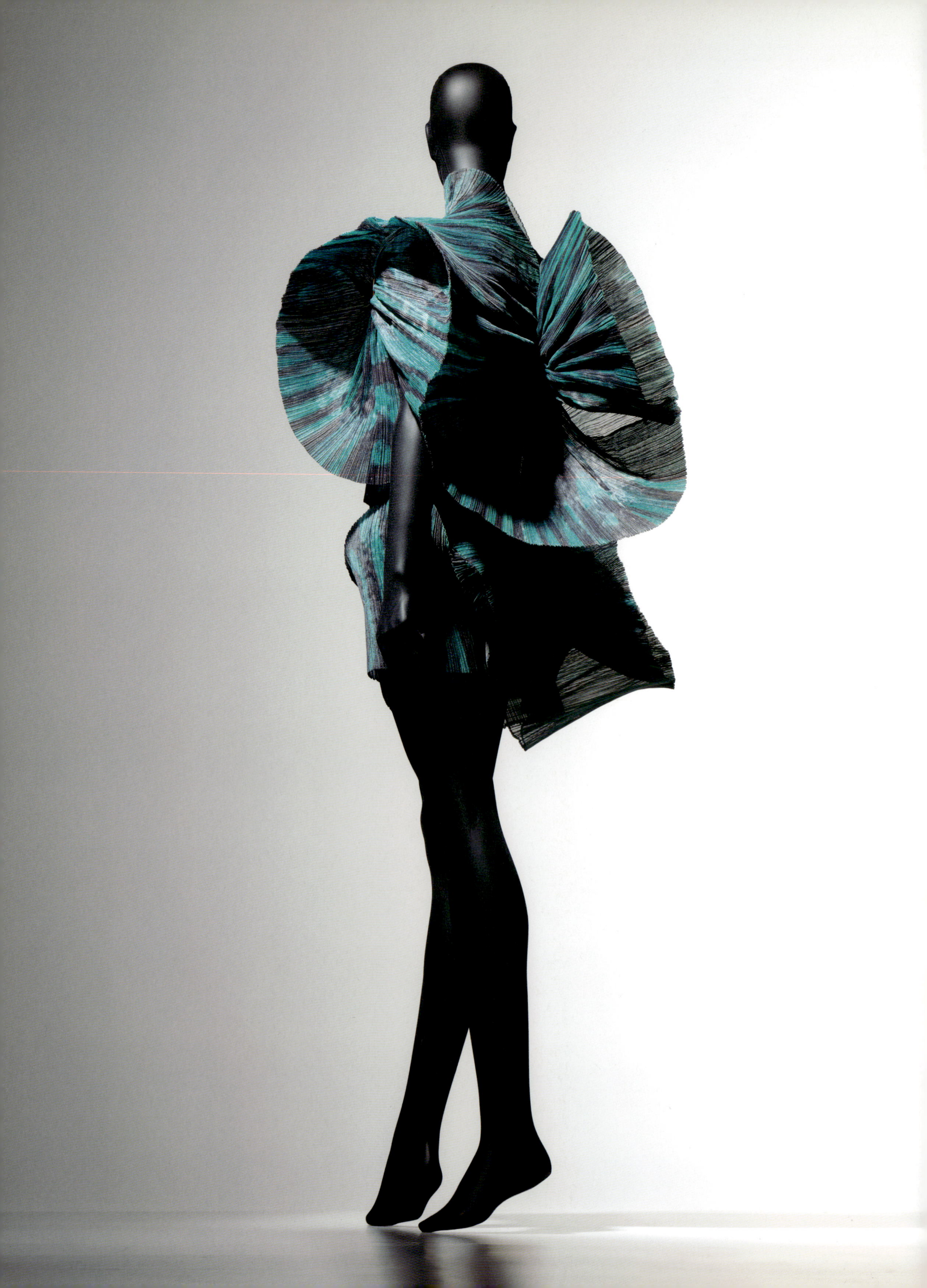

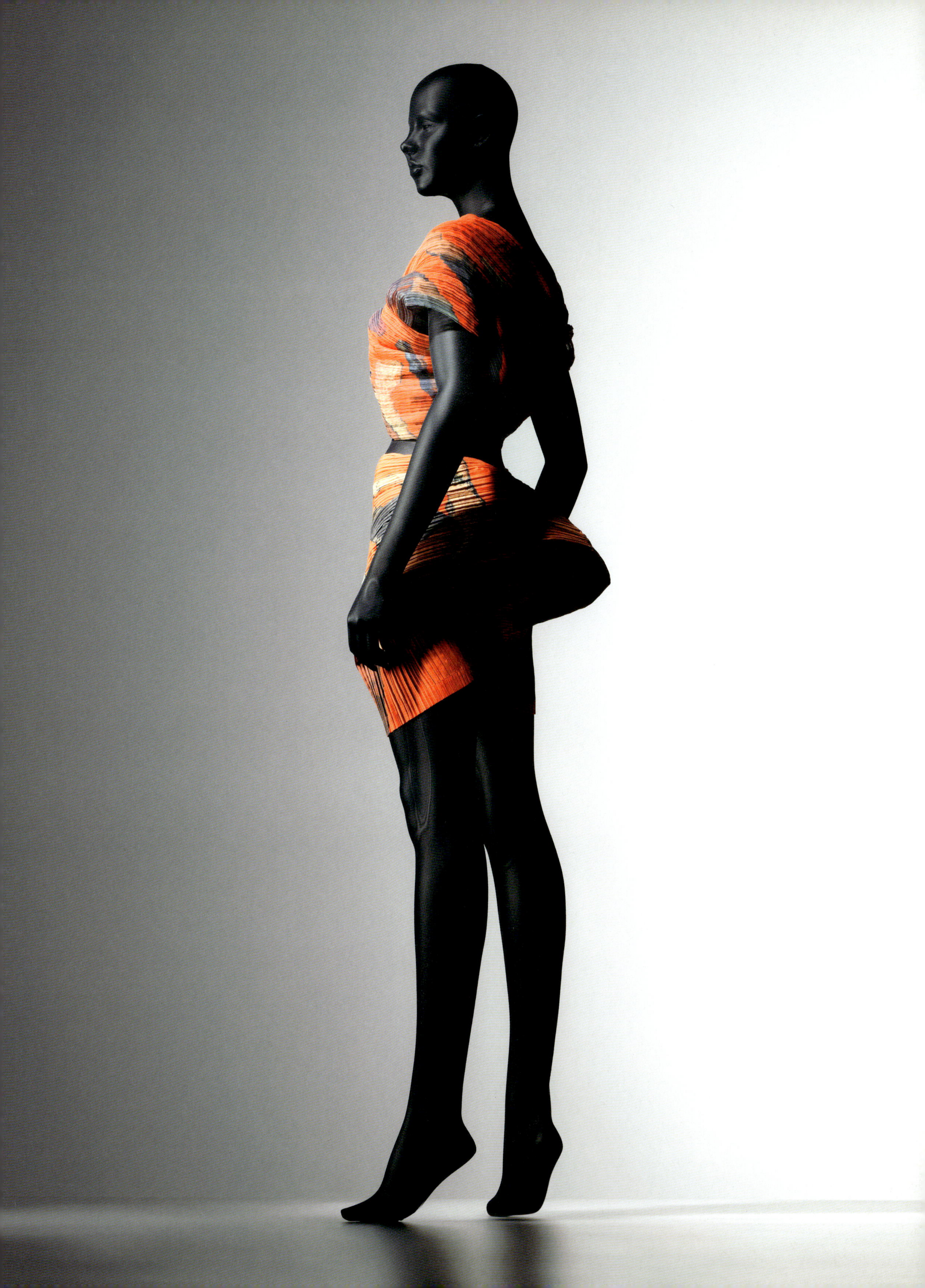

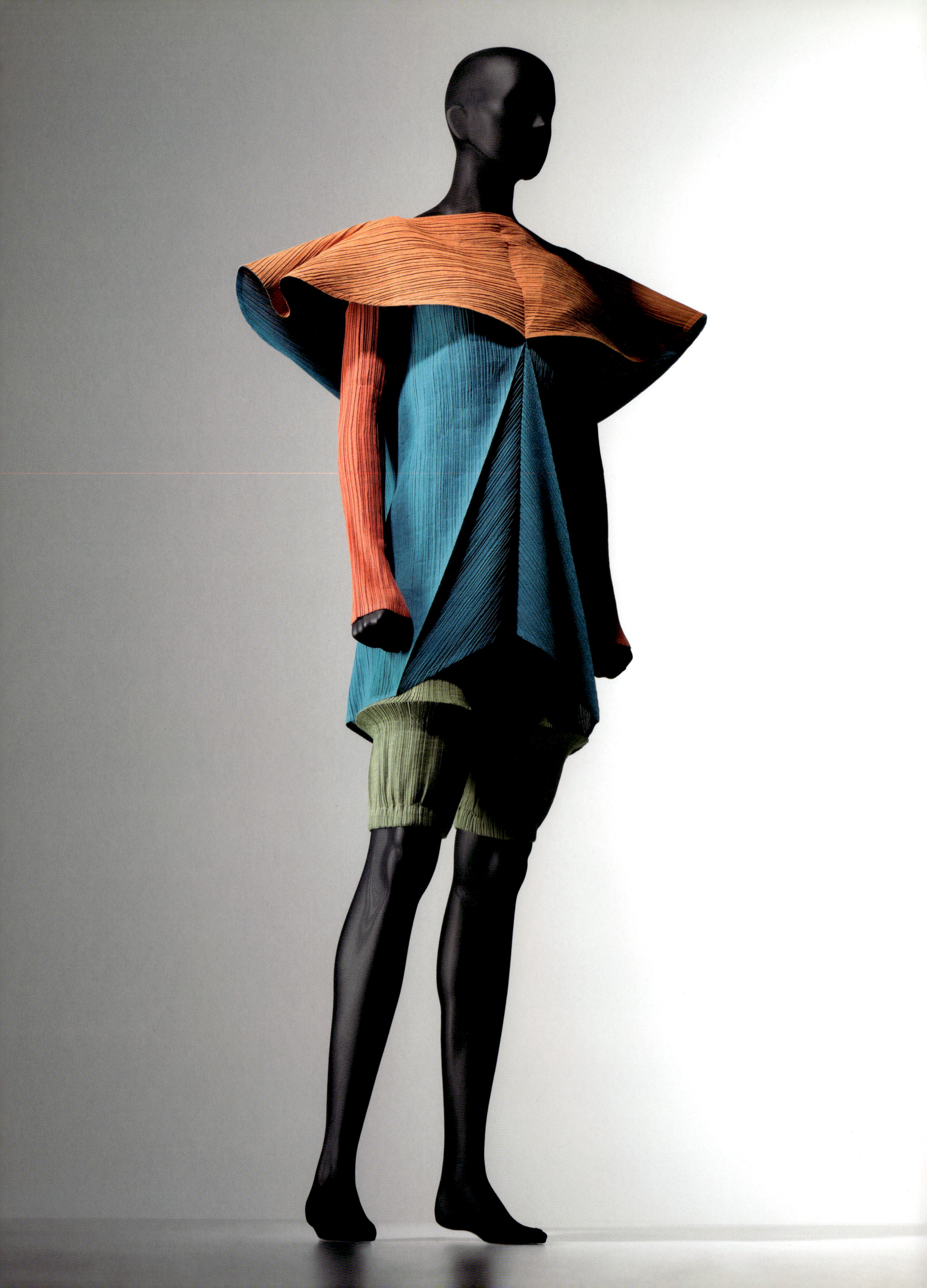

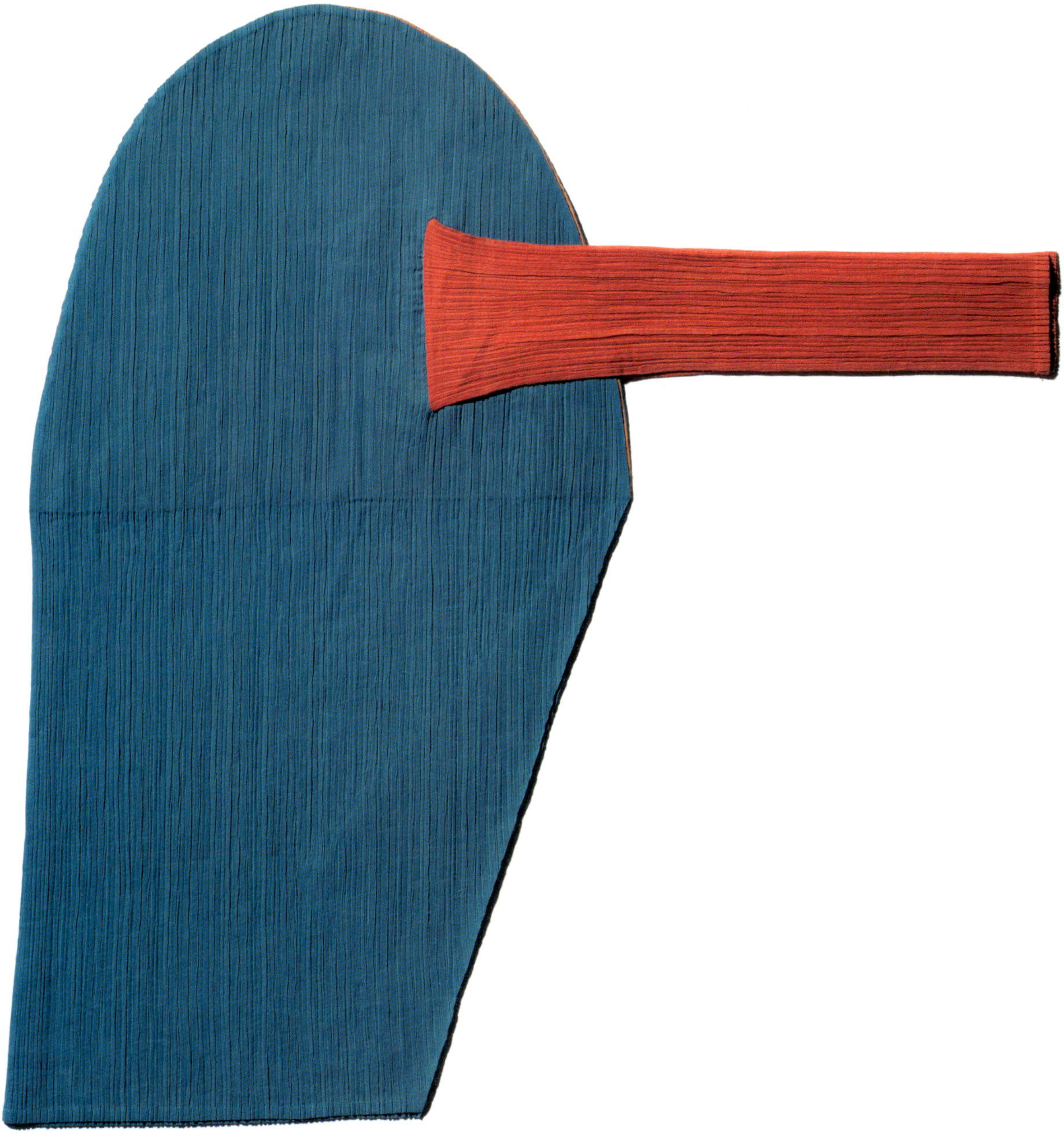

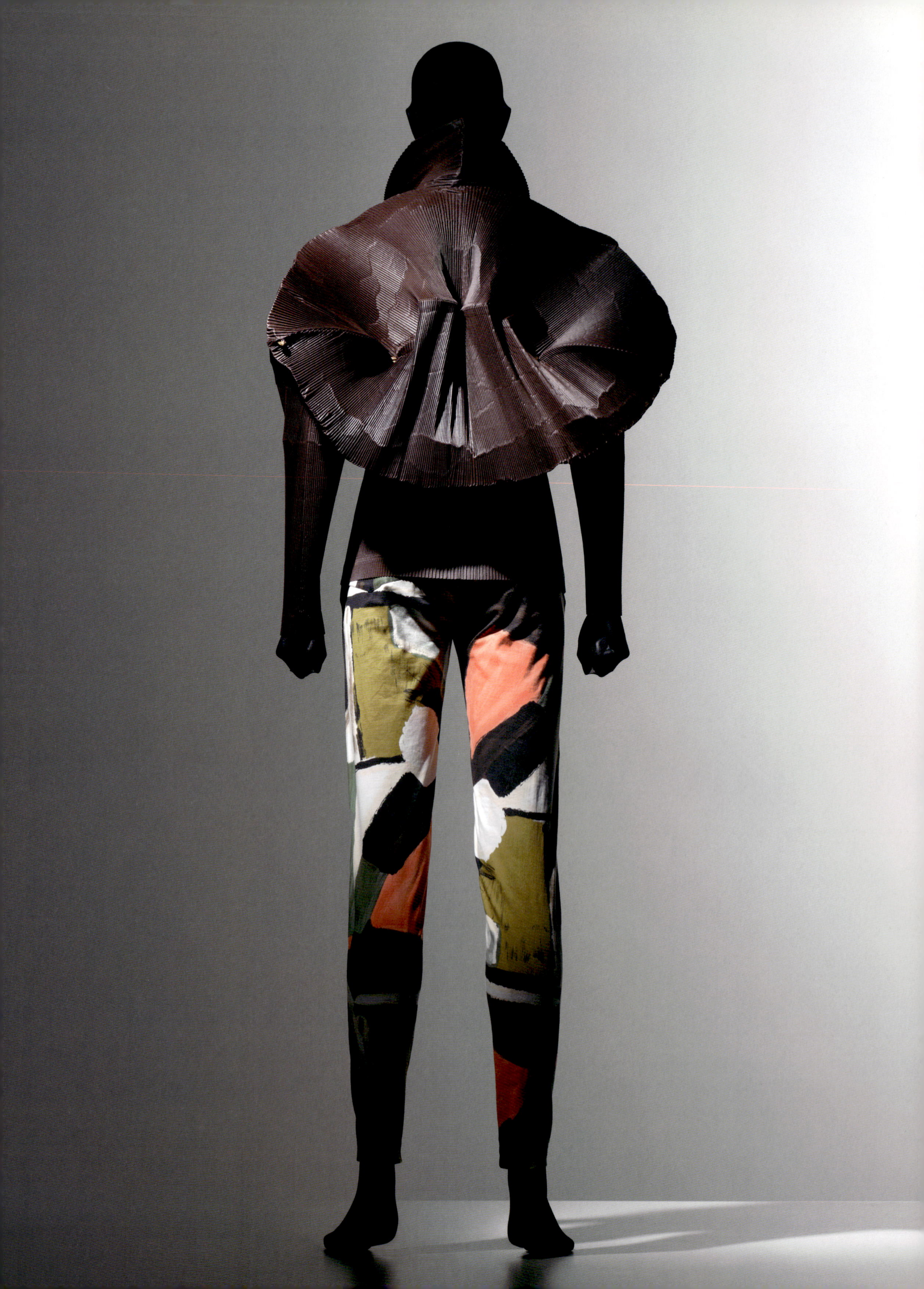

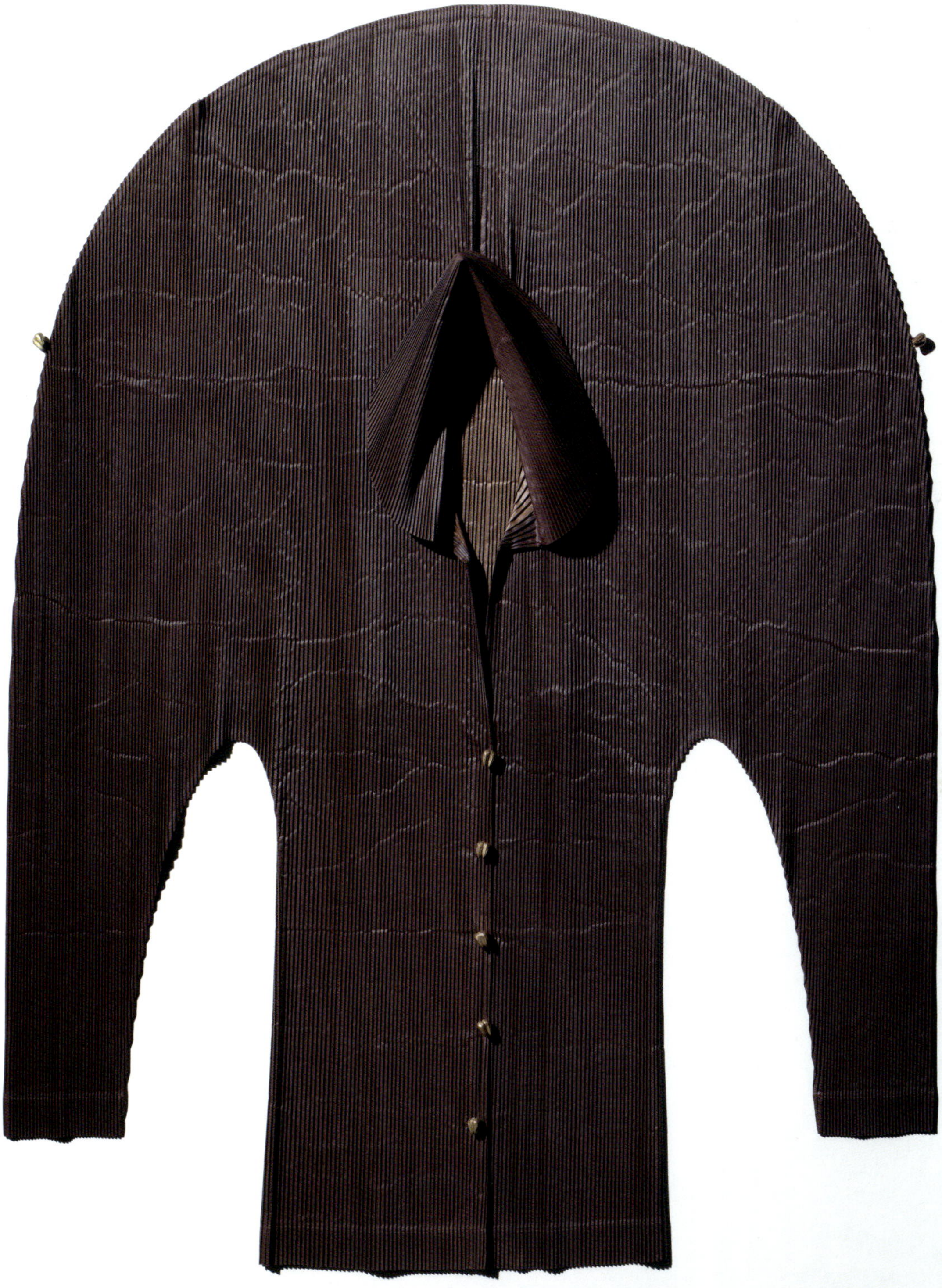

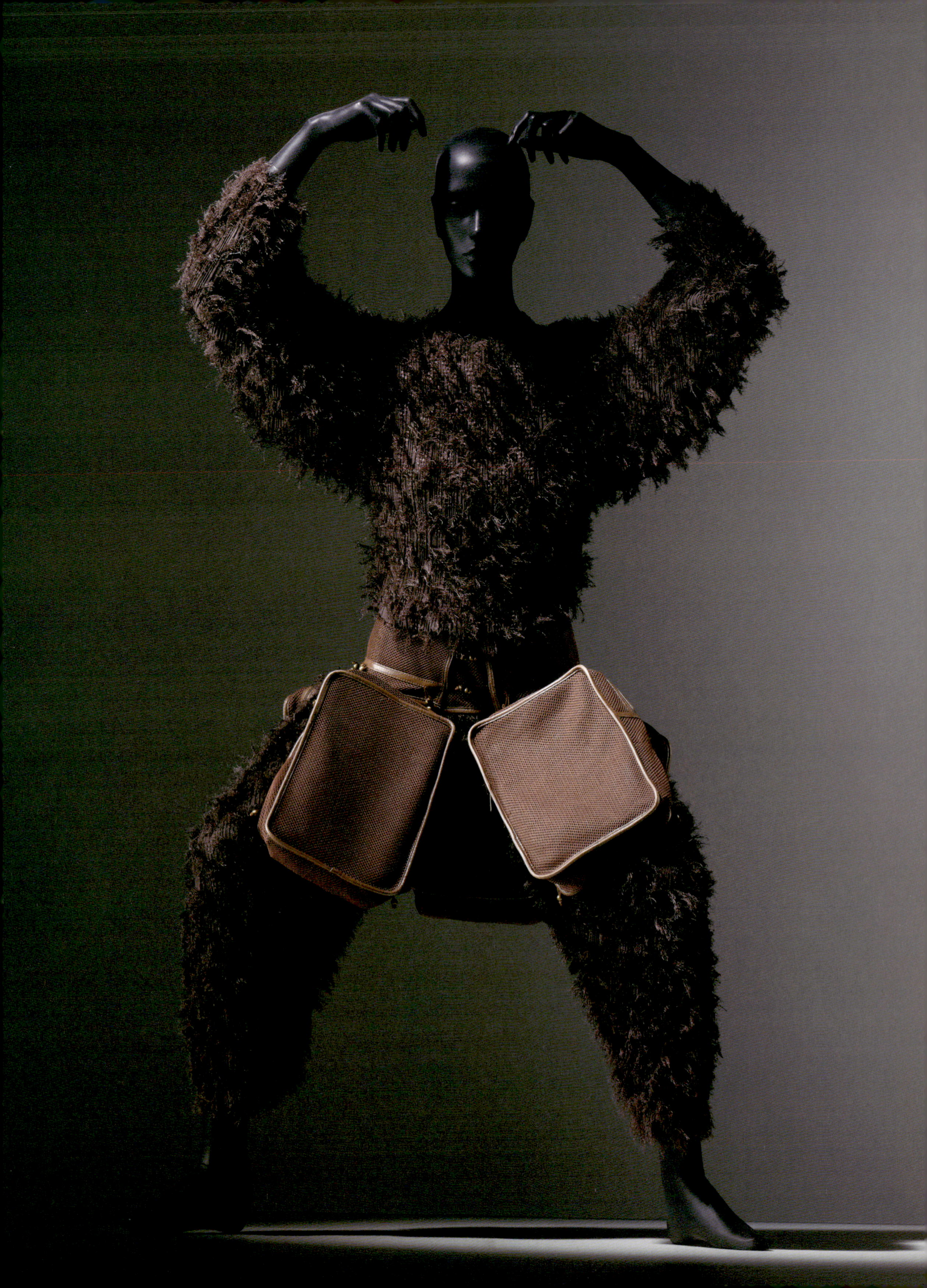

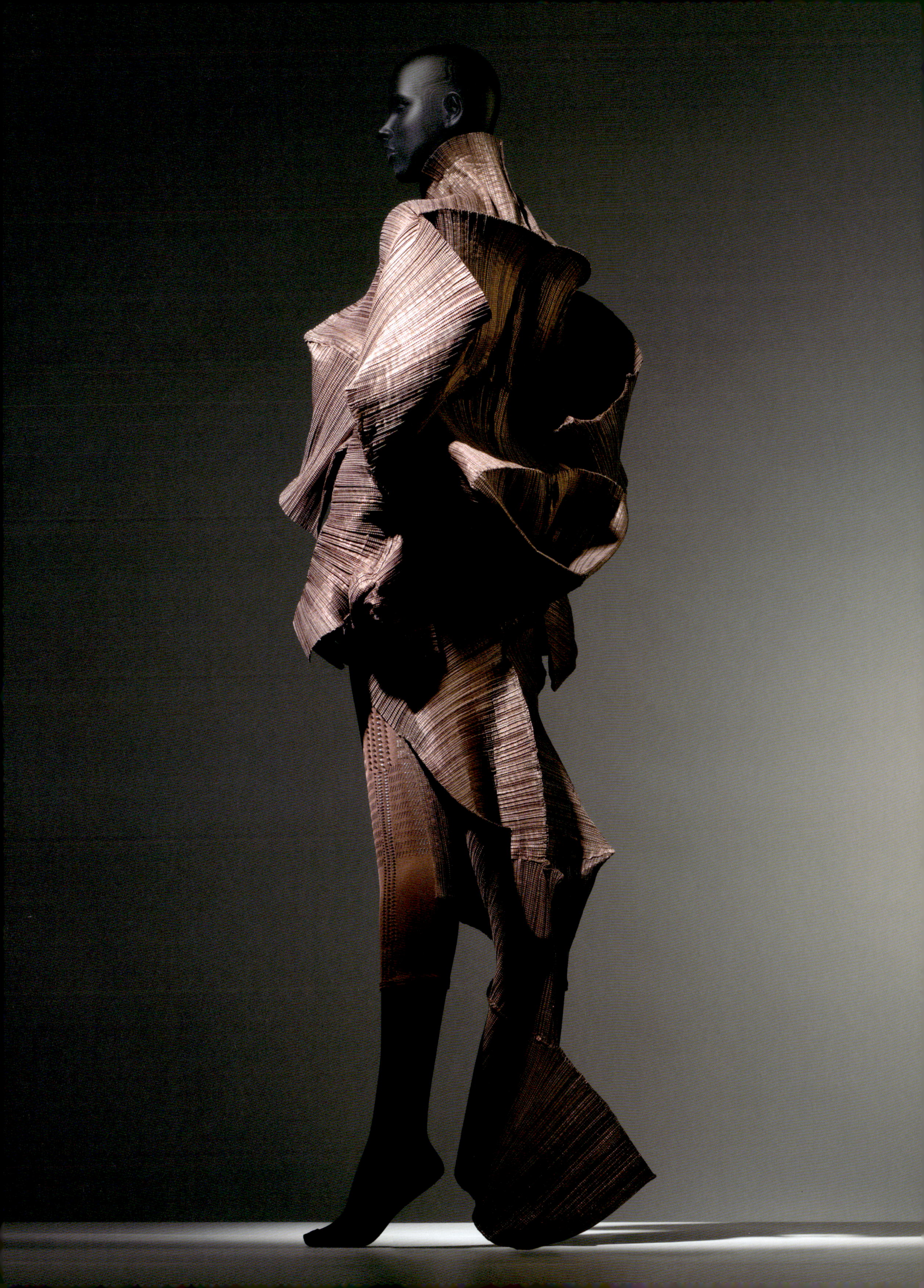

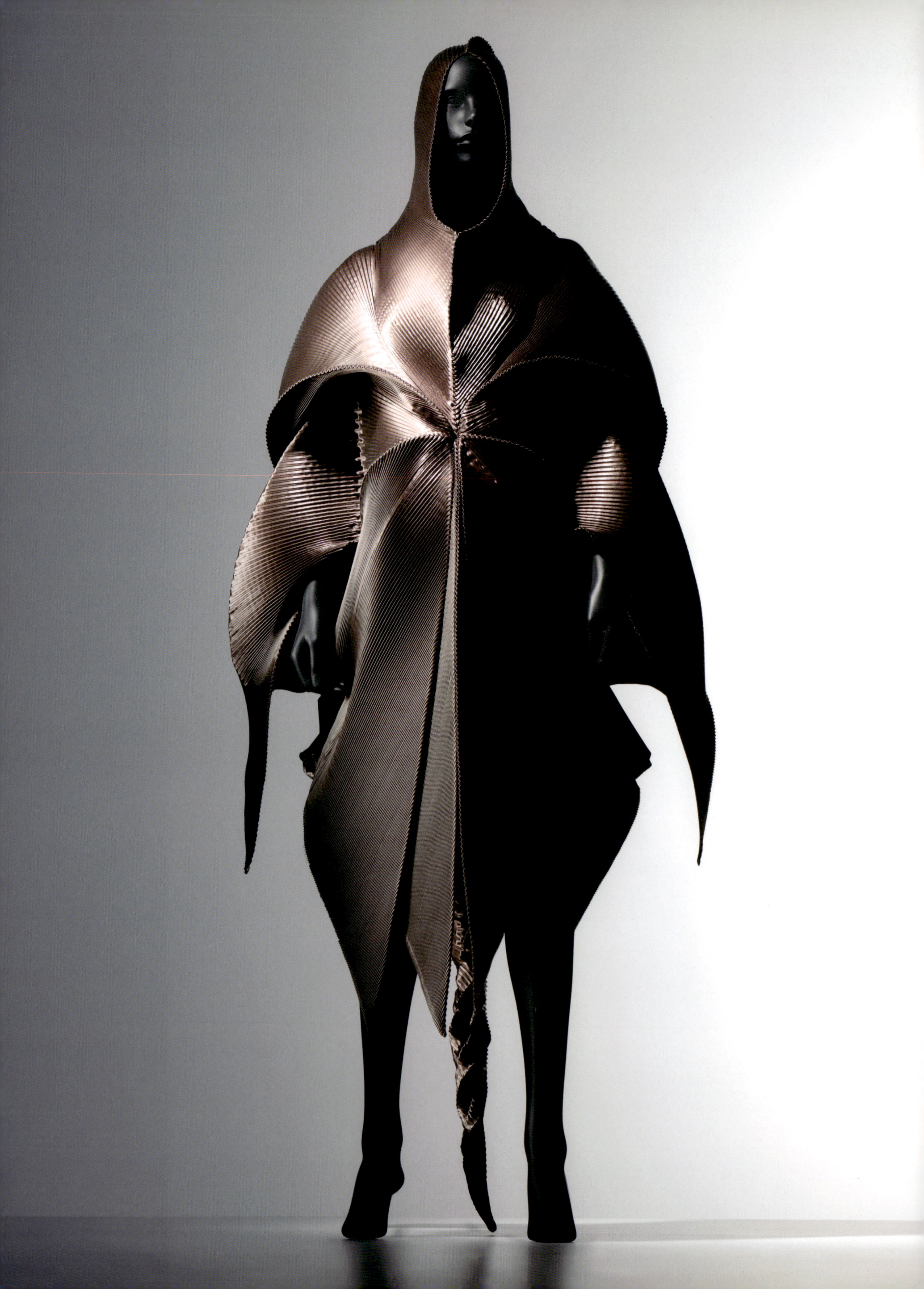

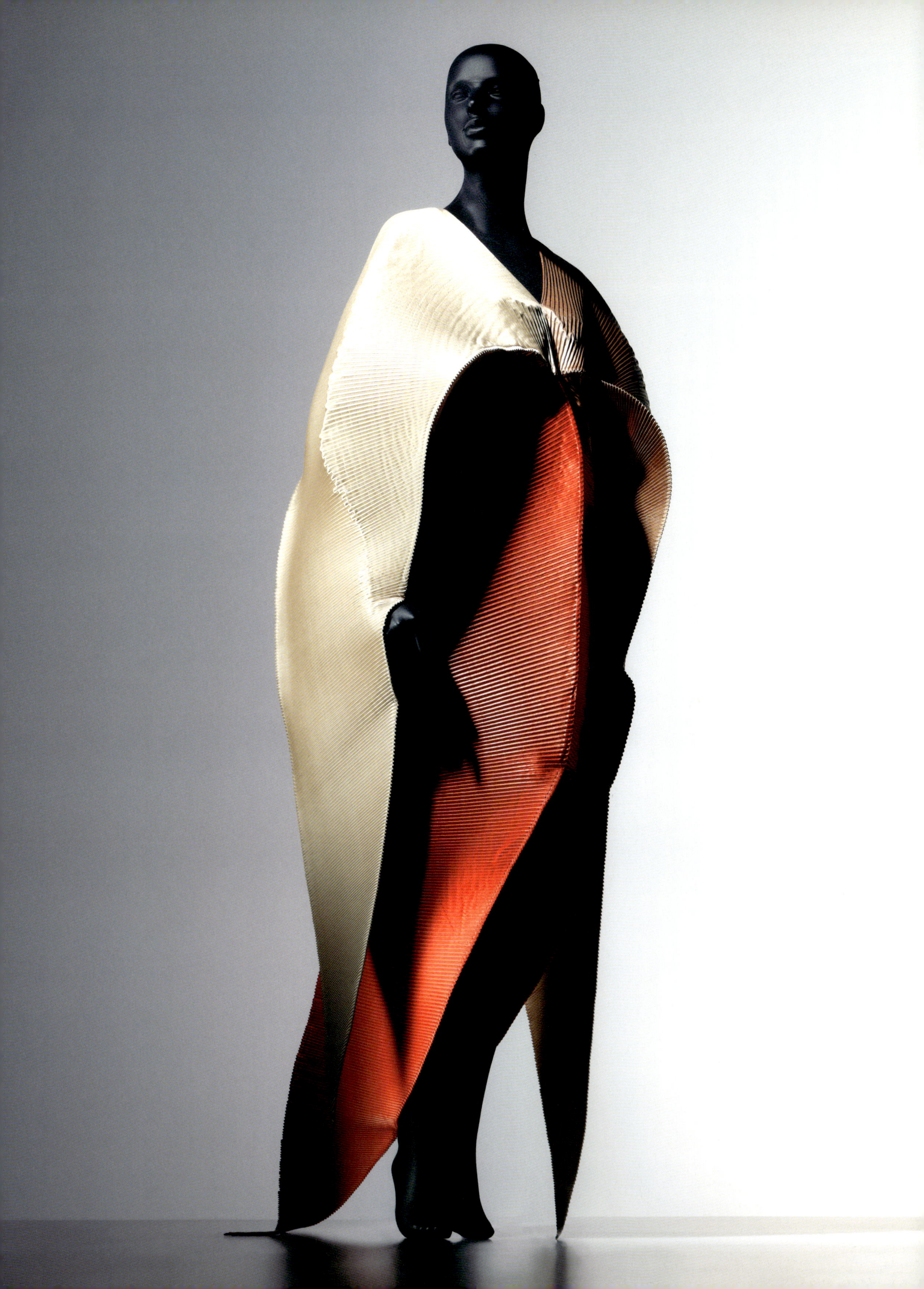

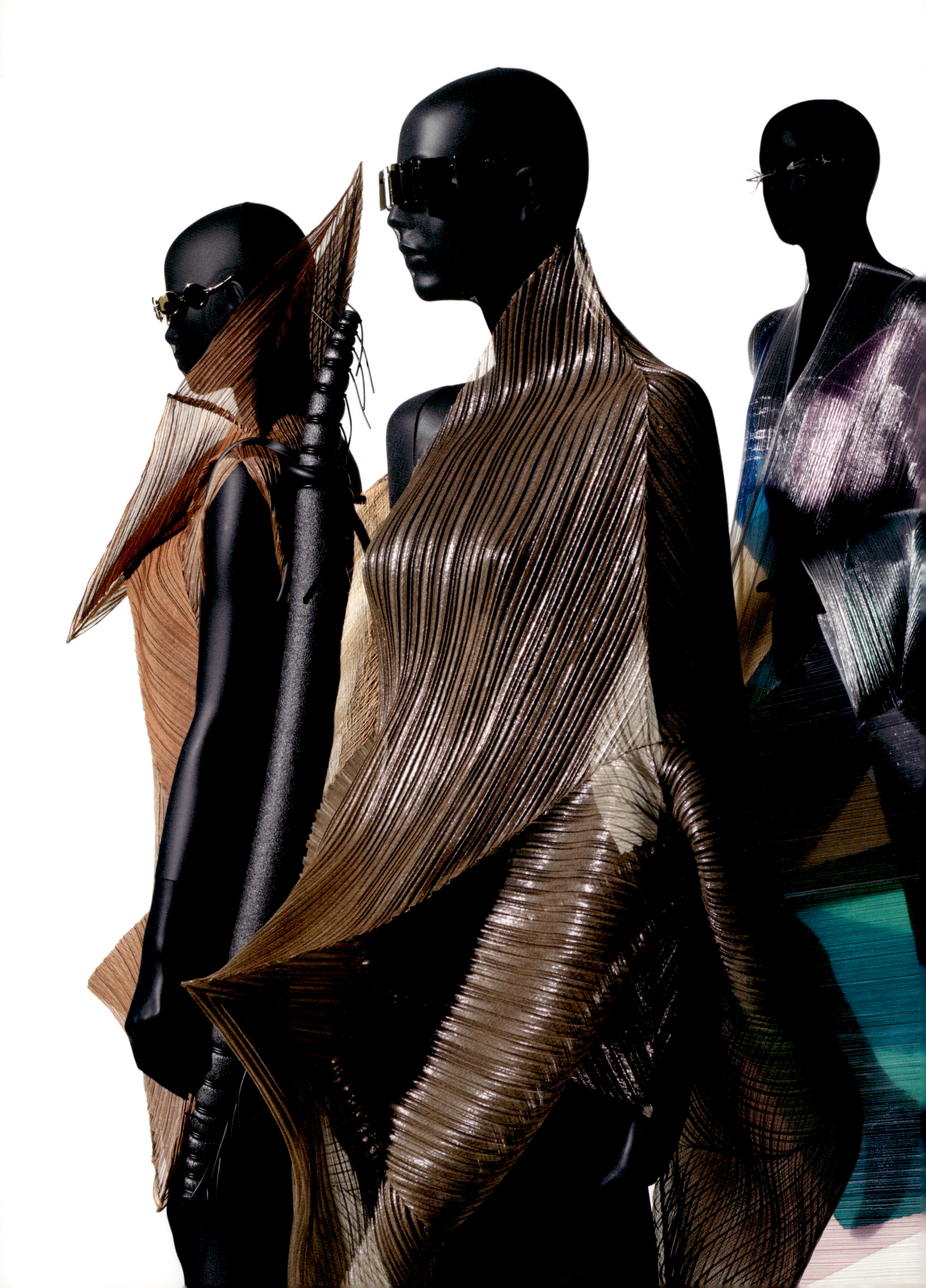

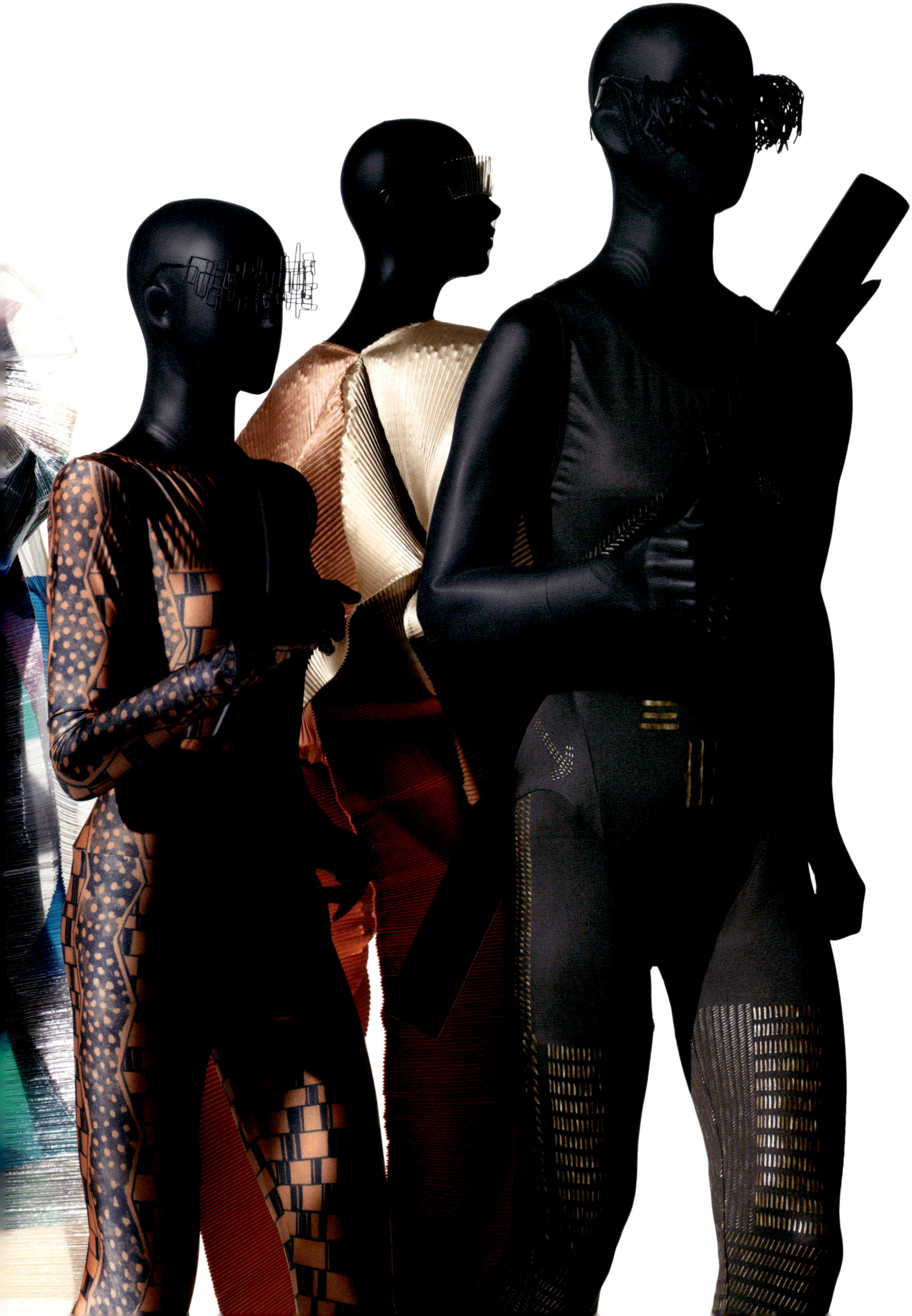

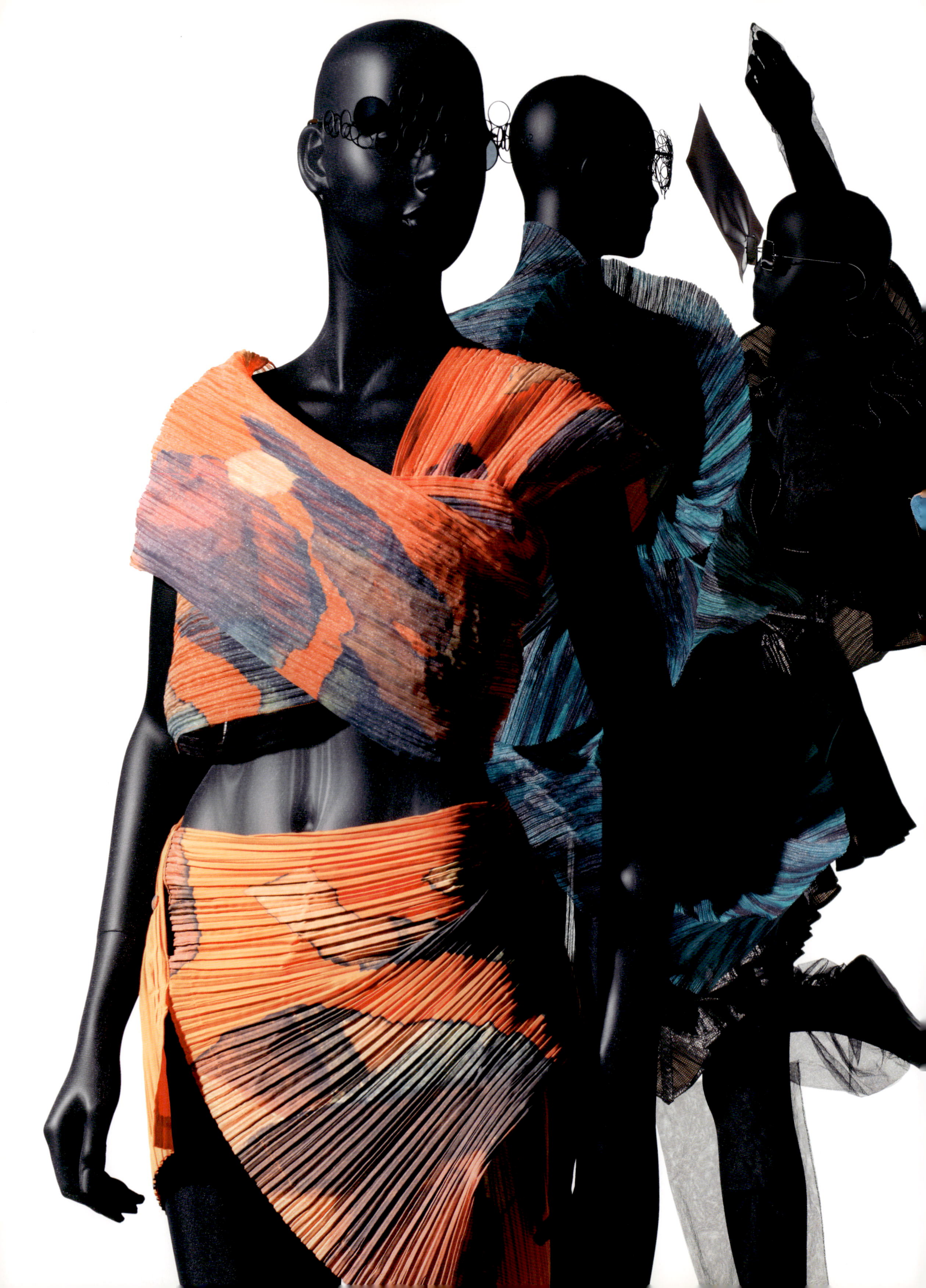

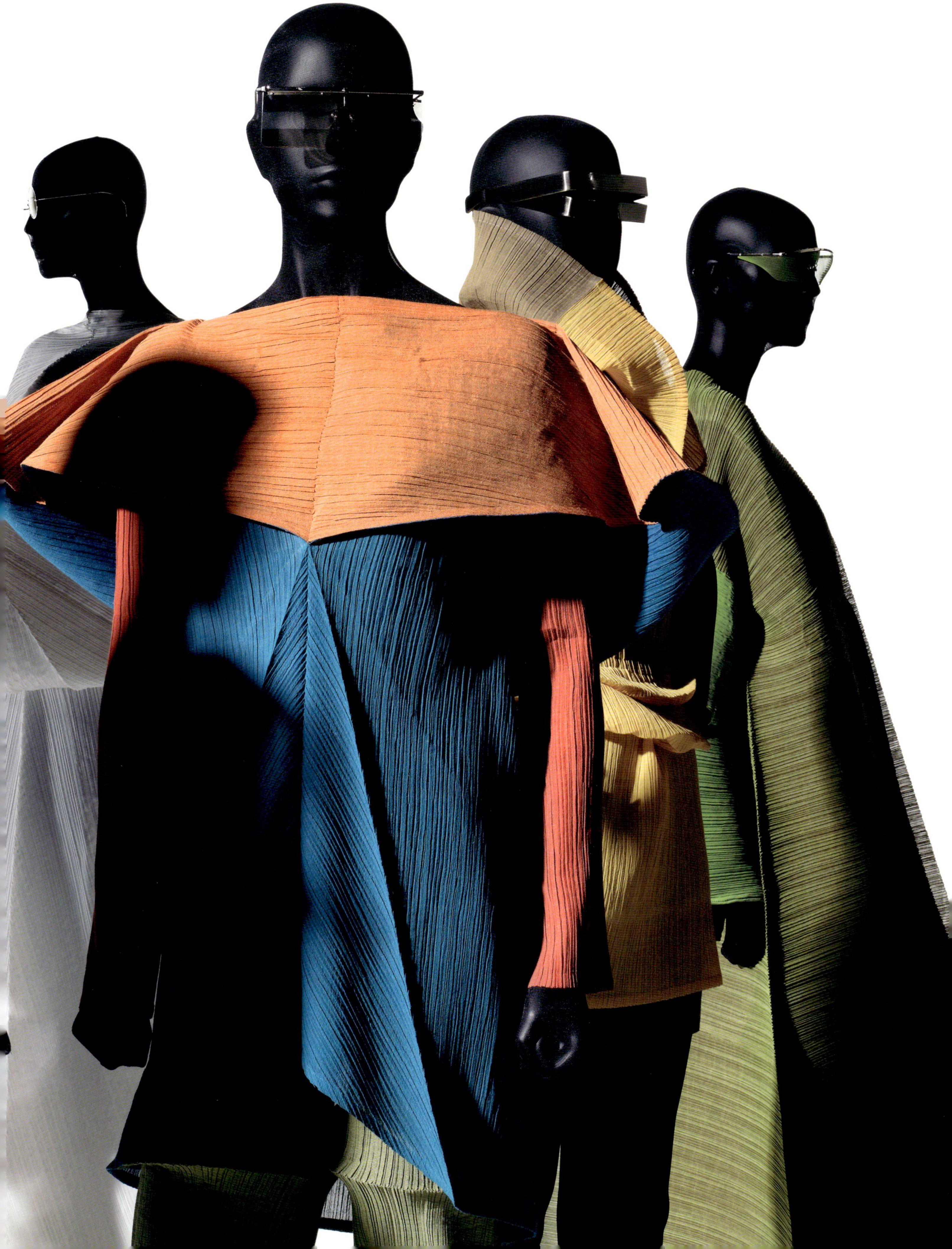

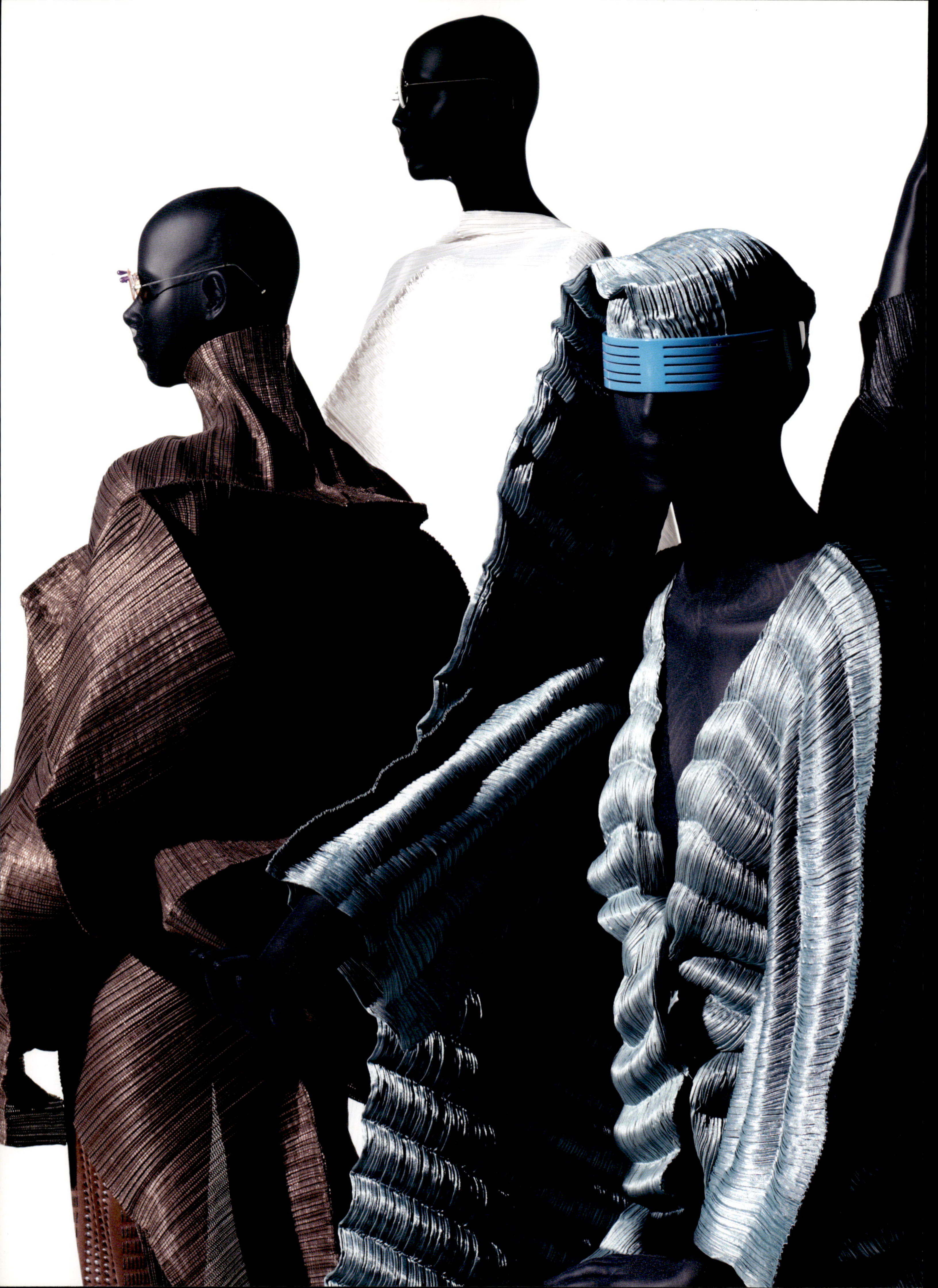

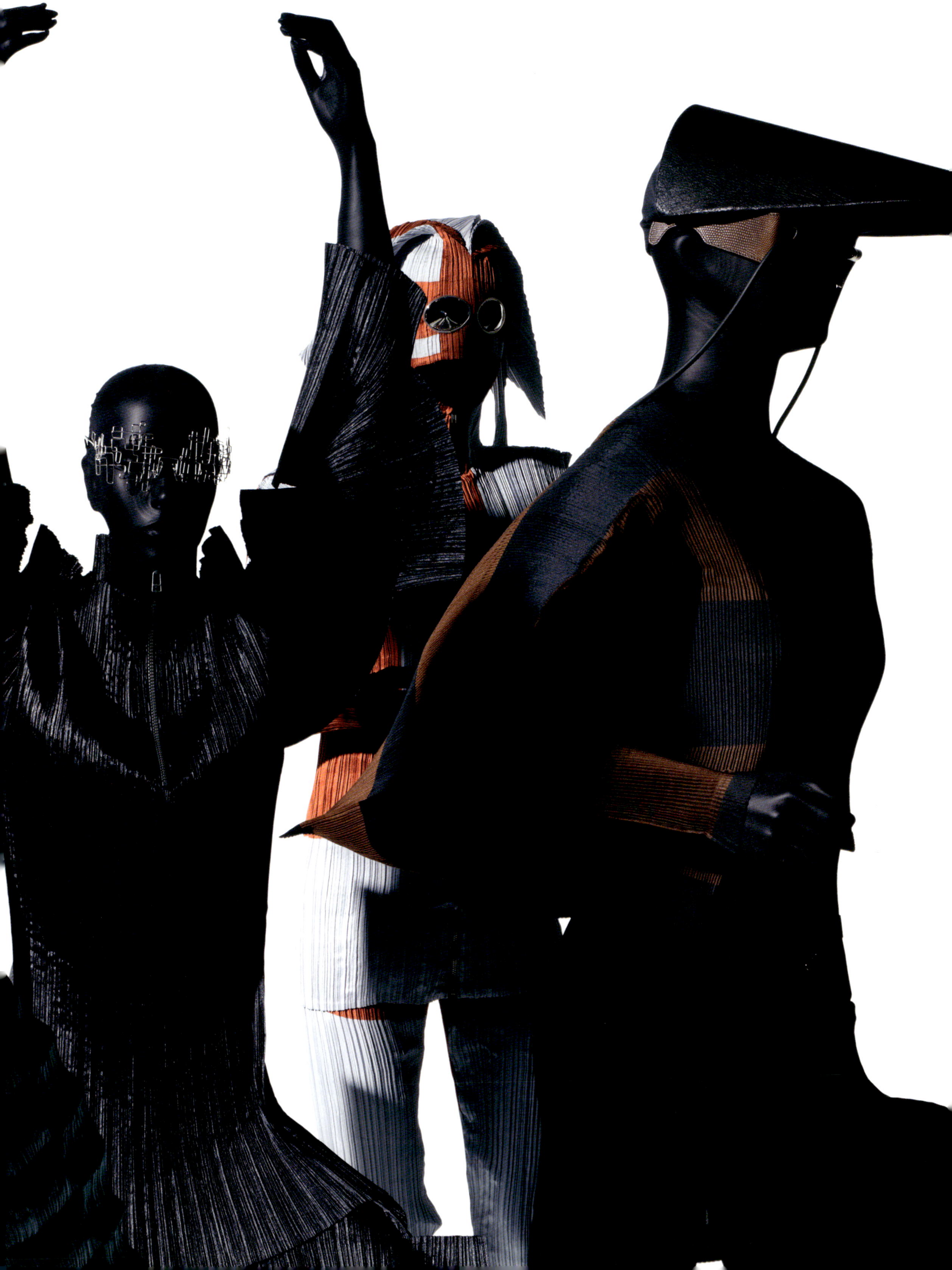

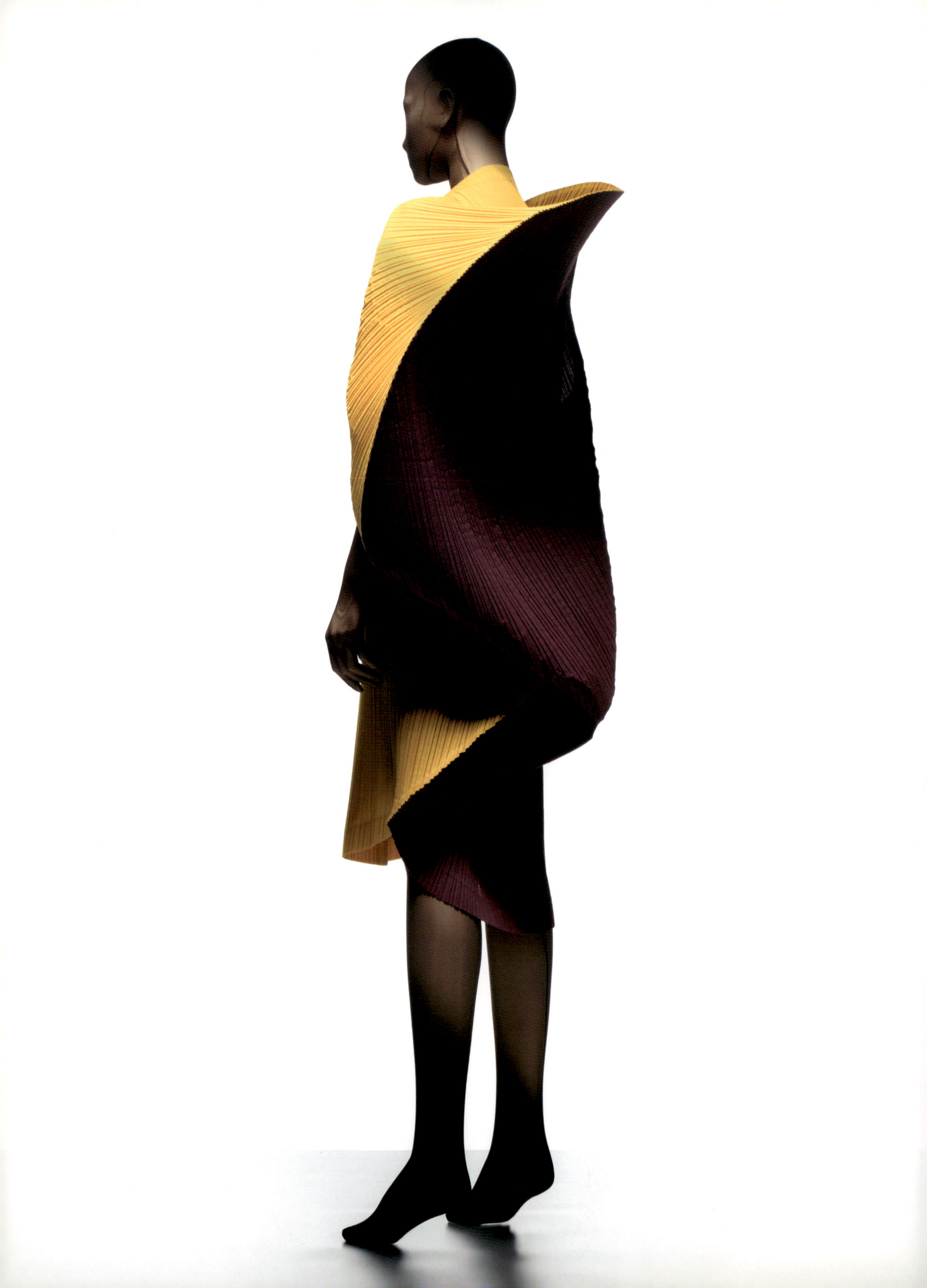

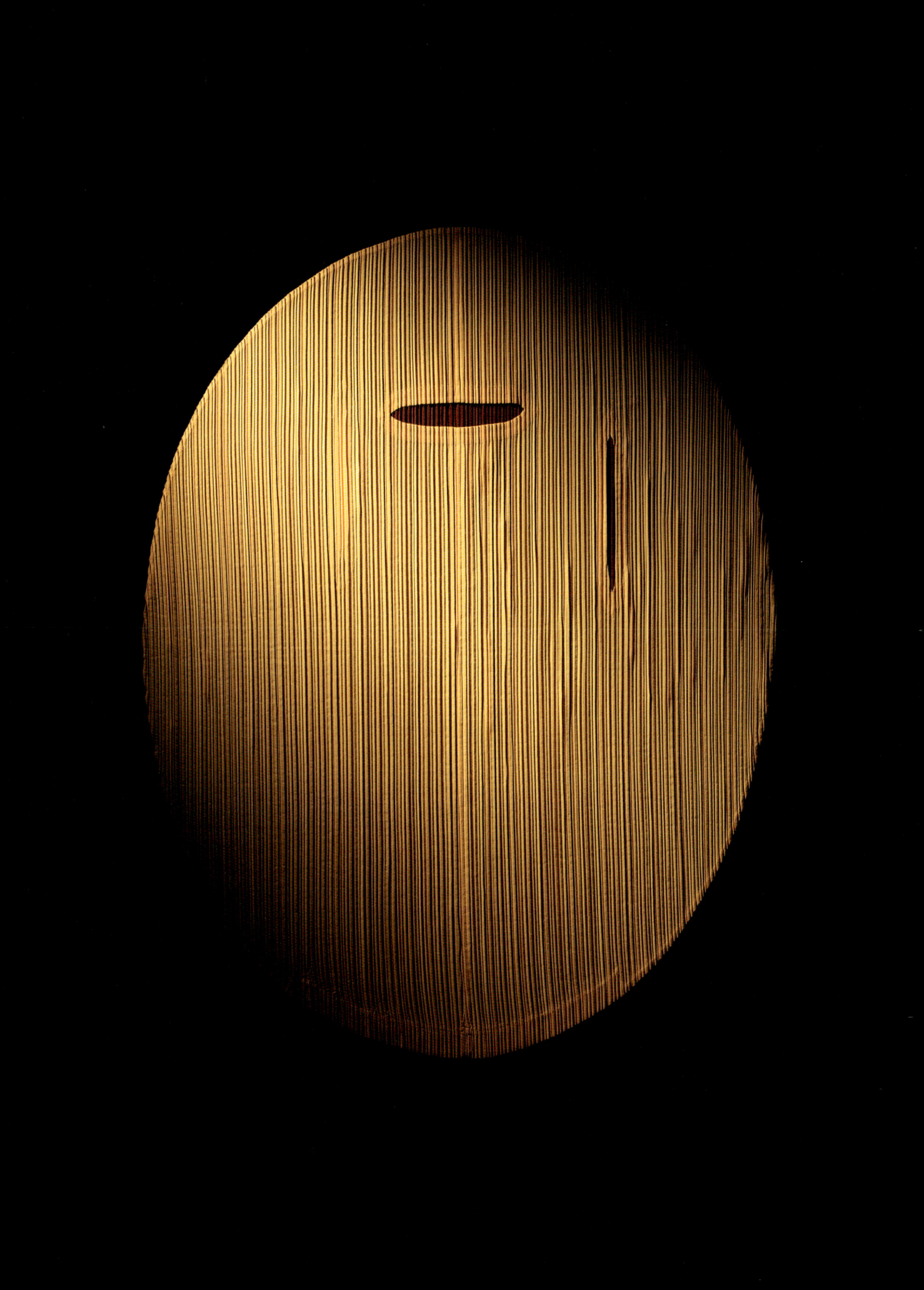

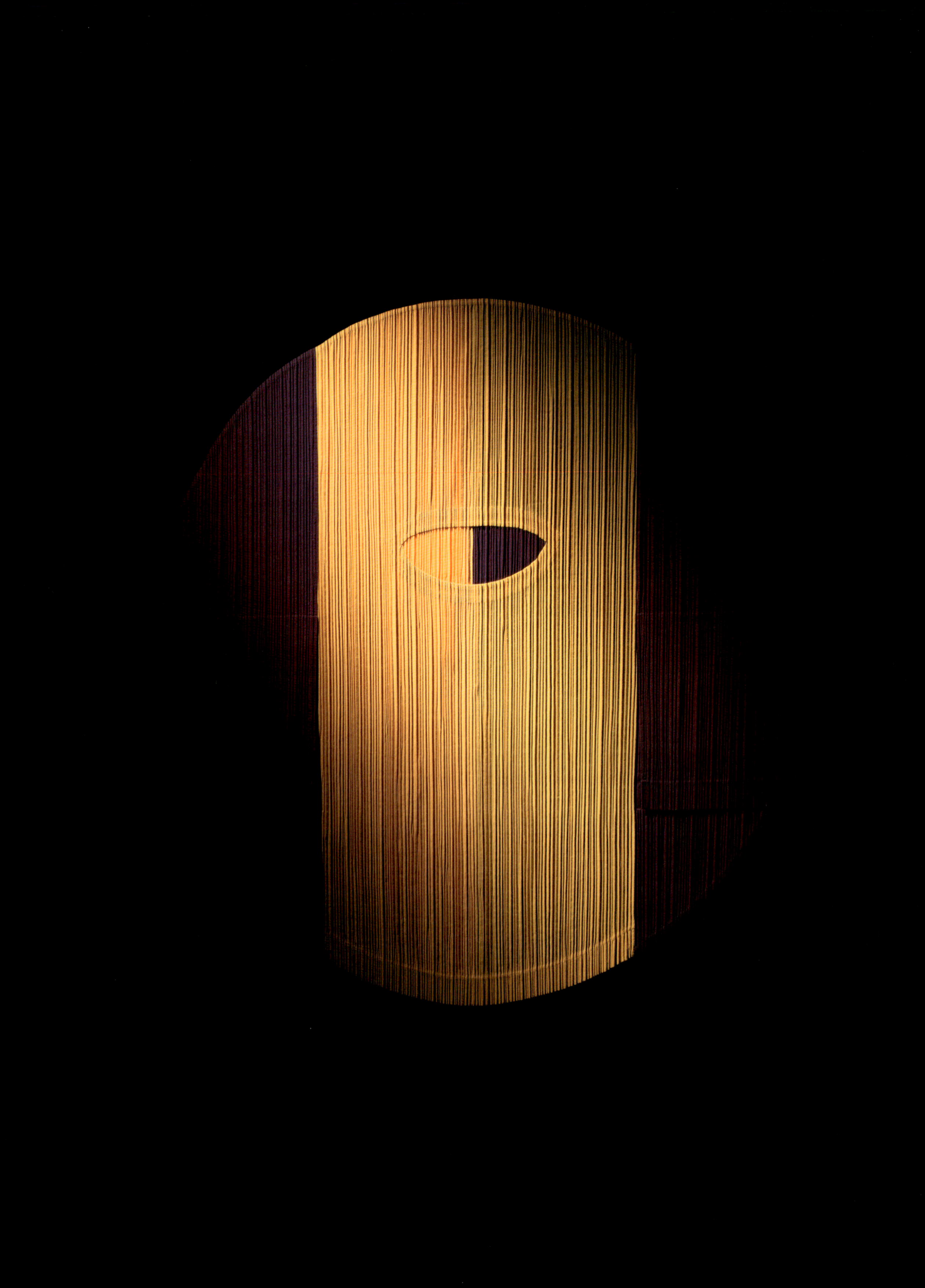

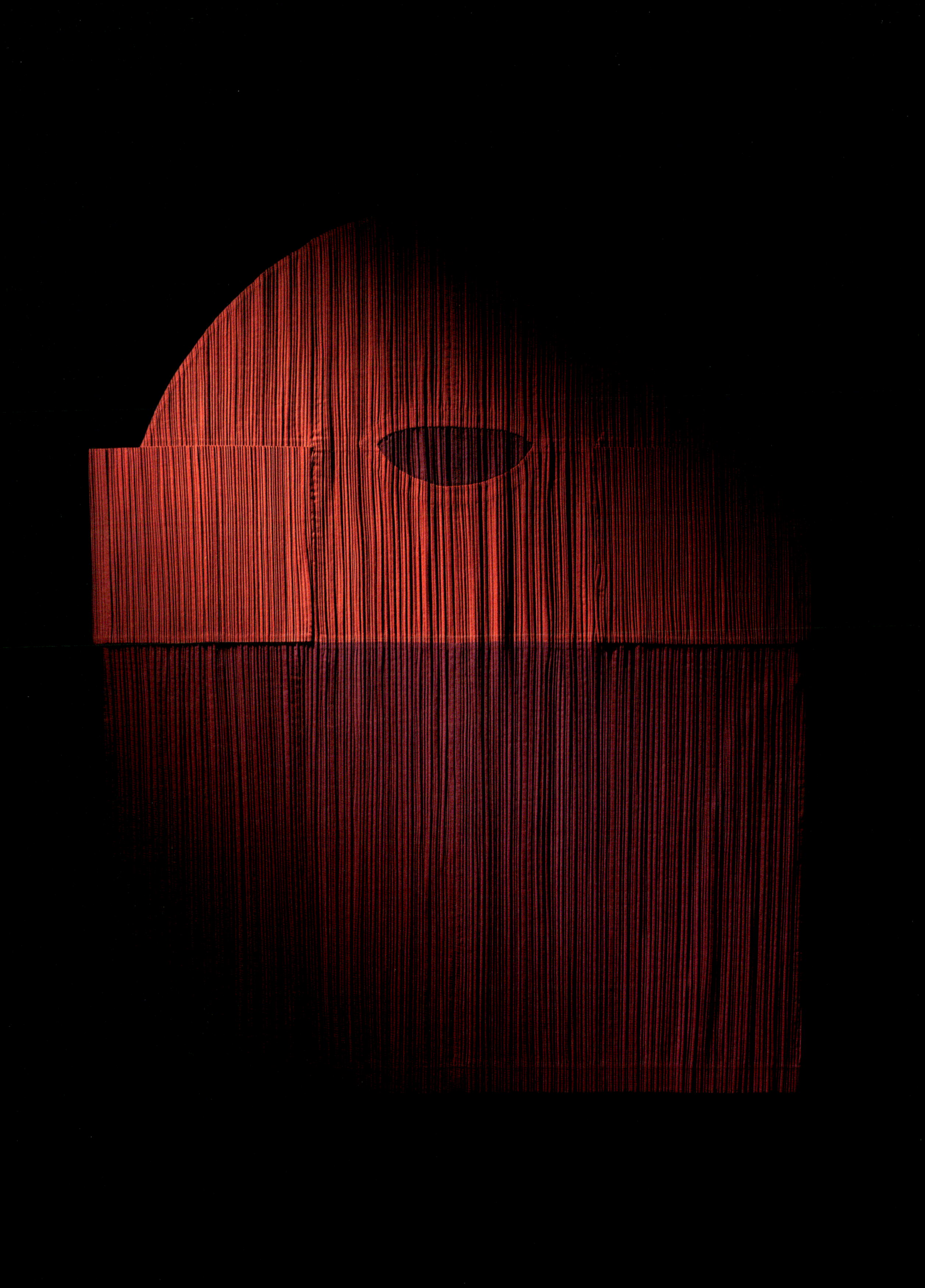

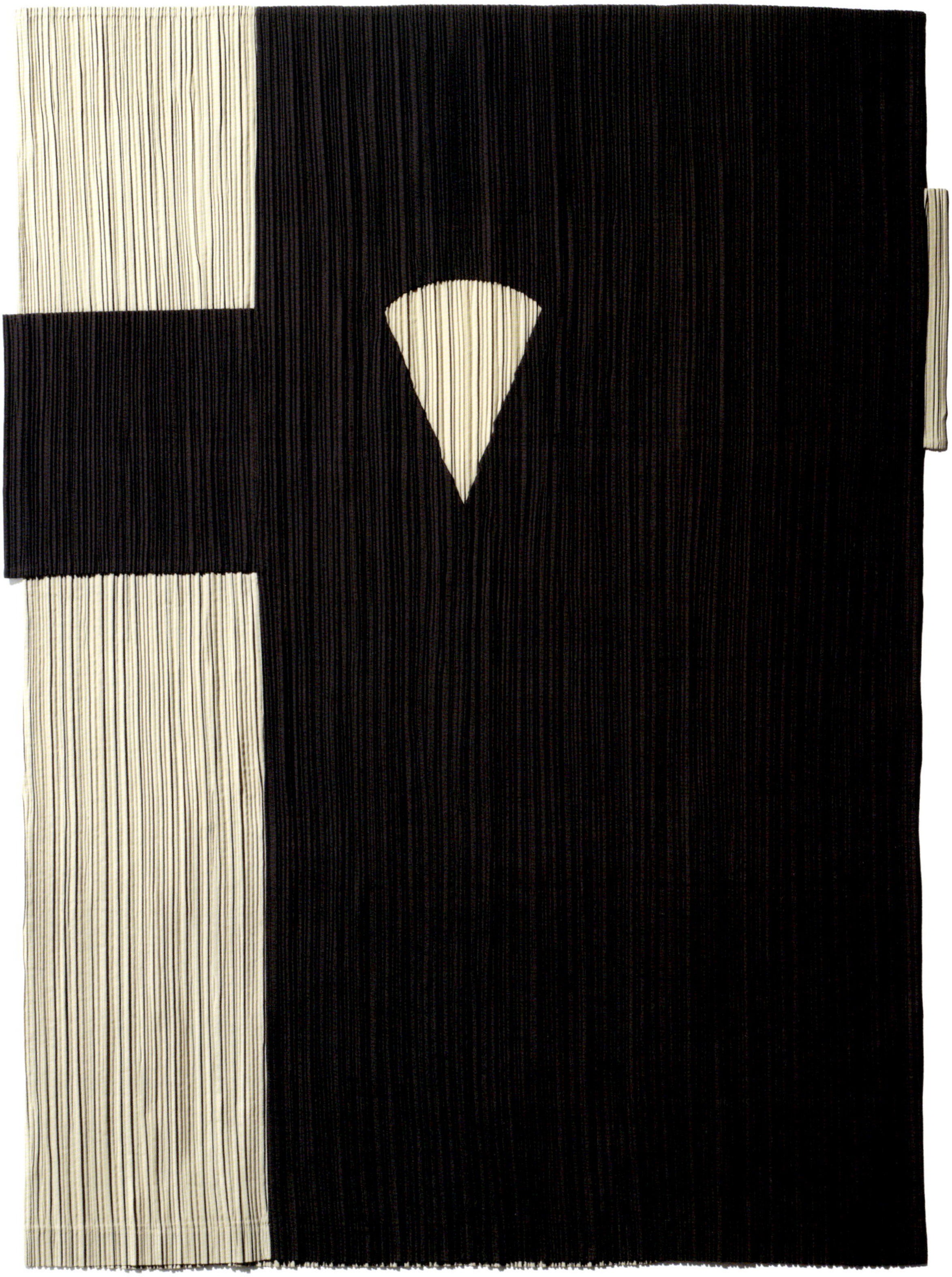

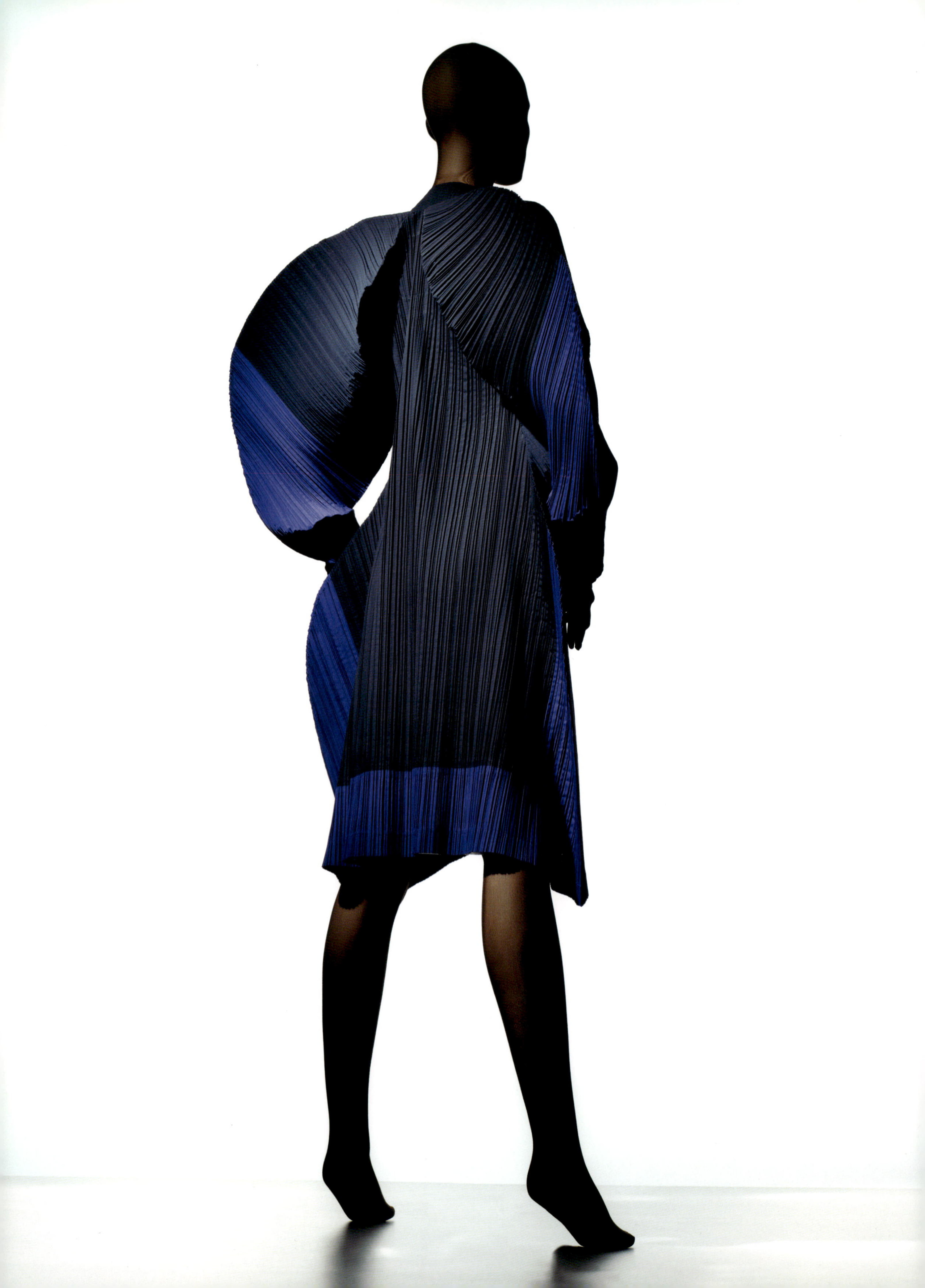

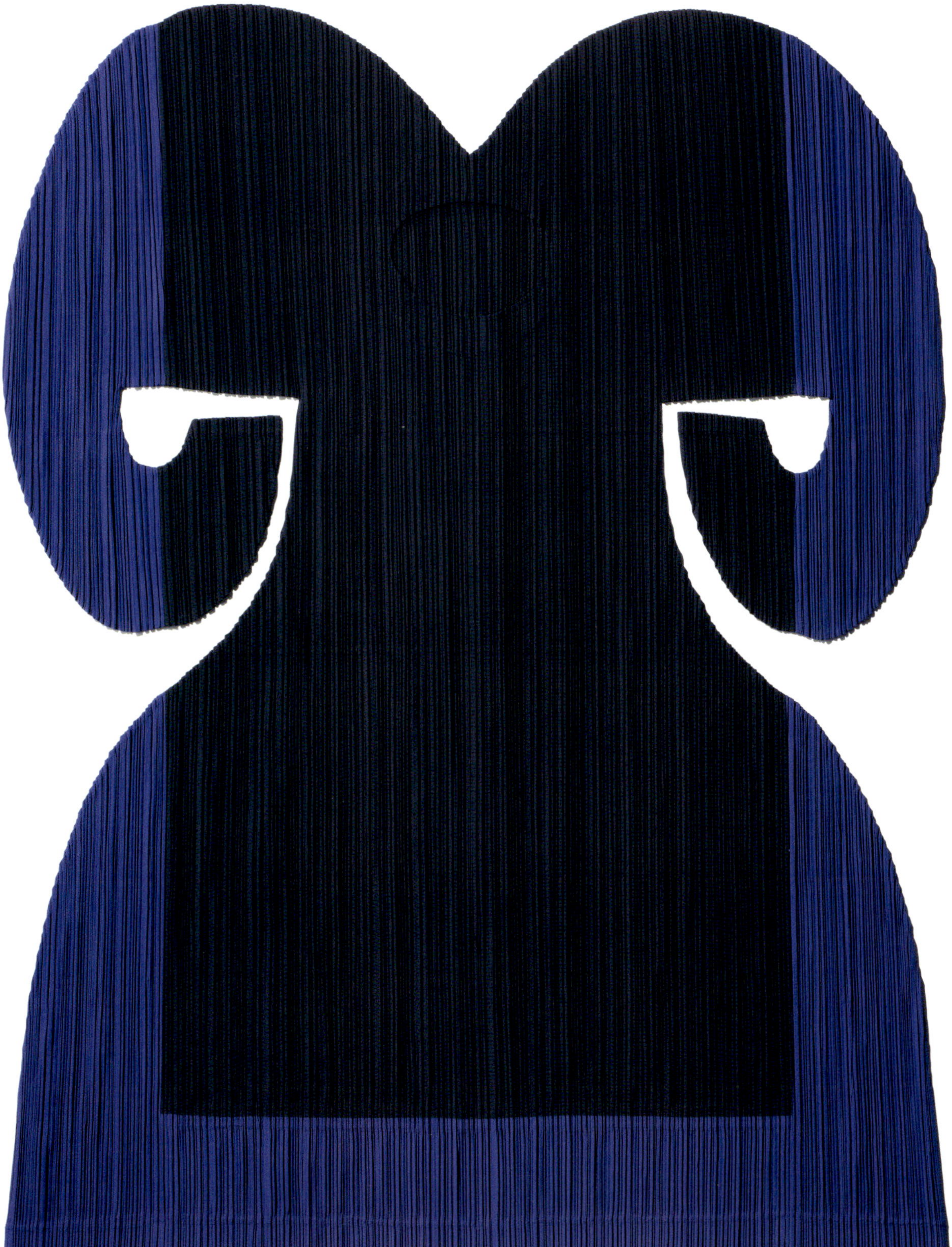

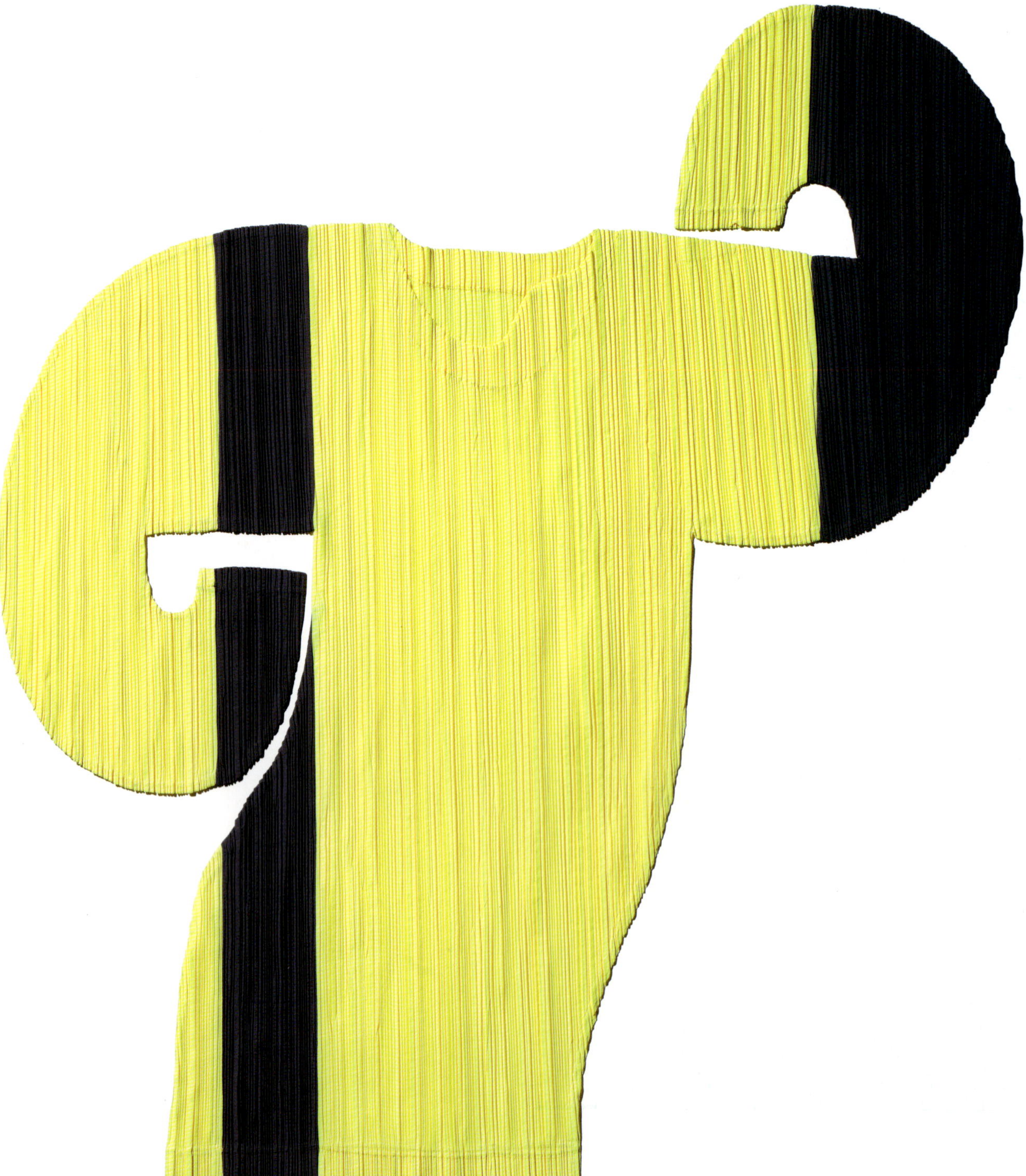

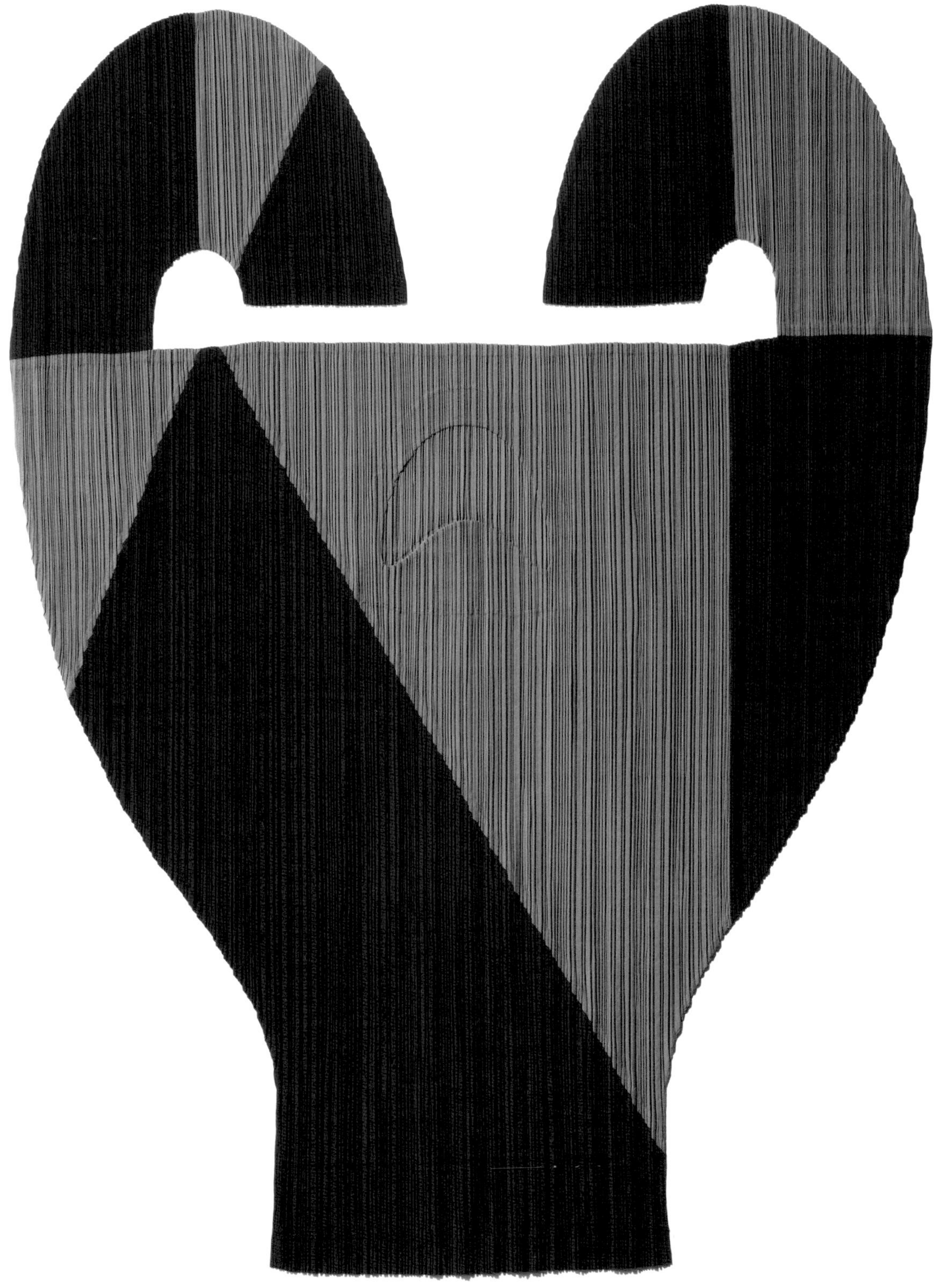

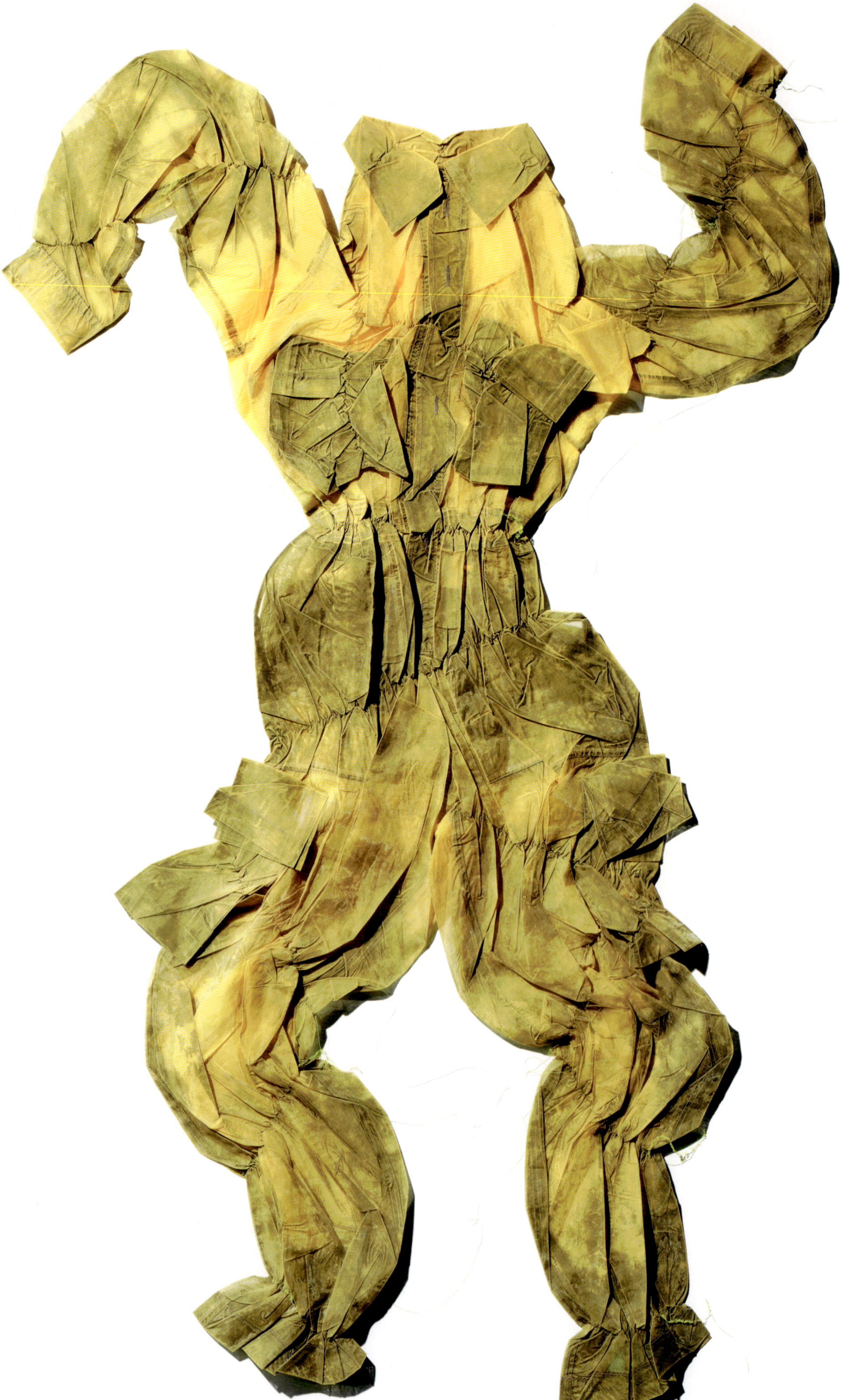

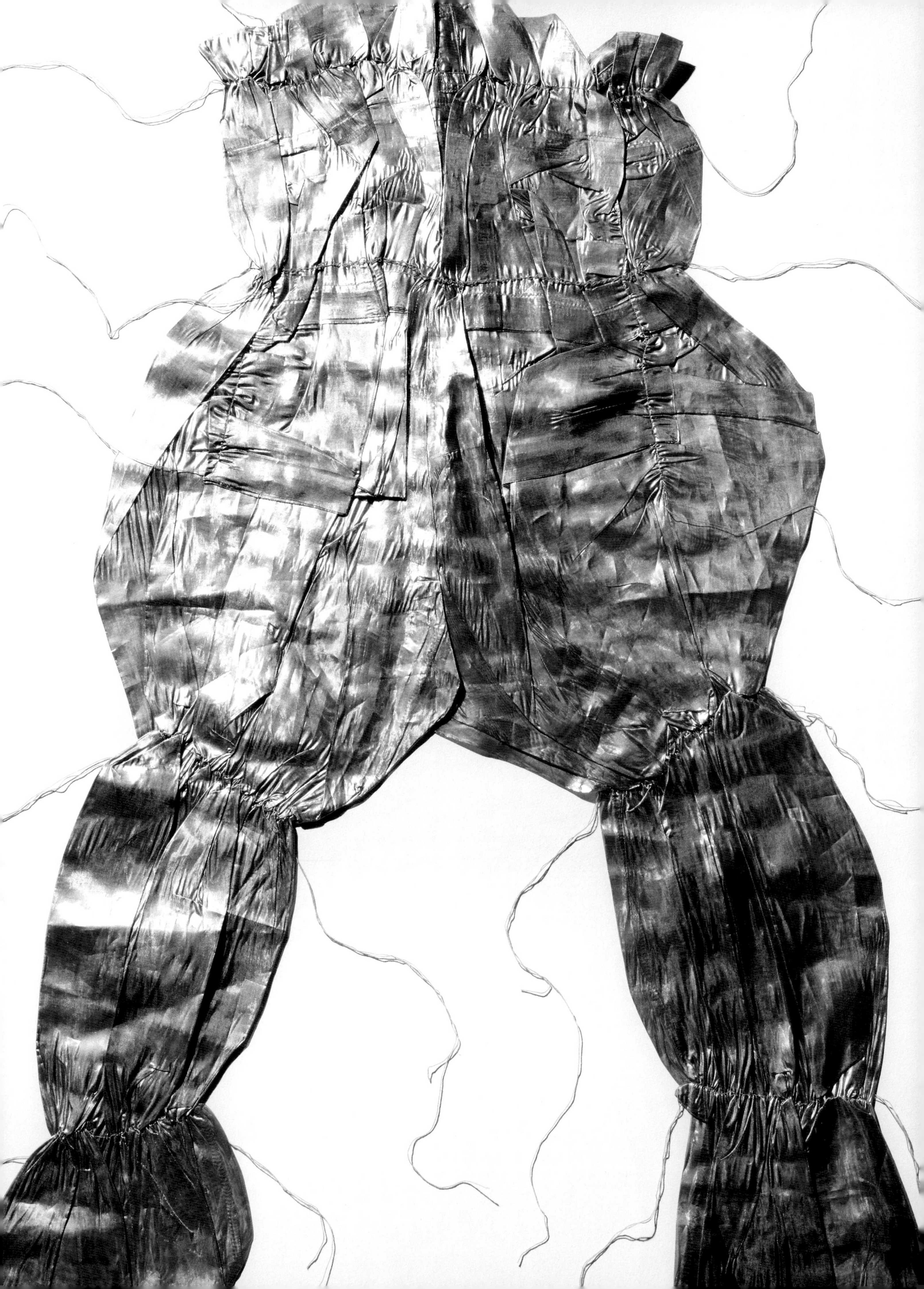

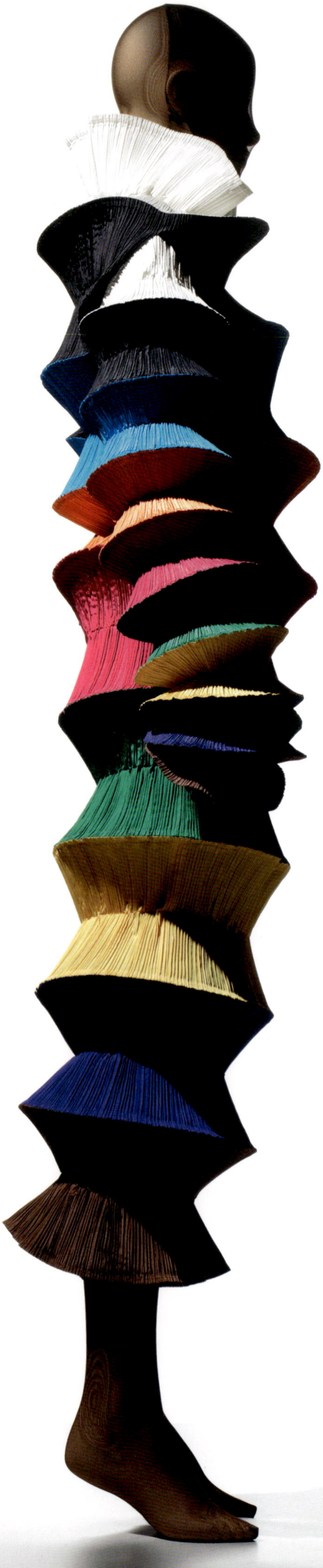

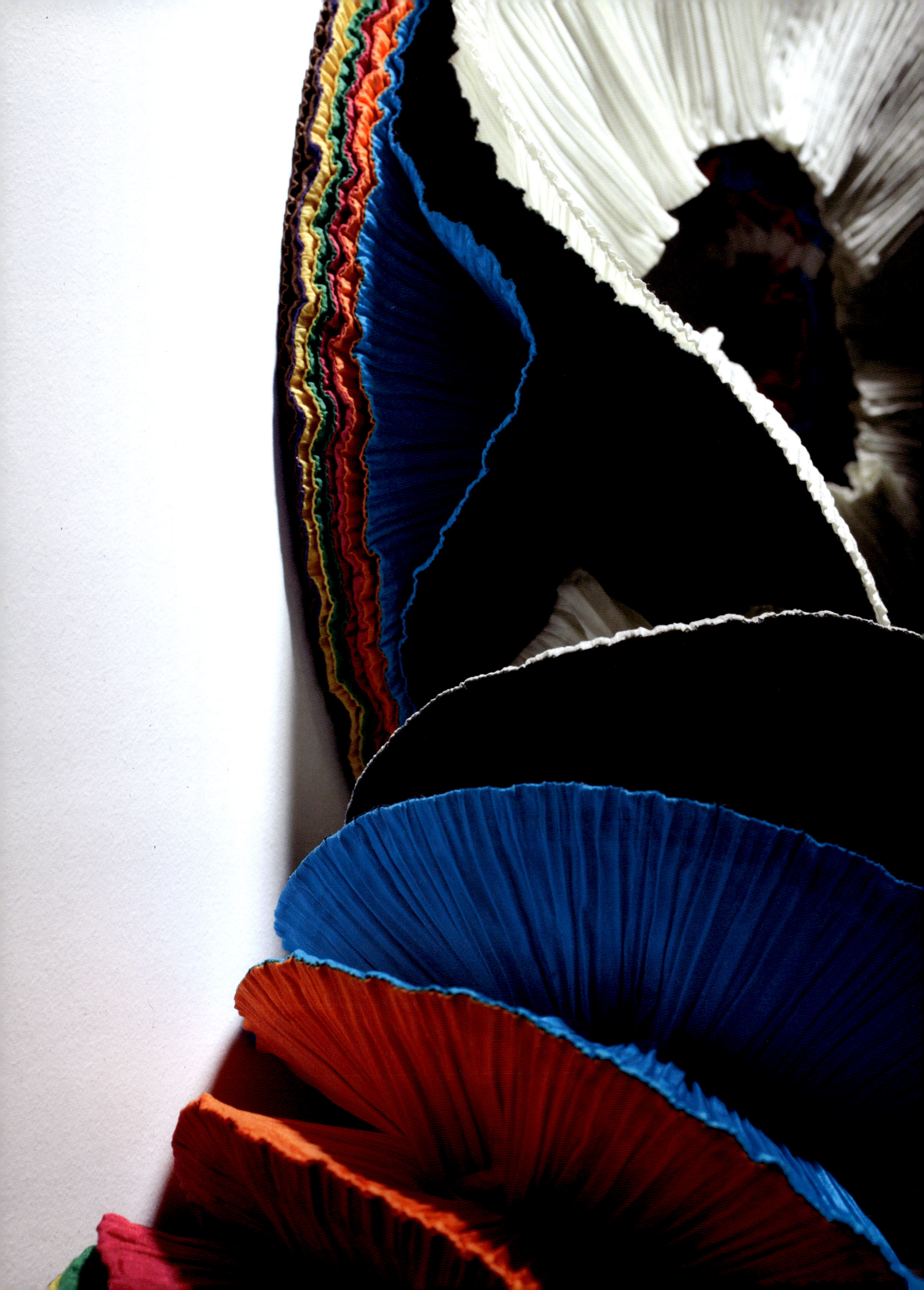

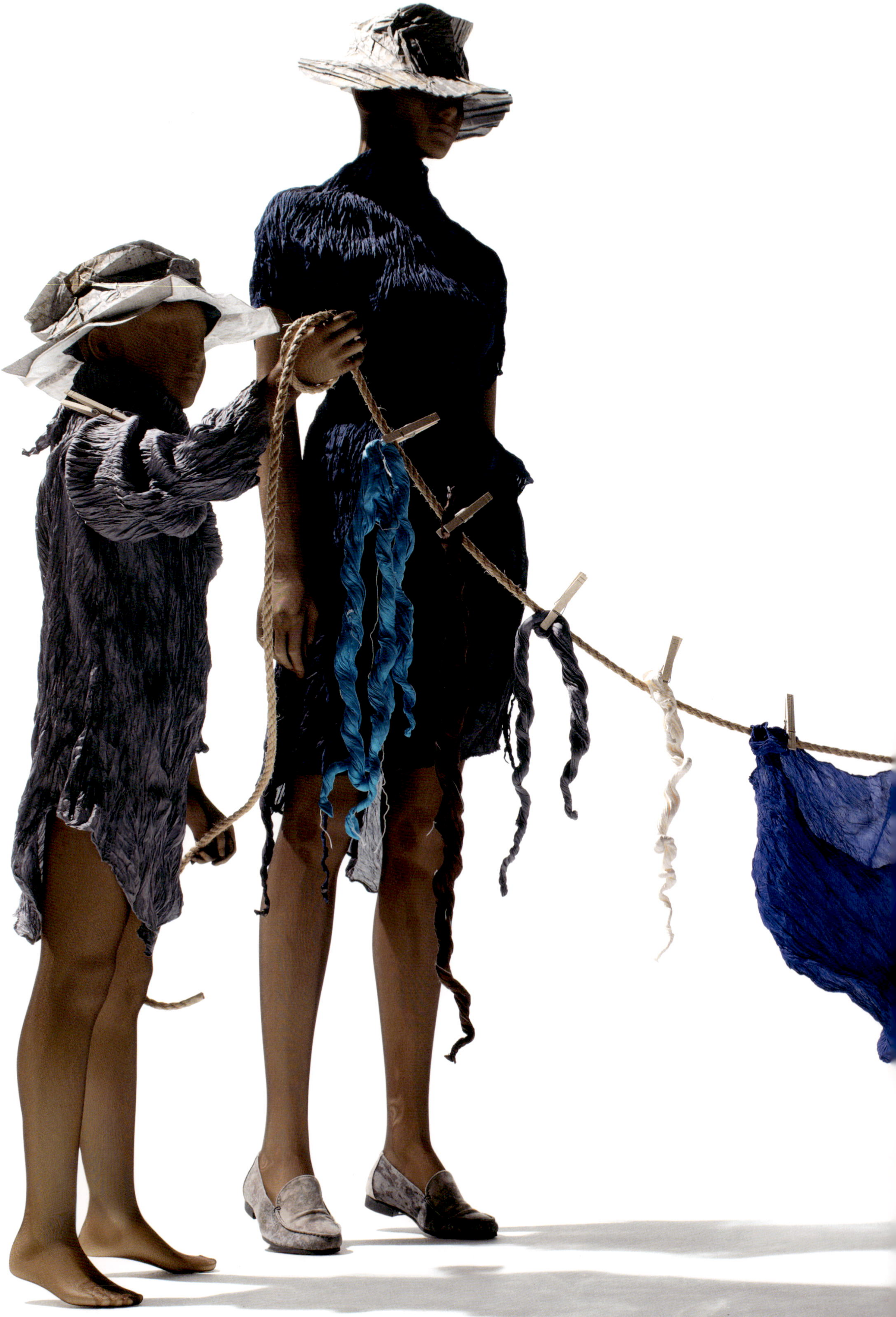

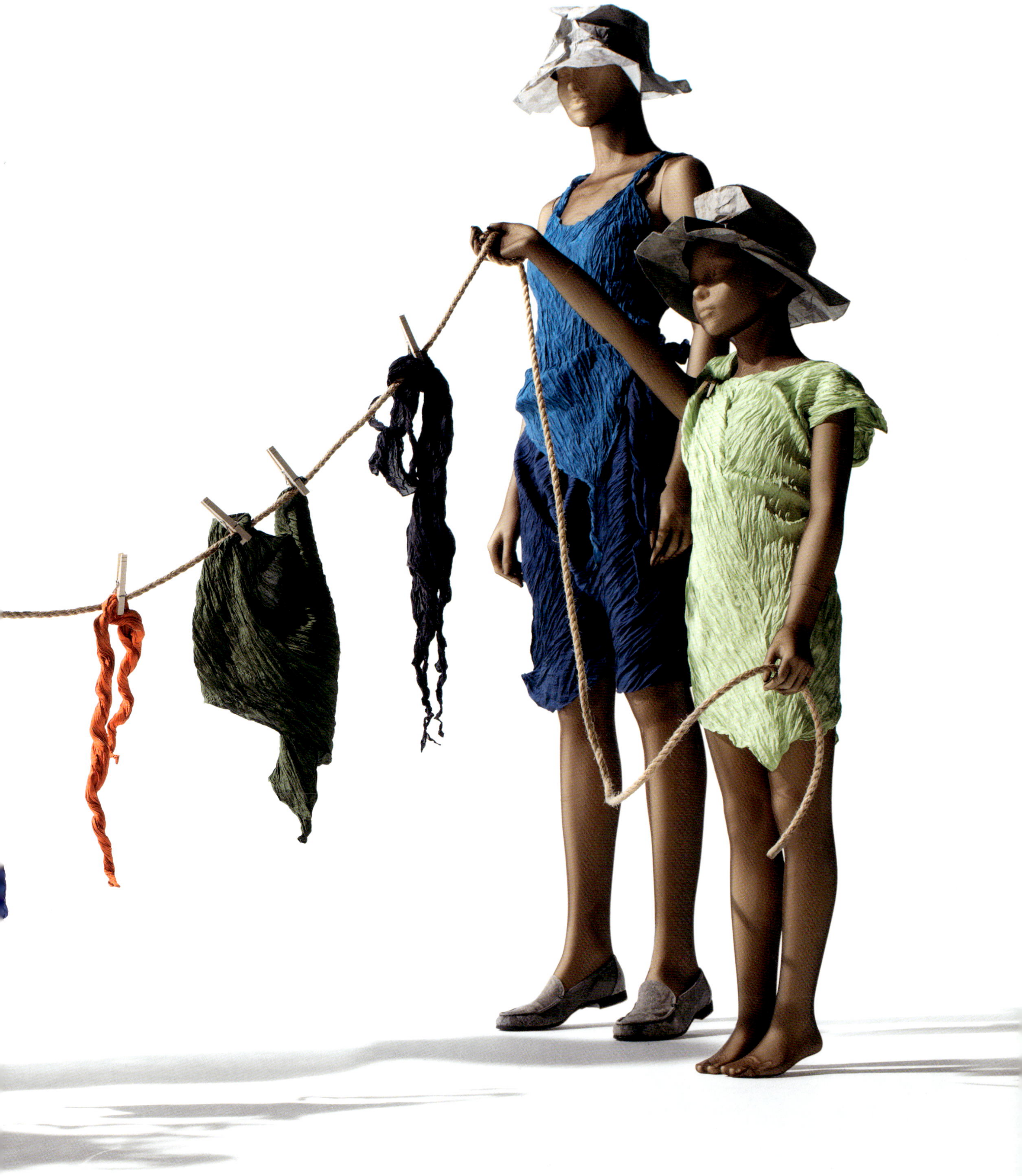

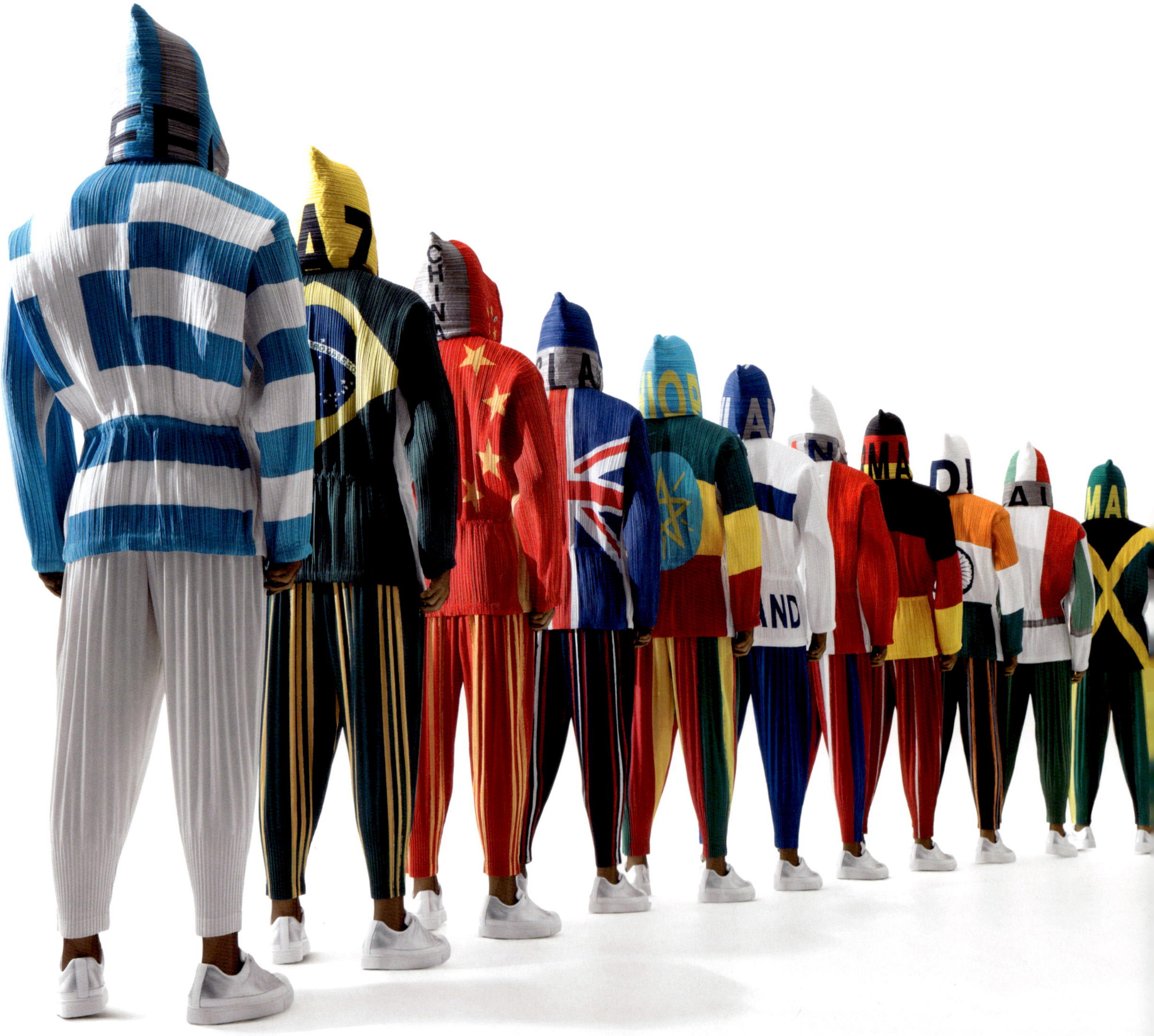
CHINA

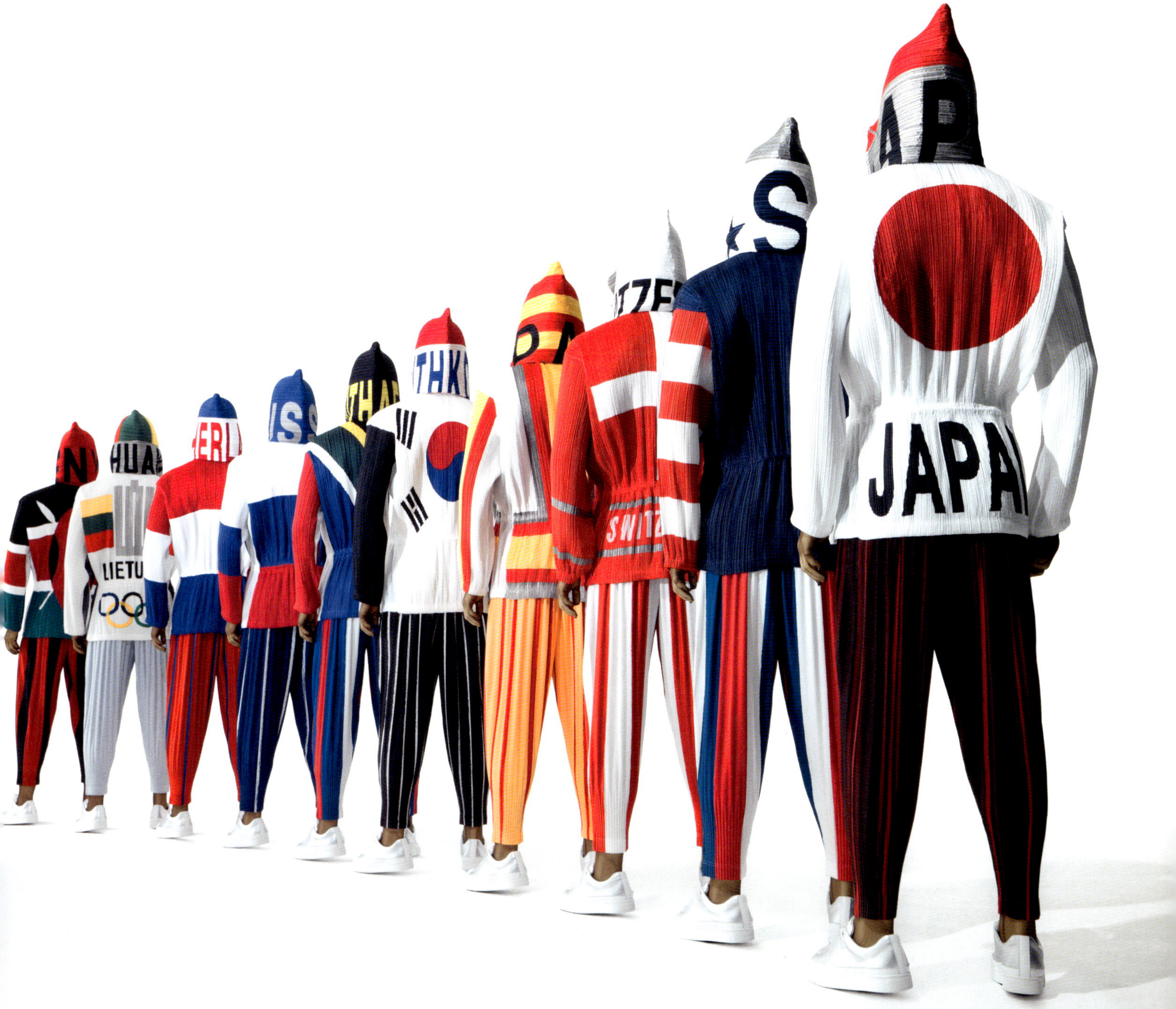

JAPA
SWITZ
LIETU

## IKKO TANAKA  ISSEY MIYAKE

　世界のデザイン史に大きな足跡を残したグラフィック・デザイナー田中一光の作品をモティーフとするシリーズ「IKKO TANAKA ISSEY MIYAKE」は、最新のプロジェクトである。大胆な発想で作品をつくりつづけた田中の仕事に刺激を受けた三宅が尊敬と感謝を込め、服づくりを通して、田中の偉大な仕事を次世代につなぐ試みだ。初回の制作は、本質的な日本の美を貫く田中の作品が、「PLEATS PLEASE ISSEY MIYAKE」の技術で表現されている。選ばれたのは、カリフォルニア大学ロサンゼルス校で行われた日本舞踊公演のポスター《Nihon Buyo》(1981年)と写楽生誕200年記念展に田中が出展した作品《写楽二百年》(1995年)。今回のシリーズは、作品を単なるプリントのモティーフとする取り組みではない。そのオリジナルの色やサイズが、忠実にプリーツ加工で仕上げられている。コートに仕立てられた田中の作品は、身体の上で動きを伴いながら平面から立体へと変化し、新たな表情を見せる。

## IKKO TANAKA  ISSEY MIYAKE

Miyake's latest project is "IKKO TANAKA ISSEY MIYAKE," a series using the work of Ikko Tanaka, one of the 20th century's most important graphic designers, as a motif. The clothing is a vehicle for conveying Miyake's deep admiration for Tanaka through the fascinating, boldly creative work that bears his name. The first in the series uses the PLEATS PLEASE ISSEY MIYAKE technology as a showcase for Tanaka's work and the Japanese aesthetic that informs it. Miyake chose the poster *Nihon Buyo* (1981) created for a performance of Japanese dance at the University of California, Los Angeles, and *The 200th Anniversary of Sharaku* (1995). Tanaka had submitted the original design to an exhibit also commemorating The 200th birthday of Toshusai Sharaku. This is more than just an attempt to turn the work into print motifs. The pleating faithfully re-creates them in their original colors and sizes. Transformed into a coat, Tanaka's work expands from two dimensions to three, revealing new dimensions and depth as the wearer moves.

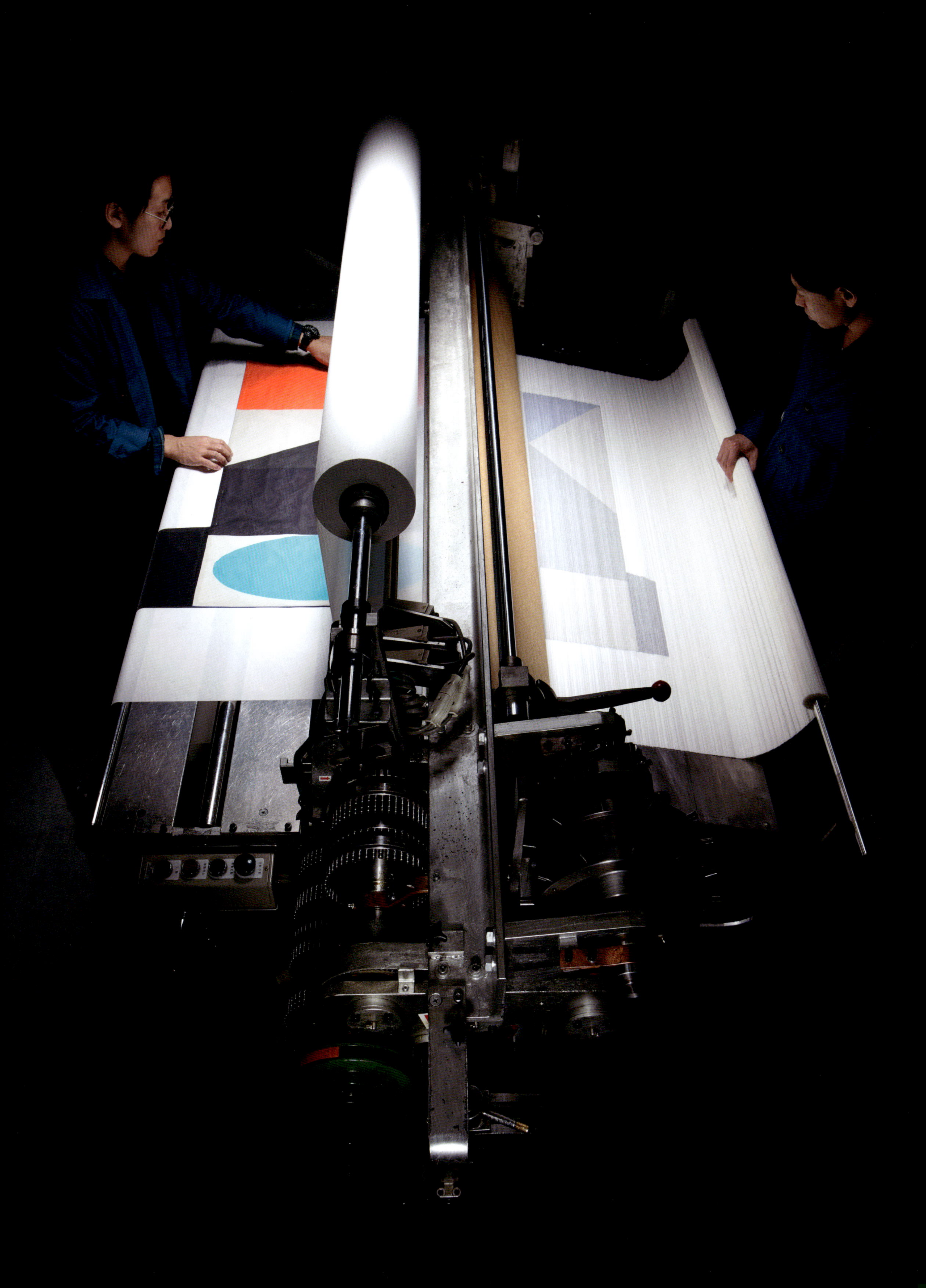

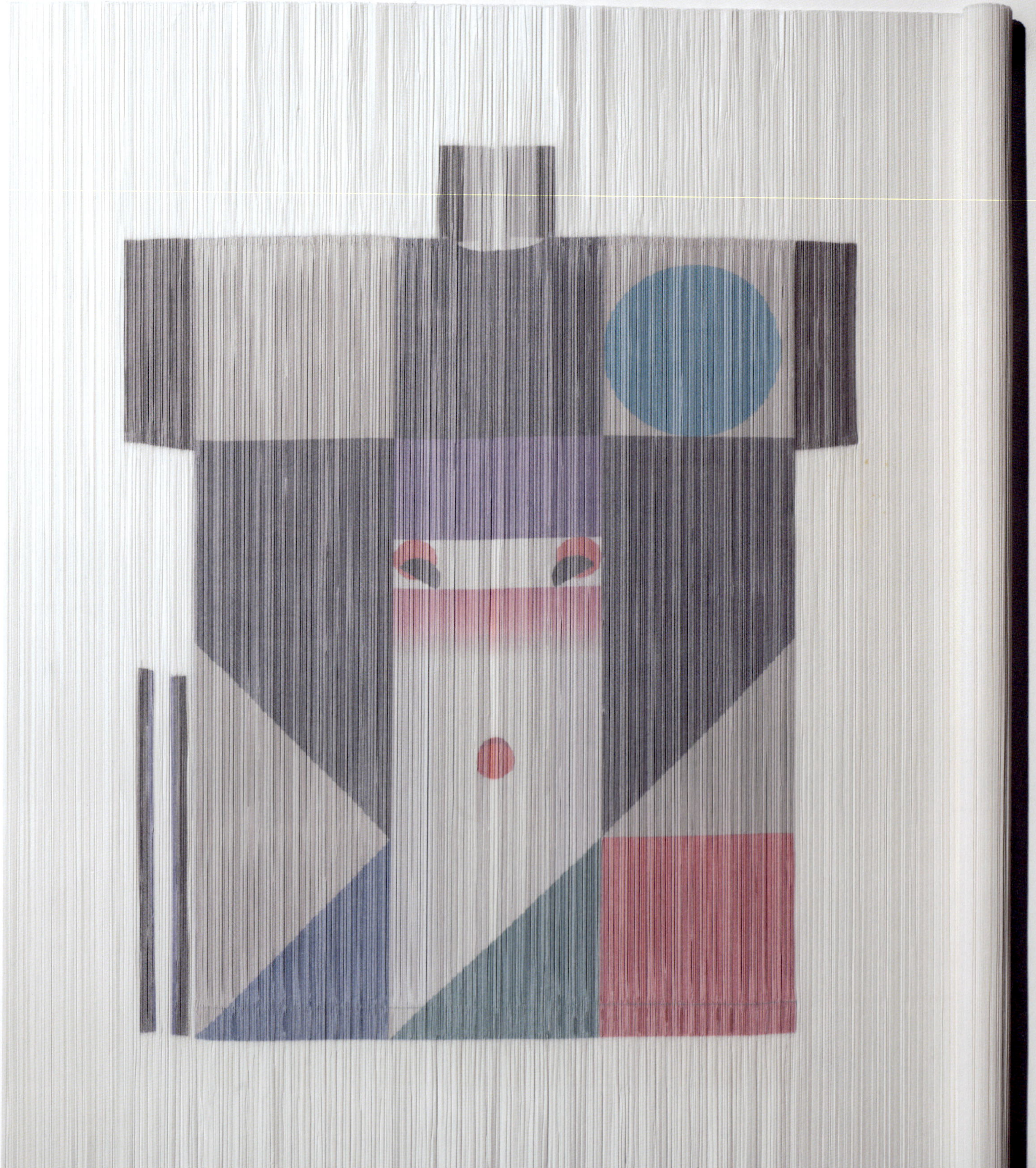

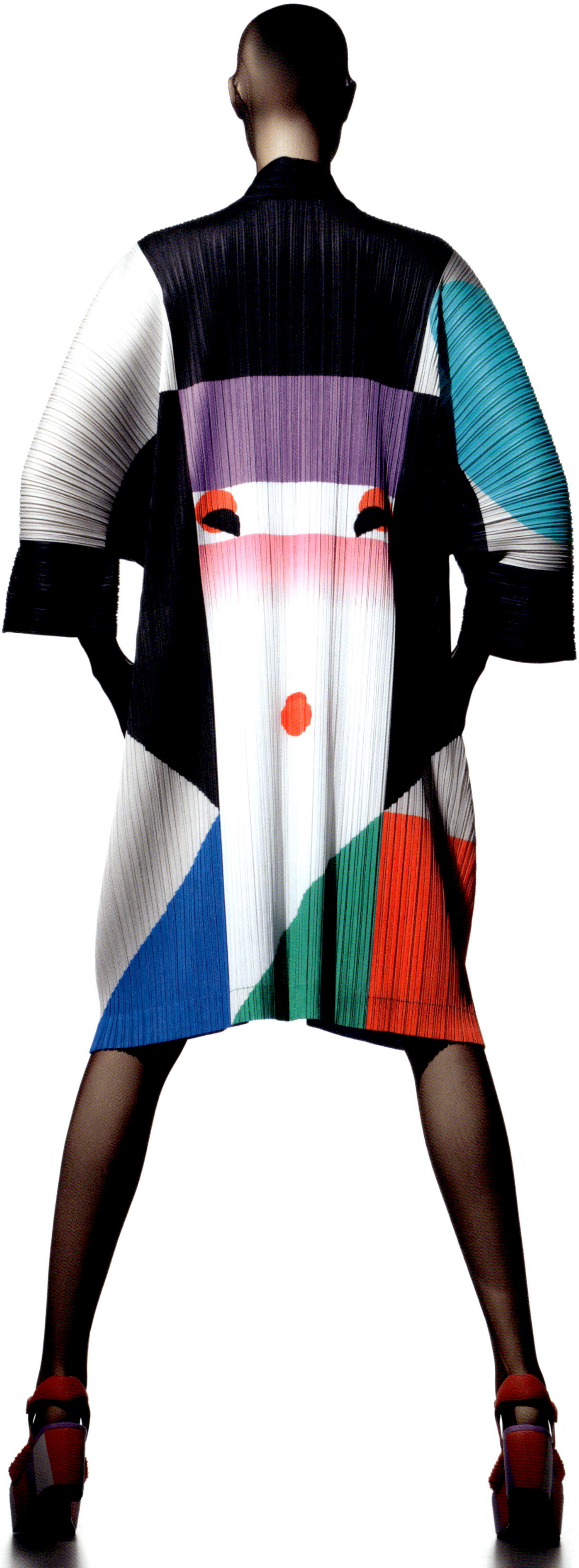

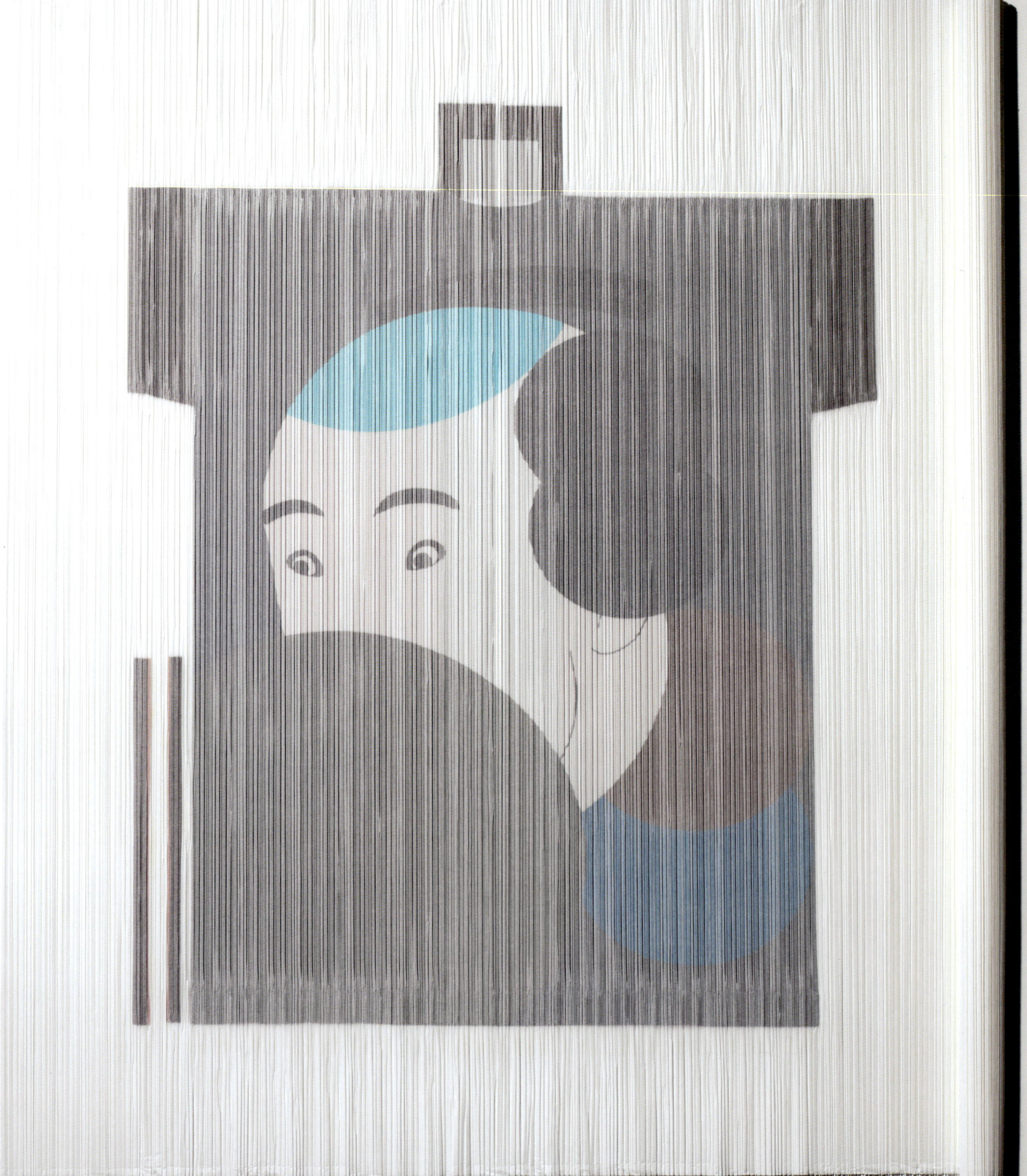

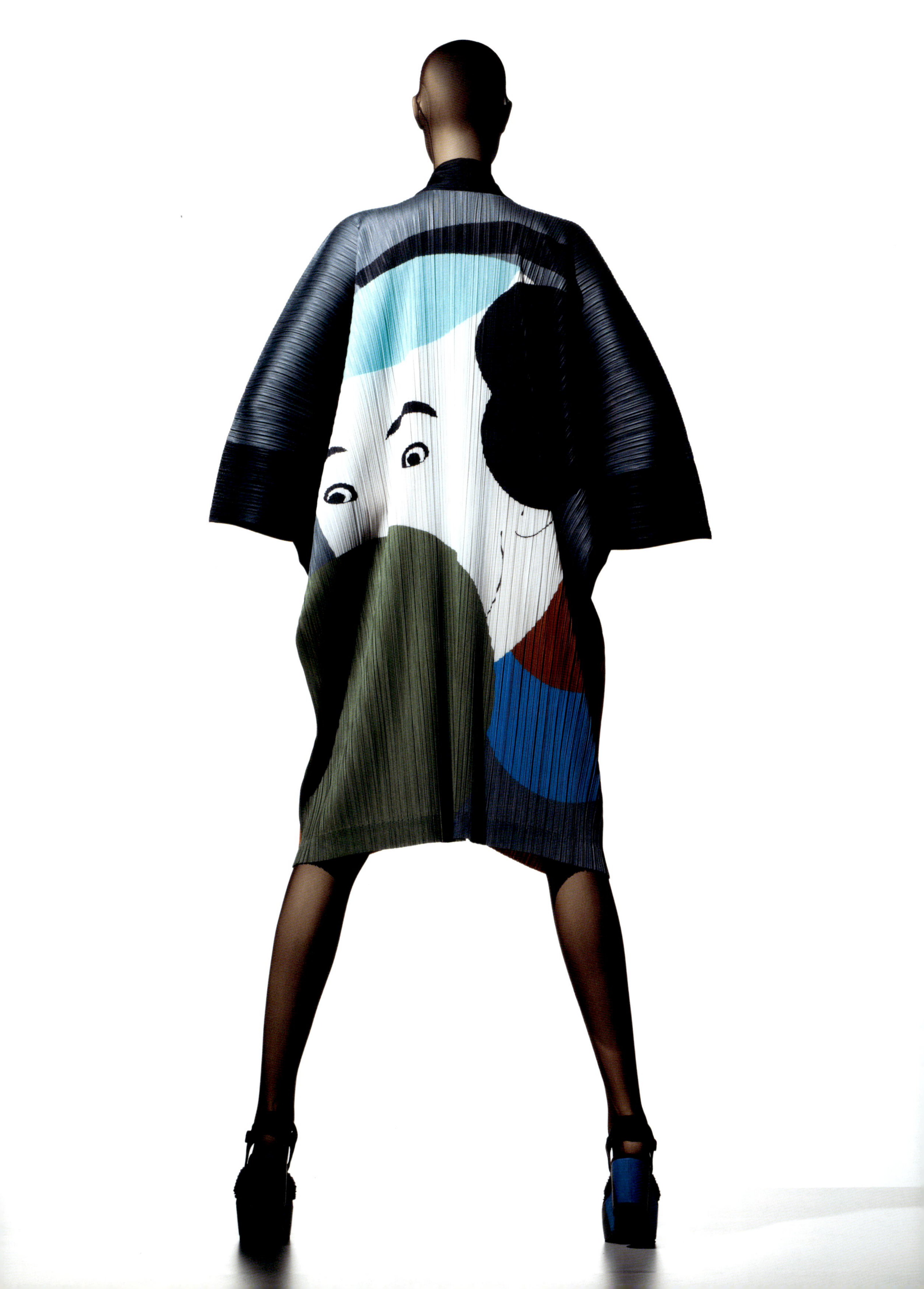

## A-POC

　コンピュータ・テクノロジーにより、一本の糸から一体成型で服をつくる、従来の服づくりの工程を変えた新しいデザインの方法論。A-POCは、三宅一生の服づくりのコンセプトである「一枚の布、A Piece Of Cloth」の頭文字と時代のエポックからのネーミングである。1998年、三宅一生は、デザイン事務所のスタッフであった藤原大とともに本格的な取り組みを始めた。分業化された生産工程を飛び越え、糸の段階からデザイナーも参加する。完成形を想定し、制作プロセスに必要な全情報を一度にプログラミングし、編機や織機を動かす。《A-POC キング＆クイーン》(1998年) ほかニットは、編み出されるチューブのなかにすでに服の形が連続して編み込まれ、ガイド線にそってハサミを入れて一着を切り取る。ほつれにくい特殊な編み方から、着る人自身がガイド線以外にもハサミを入れてデザインに参加することもできる。ブランド化された2000年には織物にも応用され、ジャカードの二重織りが多様な表現を可能にした。精密に表現される柄だけでなく縫製に必要なしるしや指示も織り込まれ、プラモデルのように、裁断してパーツを取り出し、組み立てて縫製で仕上げられる。糸から最終形をダイレクトにつくる生産プロセスでは、布の無駄は少なくてすむ。大量生産にも、少量多品種にも対応することができる。「A-POC（エイ・ポック）」ブランドで培ったものづくりの方法論は、2007年以降は「A-POC Inside」として、ISSEY MIYAKEではブランドを超えて活用されているデザイン・ソリューションである。

## A-POC

A-POC (A Piece Of Cloth) is a new design methodology that uses computer technology harnessed to an industrial knitting or weaving machine to create fabric, texture and clothing formed as an integrated whole, and from a single thread. Issey Miyake first began working on it in 1998 in collaboration with Dai Fujiwara, who was a member of the Design Studio at the time. Rather than a strictly compartmentalized production process, it brought the designer in, right from the beginning with the thread stage. The designer imagines the completed form, and then all of the information required for the production process is programmed into the computer before the knitting or weaving machines begin. A-POC KING & QUEEN (1998) and other knits build all of the components for a fully-finished garment into a single, continuous knitted tube that can be extruded by cutting along lines of demarcation, then worn. It uses a special knitting process that makes it difficult for the material to unravel; and allows the wearer to participate in the design by the act of cutting it out from the fabric and tailoring elements such as sleeve length to her or his liking. The same technology was also applied to woven garments when the A-POC brand was launched in 2000; and brought a wide range of options to Jacquard double weaves. In addition to precisely articulated color patterns, the fabric also contains all the marks and instructions required for sewing that a pattern might. While the woven group does not involve the wearer in the final process, It is a bit like a model that comes in a kit: the roll of fabric comes out, the team cuts out the parts, assembles them and then sews them together. There is less fabric wasted because the production process creates the final form directly from the original thread. This makes it suitable for different scales of production, whether mass or small-lot. Since 2007, the manufacturing methodologies developed for the A-POC brand have been used as a design solution to other brands under the name "A-POC Inside."

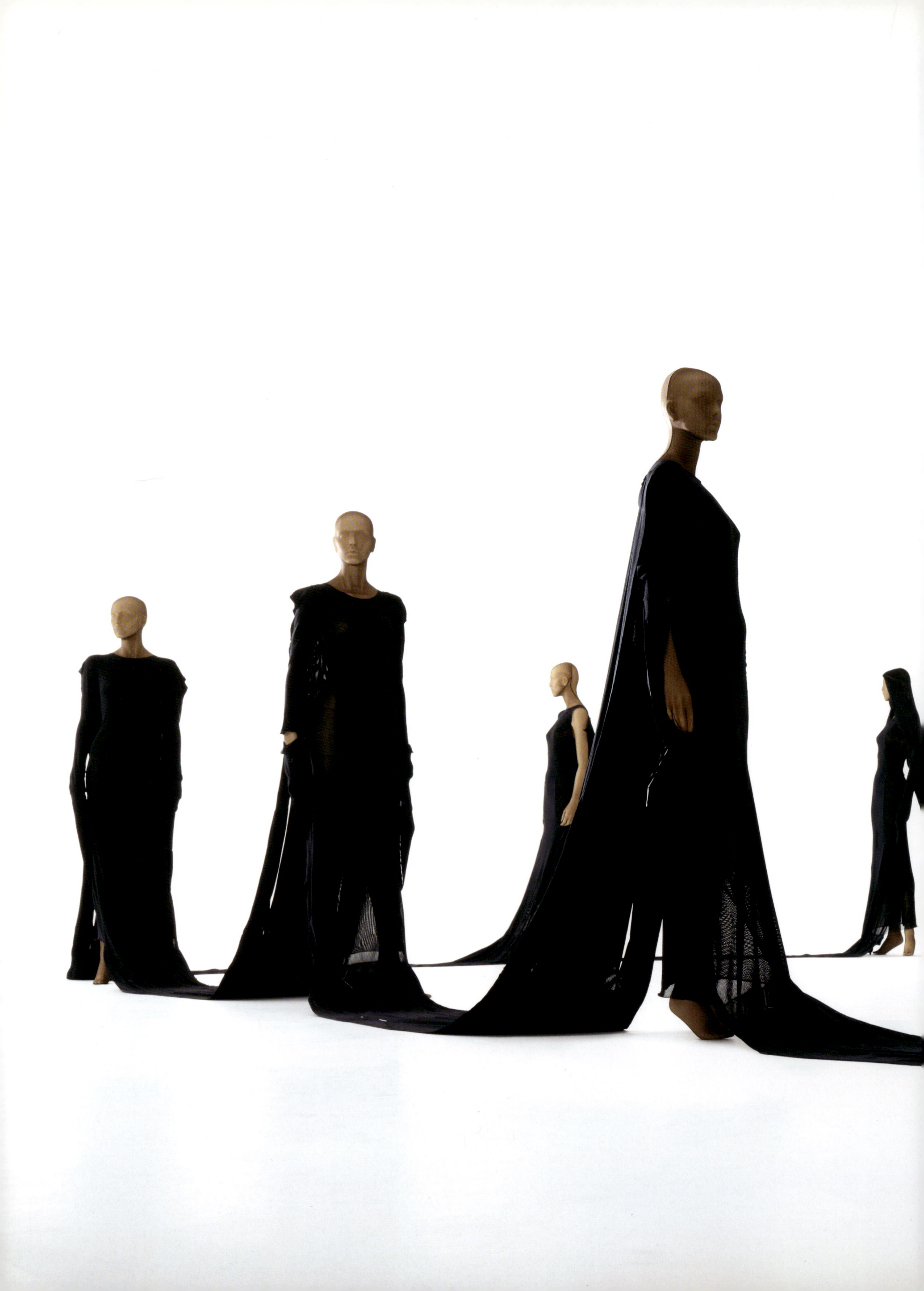

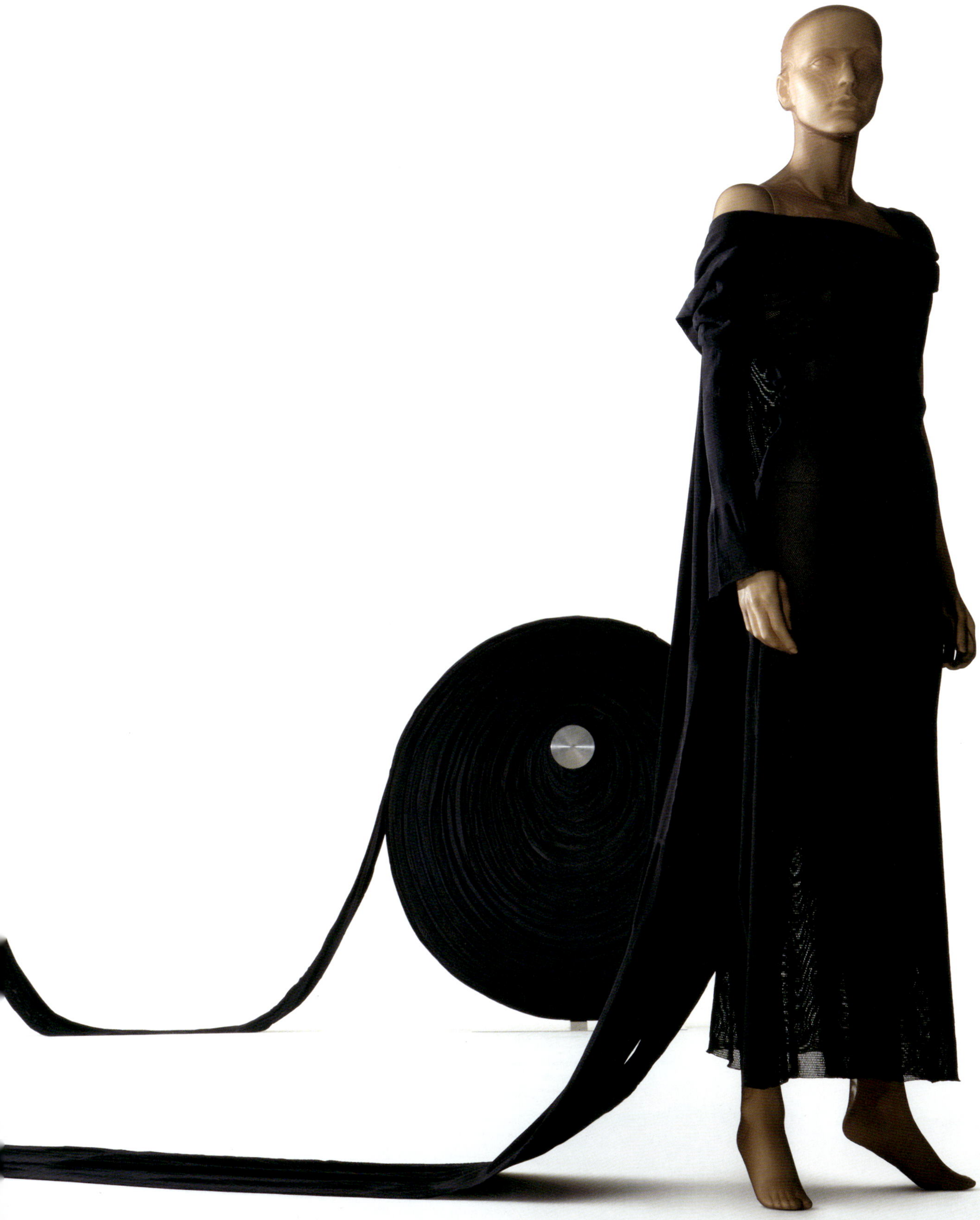

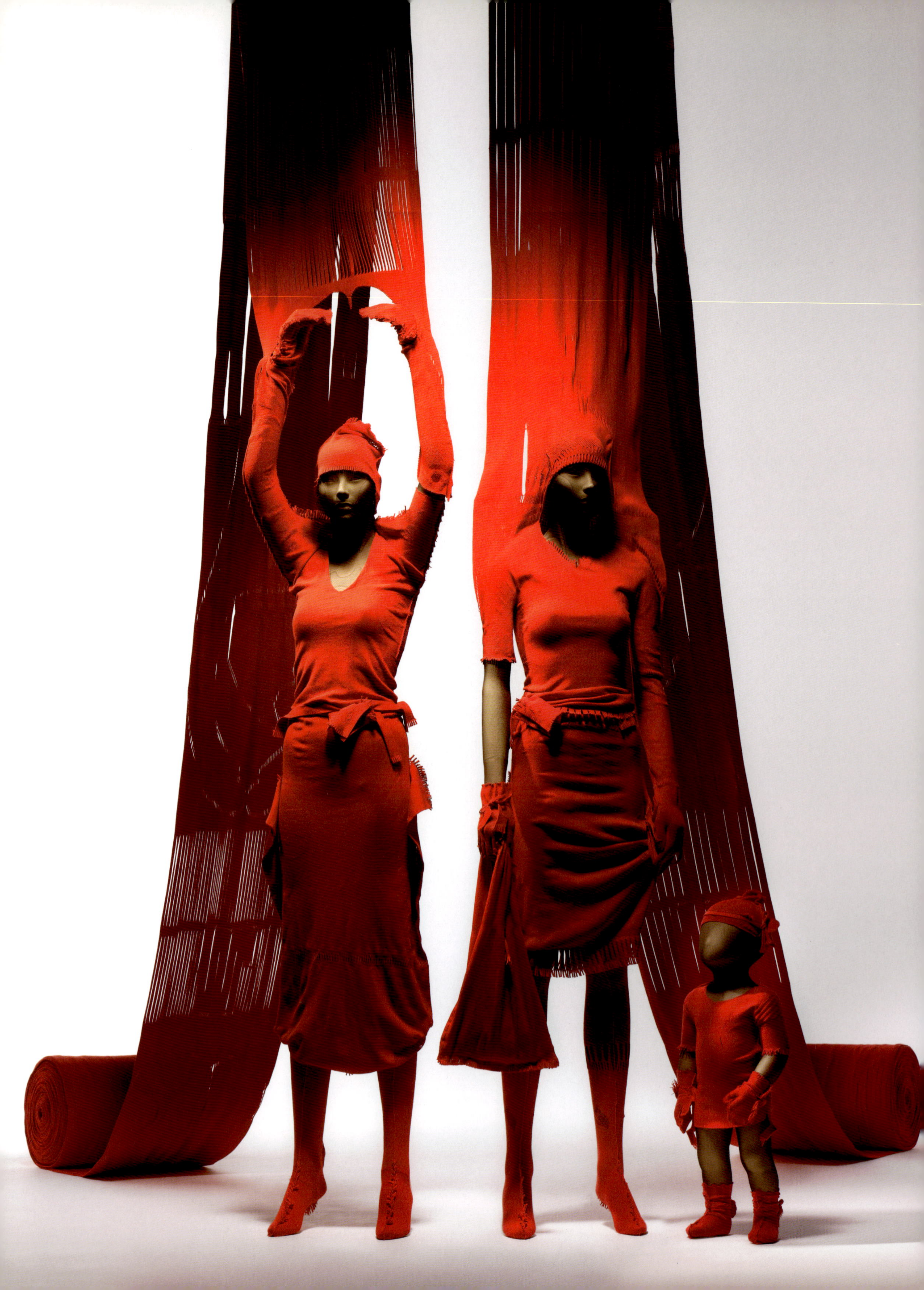

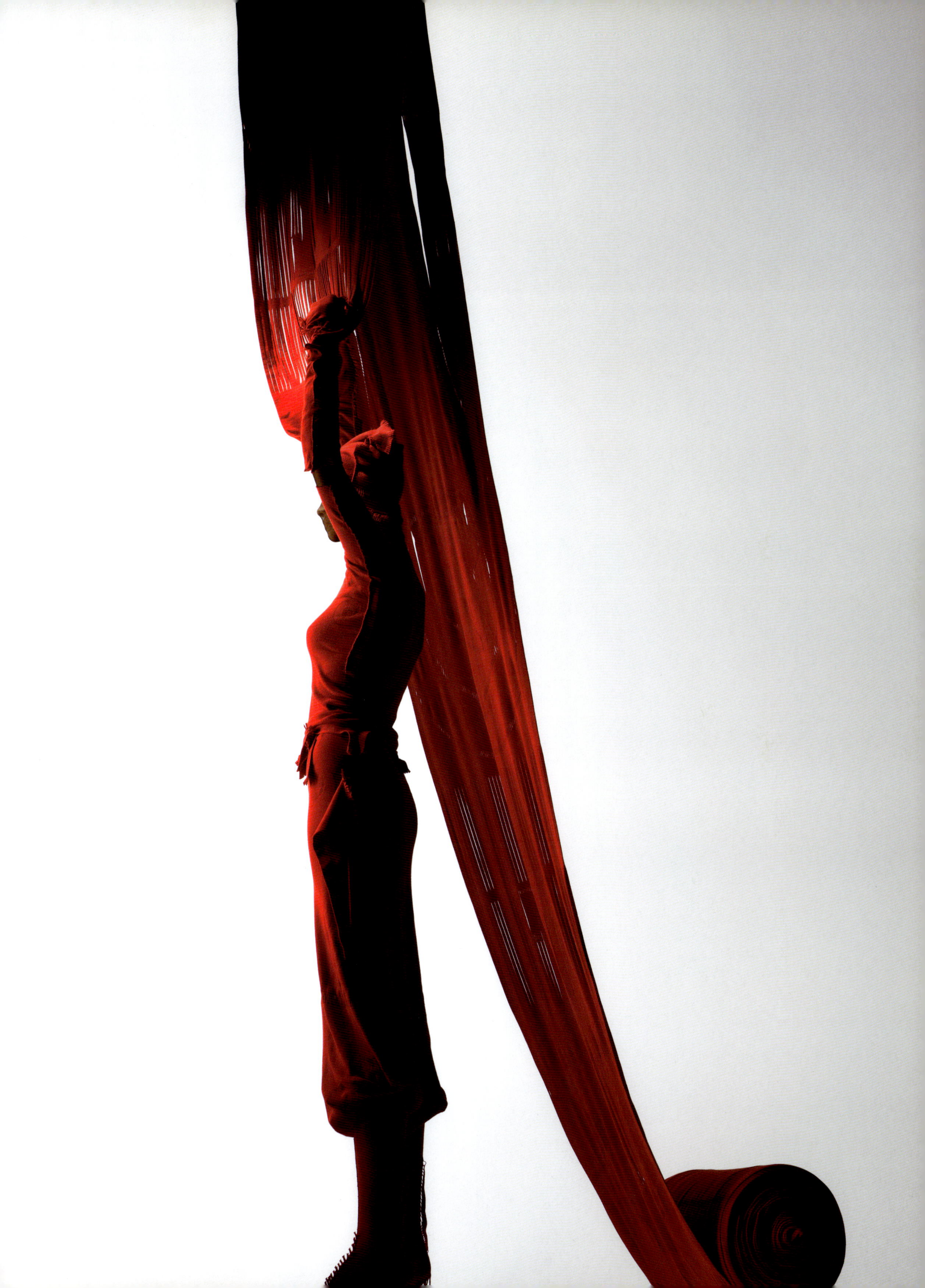

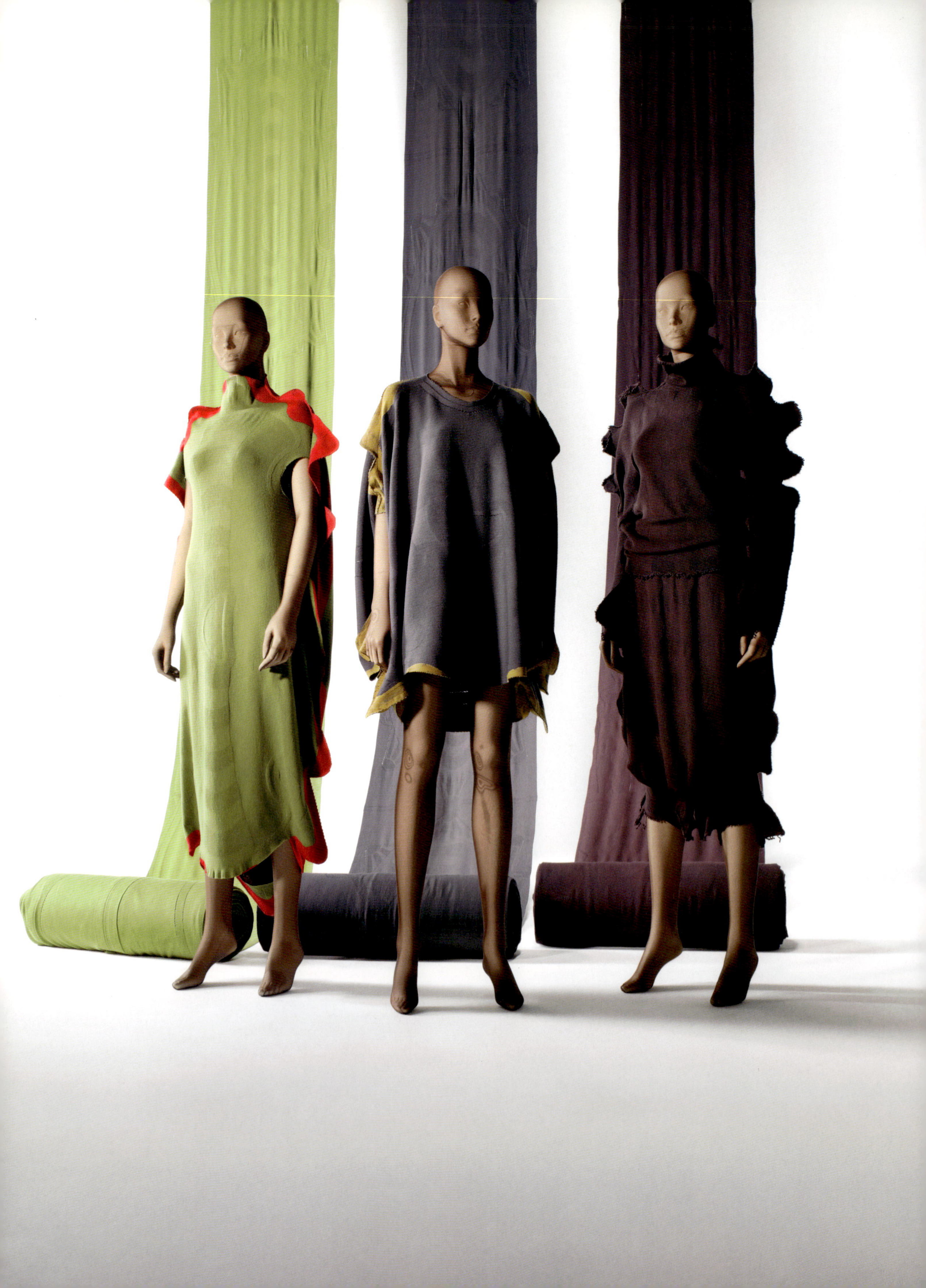

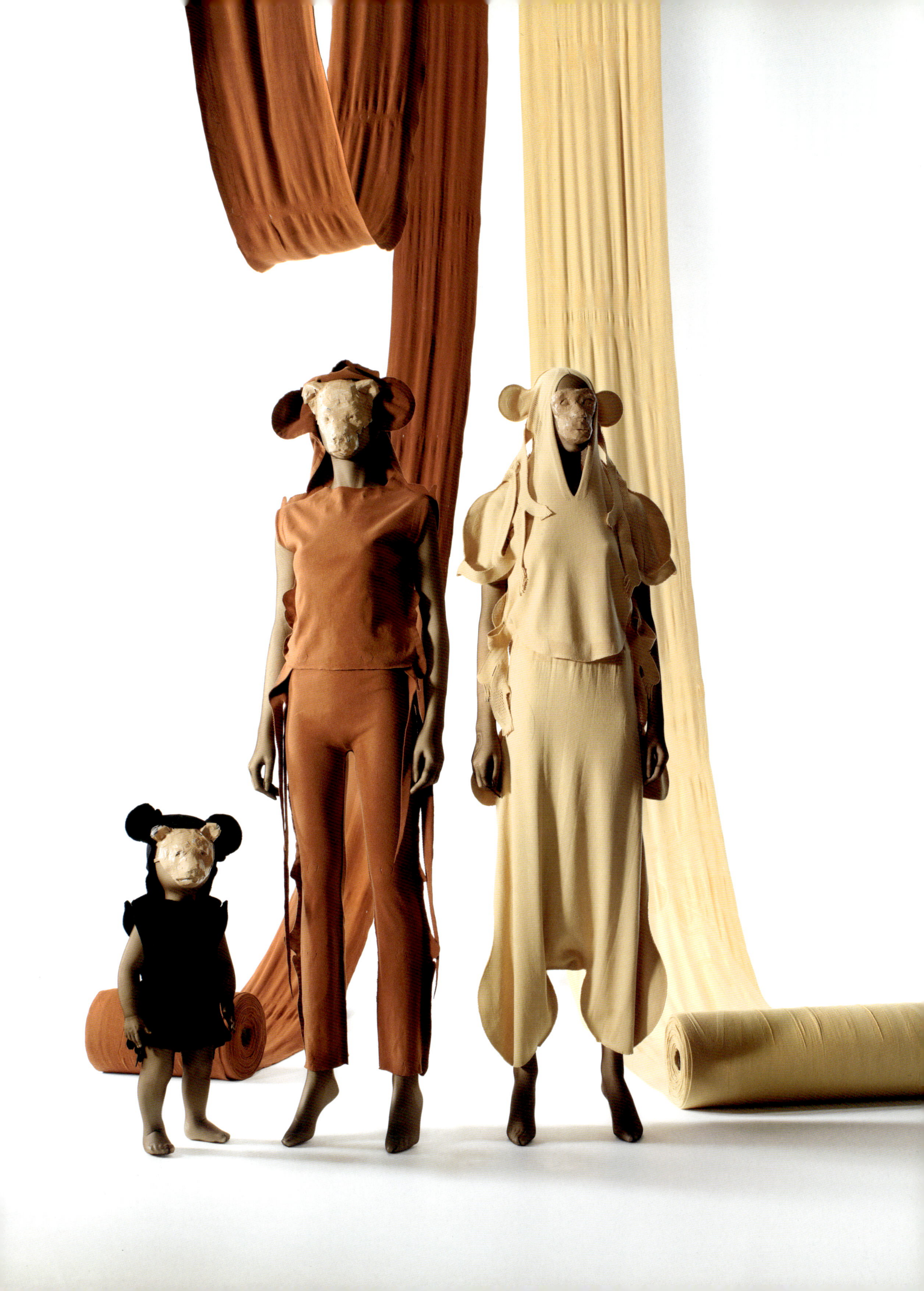

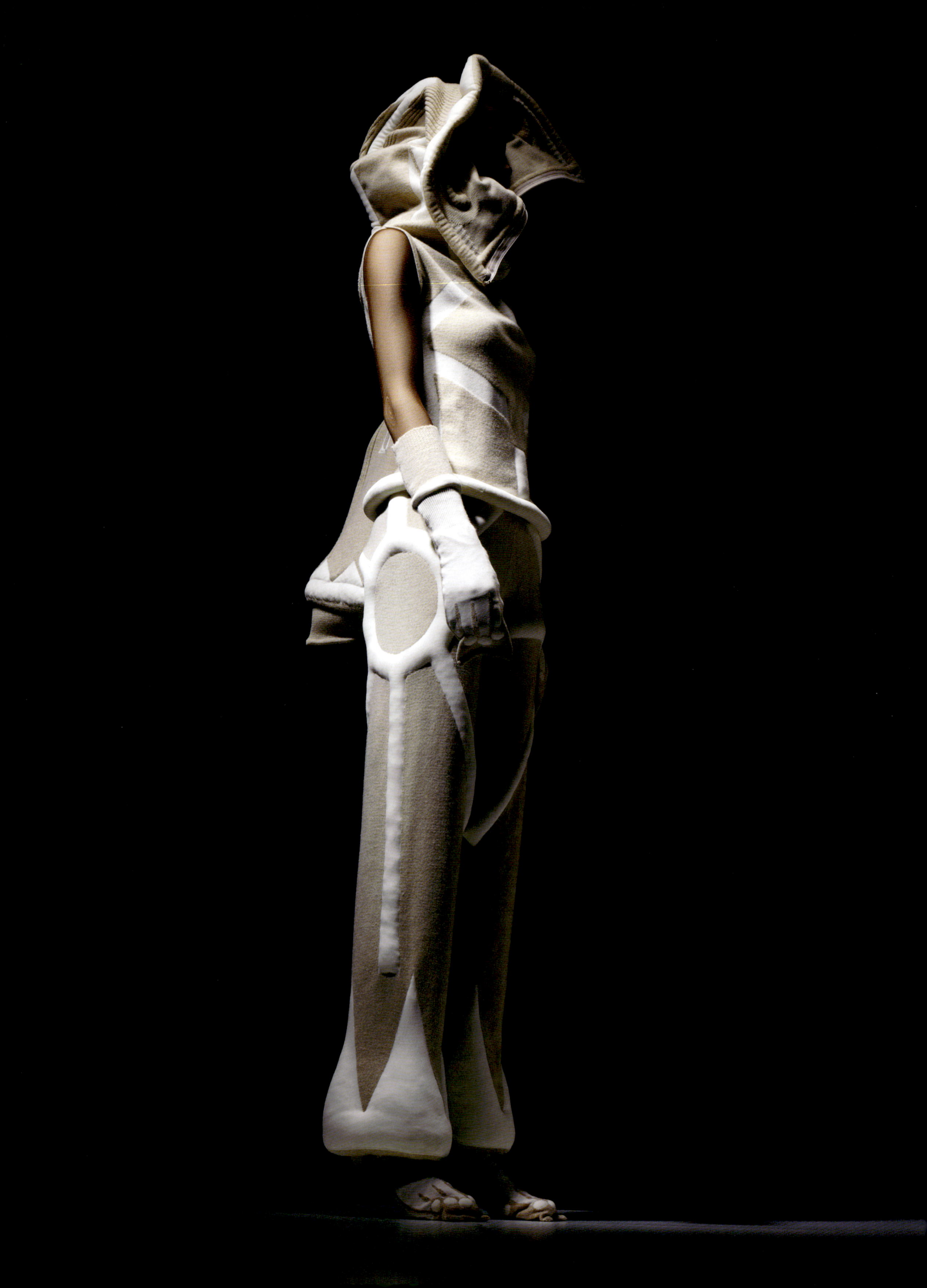

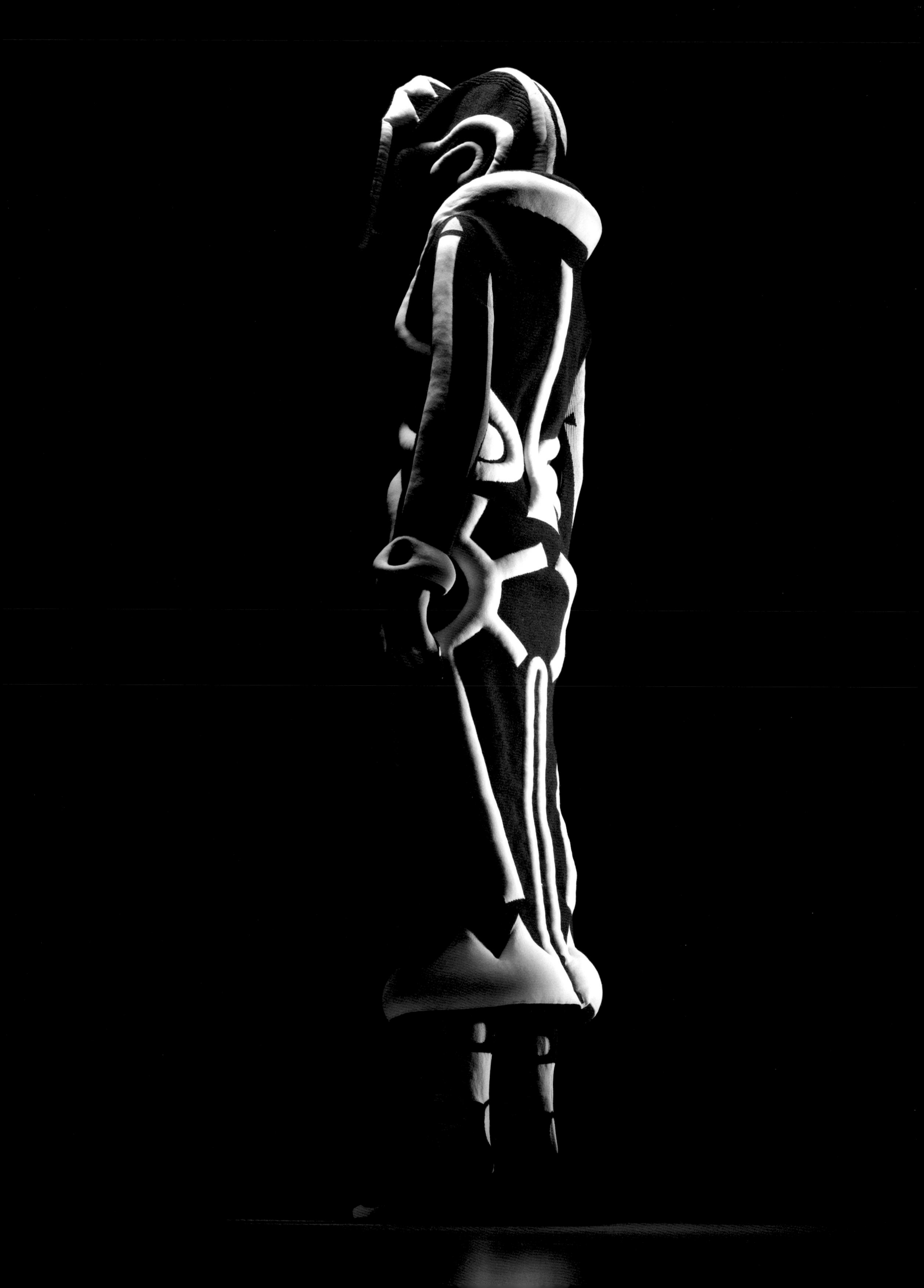

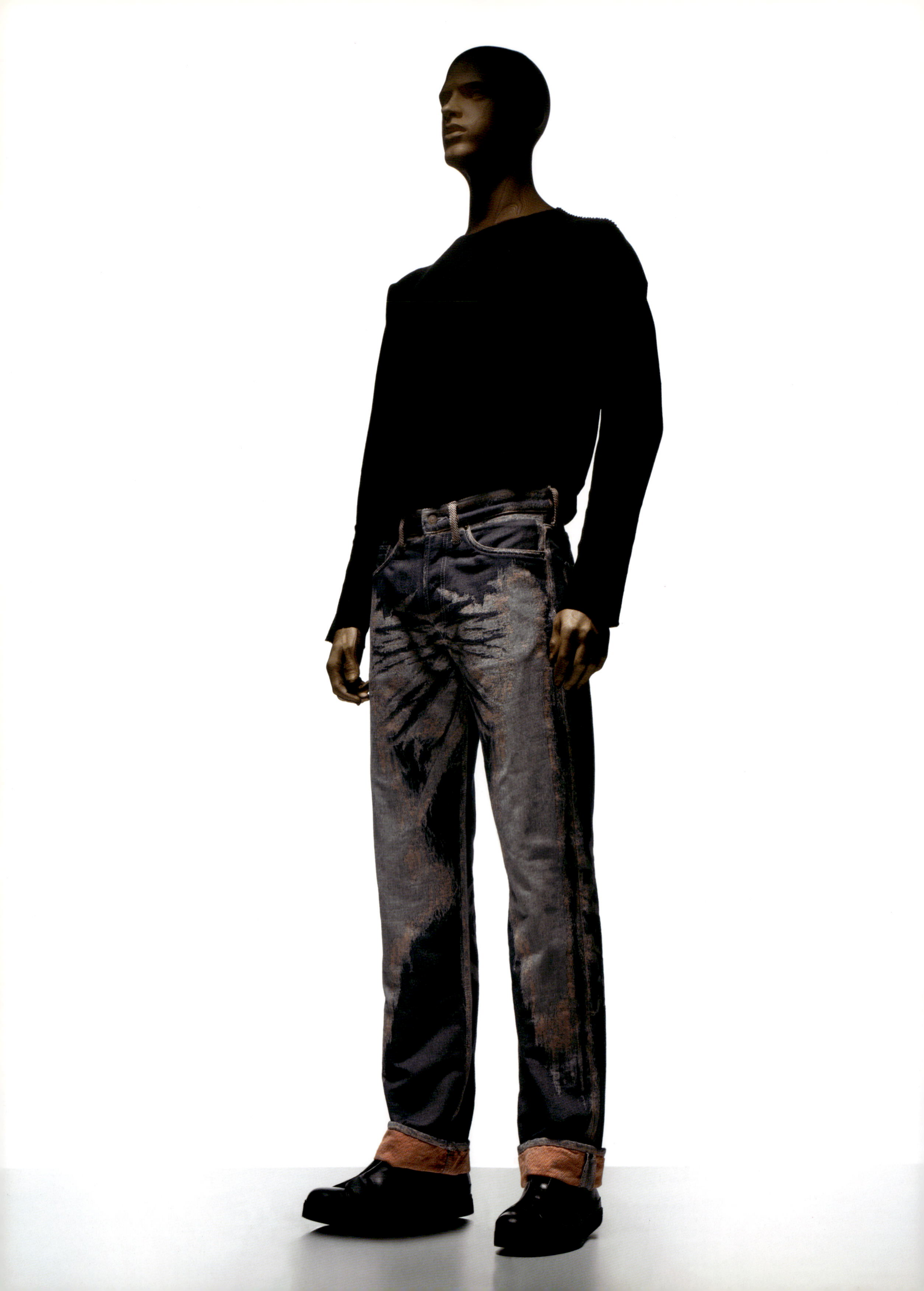

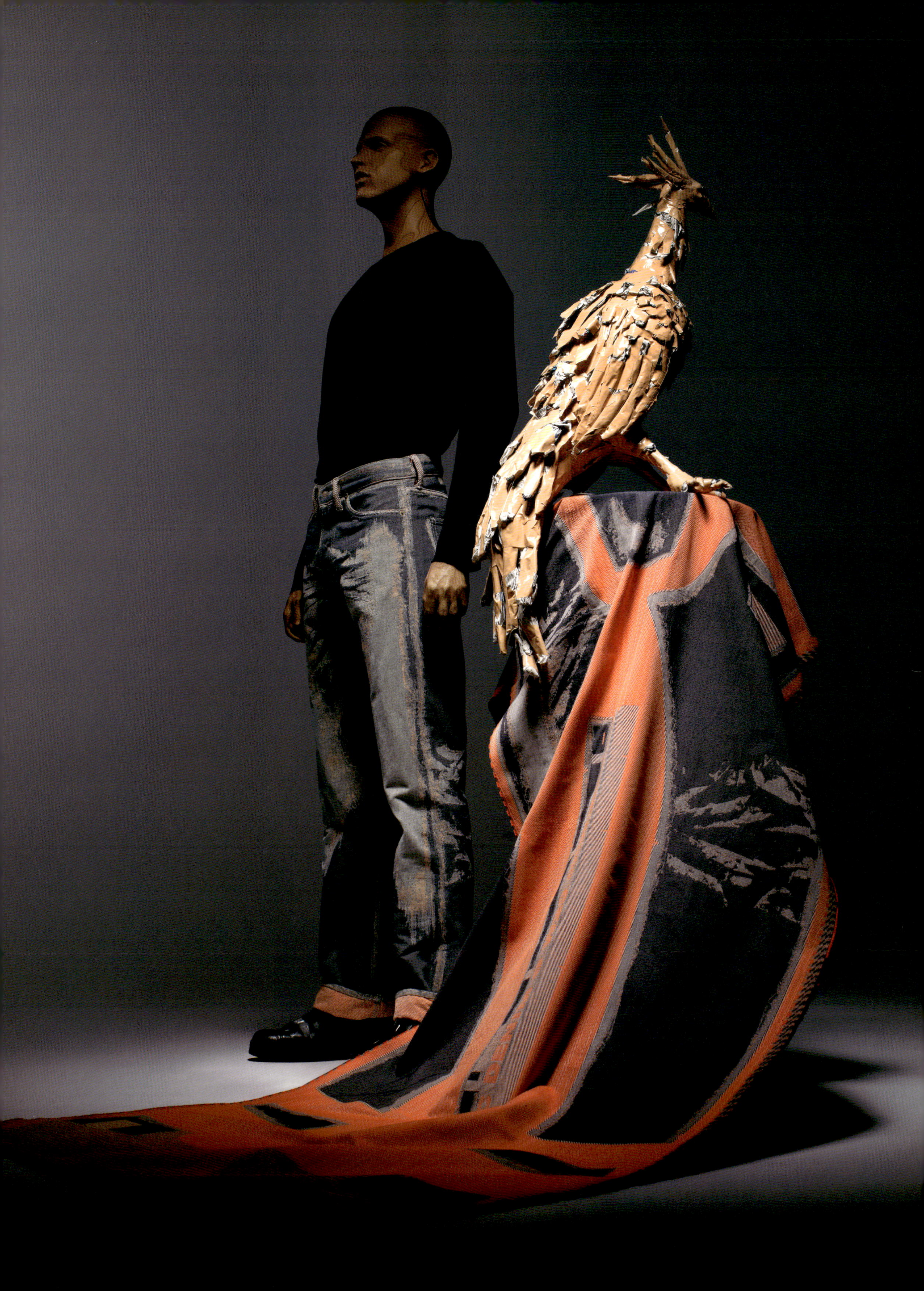

## 132 5. ISSEY MIYAKE

「132 5. ISSEY MIYAKE」は、2007年から取り組みを開始した三宅一生とReality Lab（リアリティ・ラボ）チームとの研究開発のなかから、2010年に誕生した。素材に再生繊維を用いて、コンピュータ・サイエンティスト三谷純が開発したアルゴリズムに出会い、同氏との協働を経て生み出された折りの構造による、新たな血筋をもった衣服である。一枚の布からつくられる三次元の造形を折りたたみ、プレスをかけて平面に仕上げる。幾何学的形態の平面にたたまれた服は、広げて着用されてはじめて生命が宿る。同じかたちでも、加えられた切り込み線の位置によって、異なるかたちのシャツになり、またスカートにもなる。「132 5.」の「1」は平面の一枚の布、「3」は服が立ち上がった三次元の立体、「2」は再びたたまれる二次元の平面を意味し、「5」は身にまとうことで時間や次元を超えた存在になるという思いを込めて命名されている。この折りの技術は服づくりの枠を超えて、照明器具のデザインにも展開されている。

## 132 5. ISSEY MIYAKE

132 5. ISSEY MIYAKE was established in 2010 out of a research and development project that began in 2007 as a collaboration between Issey Miyake and the Reality Lab team. They met with scientist Jun Mitani and collaborated with him to apply his algorithm to recycled textiles and create a new folding model that breathed new life into apparel. A single piece of cloth is folded to give it a three-dimensional structure before being pressed flat. Having been flattened into a geometric form, the clothing then can only take on life when it is unfolded and worn. Depending on the placement of the areas to be cut, the same geometrical form can be turned into a completely different shirt or even a skirt. In the name "132 5.," the "1" in "132 5." represents a single flat piece of cloth; the "3" for the three-dimensional form of the clothing, worn; the "2" for the two-dimensional form it takes when folded flat; and "5," the idea of going beyond and into the next dimension when the clothing is worn. Today, in addition to the clothing, this new folding technology has also been applied to the design of lighting fixtures.

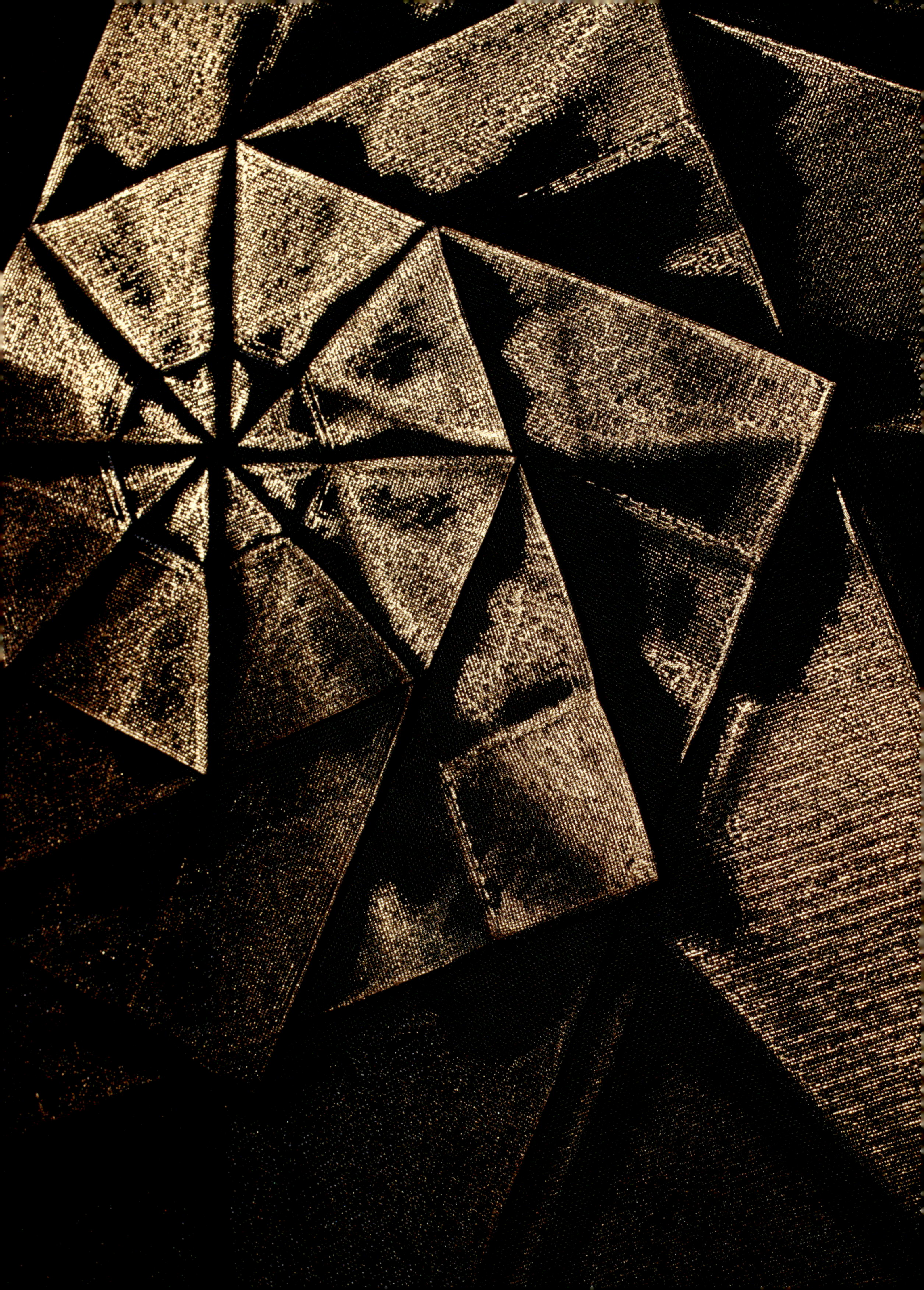

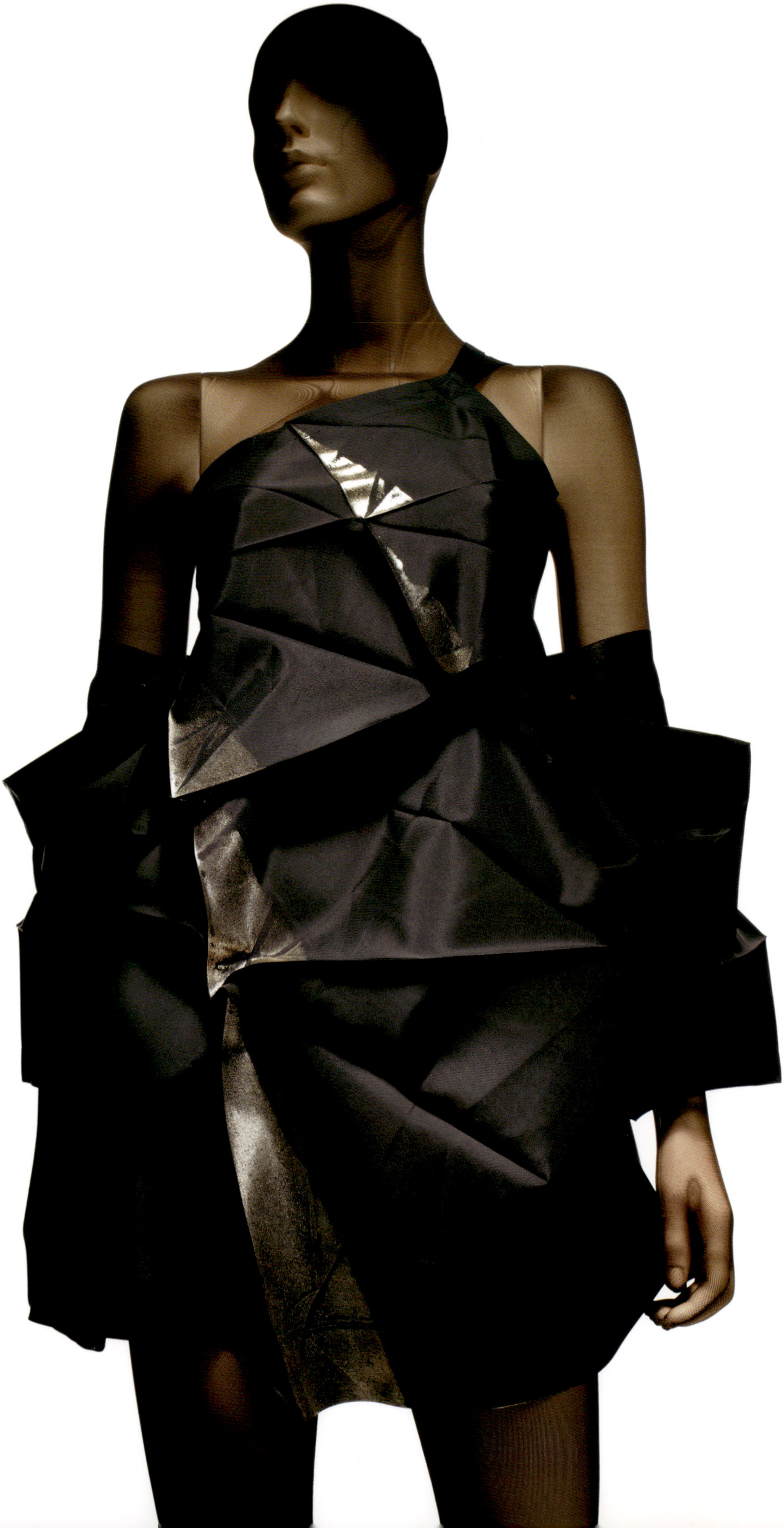

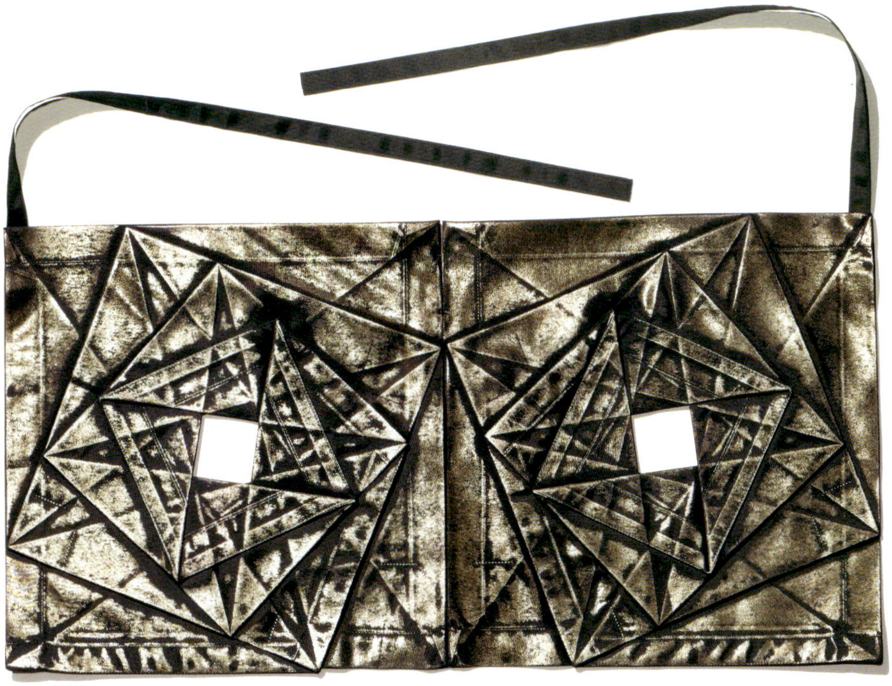
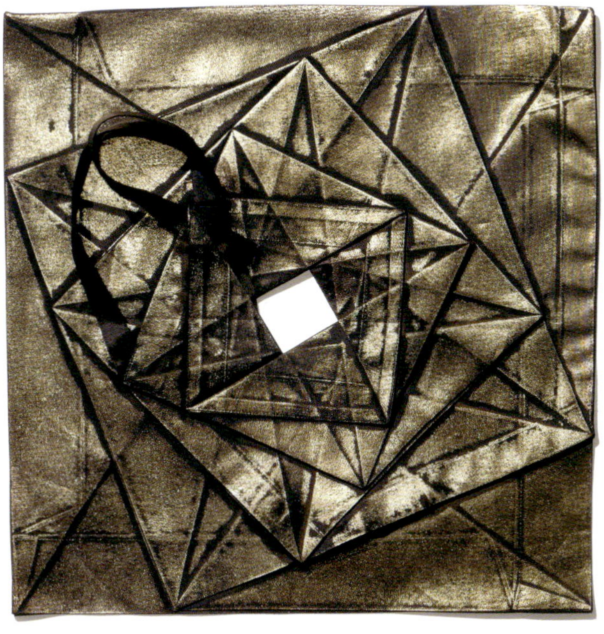

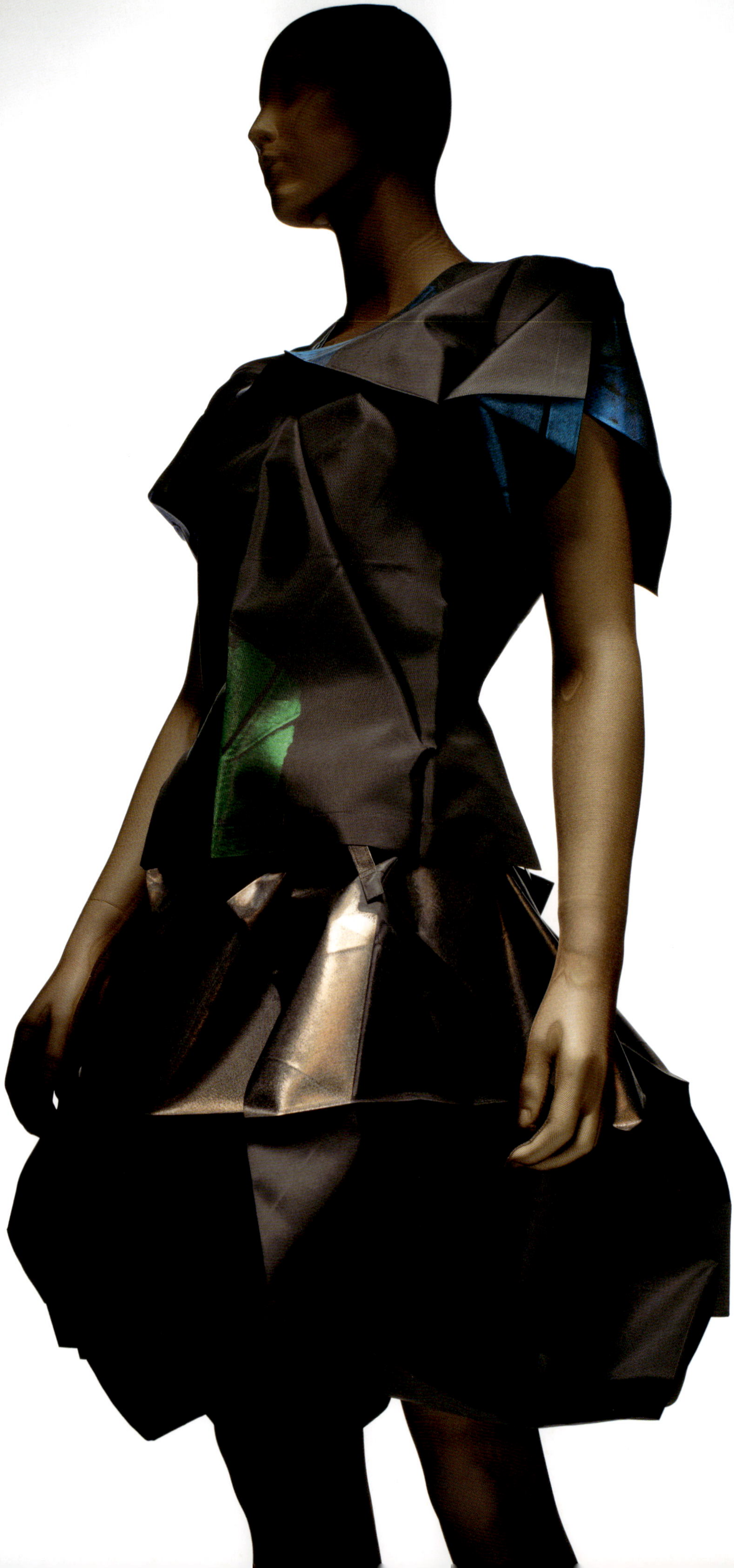

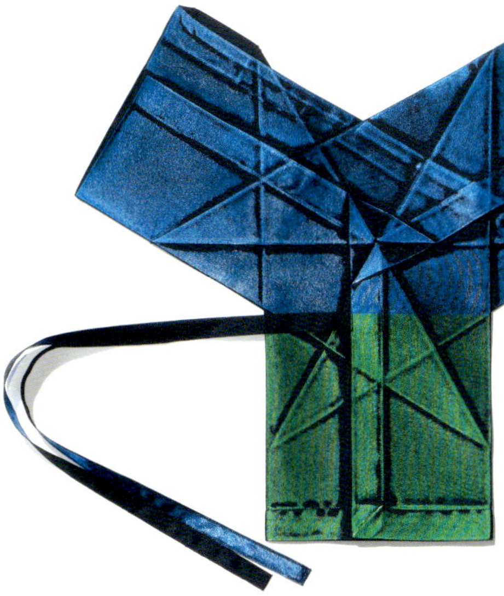
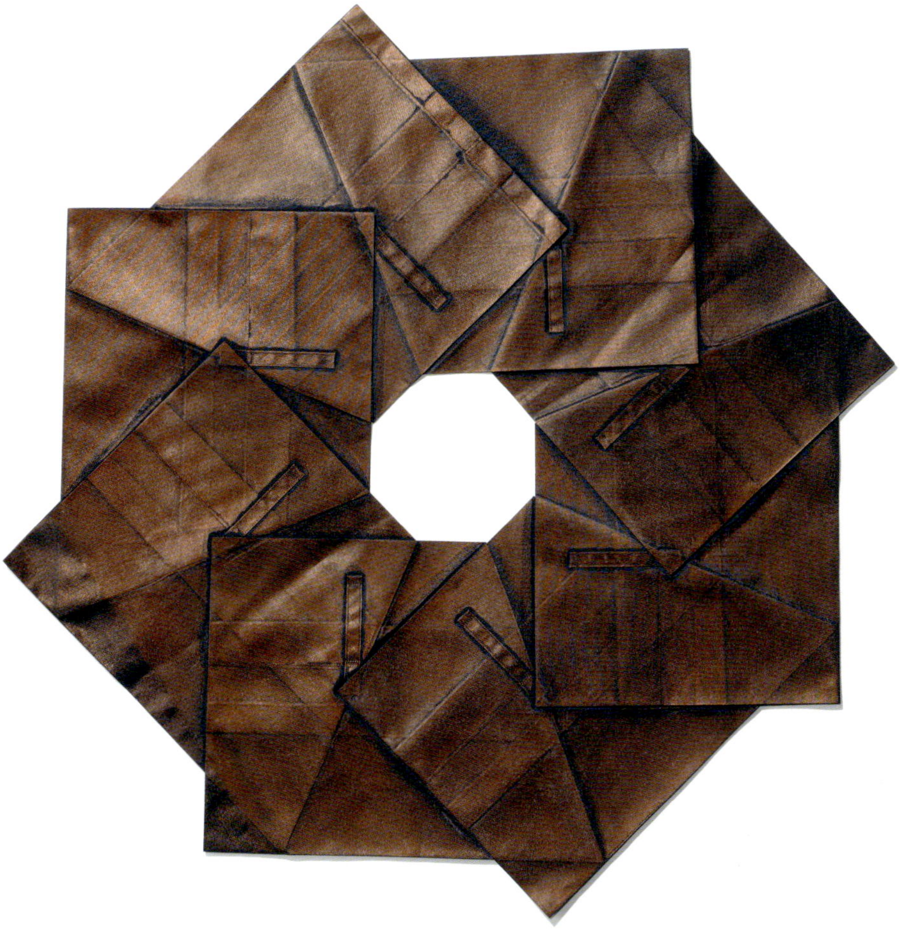

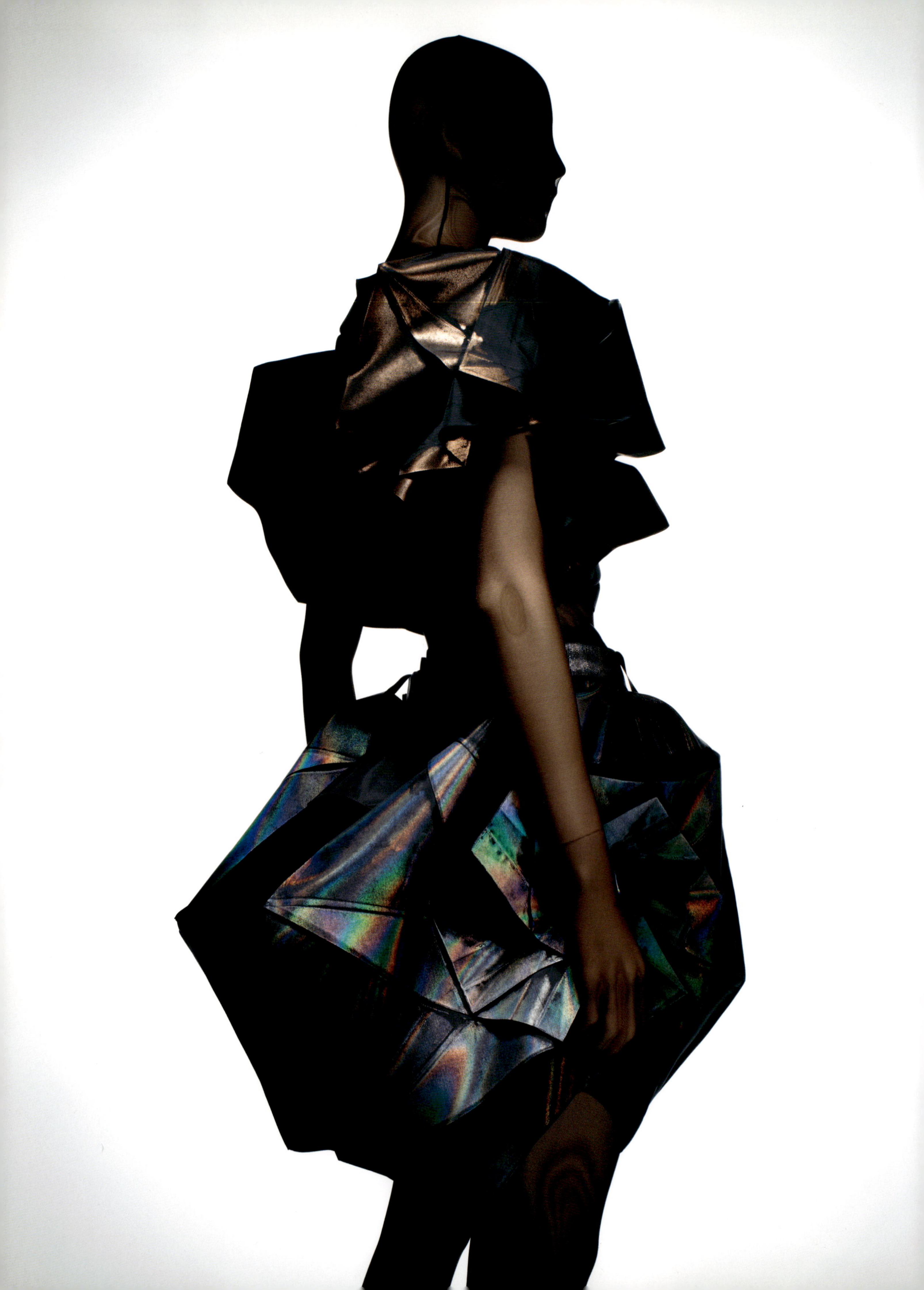

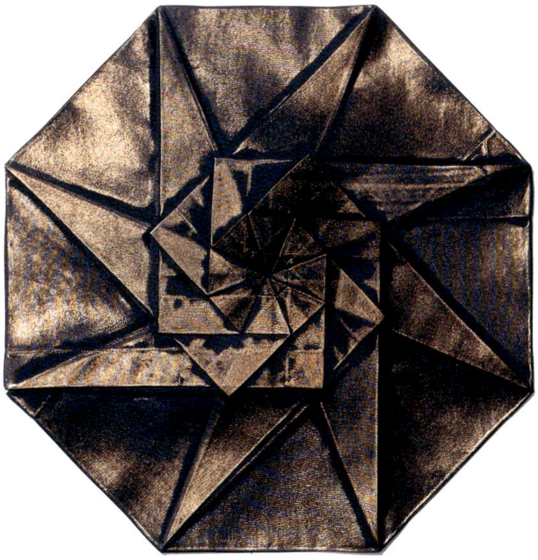

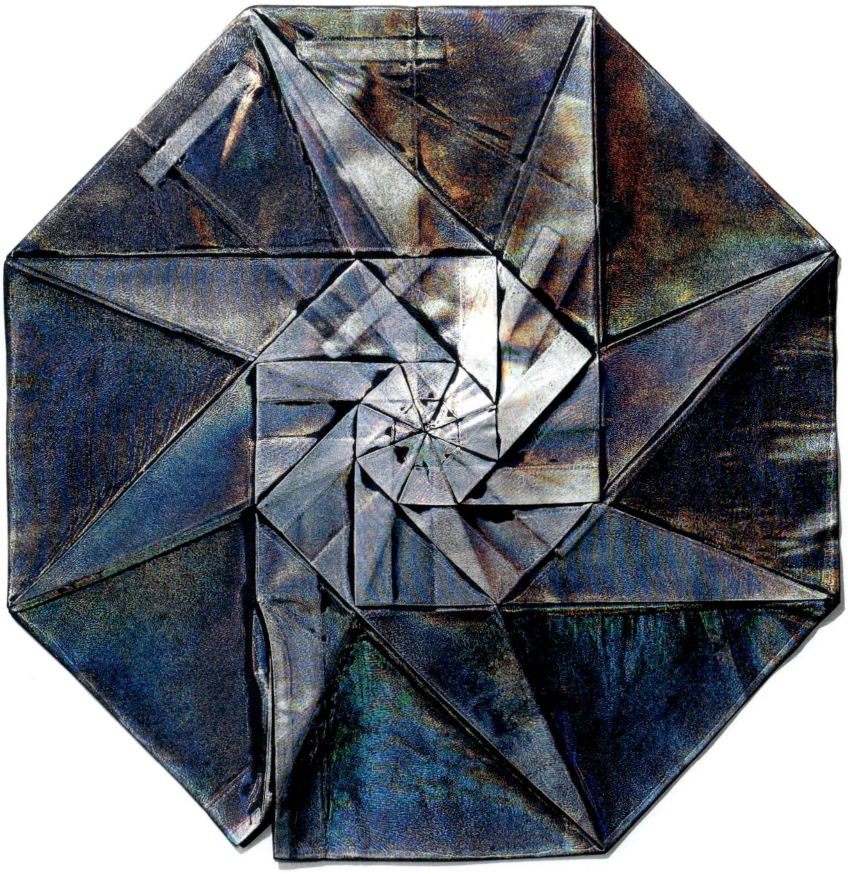

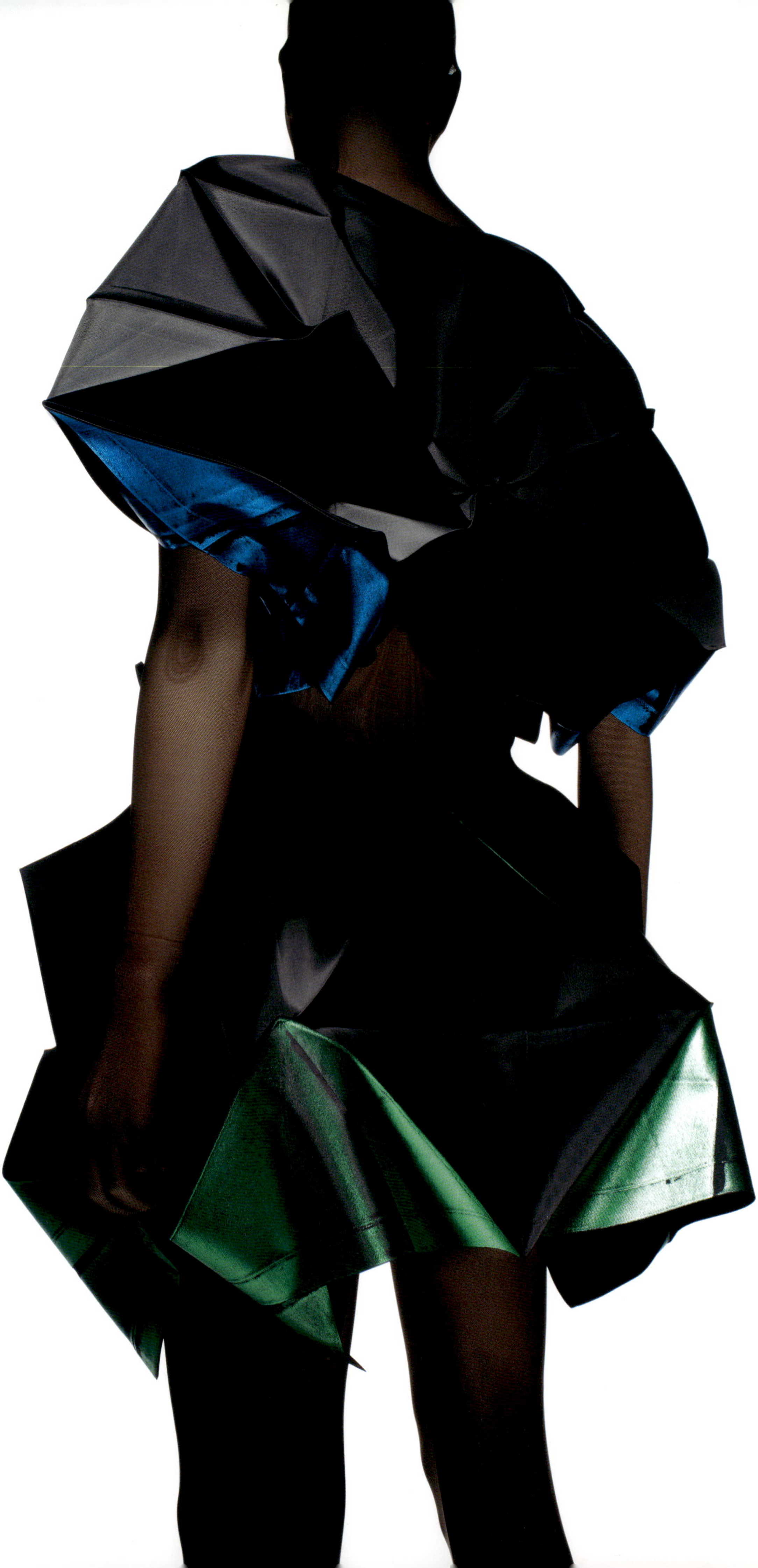

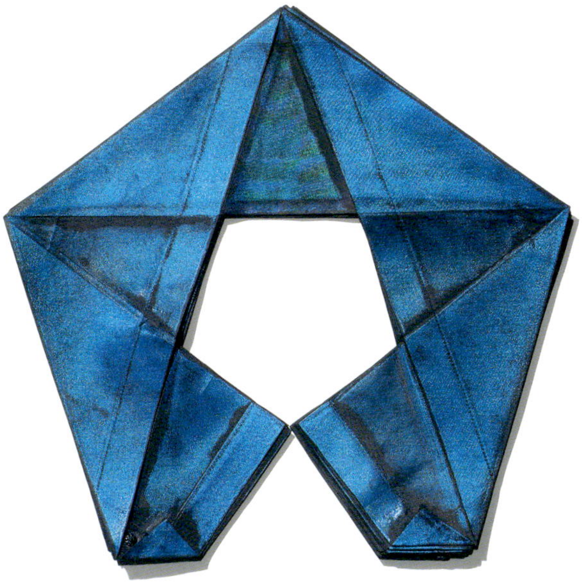

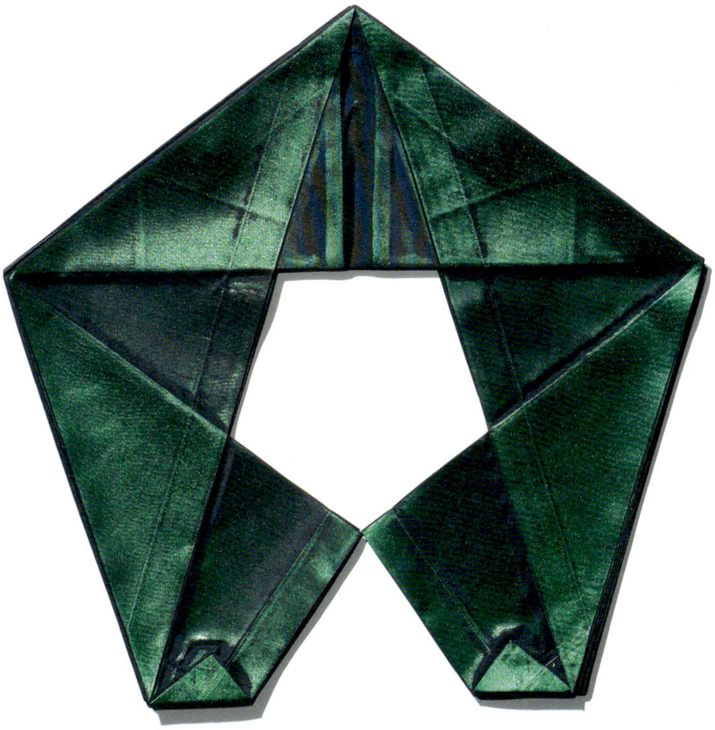

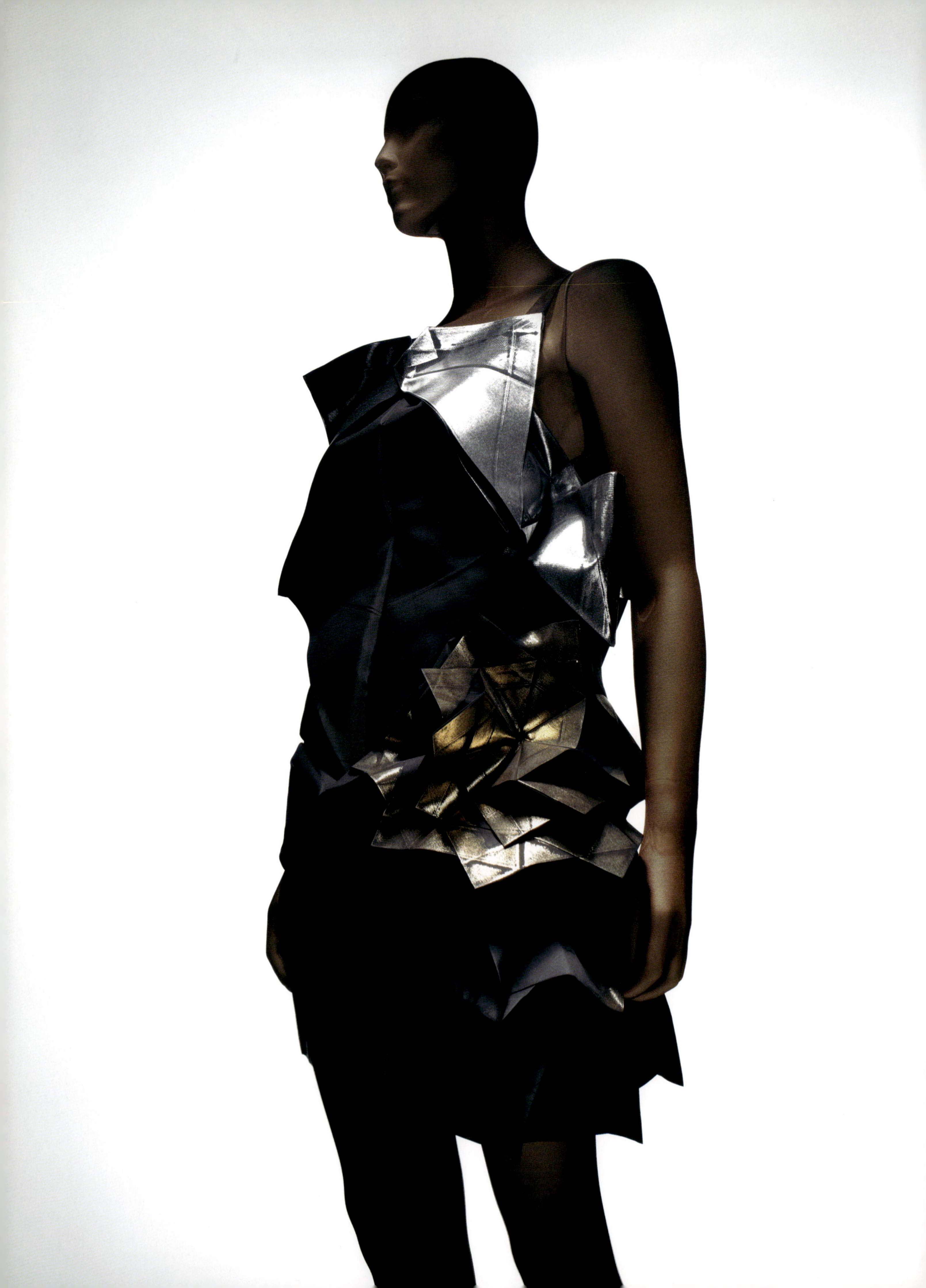

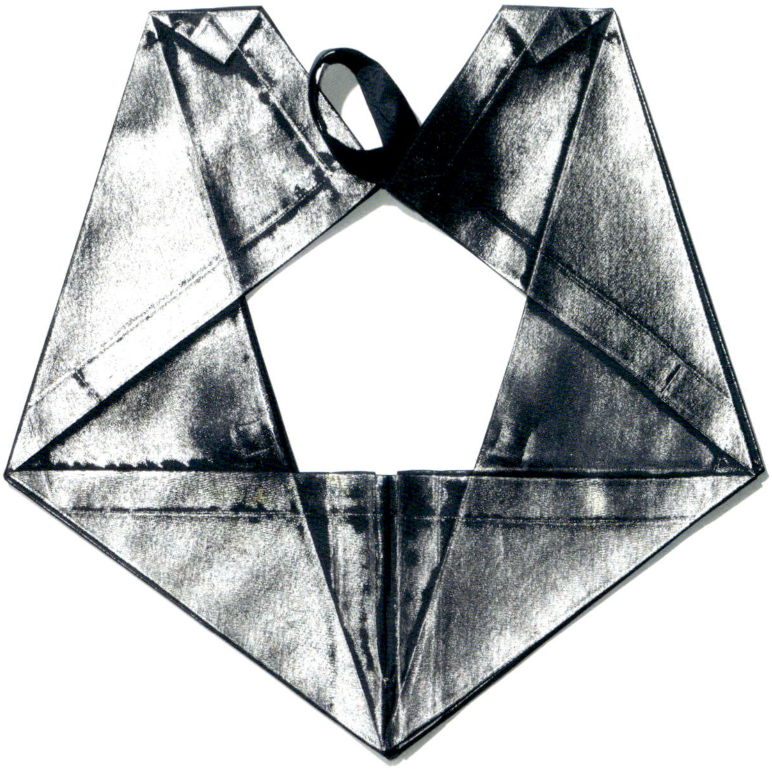

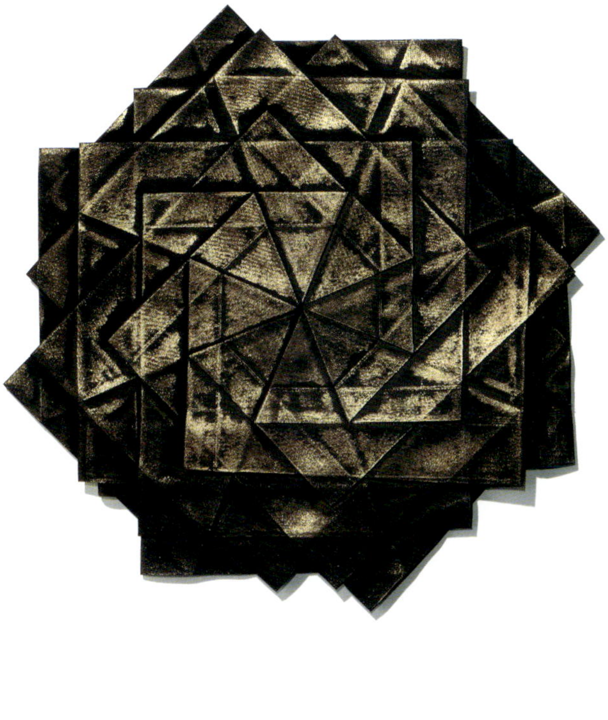

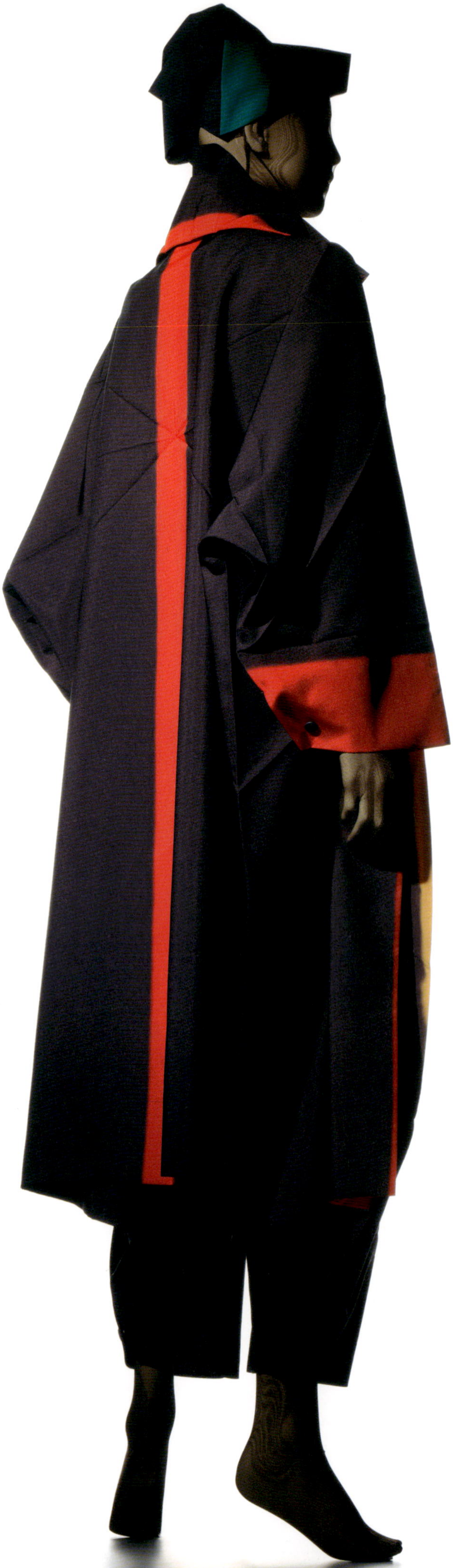

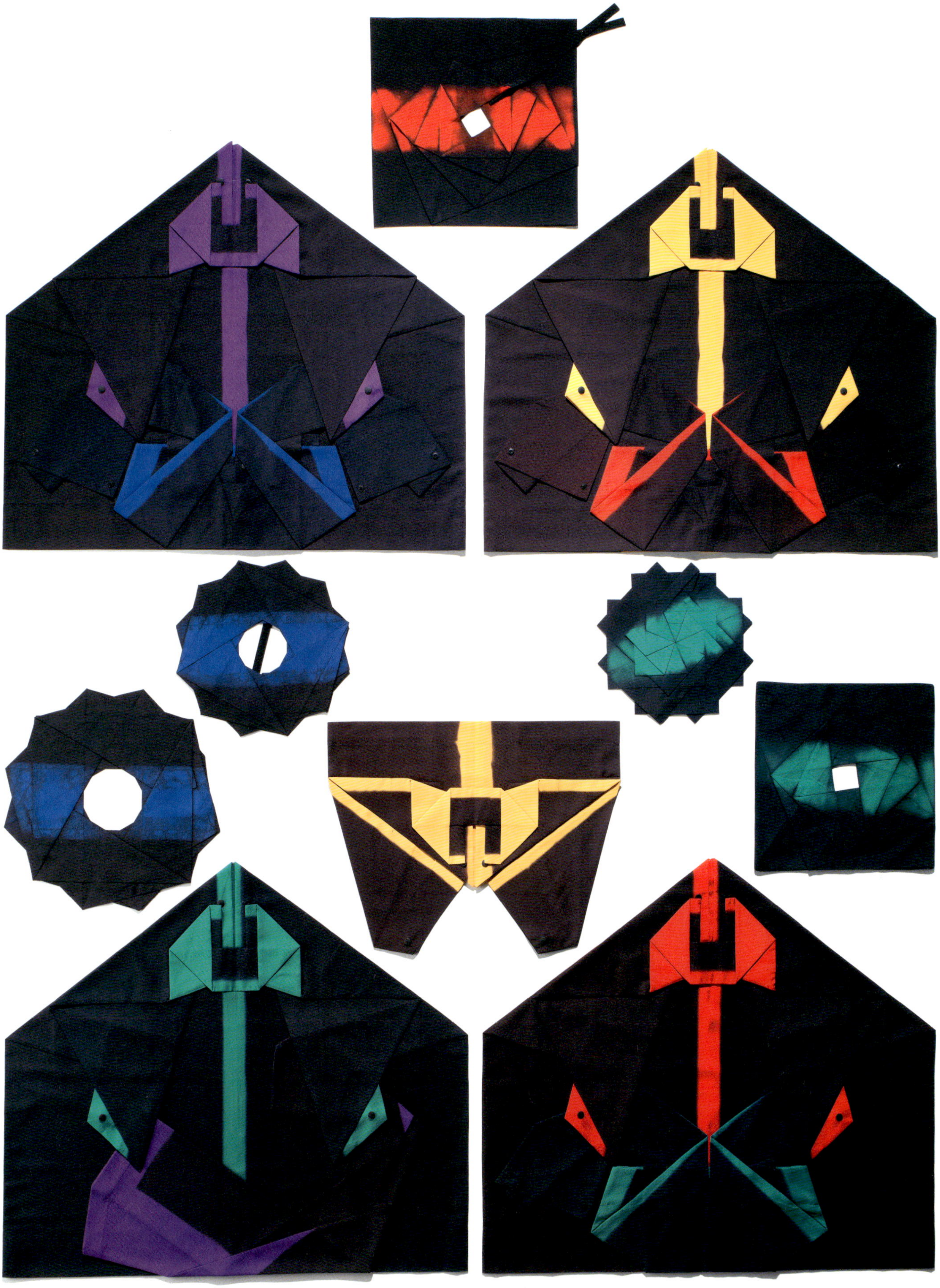

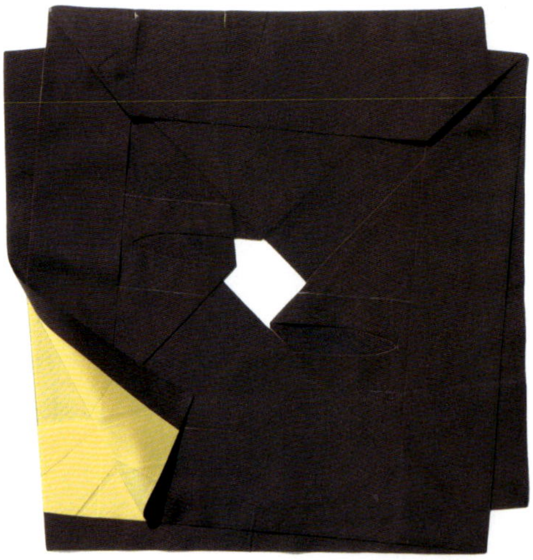
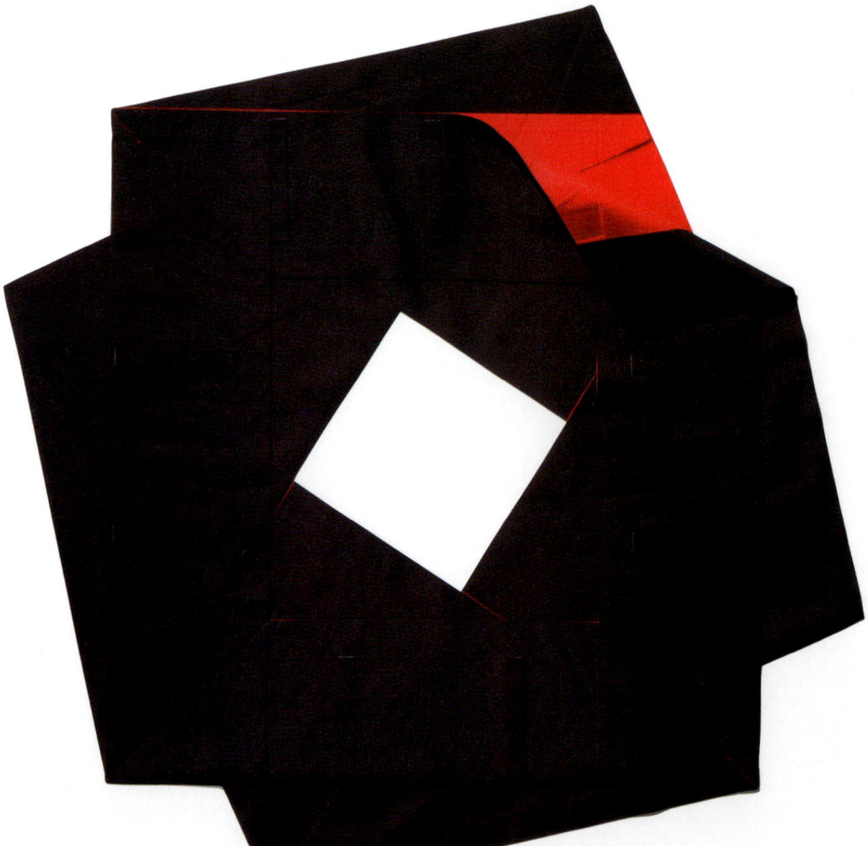

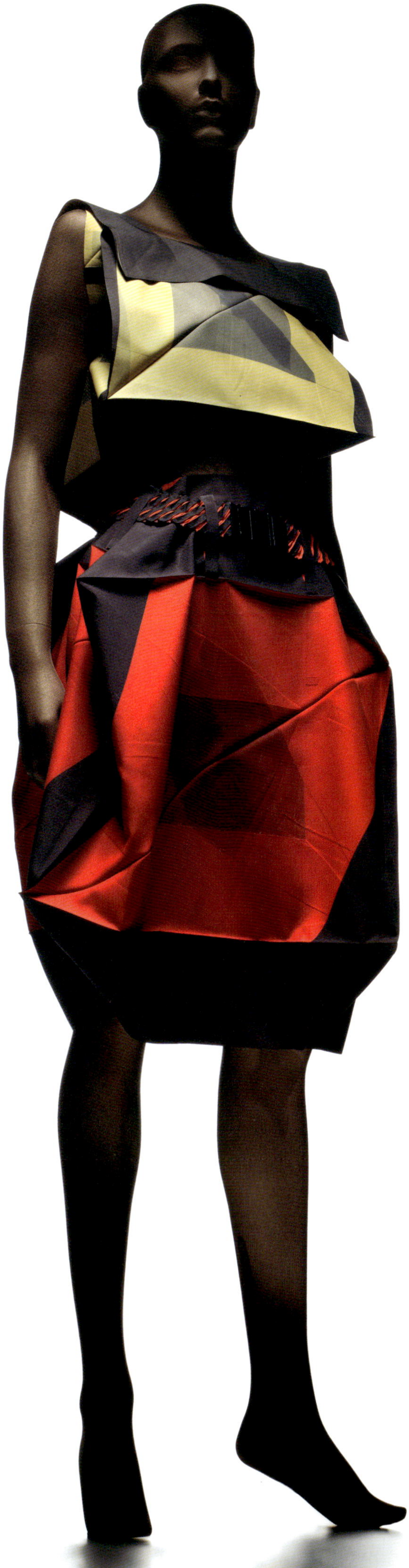

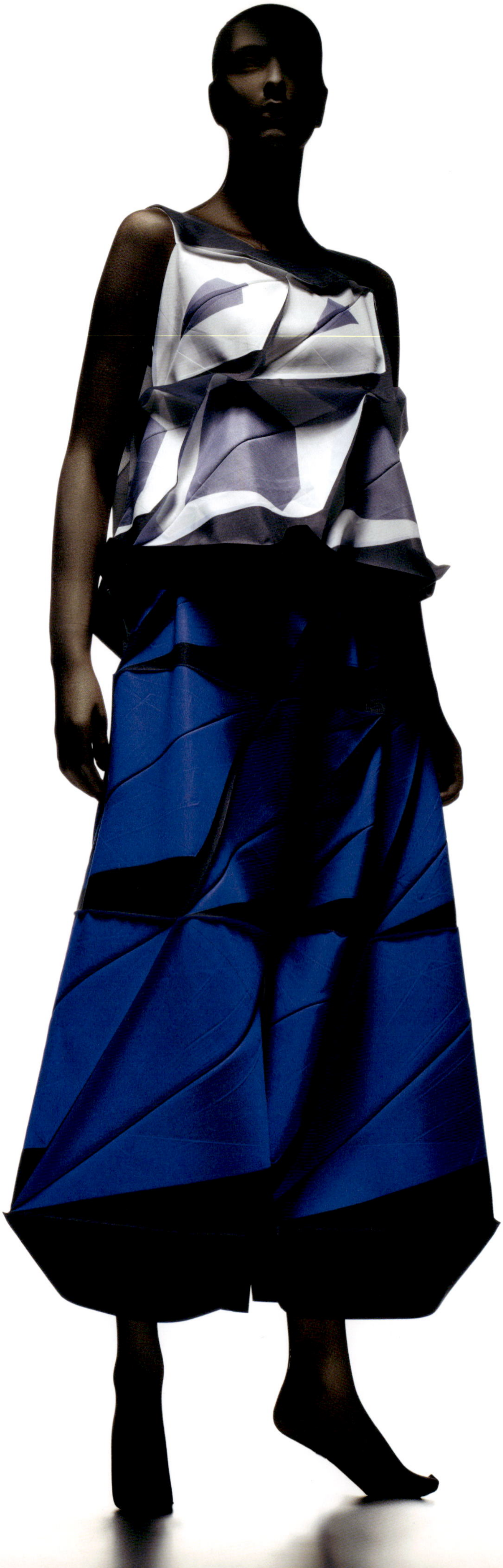

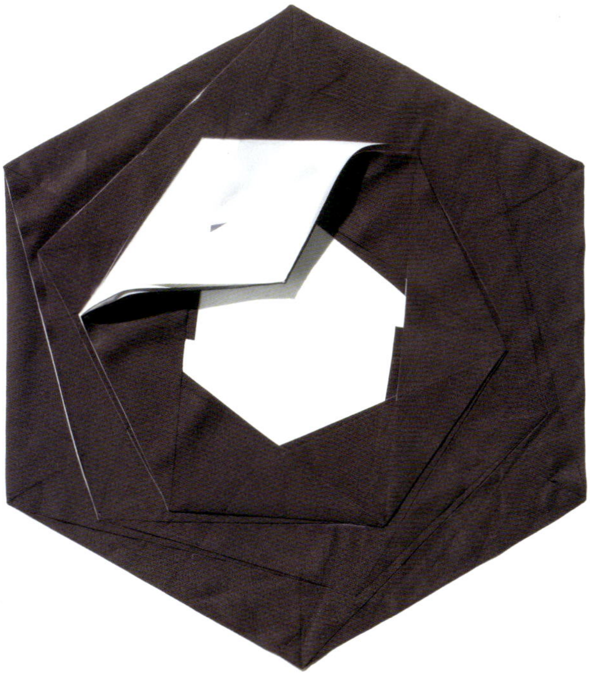

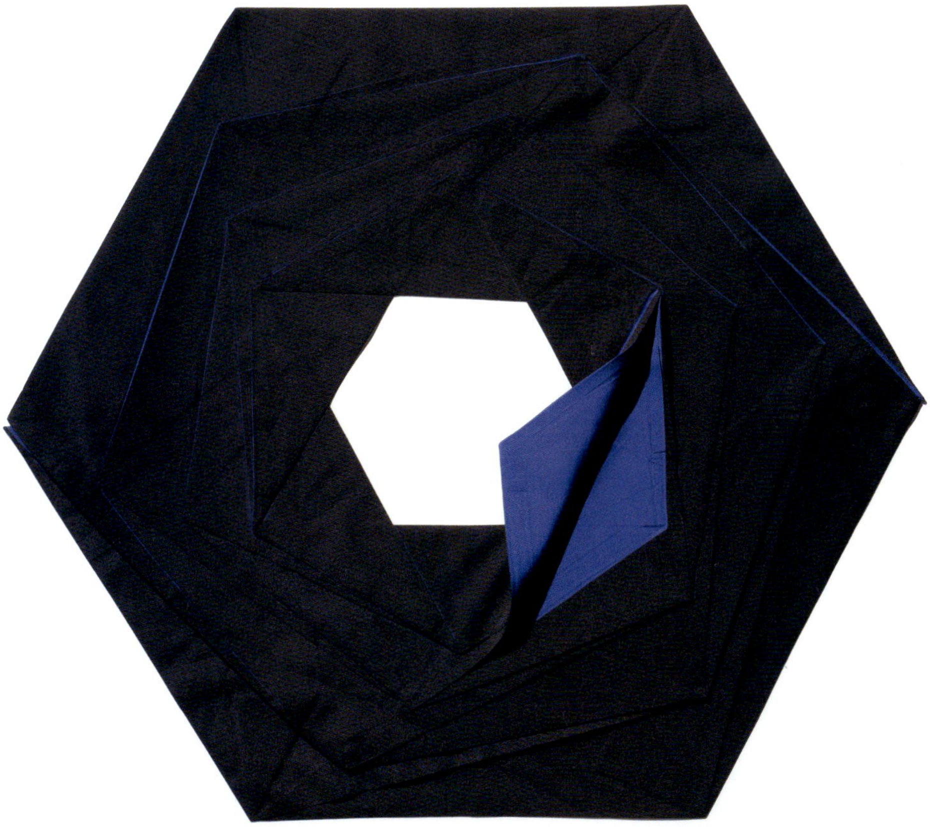

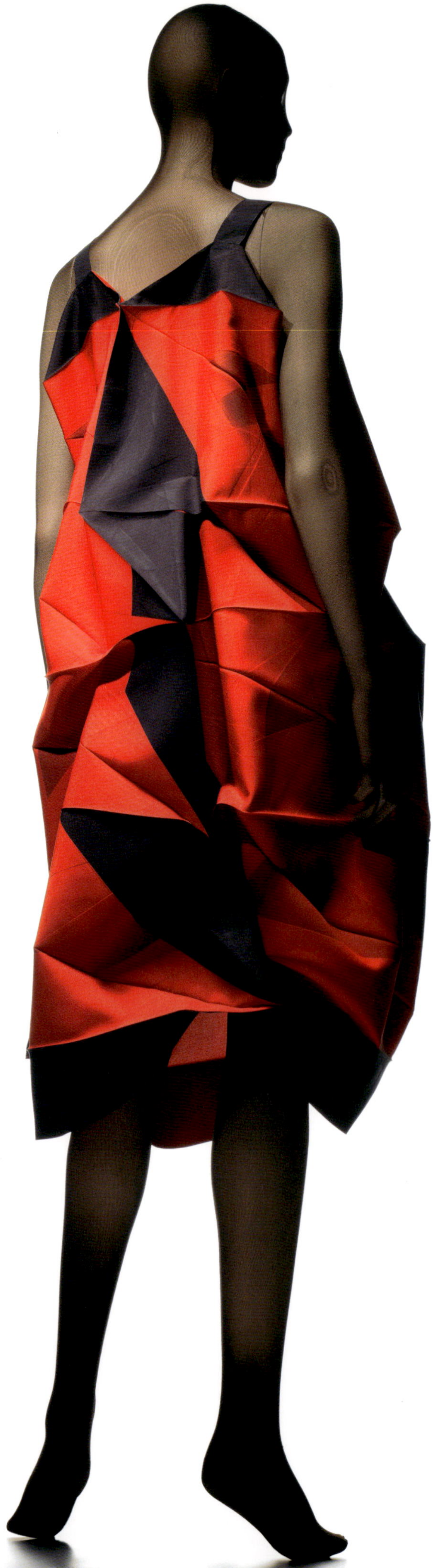

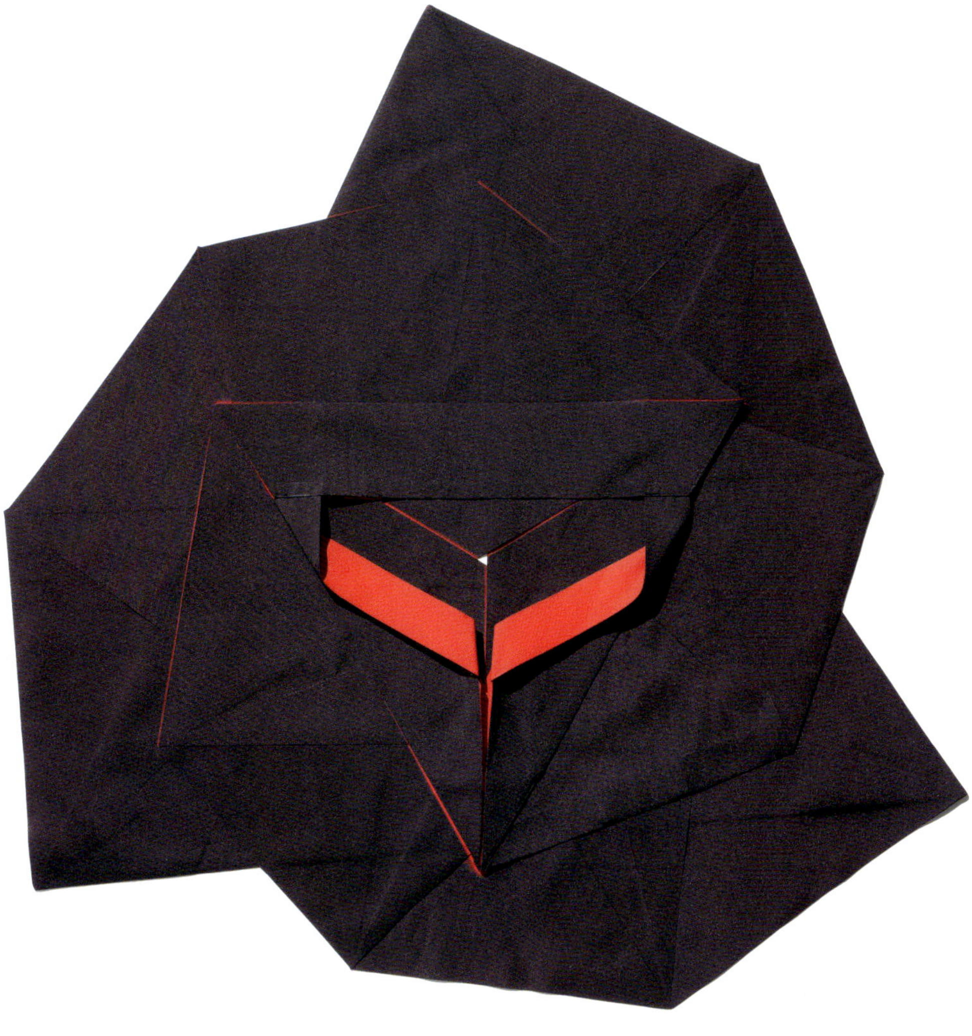

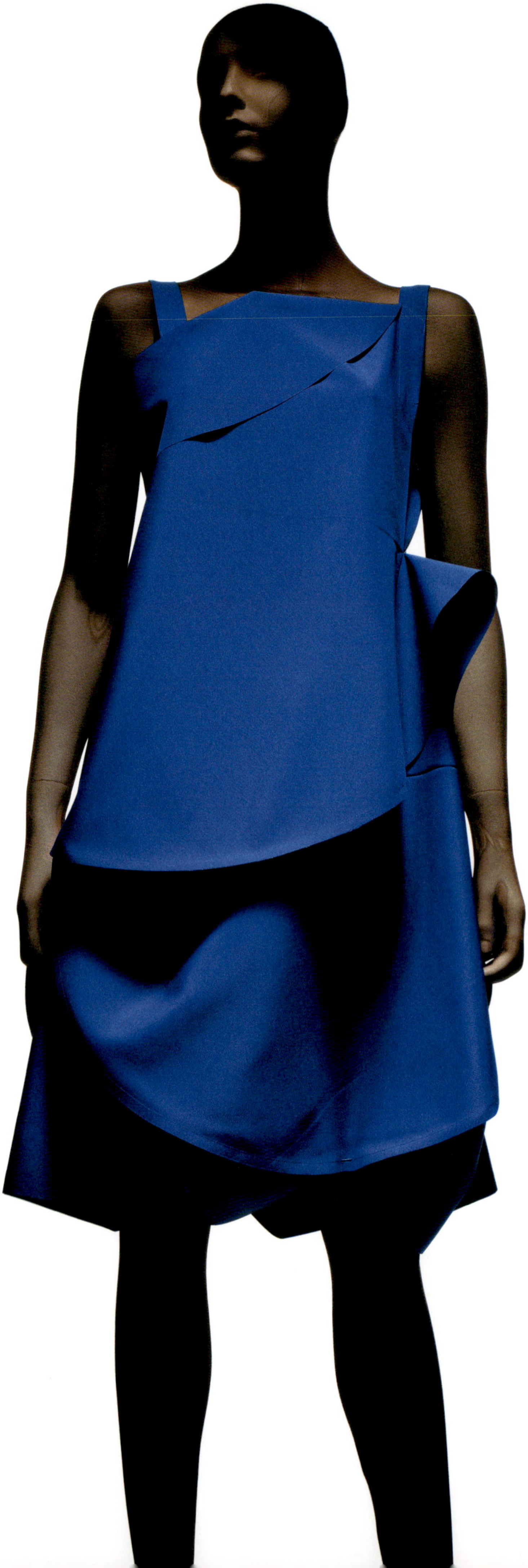

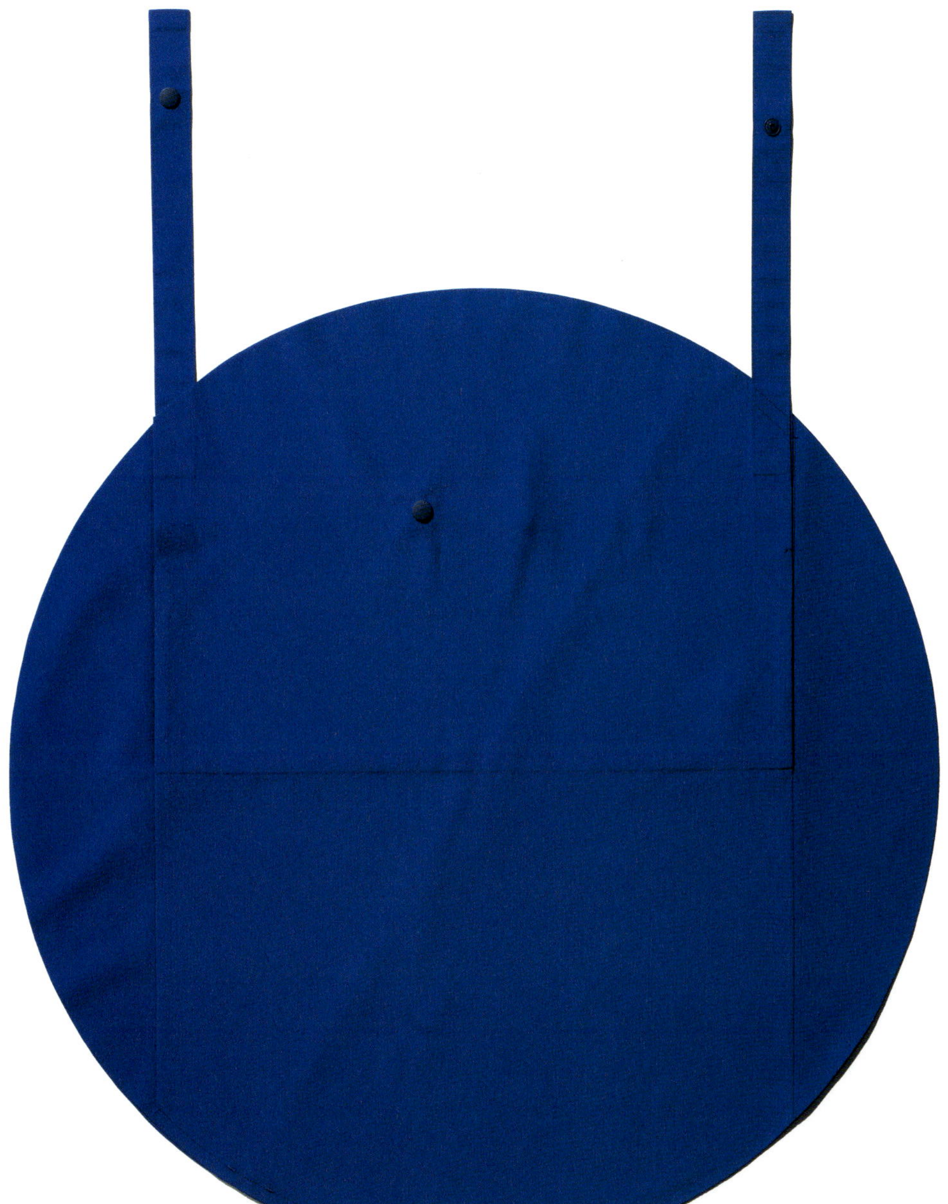

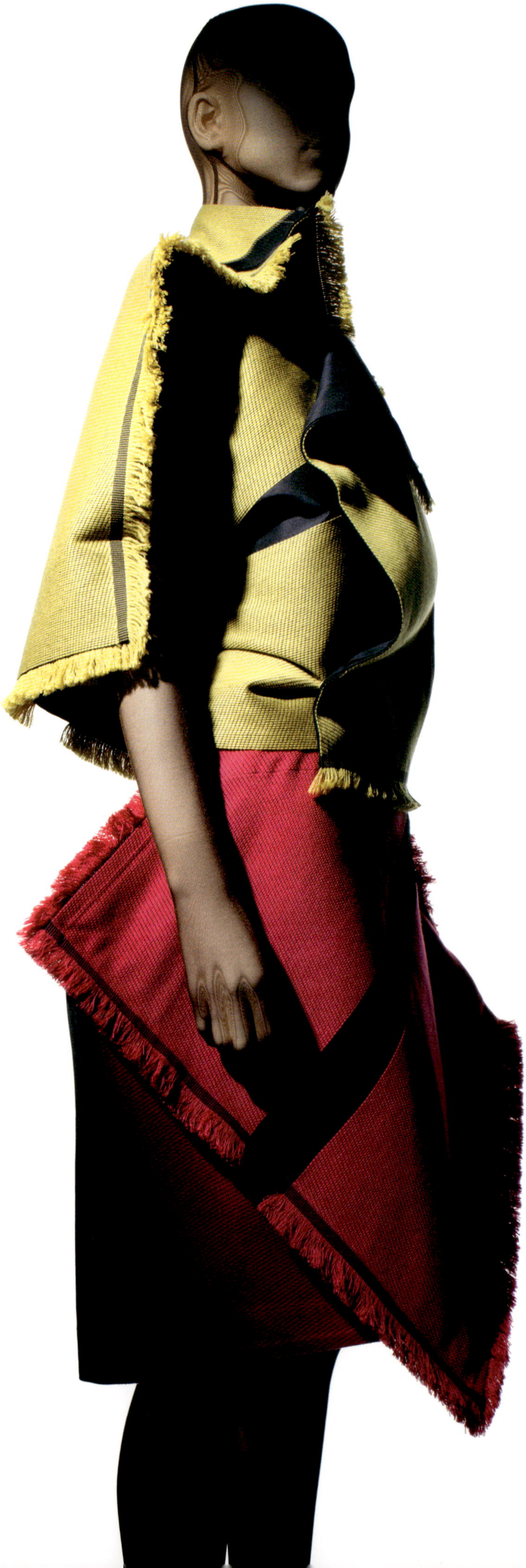

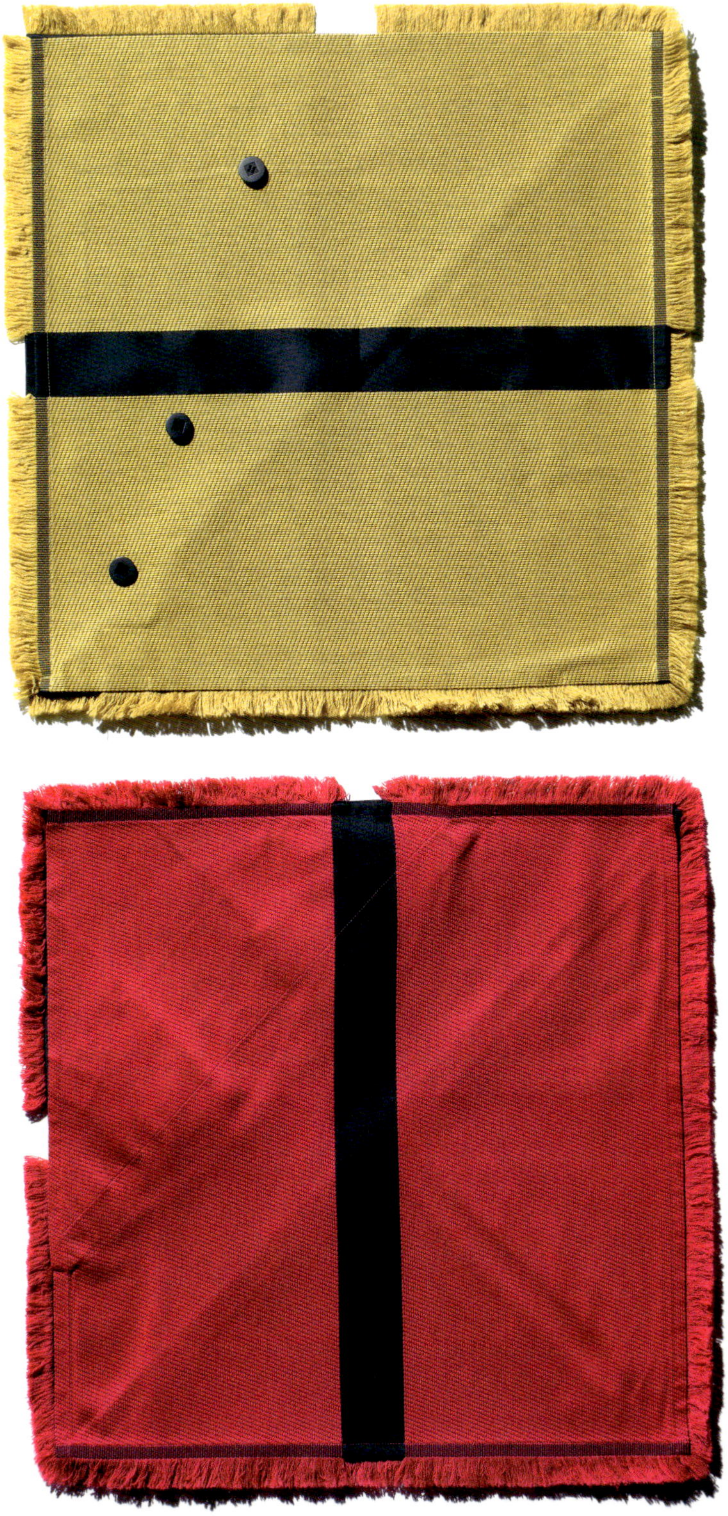

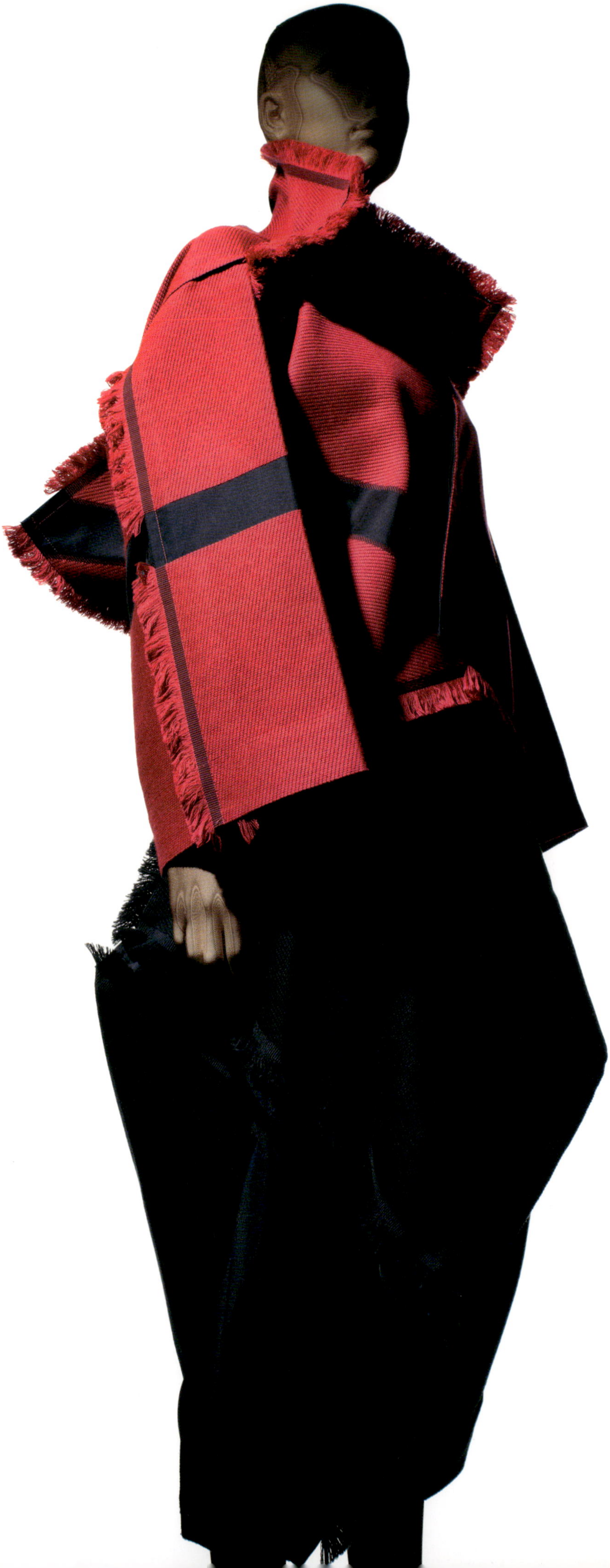

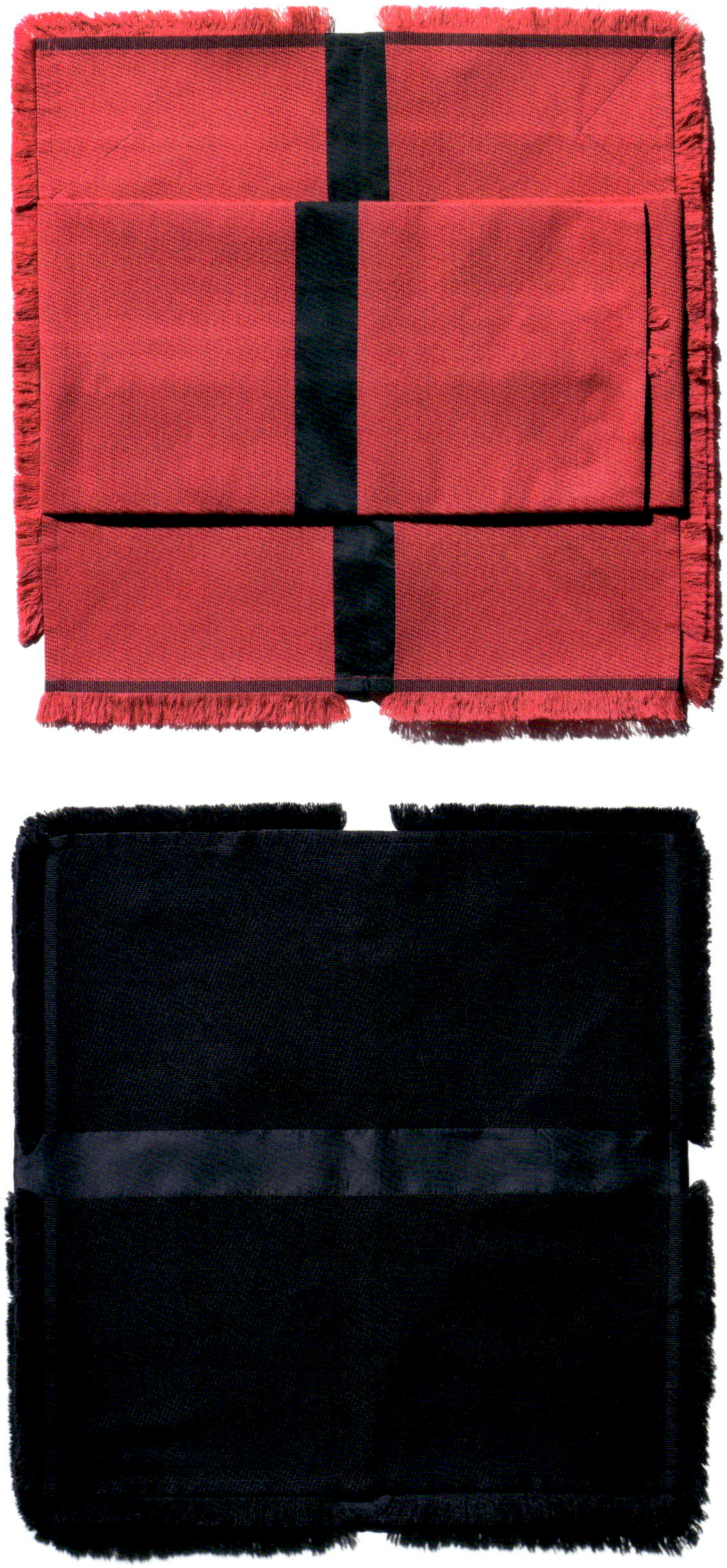

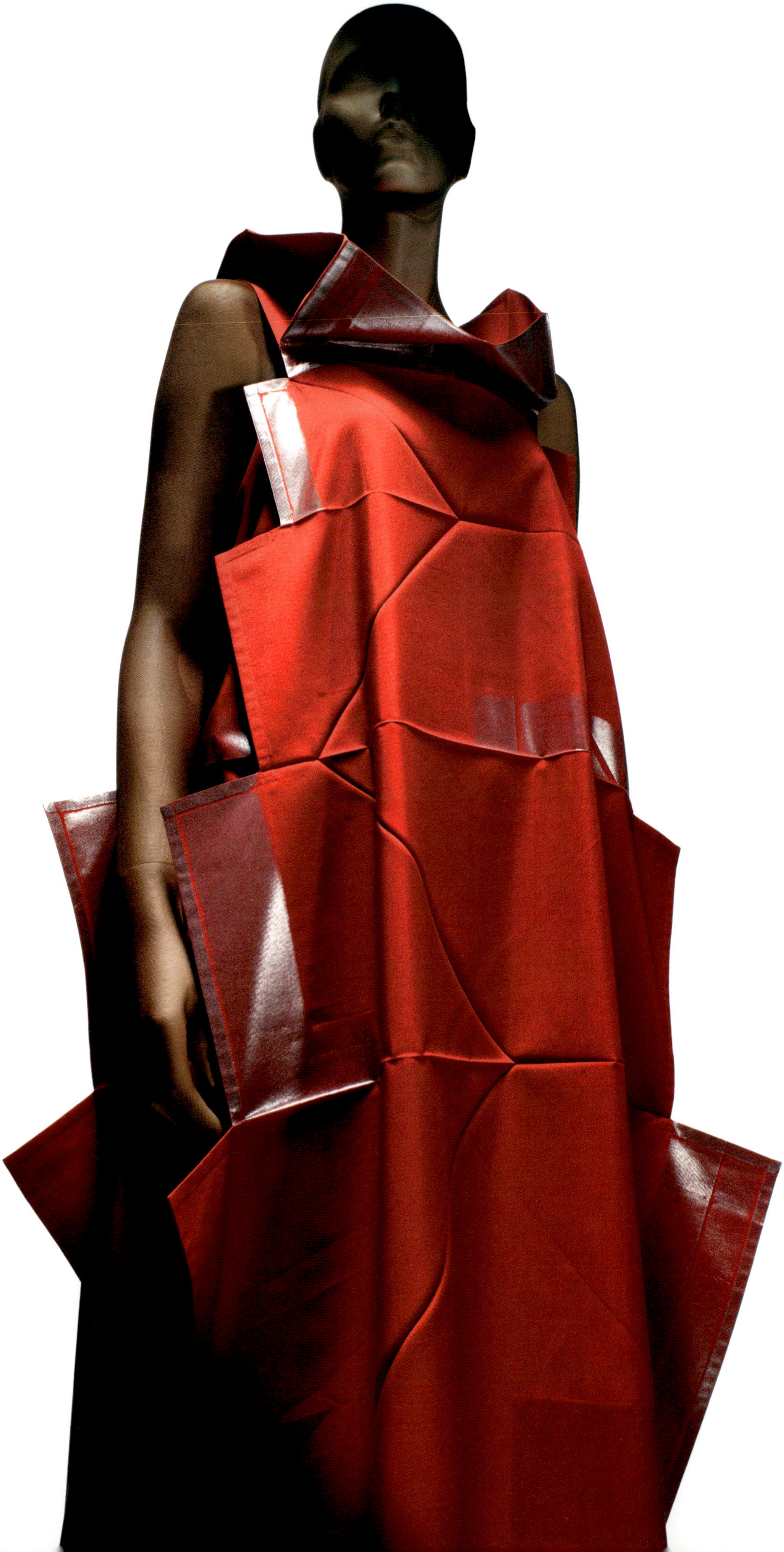

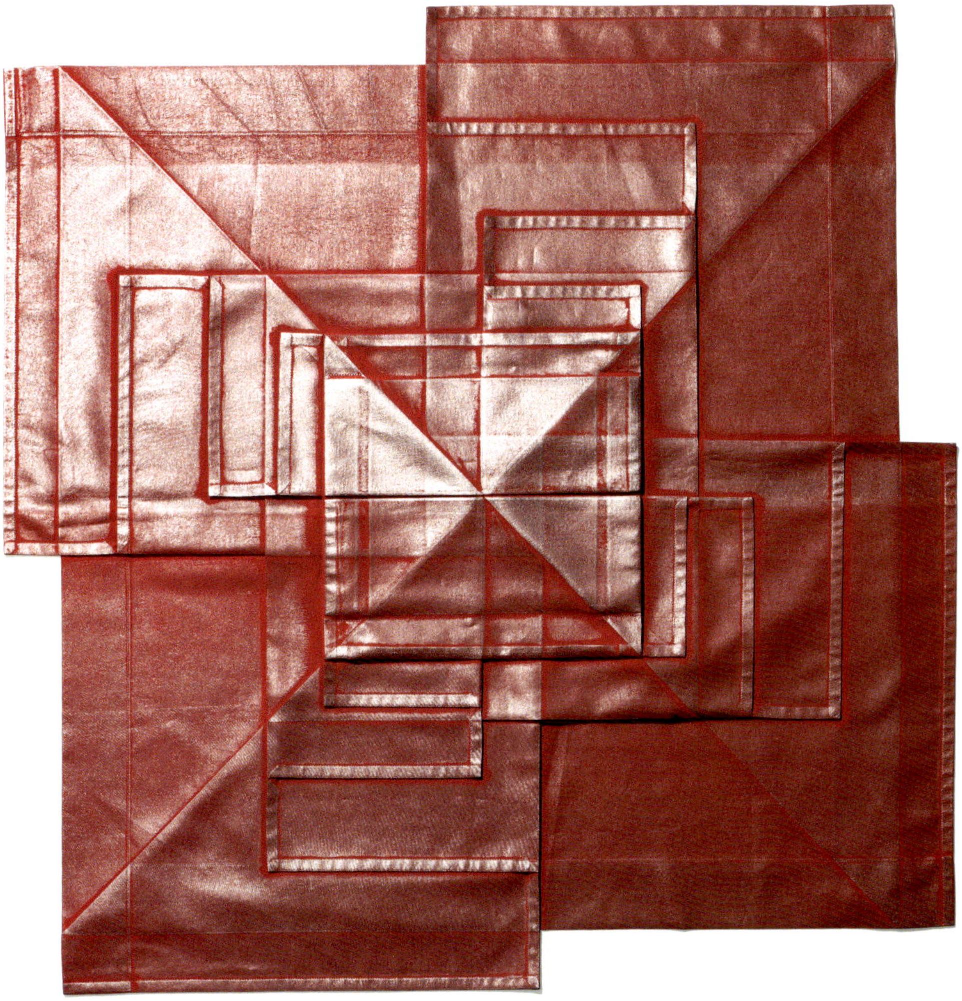

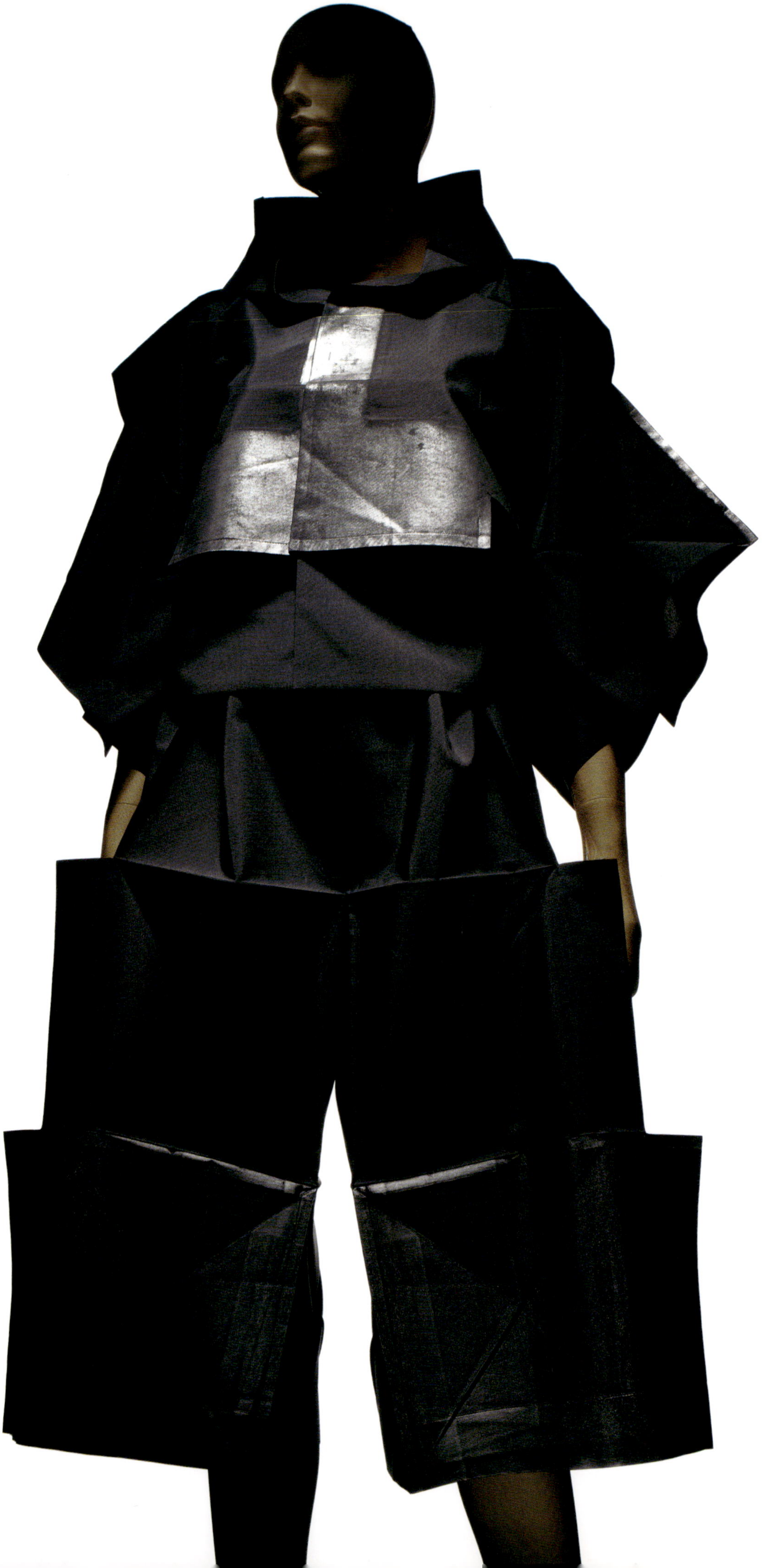

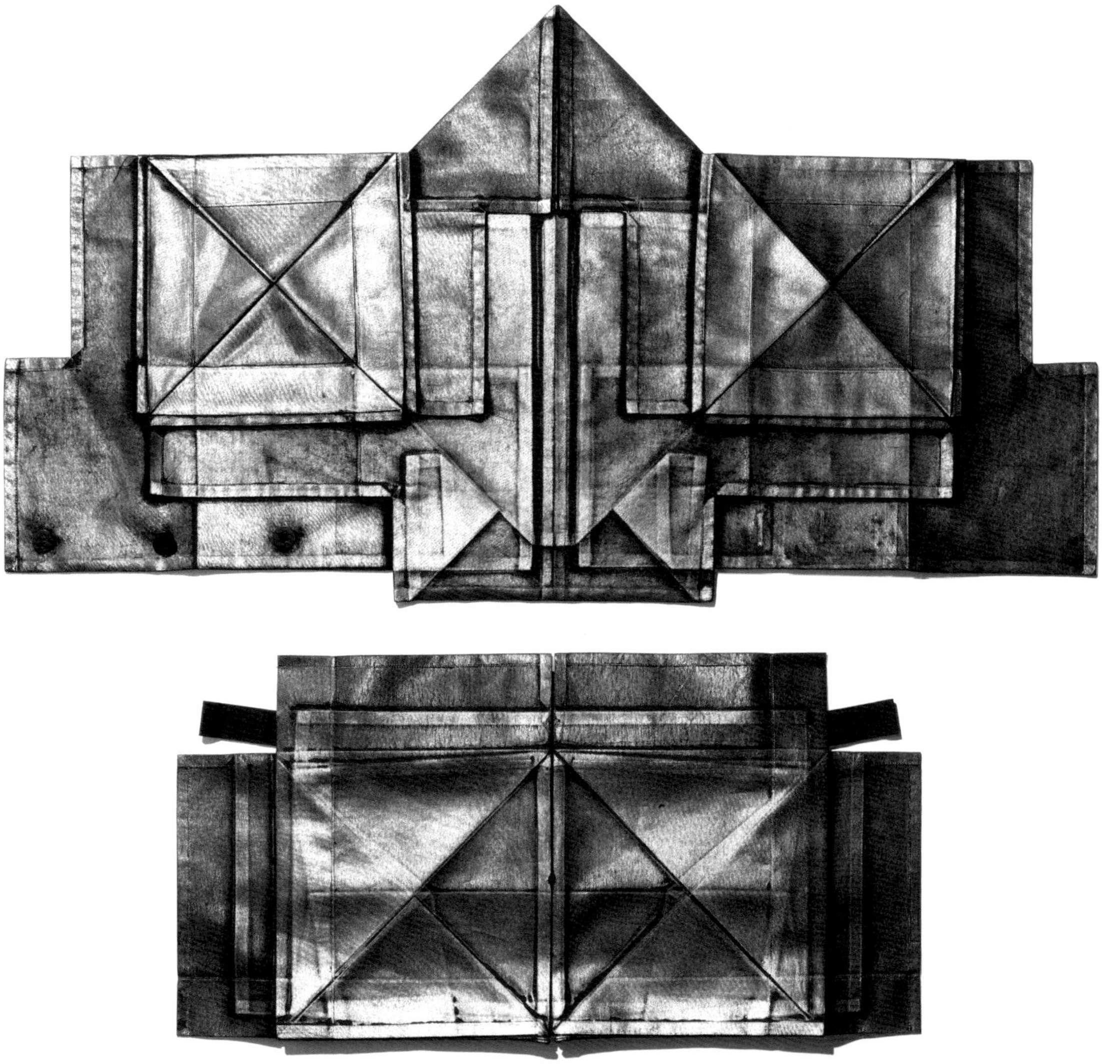

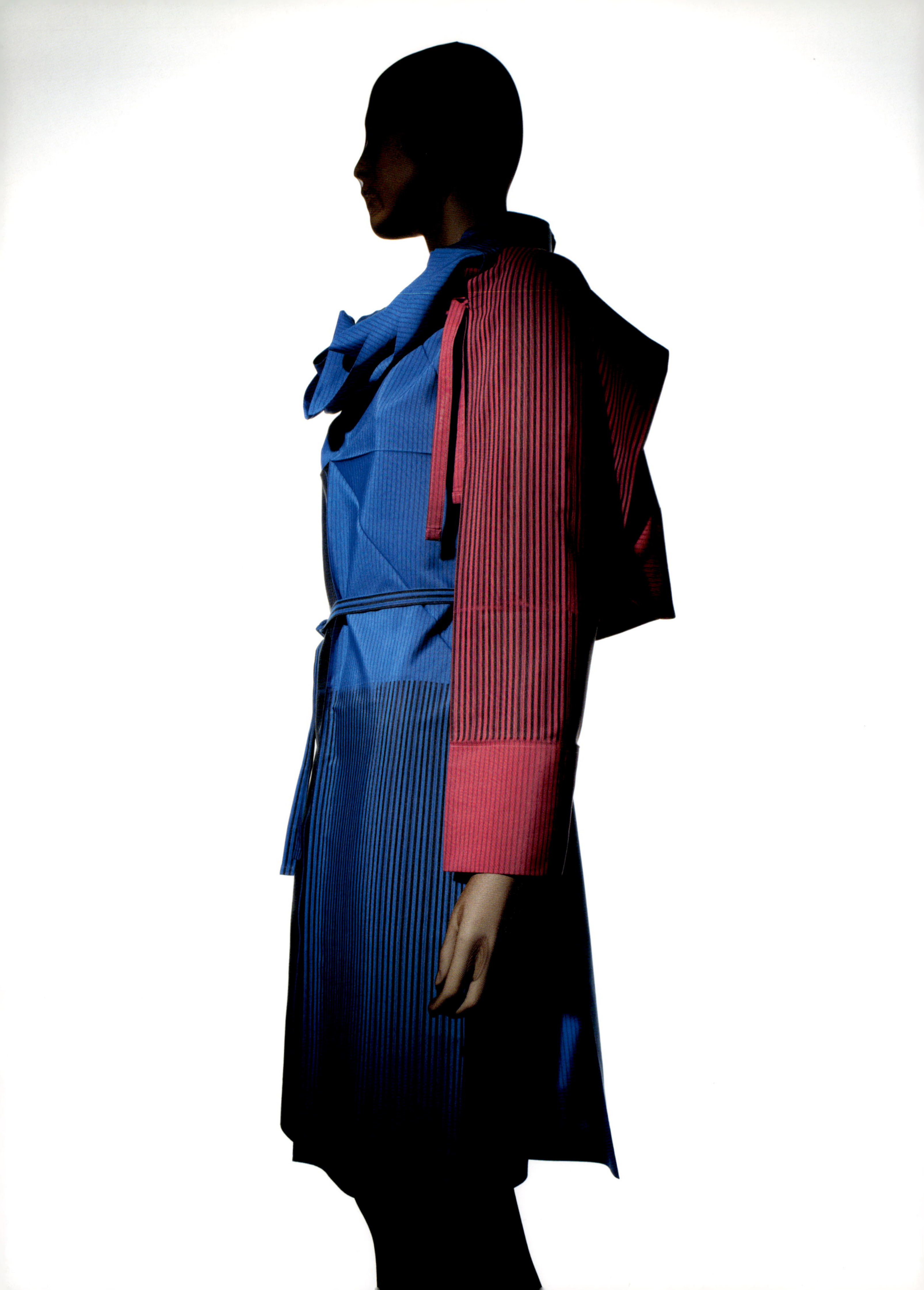

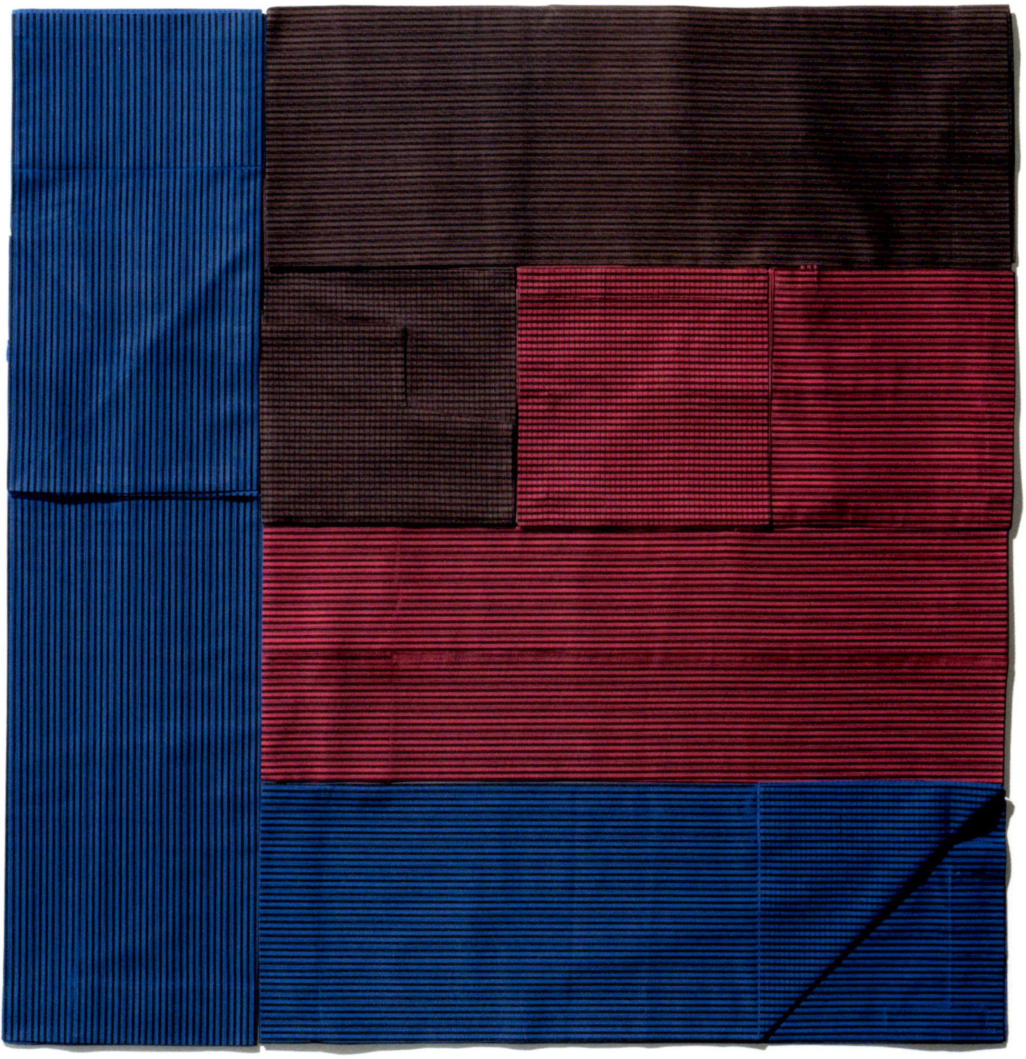

## 陰翳　IN-EI ISSEY MIYAKE

　三宅一生とReality Lab(リアリティ・ラボ)チームの思考は止まることがない。「132 5. ISSEY MIYAKE」の開発の過程で、その特徴である折りの構造は衣服デザインにとどまらず、他分野でも応用できると考えた。そこで2009年より取り組んだのが、骨組なしに折りの仕組だけで自立する照明器具だ。この発想を現実のものとするために軸となったのが、素材の開発である。132 5.のコンセプトでもある再生繊維をさらに探求し、実験を繰り返して、ペットボトルからつくられた再生繊維100％の不織布が選ばれた。そこに皺加工を施すことで強度と堅牢性をもたせた素材を開発し、照明器具メーカーとの協働で商品化が実現したプロジェクトである。平面にたたまれた形状から立ち上がる特徴ある姿それぞれに、ユーモラスな日本語の動物名がつけられている。確固たるコンセプトをもつひとつの発想からは、さらなる展開が生まれる。照明器具のかたちと折りをさらに衣服に応用した「IN-EI(インエイ)」シリーズが2013年に発表されている。

## IN-EI ISSEY MIYAKE

Issey Miyake and the Reality Lab team continue to explore new ideas. As they were developing 132 5. ISSEY MIYAKE, they realized that the unique fold structures they were creating might be applicable to other areas outside of clothing design. In 2009, they began working on stand-alone lighting built from this same folding process that could be used as lamp shades and which eliminated any supporting structures. The key to making this idea a reality was the development of materials. The use of recycled textiles has always been part of the 132 5. concept, and after numerous tests and experiments, they decided to apply a non-woven fabric made entirely from recycled PET bottles. The fabric thus created then undergoes a wrinkling process that results in a strong, hard material suitable for commercialization, which is done in collaboration with a lighting fixture manufacturer. The shades have unique forms once they are unfolded, and each of bears a humorous animal name in Japanese. When a concept is solid, new ideas allow it to develop in new directions. The forms developed for IN-EI were applied to clothing in 2013.

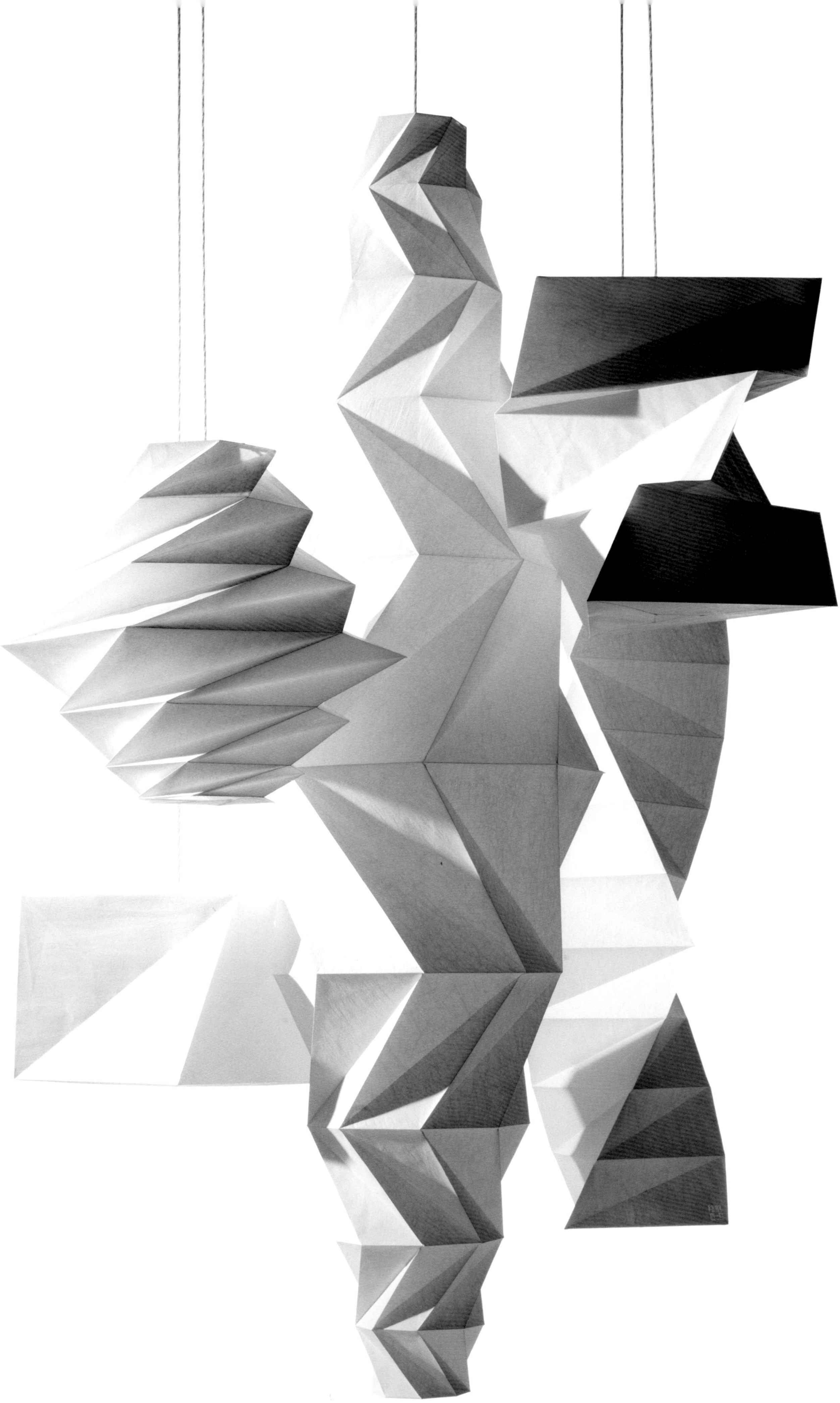

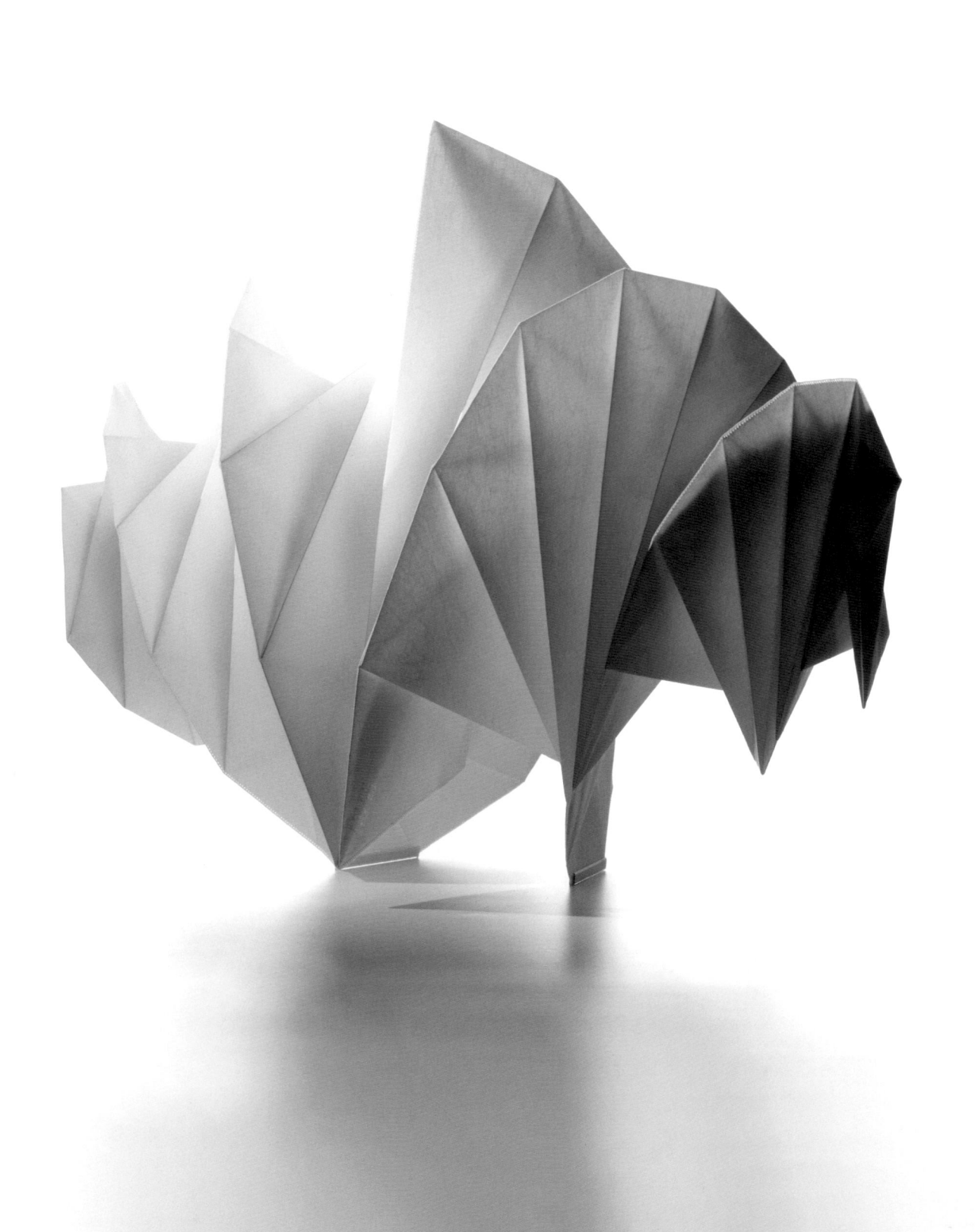

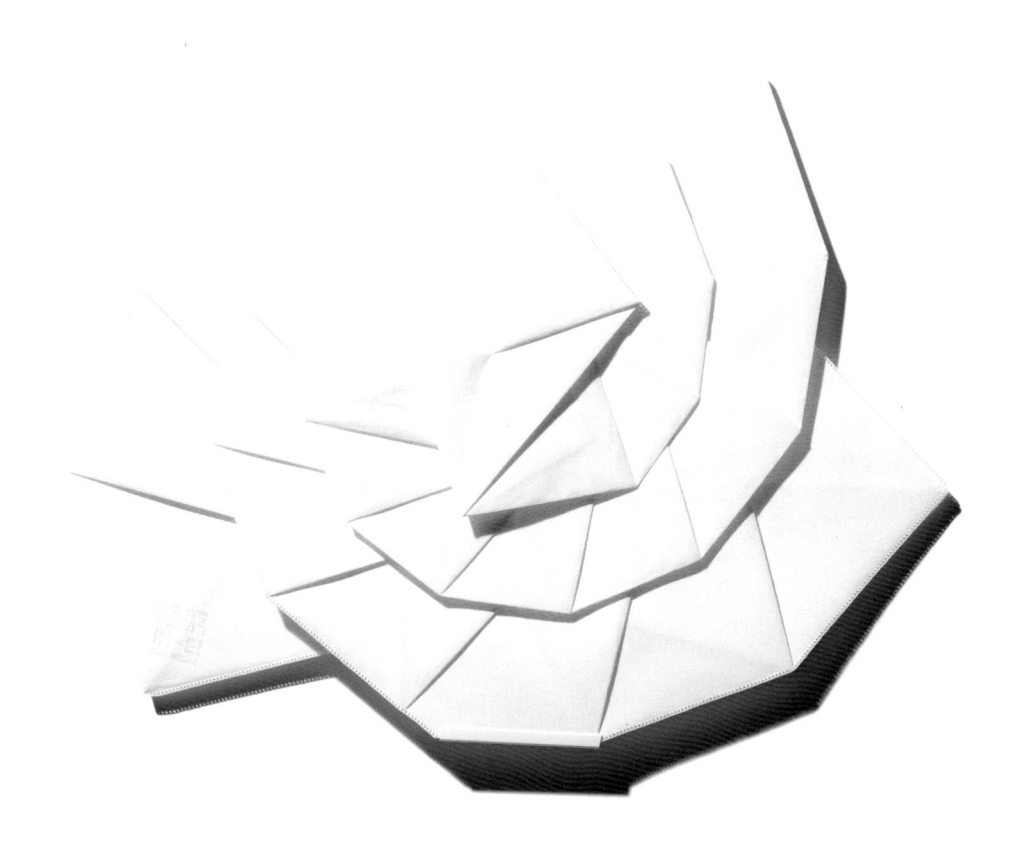

# はじめて国を越えたデザイナー

## ディディエ・グランバック

フランス国立近代美術館友の会会長、フランス・プレタポルテ連盟名誉会長、オートクチュール組合名誉会長

　プロとして専門分野を第一に尊重する私の生き方、それに、一人の人間としての私の生き方——双方ともにまたがっている数少ない人物のひとりが三宅一生だ。永年にわたって賞讃を惜しまなかった芸術家であり、何かというと接触をとってきた友人である。ゆえに、彼の仕事にしぼって取り上げる本に短い文を書いてくれと本人から依頼されたときも、正直いって心から光栄に思った。

　1971年、一生はニューヨークで初のファッション・ショウを成功裏に開催し、そこには『ヴォーグ』誌の伝説的な編集長ダイアナ・ヴリーランドの姿もあった。私はといえば、やはり同年のことだが、新たに登場したデザイナーたちを後押ししようと、パリでクレアトゥール & アンドゥストゥリエルを立ちあげた。

　1972年には、ブルーミングデイル百貨店の当時のファッション・ディレクター、ケイト・マーフィーの示唆を受けて、一生の服はパリ・コレクションズを通じてアメリカ市場に登場した。1967年に設立した同社は、当時はジヴァンシィとイヴ・サンローランのプレタポルテの流通を手がけていた。

　1973年、クレアトゥール & アンドゥストゥリエルの一翼としてコレクションを見せてはどうか。私の申し出に応えてくれた一生の快挙は大成功をおさめた。

　1974年4月にはクレアトゥール & アンドゥストゥリエルによる開催日程もパリのコレクション・カレンダーに載ることとなったが、これを勧めたのはピエール・ベルジェで、クチュリエとクレアトゥールのプレタポルテ組合の新会長の立場にあった。

　1973年3月のパリで初の一生のファッション・ショウは、三宅一生のファッション・デザイナーとしての進路を一変させ、また、以来、国際的なファッションの中心地としてパリが今日までその地位を持続する一助となった。

　それまでは、この種のイヴェントはフランスのブランドと、フランスを本拠として世界に君臨する最高の地位にあるメゾンの牙城として占有されていた。ちなみにKENZOは1970年にフランス国籍のメゾンとして設立された。

　パリでコレクションを発表すべく国境を越えて招かれた最初のデザイナーが一生だった。おかげで国際的なプレスや小売業者との接点もできたが、彼は以前とかわらずに東京を創造活動の総合的な中心地としてきた。その「ジャパニーズ・タッチ（日本の息づかい）」を支えるのは創造性、誠実な完全性を求める心、品質

である。三宅の活躍にともなって、その後、数世代にわたって日本のデザイナーたちもパリでコレクションを発表するようになった。今では、ファッション・ウィークに参加する顔ぶれは23国籍を数える。

　私がフランス・プレタポルテ連盟会長、オートクチュール組合の会長に選ばれた1998年には、三宅一生が外国人では初めてその連盟の委員に選出された。

　最後になるが大切なことをいっておきたい。2015年10月にフランス国立近代美術館のベルナール・ブリステン館長と共に東京の一生のアトリエを訪れたとき、つくづく感じたことだ。

　ファッション・デザイナーのなかには、偉大な芸術家というべき存在が何人かいる。

# THE FIRST INTERNATIONAL FASHION DESIGNER

## Didier Grumbach

President of the Société des Amis du Musée national d'Art Moderne Centre Pompidou,
Honorary President of Fédération Française de la Couture, Chambre Syndicale de la Haute Couture

Issey Miyake is one of the few persons closely linked to both my professional and my personal life, as he is an artist I have long admired and a friend I have regularly been in contact with. So when he asked me to write a few lines in a book devoted to his work, I must confess that I felt deeply honored.

In 1971, Issey successfully staged his first fashion show in New York, in presence of Diana Vreeland, the legendary editor in chief of *Vogue*. That same year I launched in Paris *Créateurs & Industriels* with a view to helping promote new designers.

In 1972, as suggested by Katie Murphy, the then *Bloomingdale*'s fashion director, Issey's clothing was launched on the American market via *Paris Collections Inc.*, a company I had founded in 1967 and which was then distributing Givenchy and Yves Saint Laurent ready-to-wear.

In 1973, I offered Issey the opportunity to show his collection in Paris under the wing of *Créateurs & Industriels*. It turned out to be a huge success.

In April 1974, *Créateurs & Industriels* was on the official list of the Paris Events Calendar at the invitation of Pierre Bergé, the new President of the Chambre Syndicale du Prêt-à-porter des Couturiers et des Créateurs de Mode.

The first Issey's Paris fashion show, which took place in March 1973 changed the course of Issey Miyake as a fashion designer while allowing Paris to continue to be the international fashion capital as it is today.

Until then the event had been the preserve of French brands and the world's highest houses were based in France. In 1970, for example, KENZO was established as a French house.

Issey was the first international designer invited to present his collection in Paris, which gave him access to the international press and retailers, while Tokyo remained the hub of his creative activities. Creativity, integrity, quality, became the hallmarks of the 'Japanese touch'. In the wake of Issey Miyake, several generations of Japanese designers were due to show their collections in Paris. Today, twenty-three different nationalities take part in the Fashion Week.

In 1998, when I was elected president of the Fédération Française de la Couture, Issey was the first foreigner to be elected to the Couture Executive Committee.

Last but not least, in October 2015, I visited Issey's atelier in Tokyo with Bernard Blistène, Director of the Pompidou Center National Modern Art Museum.

Some fashion designers are great artists.

## 未来を見つめる、人間主義、自伝的な……

アンジェロ・フラッカヴェント　　インディペンデント・ファッション評論家、キュレーター

　この一文はきわめて個人的なものになるだろう。書こうと意気込んでいるこの私の脳裏には数々のイメージが洪水のように流れ込んできており、秩序ある無秩序状態とでもいおうか。それは視覚的(グラフィック)で整然としているのだが、それでいてどういうわけか、エネルギーが身体に収まりきらず、勢いよく滲み出てきている気がして、ゆったりと解放された感覚すらある——未来へ向かって解放されているのだろうか。白い背景に塔のようにスクっと立ってポーズをとるアマゾネスがいる (アマゾネスはギリシア神話に登場する女性だけの部族)。人間というよりは、遠い宇宙から来たスフィンクスだといったほうがよいかもしれない。その両脚と両腕は明解な角度をもった位置とかたちにおさまっていて、両眼はこの世のものとは思えないサングラスで隠され、衣服はどうかといえば、純然たる幾何学的形態のドレスがごく自然に女の体格と身振りになじんでいる。そこにいるのは真っ白な、実験室のような真空にとりまかれた魔女で、透明でプリーツのある服からは鋭い釘のようなものがはえてきている。彼女のボディスーツにはどこかの部族ゆかりの彫り物(タトゥ)の柄がみっしりと描かれていて、彼女の両眼は神秘的でもの憂げな表情を押し込めるように閉じられている。ここにまた、空気をはらんで膨らんだ外套を着た、SFに出てきそうな戦闘隊員まがいの女—— 最盛期のアーヴィング・ペン氏がとらえた——彼女は宇宙船が迎えに来て出発するのを待っているらしい。だが、1970年代初頭にちなむこれより早い時期のイメージでは、異なる光景が見える——ぐるぐる回りながら情熱的で解放感いっぱいに飛び上がったりして踊るクロッグをはいたダンサーがふたりいて、ハンカチーフでつくった構成主義的なドレスを着ているのだが、そのバイアス・カットが踊りの動きを際立たせている。これまた、スナップを止めたり外したりするだけでどうやら無限にいかなるかたちにでも出来れば、ばらばらにするのも簡単な服に見える。あげくの果てには、こんな光景もある。取り憑かれたかと思うほどよく登場してくる夜の屋根の上のショットで、仮面をかぶった近寄りがたい気配の女神がおり、何種類もの液体状の布生地を羽織っているのだが、その生地は重なっては広がり、絶妙な効果で胴体をそっくり覆い、しかも、添加された秘密の化学物質の働きで、揺らぎもせずに凍ったように微動だにしない。要するにそれは三宅一生だ、少なくとも私にとっては。

　これは、記憶を無作為に蘇えらせていることになる。三宅一生の全作品を貫いて驚くべき繋がりを感じているので、私にはいっさいの年代的記録も不要だし、駄目押しの確認もいらない。まさに最初に見たときから、彼のも

のづくりのやり方のもとにある種子(たね)は何かピンときた——たしかに、創造の結果生まれたものは年月を経るにしたがって有機的に変化してきているが。三宅一生のものの考え方はこれまでつねに独特で、自身の個人的な内面に根ざし、躊躇なく他に類を見ないものだといえる。が、それはまた、歴史を踏まえ、なおかつ歴史を覆す両面をもっている。私が語るものだけでなくほかにも無数の例を挙げることができようが、それらはまさしく時間を超越していると身をもって感じられ、ファッションではふつう避けられない摩耗や損傷といった作用を受けないようだ——それらのエネルギーも新しさすらも隅から隅まで健在だ。優れたデザインは例外なくそうだが、それらは他とは一線を画してそれだけで屹立している。

　この万華鏡のような作品群は私の臓腑(ぞうふ)を掴んで離さない。事実、ラディカルな視覚言語を探しまわって、思考を伝える想像力にあふれた方法を手にしようと邁進していた十代の頃、最初にファッションに関心を寄せた時期以来、これらのイメージはつねに私につきまとっていた。そのような飛び抜けて新しい発明に印刷媒体をつうじて出会った記憶が活き活きと残っている。ヨーロッパに住んでいたため、私にとってなじみのある審美的な記号の用法や西欧流の身体と衣服の捉え方からすると、何もかも大幅に異質ながら魅惑的なものばかりだった。 私にとってそれらの表現は未知の次元に入り込む扉だった——地図のない胸躍る領域に通じる革新的な次元。イメージは性的要素をあからさまに挑発するものではなかったし、権力としての富や社会的地位を強調しているわけでもなかった—— ほおっておけば、舞い上がって元気なだけの1980年代というつまらない時代を生んでしまうところだったこれらの三要素(トリオ)とは無縁の世界だった。反対に、自由と発明について語っていた——闊達ながらも驚くほど穏やかに。ところが、一見すると異質で頭脳的なこれらのイメージは、実験が先行するとよくそこに陥るのだが、冷ややかに感じられるようなことはなかった——そこには温かな触感が宿っていて、魔法のような惹きつける魅力、触れてくるような親密さすらあり、まさにそれがページを飛び出してこちらに迫ってきた。その瞬間、掴まえられた。これらのファッションには表層的な要素がなかったことも大きい。最新のトレンドを打ち出しているのではなく、尊厳、自立、力強さを感じさせた—— 私自身が自分の問題だと感じていた心の動きそのものだった。

　自伝的な書き方になっているが、それ以外の書き方はできない。実をいえば、私自身の嗜好が形成され、ファッション批評家としての見解を確立してくる過程で、三宅一生とその日本の仲間たちのつくるものが私のなかにしっかりと刷り込まれてきた。厳格な純粋主義への私の関心、ものごとの受け止め方をめぐる疑い深さ、郷愁嫌い、進歩的な思想への情熱。すべて、発端はあの若い時代だった。端的にいえば、抽象的なものごとを愛しているが、その私にとって、三宅一生は抽象化の王者だ。いわば、実際主義的な抽象化である。彼ほど見事に引き算の出来る者はいない。少ないものでより多くを成就し、純粋なもの、表面に顕われる生(なま)の美、ものづくりの沈黙の姿勢を際立たせる。創作の主たる課題として永年にわたって三宅一生が挑んできたのは、一枚の布で服をつくること

Angelo Flaccavento

だった、そうだ。勇敢なる還元主義——これ以上に創造的な前提条件はあるだろうか？ それに、余計なものを排除するこれほど強い衝動には、ファッションづくりに賭けた抽象派の意気込みが表れているとはいえまいか？ その思想は多くの顕われとして繰り返し戻ってくる。1970年代のゆったりとして浮遊しているような服から、ごく最近の「A-POC(エイ・ポック)」に見られる熟考した末の身体感覚(ボディ・コンシャスネス)にいたるまで。この感覚は、折りたたみを取り入れた「132 5. ISSEY MIYAKE」のいくつかの服においてその真骨頂に達した。かたちをめぐるこの探究の一貫性には瞠目するが、それにもまして驚くべきなのは、後ろを振り返ることなく前へ踏み出す堅い意志だ。三宅一生は歩調を崩さずに初志を貫く。

　もっといいたいことがある。三宅一生は社会におけるみずからの固有の役割について彼ならではの考え方をたゆまずはぐくんできた。デザイナーとして早くから、数字を優先する現実主義的なアプローチをとる冒しがたい神格的存在にされるのを拒み、もっと地味でより実際的なアプローチをとってきた。そういえば、彼は自分の作業を「ものづくり」と呼んでいる。彼の作業の原動力は、具体的な機能それぞれに応じて斬新なかたちを考案し、身にまとう解答を出したいという欲求だ——そのかたちは発明であり、これまで見たことのないものであるがゆえに、まったく何かをなぞらえるものではないのだが、それでいてすぐれて実用に即している。創造性と有用性、個性と客観性とがこれほどよくバランスを保っているとは、これまでになかった快挙だ。ファッションを突き動かす作用は安定した機能よりも危ういほど実用性を欠いたスタイルを優先させがちだが、それを思うとこの点がいかに重要かわかる。とはいえ、三宅がこの世紀が生んだもっとも独創的な発明者のひとりであることは変わりない。

　ここまでで、真に決定的なことに触れていなかったとすれば、三宅一生の作業の総体は端的に、創造性の最上級の表れだ、と断言することにほかならない。その意味で、三宅が突出した存在である根拠を考えてみると、それは人間を尊(たっと)ぶ強烈な心だ。後にも先にも三宅は人間主義者(ヒューマニスト)だ——自分の世界の中心に個人を据えている。彼の仕事は身にまとう美しい衣服をつくることではなく、人間の基本的な欲求——何よりも、快適さ——に関わることであり、さらに、欲求に応えて舞台の中央に着る人——発明者の創造性ではなく——を送り出すことなのだ。これは地味な仕事ながら、尖鋭な編集技術、かなりの謙虚さ、いわんや相当な胆力がなければなし得ないことだ。この資質のすべてを三宅一生はもっていると私は見ている。この間、形態面での発明と実際主義とを融合させた解答、衣服という解答を三宅は休みなくつくり出してきたが、それらはとても軽快で、さりげなく、それでいて熟考の賜物ばかりで、西欧人として見ると、じつに詩情に溢れているとしかいいようがない。

　最後に、大胆な言い草になるが、お許し願おう。三宅一生はファッション・デザイナーではない、と思えてならない。身にまとうものをつくっているからファッションの場で仕事をしているが、彼の創造をめぐるアプローチは囲いのない生粋のデザイナーのそれだ——かたちと機能とを出会わせる、クライアントが暮らし易いようにする、

Angelo Flaccavento

その結果、より美しいものごとを実現する。彼のつくるものは実用性が高く、扱いやすく、かたちを変えることもでき、着る者は、それらを採り入れるにも、それらに自分を合わせるにも、際限なく工夫を楽しむことができる。彼がつくるものは、それぞれ異なる体型に張り切って、また独創的に応答し、存在感と安定をかもし出す。三宅一生はある種の魔法を身に付けているらしく、つくった服は自己主張せずにほとんど姿を消して人間の一部となり、人はそのおかげで、仮面をかぶっているような窮屈さを感じずに社会生活に向かっていける。心理学的にいえば、この恬淡（てんたん）としたところ、執着のなさ、それを根底に置いて、三宅一生は異文化、つまり東西の独得な交叉を実現しつづけている。それこそ、これほどの年月にわたり個人として私が応答しつづけてきたことであり、見ることをとおして初めて出会ったときから、その応答の密度はかわらない。彼の作業は歴史の枠を超えて縦横に行き来するが、それでも、たとえもっとも大胆な試みをする場合でさえ、そこにはかならず日本人としてのDNAの痕跡が感じとれる。束縛されずにこれほどの敬意を伝統に対して抱いている――未来志向としての人間主義の師匠として、私が三宅一生に私淑している所以だ――この魂を失った、反人間的な、ポスト・デジタル世界の英雄。

　さまざまなイメージが脳裏を浮遊してやまない。それは、年代的な流れから踏み出してきて私を力づけ、鼓舞してくれる。

Angelo Flaccavento

# FUTURISM, HUMANISM, AUTOBIOGRAPHY

**Angelo Flaccavento**  Independent Fashion Critic, Curator

This one will be utterly personal. As I sit down to write, a flux of images floods to my mind, in an orderly disorder. It's graphic, streamlined stuff, yet somehow oozing a barely containable zing of physical energy while conveying an optimistic sense of openness—to the future, I'd suggest. Here is a towering amazon posing against a white background, more a Sphinx from outer space than a human being, limbs and arms arranged in angular moves, eyes shielded by otherworldly sunglasses, clad in a dress that's an immaculate geometrical shape effortlessly adapted to her figure and gestures. There, a sorceress, immersed in a white, lab-like vacuum is sprouting transparent, pleated spikes, her bodysuit swarming tribal tattoo patterns, eyes closed in mysterious pensiveness. Here again, a sci-fi trooper in an inflated coat—Mr Penn at his best – looks like she is waiting for a spaceship to pick her up, and depart. In an earlier image from the beginning of the Seventies, instead, two dancers in clogs jump while performing frenzied, liberating swirls, the fluidity of their choreography highlighted by the bias cuts of the constructivist neckerchief slipdresses they wear. Here, again, it is clothes with snap buttons that can be assembled, disassembled, reassembled in seemingly infinite ways. There is, finally, a haunting, nightly rooftop shot of a masked, impenetrable goddess, bust wrapped in liquid swatches of fabric, folds ingeniously moulded allover the torso and frozen still with the aid of some secret chemical agent. That's Issey Miyake in a nutshell. At least, for me.

I am letting my memories run at random. I feel no need for chronology, not lastly because I find a striking continuity in the whole Issey Miyake *oeuvre*. The seeds of his *modus operandi,* in fact, were clearly there at the very beginning, while the outcome has kept changing over the years, organically. Issey Miyake's views have always been so distinctive, so personal and so unremittingly unique they both belong to history and defy it. The images I refer to, and the countless others that could be mentioned, are in fact so intimately timeless, they seem not to suffer from the wear and tear of time, as fashion usually does—their energy and even their newness is totally intact. They stand apart, autonomously, as good design always does.

I feel viscerally related to this kaleidoscopic repertoire. In fact, these images have been with me since I first came to be interested in fashion as a teenager looking for a radical visual language, striving for imaginative ways to convey thought. I have vivid memories of being exposed to such brutally new inventions through the printed media. Living in Europe, it all looked so dramatically yet charmingly alien from the aesthetic codes I was used to, and from the western perceptions of the body and the dress. To me, those depictions were the door to another dimension: a progressive one leading to uncharted, exciting territories. Those images were not about in your-face sexuality, not about wealth as power, not about social status—the deadly trio that marked the otherwise ebullient and lively Eighties. They, on the contrary, spoke of freedom and invention: in a commanding yet surprisingly calm way. As distant and cerebral as they seemed, however, those images were not cold, as it is often the case when experimentation rules: there was a palpable warmth to them that made them magnetically attractive, even touching, and that literally jumped out of the page. I was hooked, right away, not least because there was nothing superficial about those fashions. Those images were not about the latest trend, but about dignity, autonomy and force: urges I felt related to.

I am keeping it very autobiographic, but I cannot do otherwise. Fact is, the work of Issey Miyake—and that of his Japanese fellows – has had an imprinting in the shaping of my personal taste as well as in the forging of my views as a fashion critic. My interest in brutalist purism, my proclivity for shifting perceptions, my aversion to nostalgia and my passion for progressive ideas all stem from those early memories. I love abstraction, to put it bluntly, and for me Issey Miyake is the king of abstraction. Of pragmatist abstraction, so to speak. He masters the art of subtraction like no other. He is able of doing more with less, highlighting the pure, raw beauty of surfaces and the silent strength of surprising fabrications. Isn't Issey Miyake's main creative challenge over the years to create clothing using just one piece of cloth? Is there any creative assumption more daringly reductionist than this? And isn't such an urge to do away with the superfluous the expression of an abstract take on fashion-making? The idea recurs, in many different ways, from the roomy, floating shapes of the Seventies right through the rethought body-consciousness of A-POC only to reach its final peak in some of the folded 132 5. ISSEY MIYAKE pieces. The continuity of this formal quest is outstanding, but even more so is the stubborn will to push things forward without looking back. Issey Miyake is steady and consistent.

But there is more. Issey Miyake has always nurtured peculiar ideas about his own role in society. As a designer, he refused early on the role of impenetrable deity opting for a humbler, more pragmatic approach. He calls his activity *making things,* apropos. His practice is fueled by the urge to create innovative shapes and clothing solutions that respond to specific functions: forms that are inventive and never seen before, thus totally non-referential, yet eminently practical. Such a balance of creativity and usefulness, of personality and objectivity is an unprecedented creative achievement, if you consider fashion's drive towards the perilous impracticality of style over the stableness of function. Not for Issey Miyake, who, nonetheless, is one of the most original inventors of the century.

However, the whole of the Issey Miyake *oeuvre* would just be another expression of utter creative brilliance, if a truly defining element were missing. In this respect, what makes Issey Miyake stand alone is his adamant respect for the human being. Issey Miyake is first and foremost a humanist: he puts the individual at the center of his world. His work is not about the dress as a beautiful, wearable item, rather it is about the basic human needs—comfort, *in primis*—and how a designer can respond to them by giving the wearer, not the inventor's own creativity, the front stage. This is a mean feat that requires keen editing skills and a challenging amount of humility, but also a huge dose of boldness. All qualities Issey Miyake seems to possess. Over the years, he has endlessly kept creating clothing solutions that merge formal invention and pragmatism in ways so light, so subtle and so considered I, as a western observer, cannot help but perceive as eminently poetic.

Finally, let me get bold. I believe Issey Miyake is not a fashion designer. He happens to work in fashion because he creates things that can be worn, but his creative approach is that of a pure designer: marrying form with function, making the life of his clients easier and, as a result, more beautiful. His creations are practical, easy and reconfigurable, allowing the wearer infinite ways to adopt and adapt. They react actively and singularly to different body types, giving a sense of strength and confidence. Issey Miyake owns some kind of magic, which allows him to make clothing that almost disappears, turning into a tool for the human being to front social living without feeling like wearing a mask. In this psychological subtleness, Issey Miyake keeps creating a unique junction of cultures, of East and West, and that's what I personally keep responding to, after so many years, with the same intensity of our first visual encounter. His work moves both inside and outside of history, yet even at its most daring, a trace of Japanese DNA can always be perceived. Such a boundless respect for tradition, crowns Issey Miyake as my own master of humanism as futurism: a hero, in our soul-less, anti-human, post digital world.

Images keep floating in my mind, endlessly defying chronology while providing strength and inspiration.

Photo: TYEN

## ISSEY PAR TYEN

TYEN   Directeur Création et Photographe

Ce qui est étonnant, quand je suis en face d'Issey, son regard m'impressionne.
A la fois, il a la curiosité comme un enfant et la joie de la découverte comme un jeune premier.
En regardant Issey à son travail pour la préparation du défile, c'est son regard perçant qui coupe,
qui taille comme une merveilleuse paire de ciseaux. Mais quelle paire de ciseaux !
Ses yeux observent et transforment ses vêtements, comme un sculpteur.
Il crée les nouvelles formes pour habiller les gestes quotidiens du corps.
Ses vêtements n'ont jamais été fait pour être à la mode ou la tendance.
C'est ça la nouvelle vague.


## イッセイ氏のこと

ティエン   クリエイティヴ・ディレクター、フォトグラファー

イッセイに会ったとき、私は驚き、惹きつけられた。それは彼の瞳のせいだ。
その瞳は、子どものような好奇心と、若い見習いのような発見の喜びに満ちていた。
ショウの準備をしているイッセイを見ると、研ぎ澄まされたハサミのように、瞳が鋭い視線に変わり、
コレクションを仕上げていく。なんと素晴らしいハサミなんだろう！
イッセイはじっと服を見つめ、生まれ変わらせる。まるで彫刻家のように。
そうやって、毎日のさまざまな動きを飾る新しい方法が生み出される。
イッセイの服は、けっして流行やトレンドを追うためにつくられるのではない。
彼自身が、いつだって新しい波（ヌーヴェル・ヴァーグ）なのだから。


## ISSEY BY TYEN

TYEN   Creative Director, Photographer

What is stunning and impresses me most, when I am face to face with Issey, is his gaze.
He has the curiosity of a child and the joy of discovery of a young novice.
Watching Issey at work for the preparation of a fashion show, it is his piercing gaze that cuts,
and tailors like a marvelous pair of scissors. But what a pair of scissors!
His eyes observe and transform his clothes, like a sculptor. He creates new ways of clothing
the body's everyday gestures.
His clothes have never been made to be "fashion" or trendy.
This, is the new wave.

# 写意的衣服和情感以及思考

蔡國強　美术家

我和各种设计师有过合作，但大量都比较应景和"装饰性"。比如人家设计了建筑，有一面墙挂我的画，或一块空地让我做公共艺术…两个艺术家之间，或艺术家和设计师之间，我印象里是很难合作的。虽然我和建筑家Zaha Hadid的合作《用伏特加抚摸萨哈·哈蒂》(Caressing Zaha with Vodka)开始进行得有模有样，但结局是她有些反悔，不太开心我在开幕式上用数吨酒烧了她的冰雪建筑…想想我与一生，可算是自始至终合作愉快。

一生让我天马行空地开始。我一度想做含药材的衣服，促进穿者身心健康，又曾大谈如何让使用者因为风水而运气更好。但最后都要面对服装的现实比如能否经得起清洗…最终还是回到火药。当然火药也有问题：服装材料的化纤成分特别易燃，我想尽办法让它爆破后不会烧破，但最后无可奈何的破洞反而使我们的合作拥有非凡的特点。以至于印制的服饰也特意布上斑斑小洞的图样。每当看到自己的爆炸作品不在美术馆展示，而在马路上，派对场的人们身上，像移动的作品，也如同民众自发的行为艺术…我都莫名兴奋！

一生的友情对我人生意义远大。我的大女儿文悠最近出书《可不可以不艺术》，谈到一生对她的影响：她7,8岁时去看一生的时装秀，是在切尔西二楼的loft里。看起来那么普通，但就是有能力吸引各路崇拜者，支持者，包括媒体，让她感受到一生独特的气场。"不选择在纽约时装周里到布莱恩公园或林肯中心去搭建华丽的秀场…我觉得无比神奇…意识到自己领略了纽约市的魅力"。

这一切让我的女儿开始想做一名时装设计师，"听凭内心之美的引领，将其与整个世界分享。我想要设计的服装不只满足日常穿着的需要。还要有雕塑感，能表达自己的观念…三宅很高兴听说自己激发了一棵时装界的小苗…在与我爸妈用餐时见到我总是很开心，还常常送我礼物。在学校，我穿着无比称身的毛背心，戴着红围巾和帽子，全都来自三宅的品牌…"我渐渐"开始觉得或许自己将来不该去时装学院，而该去学习哲学或社会学…这样学习过社会运行的规律，深入了解过人类的处境，就可以通过服装设计来更好地服务于这个世界…"女儿说一生对这个想法大赞。因为他的影响，女儿从小就渴望她的创作不是为美术馆而做，而应该让大家拥有，发表在生活中。也因为如此，她在伦敦选修的硕士专业是"艺术创意产业"寻找存在社会中，可以被使用和更广泛传播的艺术。

记得有次一生来找我，临走时，从挂衣架上拿着他进来时穿的衣服对我说"好像我的衣服更适合你"。我穿上刚好合身！而我是那样瘦高…他很东方的含蓄方式让这份礼物令我有意外的温馨和收获。几乎每次见面，谈着谈着，他又送我们衣服…让我仿佛"兰亭论艺，醉意微熏"。虽然一生不仅是日本和东方的，更是世界的。但

他作品中体现的情感交流和方法论,常提醒我们东方的美和力量所在。包括易经中最重要的"易",也就是"变化",一生的作品赋予人们丰富自由的穿法和搭配。而一元复始,强调回归本真和原初的哲理,在他那里即是"一块布,一卷纸,拥天下"。东方的自然观在一生的作品里展现了谦和的自我与周遭环境的融合。对比西方更强调人体的线条和形状的美学,一生是写意的,衣服和人体处于若即若离的关系,无形而不散。

大量时候我们会困惑,东方哲学那么奇妙,但要转化为实在的创作时却那样无力,结果经常是说教般的自我声张,或是精神上的自我安慰。三宅恰恰不这样,他是实在和自足的。东方文化里人与自然的哲学不仅是设计理念或美学态度,而且是建立在工艺魅力,也就是手工的"活"上。从布料的选择,剪裁的彻底追究开始,进而到市场推广和人们穿着,参与的贯彻执行。一生世界里的东方,是用有说服力的方法和方法论来表现。这里面确实包括了日本的美学和传统工艺,但这些都随着一生的强大创造力而消化,而腾飞。

"东方的认识和思考世界的方法论,能否催生出表现世界的方法论? 始终在于创作者的重新创造和实践。"这就是一生给予我们的启示。尽管一生和我一起时,从不会去这样说话…

## 写意的な衣服と情感

蔡國強　美術家

　私はこれまで各分野のデザイナーとコラボレーションをしてきたが、それらの多くはどちらかというと相手に合わせた「装飾」的なものだった。たとえば、人がデザインした建築の壁に絵をかけたり、空いたスペースにパブリックアートを設置したり……といった具合に。私の印象では、二人のアーティスト、あるいはアーティストとデザイナーとでは、コラボレーションはとてもむずかしい。建築家ザハ・ハディドとのコラボレーション《ウォッカでザハを愛撫する（Caressing Zaha with Vodka）》（The Snow Show、フィンランド、2004年）では、はじめはうまくいっていたのに、最後に彼女の気が変わり、私が開幕式で、彼女の氷の建築の表面に数トンのウォッカを垂らして火をつけたのを快く思わなかった……。だが、三宅一生さんとのこれまでのコラボレーションは、はじめからおわりまで楽しいものだった。

　一生さんは、自由奔放にやらせてくれた。最初は、漢方薬を入れた服をつくり、着る人の心や体を健やかにしたい、さらには着る人の運気を風水でアップさせたいとも構想した。だが、洗えるかどうかなどの服としての現実に直面せざるをえず、結局、いつも通り火薬を使うことにした。火薬にももちろん問題がある。布地の化学繊維は非常に燃えやすいため、表面に火薬を置いて爆発させても燃えつきないように知恵をしぼった。試行錯誤の結果、いっそのこと焼け焦げた穴をつくろうということになり、それがかえって思いがけないコラボレーション効果を生んだ。そのかたちを布地にプリントした際には、小さな焦げ目まで再現した。こうしてできた作品が、美術館で展示されるのではなく、路上やパーティー会場で人に着られているのを見ると、パフォーマンスアートのようで、言い表せないほど興奮する！

　一生さんの友情は、私の人生にとって大きな意義をもつ。長女の文悠（ウェンヨウ）は、最近出版した著書『When You Make No Art（原題：可不可以不芸術）』の中で、一生さんから受けた影響についてふれている。7、8歳のころ、チェルシーのタウンハウスのロフトで開催された、一生さんのファッション・ショウに行った。一見普通のショウだが、各種メディア、ファンやサポーターをひきつける力があり、独特の雰囲気を感じたという。「ニューヨーク・ファッションウィークなのに、ブライアント・パークやリンカーン・センターできらびやかなショウをしない。——私にはとても不思議だった。—— ニューヨークの魅力を初めて知った。」

　こうしたことがきっかけで、長女はファッション・デザイナーになりたいと思うようになった。「内なる美の声にしたがい、それを世界とわかちあいたい。私がデザインしたい衣服は、普段身につけるという用途を満たすだけでなく、立体感があって、コンセプトを表現できるようなものだ。……三宅さんはファッション界にまいた種が芽吹いたことを知ってとても喜んだ。……両親と食事をする時、私に会うと楽しそうで、よくプレゼントをくださっ

た。私は体にフィットする毛糸のベストに、赤いマフラーと帽子で学校へ行った。みんな「ISSEY MIYAKE」のブランドだった……」。その後、こう考えはじめた。「自分は将来、ファッション・スクールへ行くよりも、哲学や社会学を学ぶべきなのかもしれない。……社会のしくみを学んで、人間がおかれた状況をより深く理解できれば、衣服デザインを通じて、世の中の役に立つことができる」。一生さんはこの考えに大賛成してくれたという。一生さんに感化された長女は子供のころから、美術館のための作品はつくりたくない、人々の生活の中で共有されたいという希望をもっていた。そこで、ロンドンでクリエイティヴ＆文化起業研究所（Institute for Creative and Cultural Entrepreneurship）の修士課程に入り、人の手に広く渡っていくようなアートについて探ることにした。

　ある時、訪ねてきてくれた一生さんが帰り際、自分のコートをフックからはずしつつ「蔡さんの方が似合いそうだ」といって差し出した。着てみると、私はやせてのっぽなのに、なぜかぴったりだった。一生さんは東洋式の含蓄のあるやりかたで、思いがけない温かい贈り物をしてくれたのだ。ほぼ毎回、会って話しこんでいるうちに、いつのまにか服を受けとっている。何だかまるで、気の合う仲間と詩作をしようと集まったのに、いつのまにかほろ酔い気分になっている、蘭亭での曲水の宴のようだ。

　一生さんは日本、東洋のみならず、「世界の」といった方がふさわしい。ただ、作品の情感や方法論は、東洋の美と力のありかをいつも気づかせてくれる。その中には『易経』が説く重要な思想である「易」、つまり「変化」も含まれ、一生さんの衣服は自由な着方やコーディネートが可能だ。あらゆるものを刷新し、本質への回帰を説き、一枚の布、一枚の紙で宇宙を生む。東洋の自然観は、一生さんの作品において、謙虚な自我と周囲の環境との融合としてあらわれる。西洋が人体の線やフォルムの美を強調するのに対し、写意的で、衣服と人体とがつかず離れずの関係をたもち、かたちがないようでしかも一体感がある。

　いつもとまどうのは、東洋の哲学はあれほど神妙なのに、実体をもたせると無力になってしまうことで、往々にして説教くさい主張か、精神的な自己満足におちいる。だが、一生さんは決してそうではない。しっかりとそこに実在し、自足している。東洋における人と自然とのかかわりの哲学が、単にデザイン理念や美学としてではなく、ものづくりの魅力、つまり手仕事に生かされている。布地の選択、カッティングの徹底的な追究にはじまり、製品化し、着る人に加わってもらうまでを一貫しておこなう。一生さんの東洋は、説得力のある方法と方法論で表現される。そこには確かに日本の美や伝統工芸が含まれているが、一生さんの豊かな創造力がそれを消化し、また昇華していく。

　「東洋の考え方と世界観によって、世界そのものを表現する方法論を生み出すことは可能か。それはアーティストの絶え間ない創造と実践にかかっている。」これは一生さんが与えてくれた啓示である。一緒にいる時には、こんな話はしたことがないのだが……。

# FREEHAND CLOTHING AND AFFECTION

**Cai Guo-Qiang**   Artist

I have collaborated with many designers, typically in a "decorative" vein, creating pieces of work for specific sites – a painting to hang on a wall, or public art to fill the empty space in an architectural project. My impression has been that collaboration between artists, or artists and designers, is extremely difficult. Zaha Hadid and I got off to a good start while working on CARESSING ZAHA WITH VODKA (The Snow Show, Finland, 2004), but by the end she had developed certain reservations about working with me – a little unhappy about the fact that I set her ice-architecture on fire with a few tons of vodka, melting it to the ground at the opening ceremony⋯ Looking back at my collaboration with Issey Miyake, it was a joy from start to finish.

Issey gave me total freedom straight out of the gate. For a while I thought of creating "clothing with herbs" that would boost the physical and psychological health of the wearer. Then I talked a lot about *feng shui* clothing to bring the wearer good fortune. In the end my efforts were stymied by practical limitations: for example, clothing must be able to survive being washed. Thus I returned to my old standby, gunpowder. Naturally gunpowder presents problems of its own, since clothing fibers tend to burn easily. I racked my brain for a means to explode the garments without burning away the fabric. The burned holes had turned out to be nearly unavoidable, but it in turn led to an extraordinary breakthrough – we even printed patterns of scorched holes on printed fabrics. Every time I see my artworks—the exploded Issey Miyake garments—not in a museum but worn on the street or at a party, I feel as if I am witnessing art in motion. These "spontaneous works of performance art" bring me an inexplicable sense of excitement!

My friendship with Issey has had an enormous impact on my life. Even my daughter Wen-You discusses Issey's influence in her recent book *When You Make No Art*. At the age of 7 or 8, Wen-You attended one of Issey's shows at a second-story loft in Chelsea. The venue looked nothing special, but my daughter observed that Issey's unique aura had the power to draw all manner of adoring fans, supporters and media. "He chose not to put on an extravagant show at Bryant Park or Lincoln Center for New York Fashion Week... It was unfathomable to me... and helped me to appreciate New York's charm."

This event served as my daughter's inspiration to become a fashion designer, "...to listen attentively to the voice of beauty within, and share it with the world. I want to design clothes that do more than satisfying the needs of daily life. I want them to be sculptural. I want them to express my point of view... Miyake was delighted to hear that he had inspired a small seedling to take root in the world of fashion... He was always happy to see me when dining with my parents and frequently brought me gifts. I often wore a superbly fitted sweater-vest, and a red hat and scarf to school, all of them from Miyake's label." Later, "I began to think that I should study philosophy or sociology instead of going to fashion school... If I could learn the rules by which society functioned, and gain a deeper understanding of our current predicament, then I could use the medium of fashion design to better the world." My daughter told me that Issey enthusiastically supported this idea. Because of Issey's influence, my daughter's interest in creating art was never directed toward museums. She wanted to release her work into the world, for everyone to share. When she left to pursue her Masters degree in London, she chose a program in Creative & Cultural Entrepreneurship, hoping to understand how art can be more broadly transmitted and applied within our society.

Once, as Issey was leaving my home, he took his coat from the coat rack and said, "I think this coat you better than it does me." I put on the coat and found it fit perfectly! But think about my unusually long and lanky frame⋯ This was Issey's indirect and thoroughly Eastern way of giving me a gift, and I felt deeply touched by this unexpected gift and his warm gesture. Nearly every time we see each other, somewhere along our conversation, he would find a way of giving me more clothes. These experiences make me feel as if I were the ancient Chinese literati who met his like-minded friends at the "Orchid Pavilion gathering" to discuss art over the pleasantly lingering headiness brought on by wine.

Issey is not just Japanese, or Asian—he belongs more to the world, the methodology and interflow of feeling found in his work reminds us of the existence of a distinctively Eastern beauty and power. Recall that the *Yi Ching* is the book of *changes* — Issey's clothing has always been about creating a multitude of options for wearing and matching. He also embodies an Eastern philosophy "with the beginning of each new cycle, all is renewed", which emphasizes a return to our original nature, to universal principles. Within a piece of fabric and a piece of paper, he finds the entire world. The Eastern view of nature manifests in Issey's works as an unassuming modesty, the merging of the individual into the environment. In contrast, the Western fashion designers usually emphasize the contours of human bodies and the aesthetics of form. Issey's work is freehand: the garment and the wearer merge yet remain distinct. Defying form, his works are nonetheless coherent.

Often times we wonder why attempts to convert Eastern philosophy into concrete creations have failed on more than one occasion, devolving into a kind of preachy propaganda, or spiritual self-consolation. But never Issey. He is down-to-earth and self-contained. The Eastern philosophy of the relationship between humanity and nature is not merely a concept of design or aesthetics; it is equally found in the allure of technical manufacture, and in the lifeblood of handicrafts. It begins with the selection of fabrics and the fastidiousness of the cut, and carries through into real-world operations, from marketing to end-consumer participation and use. Issey's concept of the East is best expressed through his persuasive methods and methodology. Japanese aesthetics and traditional craftsmanship played a part in Issey's achievements, but it took Issey's considerable creative talent to assimilate these elements, and send them soaring into the world.

Can an Eastern methodology of understanding and reflecting upon the world induce a methodology of representing the world? The answer always lies in the artists' ability to create as well as in the latter's artistic practices. This is a lesson Issey leaves us with, but of course, while together, he would never have spoken in this way⋯

# ホップ・ステップ・三宅一生

**森山明子** デザイン・ジャーナリスト、武蔵野美術大学教授

　三宅一生はデザインの匿名性を身上とする。展覧会の題名がそれを端的に表している。本展は「デザインの仕事」、そしてパリ、ニューヨークの巡回展に新企画を加えて東京都現代美術館で開催された「Making Things」（2000年）——仕事とものづくりなのである。スタジオの活動と全スタッフの声をまとめた書籍『一生たち[※1]』でも、テキストの特別扱いを望んだ形跡はない。そうした姿勢は今に至るまで変わることがないためか、三宅自身の全貌はベールに包まれている感がある。

　私にとって、〈ホップ・ステップ・ジャンプ〉の"ジャンプする者"こそが三宅一生であって、ここでは、いくつかのエピソードをまじえて、"アスリート"としてのデザイナーの人となりと心情の一端に触れてみたい。

　あまり知られていないことだが、三宅はリトアニア選手団がオリンピックで着る公式ユニフォーム（1992年）を皮切りとして各国ごとの選手団向けに同じ提案をしており、今回その全容が明らかにされる。縫製してからプリーツ加工することで「トースターからポンとパンが上がってくるようだ」と新製法の完成を喜んだプリーツを舞台で最初に着たのはウィリアム・フォーサイス＆フランクフルト・バレエ団だが、それが「ジャンピング」するこころ躍る展示もあった。さらに、2013年夏の国立代々木競技場第二体育館では、新体操で国内連覇する青森の男子チームによる一夜限りのパフォーマンス「青森大学男子新体操部」を企画し、選手たちは三宅がデザインしたウエアを身にまとって躍動した。

　身体の自由に寄り添うデザインは、アスリートとダンサーにおいて究極の輝きをみせるのである。

　カール・ルイスが4度のオリンピックでメダル10個を獲得していたころ、三宅がポートレートとしていた操上和美撮影のモノクロの写真には、このアスリートを思わせる精悍（せいかん）さがあった。陸上競技で日本選手が初の金メダルを手にしたのは1928年アムステルダム大会における織田幹雄だが、それ以来の三段跳オリンピック三連覇は世界を驚嘆させて、「跳躍日本」と呼ばれることとなった。優勝三度目のベルリン大会から2年後の1938年、三宅一生は広島で誕生している。

　身体に向きあう服づくりは、生きた植物を相手とするいけ花に通じるのだろうか。前衛いけ花作家として知られる中川幸夫の作品から、三宅が「これ2点」と所望したのが、代表作の「花坊主」とその直前の「ひらけない拳」だったことに虚を衝かれたことがある。「ひらけない拳」は馬蹄形にたわめたゴムチューブの両端に仏手柑（ぶっしゅかん）がのぞくもので、幼くして罹った脊椎カリエスのために背骨が曲がって短躯だった中川幸夫の自画像とおぼしい（初期の作品に「被爆者の眼」がある）。身体と服の関係を探求した三宅の実作としては、綿ジャージーにプリントした「タトゥ」が印象深い。事務所開設翌年の1971年、三宅自身がモデルを買ってでて発表したこの作品[※2]は、亡くなったロックミュージックの勇者、ジミ・ヘンドリックスとジャニス・ジョプリンに捧げた。負の歴史もある

刺青だが、その文様は本来、施された人を守護するものなのだ。いけ花と刺青。三宅は日本のかたちの伝統に対して偏見をもつことがない。

*

「大量のゴミを生産するという意味で、デザイナーの仕事の半分は罪悪だと思うくらいです」とはデザイナー・柳宗理の発言である。三宅がみずからの仕事を「本当にアイディアと呼べるものは少ないです」と述べたのち、話題は製品の計画的陳腐化におよび、デザインのゴミ談義が始まった。司会者として日本民藝館でのその対談記事を「アノニマウスデザインに向かって」[※3]としたのは、「匿名のデザインが最高」と二人が笑い合って手を叩かんばかりだったからだ。

ゴミになる服を極力つくらないという志向は三宅の創作で一貫している。

最近の仕事では、再生ポリエステル素材を使った「132 5.」が目覚ましい成果である。再生素材にコンピュータ・サイエンティストの協力によるアルゴリズムを組み合わせる進化形であるため、リサイクリングではなくアップサイクリングと呼ぶものだ。これが三宅にとっての21世紀の素材であり、多彩な陣容のチーム「Reality Lab」（リアリティ・ラボ）開設の意味なのである。

この期に発売して人気沸騰の柔軟で堅牢なバッグシリーズ「BAO BAO」（バオ バオ）は、「PLEATS PLEASE」（プリーツ プリーズ）から生まれた三角形のパーツが連続する「BILBAO」がもととなっている。フランク・ゲーリー設計のグッゲンハイム美術館・ビルバオに敬意を表しつつ、チタン合金の不定形の外壁を一週間に二回、何人かがロッククライミングのようにして拭かざるをえないことに三宅は疑問を呈する。これは柳宗理との先の対談での発言だが、それにしても、ビルバオ開館は1997年10月、柳との対談は翌年4月だから、行動の素早さには驚かされる。好奇心と冷静さが同居するのが、三宅一生という人なのだろう。

*

素材と技術と地場を重視するものづくりにおける三宅の〈ジャンプ〉は、「ISSEY MIYAKE」ブランドを次世代へバトンタッチしたことが契機である。同じ1999年に発表した「A-POC」（エイ・ポック）[※4]はその最初の成果といえ、大胆な製法技術がみる者すべての度肝をぬいて、新世紀を予感させるに十分だった。

パリとニューヨークを助走のフィールドとした三宅の〈ホップ〉に相当するのは、本展で［A］のセクションに並ぶ70年代の作品であり、その思考は毎日デザイン賞受賞記念のショー「三宅一生。一枚の布」（1977年）で代表できそうだ。

〈ステップ〉としては、海外でのコレクション発表とともに、「BODYWORKS」（1983年）、「A-ŪN」（1988年）と記念碑的な展覧会を実現させる。1988年に独自の製法によるプリーツを発表してから3年後、ニット素材によるプリーツが加わり、1993年にはブランド「PLEATS PLEASE」としてマーケット投入で成功を収め、世界的な定番商品となって今日に至っている。同じように、「Plantation」（プランテーション）は男女共用できるさりげない日常着、「ASHA BY MDS」（アシャ バイ エム ディー エス）はインドの素材のよさを現代に生かすべく技法を駆使したもの、長く着られる服を目指してその名も「PERMANENTE」（ペルマネンテ）と、80年代の仕事は流行を追わない理性的なブランドに結実しているのだ。

本展の［C］のセクションでは、これら二つの時期の、発明と呼べそうな開発による独自のスタイルを目にすることができるだろう。「紙衣」にはじまり、「ゴボウ・フリンジ」、韓国モシを素材とするジャケット、「スターバースト」など。三宅の情熱は、素材と製法の革新とともにある。

そうした服を着る人には、三宅の女性観が反映している。市民運動の政治家・市川房枝、エッセイストの白洲正子、ピアニストの内田光子、フォトグラファー・高木由利子、彼女らに連なる自立する世代にも……。服で自分を飾り立てることなく、肩肘はらず、しなやかな女たち。「三宅一生と12人の黒い女たち」（1976年）を思わせるほどに、三宅のかたわらで働く女性スタッフは、仕事場のそこここを、日々生き生きと闊歩している。

＊

オリンピック北京大会の開会式で、映画監督のチャン・イーモウは中国の四大発明である火薬、方位磁針・羅針盤、造紙術、印刷術を、流れるような構成でみせてくれた。人民軍兵士たちが頭上のパーツを高く持ち上げることで三書体の巨大な「和」が出現する活字のシーンが圧巻で、そのさまは「デザイン立国宣言」のようだった。

三宅一生デザイン文化財団と21_21 DESIGN SIGHT、「国立デザイン美術館をつくる会」における三宅の活動は、チャン・イーモウの演出に似て、"デザインの国・日本"を取り戻そうとする切実さを感じさせる。イサム・ノグチ、ルーシー・リィー、エットレ・ソットサス、クリストとジャンヌ＝クロード、アーヴィング・ペン、田中一光、倉俣史朗と、三宅が深く交流し、21_21 DESIGN SIGHTで取り上げた人々には、創造のスピリットによって離陸し、困難を乗りこえてデザインに着陸するたしかな軌跡が、歴史となるべく刻まれている。

三宅は言葉でも跳躍する。私が好きな「HaaT」「PLEATS PLEASE」「A-POC」、照明器具「陰翳 IN-EI」のメンドリやモグラやタツノオトシゴといったネーミングは、発想の種、生産の現場、使われる情景を思い描いて、瞬時に生まれただろう。そんな場面に遭遇したこともある。

そう、デザイナー・三宅一生は三段跳のジャンパー、アスリートでもあるのだ。

※1 『一生たち』旺文社、1985年
※2 雑誌「アミカ」1971年5月号、pp.113-114。同写真は、書籍『三宅一生の発想と展開――EAST Meets WEST』(1978年)、pp.18-19にも掲載されている。
※3 『approach』1998年夏号、竹中工務店
※4 「A-POC キング＆クイーン」が1998年10月のISSEY MIYAKE 1999年春夏パリコレクションで発表され、翌年、2000年春夏より A-POC がブランドとなることが発表された。

# HOP-STEP-JUMPING ISSEY MIYAKE

**Akiko Moriyama**  Design Journalist, Professor at Musashino Art University

Issey Miyake prizes the anonymity of design. The very titles of his exhibitions are a clear indication of this fact. This exhibition is called simply *MIYAKE ISSEY EXHIBITION: The Work of Miyake Issey.* The 2000 show at the Museum of Contemporary Art Tokyo (an expanded edition of a show that had also been in Paris and New York), was also titled simply, *Making Things.* The ISSEY MIYAKE & MIYAKE DESIGN STUDIO 1970–1985[*1], provided an overview of the studio's activities and brought together the voices of all the staff, without any special treatment beyond the work itself. And thus the focus has remained – on the work, on the making of things. That this stance remains unchanged may account somewhat for why Miyake himself seems to be cloaked in mystery.

Issey Miyake, I feel, is like an athlete in the triple jump, which is also known as the hop-step-jump. Here, I want to look at a few anecdotes that might illuminate the personality and mind of this designer-as-athlete.

It is not well known that since 1992, when Miyake created the official uniforms for the Lithuanian Olympic team, he has continued to propose even more Olympic uniforms for national teams, and this exhibition will represent the first time that the total scope of this part of his work will be unveiled. In the summer of 2013, there was a one-night only performance at the Yoyogi National Stadium, which featured the Aomori University male rhythmic gymnastics team from northern Japan – who are known for their exuberant routines, and who continue their winning streak as Japan's top team – wearing Miyake-designed outfits. The innovative technique of pleating finished garments was, he said with pleasure, "like toast popping up from a toaster", and the first Pleats were worn as costumes by William Forsythe & the Ballet Frankfurt. There have been many happy installations of pleated clothing since then.

In sum, designs that think of the body's freedom shine most brilliantly when they embrace athletes and dancers.

*

When Carl Lewis won his tenth medal at his fourth Olympic games, Miyake chose by chance a black and white photograph by Kazumi Kurigami for his own official portrait, which had an athlete-like virile aura somewhat reminiscent of Lewis. Mikio Oda was the first Japanese Olympic gold medalist in track and field athletics at Amsterdam 1928, and the world was amazed when Japanese triple jumpers triumphed in two further Olympic games, leading to the country becoming known as "leaping Japan". Two years after a Japanese athlete won the third successive gold medal was won at the Berlin Olympic Games, Issey Miyake was born in Hiroshima in 1938.

Does making clothes, an act that deals with the body, resonate with ikebana (flower arrangement), which works with living plants? I was taken aback once when Miyake and chose FLOWERY PRIESTESS and CLENCHED FISTS from out of the oeuvre of the avant-garde ikebana artist, Yukio Nakagawa. The first, from 1973, is considered to be Nakagawa's masterpiece, while its immediate predecessor, CLENCHED FISTS, consists of a horse-shoe-shaped rubber tube with a buddha's-hand-shaped citrus peeking out from both ends, and may be a self-portrait of the artist, whose spine and body were left disabled by childhood spinal tuberculosis (one of his early works is called ANGUISH OF ATOMIC BOMB SURVIVOR). One very impressive work by Miyake in which he particularly explored the relationship between the body and clothing was TATTOO. This was announced in 1971, just one year after he opened his own studio. TATTOO was printed on cotton jersey, and was dedicated to such Rock music heroes as Jimi Hendrix and Janis Joplin. Miyake even volunteered to model it himself. Despite certain negative associations attached to them, tattoos were originally thought to protect the persons wearing them. Flower arrangement and tattoos: Issey Miyake shows himself[*2] to be free from prejudices stemming from traditional Japanese aesthetic and plastic forms.

∗

I was the moderator at an event held at the Japan Folk Crafts Museum, and chose to title an article about a talk between Miyake and the industrial designer Sori Yanagi, The Anonymous Design.[*3] Yanagi said, "In the sense that we generate massive amounts of waste, I even think that half of any designers' work is sinful". Miyake summed up his own work by saying that "there are very few things that could be described as ideas." Following this, the discussion touched upon the planned obsolescence of products and design-as-garbage. In the end, the two were almost applauding each other, laughing as they agreed that "anonymous design is the best".

Miyake has always striven to avoid generating clothes that could become garbage.

One outstanding recent work has been the 132 5. line, which is made out of recycled polyester. This combines recycled materials with an algorithm developed through a collaboration with a computer scientist; the process is referred to as upcycling, rather than recycling. 132 5. is 21st century material as Miyake perceives it, and the reason why the multi-talented Reality Lab was established.

BAO BAO, launched in 2010, features a flexible and durable line of bags that has become wildly popular, and grew out of BILBAO, an off-shoot of the PLEATS PLEASE line that was based on continuous triangular parts. While paying homage to the Guggenheim Museum Bilbao designed by Frank Gehry, Miyake questions the need for workers to clamber up the irregularly shaped, titanium alloy exterior walls once or twice a week in the manner of rock-climbers in order to clean and maintain the building's surfaces. This was a point that he made in the talk with Sori Yanagi, but when one realizes that the museum opened in October 1997, and that the talk with Yanagi was in April of the following year, the speed of his actions is staggering. Curiosity and level-headedness seem to co-exist in Issey Miyake.

∗

Miyake's design "jump"–ever mindful of the importance of materials, technology, and locale–was instigated by the passing of the baton of the ISSEY MIYAKE brand to the next generation. A-POC,[*4] launched in 1999 showed its first achievements the following year with its bold manufacturing technology; this was enough to foreshadow the dawn of the new century.

For Miyake, whose artistic formation took place in Paris and New York, the equivalent to the "Hop" stage is featured in Section A of this exhibition, which brings together his work from the 1970s, and where, in particular, his philosophy can be summed up by the show, *A Piece of Cloth – Issey Miyake in Museum* (1977), which commemorated his winning of the Mainichi Design Award. "Step" would be represented by his international fashion shows, and the milestone exhibitions, *BODYWORKS* (1983) and *A-ŪN* (1988).

PLEATS items, manufactured with a unique method, were first unveiled in 1988, and, with the addition of pleated knit items three years later, they proved successful following the market launch of PLEATS PLEASE brand in 1993. They have, of course, gone on to become a worldwide wardrobe staple. Other clothing lines included Plantation, unassuming everyday wear that can be worn by both men and women; ASHA BY MDS, which utilized techniques that drew out the qualities of materials from India; and PERMANENTE, which, as its name implies, aimed to create clothes that can be worn for many years. Miyake's work during the 1980s resulted in brands that spoke to reason, and were not simply momentary fashion statements.

In Section C of this exhibition, the audience will see distinctively original styles that were born from the inventive developments since 1980's. Beginning with KAMIKO washi paper, GOBO FRINGE, the jacket made with Korean-origin *karamushi* woven fabric, STARBURST, and many more, Miyake's passions have always been engaged with innovations in materials and production techniques.

Those who wore and wear these clothes reflected and reflect Miyake's vision of women. The late politician and citizens-movement activist, Fusae Ichikawa; the late essayist, Masako Shirasu; the pianist Mitsuko Uchida; the photographer, Yuriko Takagi, and the many independent-spirited women that came after them as well. Women who do not adorn themselves with their clothes, who are not rigidly formalistic and who know how to be responsively flexible. Just as in *Issey Miyake and Twelve Black Girls* (1976), the women staff who work with Miyake stride confidently in their work place.

∗

At the fluidly orchestrated opening ceremony of the Beijing Olympic games, the film director Zhang Yimou showed China's four great inventions—gunpowder, the compass, papermaking, and printing. A particularly stunning moment took place during the movable type sequence, when soldiers from the People's Liberation Army raised parts high above their heads to form gigantic variations of the Chinese character for harmony —和—in what seemed to China declaring itself as a country of design.

Miyake's involvement with such organizations as The Miyake Issey Foundation, 21_21 DESIGN SIGHT, and the Society for a Design Museum Japan, is comparable to Zhang Yimou's direction of the Olympic ceremony, and one senses his urgency to reclaim Japan as a country renowned for its design. Isamu Noguchi, Lucie Rie, Ettore Sottsass, Christo and Jeanne-Claude, Irving Penn, Ikko Tanaka, Shiro Kuramata—these were all close friends of Miyake, and have been featured in exhibitions at 21_21 DESIGN SIGHT. Their creativity allowed them to soar high, to overcome difficulties and then come to ground upon the field of design—and the incisive trajectories that they traced are already part of the historic record.

Miyake also takes great, pleasurable leaps in language. I am particularly fond of names such as HaaT, PLEATS PLEASE, A-POC, and the IN-EI lighting fixtures which include names like MENDORI/Hen, MOGURA/Mole, and TATSUNO-OTOSHIGO/Sea-dragon. These many names were probably bestowed instantaneously, combining the idea, their place of creation, and the function all imagined together. I have, in fact, been witness to such creative scenes.

The designer Issey Miyake is truly a triple jumper—a real athlete.

*1　*THE ISSEY MIYAKE & MIYAKE DESIGN STUDIO 1970–1985*, Obunsha Co., Ltd, 1985
*2　Magazine *Amica*, May issue, 1971. pp.113-114, The same photo appeared in the book *EAST Meets WEST*, 1978, pp.18-19
*3　*approach*, 1998 summer issue, Takenaka Corporation.
*4　A-POC KING & QUEEN was announced as a part of ISSEY MIYAKE spring/summer 1999 collection; in 2000 it was announced that A-POC would be launched as a stand-alone brand from spring/summer 2000 season.

# プリーツ

小林康夫　哲学者

　それは、——「価値の転倒」という言葉の真正な意味において——紛れもなく一個の《革命》であった。すでに四半世紀の時間が経過しているのに、その鮮やかさは一向に色褪せることはない。いや、それどころか、《革命》は、いま現在もなお、深化＝進化しながら、ますます激しく続いている。見たことのない《未来》、来るべき《未来》に向かって。

　1988年《プリーツ プリーズ》の前身《製品プリーツ》誕生——このとき三宅一生は、《流行》la mode という《現在》の呪縛にとらわれたファッションのなかに、《未来》へと伸びていく《途》という新しい《様態》le mode を切り拓いた。時代はいわゆるポストモダン状況が一気に顕在化し、歴史が過飽和の状態になって、クリエーションが過去のもののリメーク remake の意匠を競う方向へ流れるなか、かれは、一刀両断、ノスタルジーへの誘惑を断ち切って、——すでに「プリーズ！」と優しく微笑みながら——断固、見たことのない《未来》を手繰り寄せると、宣言したのだった。

　**そう、《プリーツ プリーズ》をまとうあなたは、遠い《未来》をまとっているのでもある。**

　だが、ここで《未来》とはなにか。驚くべきことに、——はっきり言っておかなければならないが——それは、《人々》people であり、かつ《地球》という惑星、つまりこの惑星に住むすべての人々（いや、それ以上にすべての《生命》と言うことすらできるかもしれない）である。すべての《人々》のための服なのだ。これがどのくらい革命的なことであるか。ファッションは、なによりも社会的な差別化のシンボルとして機能していたのだから。もちろん、《美》。だが、同時に、社会のなかの拘束の表現。この拘束を、ファッションのまっただなかで解除し、解放する——それこそ、三宅一生が、活動の最初から挑戦してきたこと。かれは、はじめから《革命家》であったのだ。いったいどんなファッション・デザイナーが、鳶職など市井で働く人々の作業衣に、さまざまな国の民族衣装に、さらには、皮膚を《衣装》に変える刺青までを含めて——それを自分のクリエーションのために「使う」ためではなく——心からの共感をこめて「美しい」という言葉を発しただろうか。かれにとっては、デザインとは、この惑星に住む《人々》common people という絶対的な「共有」の地平を開くことなのだ。

　**だから、《プリーツ プリーズ》をまとうあなたは、なによりも自分が地球という惑星に住む《人々》のひとりであることを、あらためて確認する。**

しかし、言うは易し、この理念をいかにして具体的なプロダクトにおとしこめるか。そのためには、まずなによりも素材が問われなければならないのは言うまでもない。少量しか生産されない稀少な素材を使うことは問題外。地球上のどこにでもある廉価な素材でなければならない。だが、廉価な素材をそのまま使ってしまえば、《未来》という《夢》ははぐくまれない。では、どうするか。この困難の極点において「プリーツ」という言葉が響いたのだったか、わたしは知らない。が、論理的な隘路が、思いがけないシンプルなプロシージャーによって一挙に解決されるのは歴史が示すところ。一枚のポリエステルの布が折りたたまれて熱を加えられると、まるで魔法のように、襞が現れ、襞が波打ち、あまりにも平凡でもあった布が、まったく新しい《質》をはらんで生まれ変わる。襞のひとつひとつが無数の可能性の《時間》をはらんでいるかのように —— それこそ《未来》でなくてなんだろう ——、布は、2.5次元というフラクタルな《質》をあらたに獲得して、晴れやかに伸び、縮む。もはや2次元の形にも3次元の形にも拘束されない。両者の「あいだ」には、絶えず生成し、動き続けるダイナミックな《時間》が流れている。驚くべきことに、ここでは形とは運動なのだ。デザインは、ここでは運動へのはてしない呼びかけなのである。

とすれば、《プリーツ プリーズ》をまとうとき、あなたは、出来上がった形を着るのではない。形は、あなたが動くことで生まれてくる。そう、あなたはダンスをするように誘われているのだ、《もうひとりのあなた》というダンスを動くように、と。

それは、《プリーツ プリーズ》がそれをまとう者の身体に《軽さ》を与え返してくれるということ。一枚の布に包まれているのに、身体は、その分、より軽くなる。より軽快になる。より自由になる。おそらく、人間の使命とは、地上という物質の重さを引き受けて、それをより軽く、より高く、より開かれたものへと変換させることなのかもしれない。そして、人間がそのような変換の運動を行うとき、人間の身体は《光の痕跡》をあとに残すだろう。オーラのように、コロナのように、鮮やかな《色》が空間を流れて行くだろう。《色》と《軽さ》が密かに結びついている。一枚の布に先導されて、そこでは身体の《時間》が、《色》の神秘的な《明るさ》へと変換させられるのだ。

だから、《プリーツ プリーズ》をまとうとき、あなたは、鮮やかな翼を得て、ほんの少しだけなのだが、天使的になるのかもしれないのだ。

※ このときはまだ、織物の布を形にしたあとでプリーツをかけるという方法であった。それが、1991年、編み物ニットの布地を使うようになる。さらに毎シーズンごとに素材も方法も改良され、1993年に現在のブランド《 PLEATS PLEASE (プリーツ プリーズ) ISSEY MIYAKE 》として確立した。ここでは、数年に渡るこの《連続革命》の具体的な詳細には立ち入らず、全体をひとつの《革命》として透視していることをお断りしておく。しかし、このブランド化への最後のジャンプの契機となったのが、世紀の振付家であるウィリアム・フォーサイスのダンスのためのコスチュームのデザインであったことは特筆しておくべきかもしれない。ダンスという全身の《自由》のために、《軽さ》そのものが折りたたまれなければならなかったのだ。

# PLEATS

### Yasuo Kobayashi  Philosopher

Obviously – in the real sense of an overturning of values – it was a **revolution**. A quarter century has passed since then, but it yet remains whole and strong; indeed, this **revolution** continues to evolve, grow deeper, and increase in intensity towards an unseen but inevitable **future**.

In 1988 **PLEATS** made by the garment pleating technique, the precursor of **PLEATS PLEASE ISSEY MIYAKE** was launched.* This was the very moment when Issey Miyake initiated a **brand-new way** that would lead to the **future** in mode, the prevailing world of fashion that had limited itself to being of the **present moment** alone. Historically, we were at a time when the so-called post-modern situation had fast emerged, oversaturating history and creativity and tending only to a competitive remaking of things of the past. In spite of this, Miyake determinedly dismissed the persuasions of nostalgia, and, while smiling nicely to even say "PLEASE", envisioned the yet-unseen **future**, and pulled it close as he declared:

**"You are wearing the clothes of the distant future when you wear PLEATS PLEASE."**

But what **future**? Surely, explicitly, this 'future' denotes both the **people** and their habitat, this planet **Earth**. (Shall we go so far as to include all the **living organism** on Earth?) Clothing for **everyone** then – how revolutionary a concept is that!

We need only remember that fashion has functionally been a symbol of anything but social segregation. Of **beauty**, needless to say. But fashion has also represented social restriction and control. To try and denounce this and do away with it while working in the fashion world – this has been Issey Miyake's challenge since the beginning. He started out as a **revolutionary**. Who, which fashion designer, has dared to work the way he has? From laborer's outfits to various ethnic costumes, and even tattoos that turn one's own skin into a **costume** – who else would have found and declared them beautiful? And to do so with profound sympathy and without any sort of exploitation. The task of design, for Miyake, is to reclaim the common horizon, that of we **commoners**, inhabitants of Planet Earth.

**Thus it goes:**
**"Yes, wearing PLEATS PLESE, you confirm, above all, that you are an inhabitant of Planet Earth."**

It may be easy to say, but really, how can one translate such an idea into a specific product? Obviously, first, one has to deal with the material. Using rare materials produced in small lots is out of question. They have to be reasonably priced and available anywhere in the world. Yet, to use such materials just as they are, and without any flair, what becomes of the **future** we are **dreaming** of ? So – what to do?  I have no idea if it was at such a moment – of being at his wits' end – that Miyake heard the ringing of the word "pleats." But, as history shows, unpredictable, simple procedures sometimes break through the most complicated impasses. A piece of polyester fabric is folded and heated, and – like magic! – pleats appear and move in waves; a simple, flat piece of fabric has been reborn and become something possessing a whole new **quality**, as though each fold contains a **span** of countless possibilities. That's the **future**, isn't it? The fabric acquires the new fractal **quality** of being 2.5–dimensional as it joyously stretches and shrinks. It is no longer controlled by two or three dimensional form. In fact, in–between the two and three, a dynamic **time** flows. Here, form is undeniably movement. Design is the interminable invocation of movement.

**Thus it goes once more:**
**Wearing PLEATS PLEASE, you don't put on a fixed form; forms will be born from your movement. Yes, you are persuaded to dance, to dance another you.**

The truth is that **PLEATS PLEASE** reciprocally gives its wearer a sense of **lightness**. Though the body is covered by a piece of cloth, it feels lighter, more supple and free. Imagine that it is our mission as human beings to first acknowledge the physical weight of things on Earth, and then to convert it to a lighter and more ethereal realm of being. And when we thus convert, what will emanate from the body and remain ever afterwards will be **traces of light**: bright **colors**, auras, coronas of light flowing through space. **Color** and **weight-free**, subtly bonded. **Time**, carried by the body, converted into the mystic **brightness** of color – all of it guided by a piece of cloth.

**Thus, once more:**
**Wearing PLEATS PLEASE, endows you with wings and you become angelic.**

✴ At this point, the dress was sewn first and then the woven fabric was pleated. In 1991 knit materials were introduced. Subsequently, materials and methods underwent a variety of improvement with each season. The current brand – PLEATS PLEASE ISSEY MIYAKE – was established in 1993. This brief text does not delve into the concrete details of subsequent years, but it is true that Miyake's entire effort is a revolution. But it should be noted that what led to the final launching of PLEATS PLEASE as a singular brand was the 1991 commissioning of Miyake to design costumes for dance works by William Forsythe, one of the great choreographers of the century. Lightness itself had to be folded into the clothing in order to allow a dancer's entire body its freedom of movement.

# 「132 5. ISSEY MIYAKE」の数秘術

リー・エデルコート　トレンド・フォーキャスター

『数秘術では数と、それぞれの数がどんな性格や魂を反映しているか、それを研究する。並んだ数字を合わせた数から概念を生み出して、人生における目的を明らかにしたり、才覚を発揮したりすることもできる。』

　数字の1は一枚の布をさし、3は布の三次元の形を呼び起こす。2は当初は平らな二次元の素材を示し、一字分の空きスペースで分かれている数字の5は折りたたまれたかたちと服を着ることの間の時間をさすが、これは、着る人が衣服に生命を吹き込むまさしく詩のような瞬間だ。最後のドットは使命の達成を表す。

　もっとも若い（最近の）三宅の冒険的事業（2010年以来の）では、その強烈なブランド名がいくつかの数字で表現されており、その内容は上記の通りだ。とはいえ、私がすぐさま見てとったことはこうだ。このコレクションや創作は、また別の数字に関する知識をもって分析も理解もできる。目の前にある命題をより精神性の高い読み方をすれば、それは可能ではないかと思う。ということで、私は調査を始め、まとめて書くことにした。その考え方（コンセプト）の背後に隠されたいくつもの力を理解すべく。

　数字の1は普遍的な統一の象徴で、直立する1という数字に凝縮されたエネルギー、つまり、もうひとつのそそり立つものであり、感嘆の頂点を表象する！掛け算のような増加する性質をもつシステムだと解読することもできるし、幾重にも折り畳める単一の総体を表すともいえる。広げると、摩訶不思議で希有な何枚もの抽象的で平らな布に変貌する「132 5. ISSEY MIYAKE」は、まさにそうではないか。ある数に1を掛けても、解は最初の数と変わらない。ことほどさように、このシリーズの服もそういう尊厳と自立を体現している——1であることの力は他のものたちに影響を及ぼさない……そうだとすれば、なんと美しい存在のあり方だろう。

　我々の身体に寄り添うとき、これらの服はたった一枚で唯一（ワン・アンド・オンリー）なのだと思うと、これまた美しいことだと感嘆する。つまり、1である、「ひとつ」であるということは、それ自体のみで自身が構成されている、運命が成立している、数学的な衣服になりきっている、ということになる。三宅はこの掛け算に興味をもち、何度も何度も革新に取り組んできた。折り目ひとつから如何にしてもっと多くのプリーツ（襞）をつくり出すか、如何にすれば構成を符号化して概念を表すことができるか、全体がひとつのチームとして一緒に作業しているなかで、1であることの力を如何にして抽出するか？　三宅はプリーツや折りを取りまとめるごとく、人々を取りまとめる。「132 5.」のために Reality Lab（リアリティ・ラボ）を結成するにあたり、ひとつの声で3までを語りきるスーパー・チームを選定した。

　1、2、3、1、2、3……リズムを定め、タイミングを決め、集合体としての前進、世代を超えた作業、繊維をつくり出すことからコンピュータ・プログラムを書くことまでさまざまな技術の配合——それらの美点を示すひとつの声を見つけ出す。現在のなかでデザインをしながら、このチームは過去、現在、未来の統一を何よりも大切にし、未来を探り、永年の由緒ある日本のものづくりの原則を基盤にして、現代の再利用された布と統合して重層的な作業

をする。結局、3という記号は普遍的であるが故に、あらゆる時代からも文明からも採集できる。けだし、3は符号の証しであり、すべての物や問題が相互に補完し合っている事実を解く鍵でもある。

　核心をなすこの3という数字の優れた特質を考えると、それは一連のプロトタイプ（原型）の結晶化であると見ることができる。また、こうもいえないだろうか。数の用法とその幾何学的な相関関係に象徴される精密で普遍的な法則に従い、秘教的ともいえるほどの方法で具現化されているにちがいない創造的思想——それが、このたびの三宅たちの作業のおかげで物として存在をあらわにした、と。このコレクションが表現することには明らかに次の要素が含まれている。それは根源にあるもので、これまでとは別の隠れた精神的な要素（ルーツ）であり、実は、コレクションをつくった当人たちでさえそのルーツを理解しきっているわけでもないと見てもよい。だが、コレクター諸氏や購買者たちとなると、何らかの作用のおかげだろう、このコレクションの精神的ルーツを身をもって体験したり意識したりすることが可能なようだ。その力、人々はそれを感じることができる。肉体、魂、それに精神（スピリット）——こういったものが、この新しいいくつかの方法に関係しているようだ。従来の服づくりや裁断の常套手段を排して、衣服は内面の聖域であることを標榜し、人体と布が合体する方法を提示する……こういった企図が新たなる服の着方をもたらした。

　陰と陽というふたつの力の作用が功を奏し、足元のしっかりした三宅の宇宙を支え、完璧な均衡を維持していることはいうまでもない。「132 5.」のうち、2という数字は二元論や二重性を代表する。「組織という、苦痛をともなうが必要なものに応えると同時に、取捨選択も行なう」、こういった行動形態も辞さない。この説得力が数字の2には込められている。考えてみれば、人は選ぶことを先送りして未決定の状態を長引かせるものだが、2という数は我々をそこから引きずり出し、同じような精神をもつメンバーが集まる工房（アトリエ）をひとつにまとめる役割を果たす。つまり、2に宿っているのは、考えを実際の物にする作用である。ある意味では、デザインするあらゆる物に必ず疑問を投げかける2という数は、創造の過程そのものを象徴している。

　よいものごとは対（つい）であらわれるものだ。だから、2の素晴らしいところはこうではないだろうか——支え合う関係（パートナーシップ）や縁戚関係などのごく親しい関係を象徴していて、白と黒、男と女、旧と新といった対の均衡を保っている。カップルをつくり、パートナーシップを支え、サンドウィッチを出現させ……と、例はまだあるが、こうしたことを成し遂げてきた素晴らしい記号が2という数字だ。2という数がなかったら、正も否も存在できないだろう。斬新な展望や刷新をもたらす新たな可能性をつねに気付かせてくれる——それには、均衡という名の力が必要ではないだろうか。太陽と月——「132 5.」コレクションのなかでもメタル・フォイル・プリンティングは、全体を際立たせる活躍をしている。明と暗——このコレクションでは、古来の染色方法が試練にさらされている。昼と夜——出かけていって踊りましょう——こういう誘いが、ここでは概念として打ち出されている。生と死——ここに見られるデザインは長持ちする、蒐集に耐える、つまり、未来まで生きのびる「後世に残すべきもの」となることを意図して創られている。再生や再創造という三宅にとって非常に大切な思想をこれらのコレクションははらんでいる、そういうことだ。

　ココ・シャネルはそれなりにわかっていた——数字の5は完璧に近かった！ 一桁の数のすべてのなかでも、5は

もっともダイナミックにしてエネルギーがある——予測不可能で、つねに動いていて、いつだって変化したがっている。だから、5は多才で、利口で、即座に変化をもたらさなければならない。5にまつわるすべてのものごとは心も魂も独立しており、決まり事（ルーティン）や繰り返し（レペティション）の逆だ。なんといおうと、変化こそ必須であり、完成品を云々する以上に革新的な工程を求める。成功したからといってけっして充足しない一生は5を体現しているといえようか。彼はこれまでも、たえず好奇心をさらに一歩前に進めることを続けてきたし、休みなく無理難題を突きつけてチームを困らせてきた。彼の人生を物語として見ると、創造的な出会いに満ちた景色が見える——芸術家、デザイナー、振付師、写真家など、彼自身とは異なるあらゆる分野や学問に携わる面々が、もっと知りたいという彼の飢餓感に応えて、栄養分を提供してきた。匠（たくみ）と呼びたくなるような存在となった彼は今、この時代に先行して科学に関心を寄せている。その領域から触発を受けて、ものを見る力を強化しようというのか、電子工学オタクや布地の専門家の話に熱心に耳を傾けては、数学的な手掛かりを着るものとして楽しむ抽象の世界に活かそうとしている。

　ピタゴラスから三宅一生まで数学的思考の力が発揮された結果、21世紀最初の現代ファッションの宣言が創造されることとなった。

　数字をゼロから見ていくと、いちばん早く来る奇数にして偶数を内含しているのは3である。始めの1から3までの数には、ほかのすべての数の性質がもりこまれている——そう考える根拠ともなる見方ではないだろうか。1たることと2であることが、3という数において一緒になっている。ほかのすべての数はこの合体から発し、また、三角形という形態からすべての形が派生している……固定された形態のもっとも単純なものは立方体で、それを構成するには長さ、幅、高さが必要だ。3（コレクション）が立方体の象徴だとすれば、2（チーム）は正方形（スクウェア・広場）であり、1（精神）はチームの統一（ユニティ）を表す。いっぽう、5（デザイナー）はすべての論理から自由で、革新に没頭している……。

　現代のシャーマンともいえるだろうか、一生はこれらすべての象徴的な形態の交叉地点に立って、次は何処へ行こうか、どんな挑戦を受けて立とうか、崇敬され奉られるようになった自身のスタジオには、どんな刺激をぶち込むべきか、などと考えにふけっている。さて、今後はどの数を身の内に抱（いだ）くつもりなのだろうか？

　推量するに、ゼロというのもあり得るのではないだろうか。

パリ、2015年11月

Lidewij Edelkoort

Lidewij Edelkoort

# THE NUMEROLOGY OF 132 5. ISSEY MIYAKE

**Lidewij Edelkoort**  Trend Forecaster

*Numerology is the study of numbers and the way in which they reflect character and soul. The sum of these numbers is able to connect to create a concept, forming a vision about purpose in life and discovering where talent is located.*

The number 1 refers to a single piece of cloth, and the number 3 evokes its three-dimensional shape. The number 2 designates the initially flat, two-dimensional material, and the number 5, separated by a single space, refers to the time between folding forms and putting on the clothes, that poetic moment when the wearer brings a garment to life. The dot stands for mission accomplished.

This is how the latest Miyake venture (since 2010) explains its striking brand name in numbers. Nevertheless, I realized at once that one could also analyse and understand these collections and creations by using another knowledge of numbers, giving another more spiritual reading to the matter at hand. So this is what I sat out to research and write, trying to understand the hidden powers behind this concept.

The number one is seen as the universal symbol of unity and represents the compacted energy of the erect number one, the phallus, the tower and the exclamation point! It can be understood as a system with a multiplicative identity, it represents a single entity that can fold into manifold, just as the folded flat pieces of cloth in 132 5. ISSEY MIYAKE unfold in multiples of strange and unusual abstract clothes. It stands for integrity since any number multiplied by one is itself; how beautiful it is to understand that the power of oneness doesn't influence others…

How beautiful to realise that these clothes are one and only when they espouse our own body. As a result, one is its own composition, its own destiny, its own mathematical dress. This multiplication is what interests Miyake and what has steered him to innovation time and time again; how to construct more pleats from one fold, how to code construction to conceptualise, how to derive power from oneness in working together as a holistic team. Miyake gathers people like he gathers pleats and folds. In formulating the Reality Lab for 132 5., he has selected a super team that counts to three in one voice.

One, two, three, one, two, three… setting a rhythm, deciding on timing, finding one voice to express the virtues of joint progress, working amongst generations, blending skills between crafting textiles and writing computer programs. The team worships the unity of past, present and future as it designs in the present, researches the future and dwells on the principles of age-old Japanese craft that is integrated into and layered on the contemporary recycled cloth; after all, the symbol three is universal and can be sampled through all times and all civilisations. As such, it can be seen as a sign of integrity and the key to the interdependence of all matter.

The positive properties of this central number three can be considered as the crystallization of prototype sequels, embodiments of creative ideas that seem to materialize in an almost esoteric fashion by obeying precise, universal laws which the numerical codes and their geometrical correlations symbolize. The expression of this collection clearly has other, hidden spiritual roots that even its makers don't seem to comprehend; yet its collectors and customers somehow can experience. People can feel the power. Body, soul and spirit are concerned with these new ways of dressing that break with the traditional way of making clothes and cutting patterns, pointing at dress as an inner sanctuary, a way to become one with cloth.

The forces of Yin and Yang are definitely at work and keep the Miyake universe on their toes, poised in perfect balance. The number two represents duality, beckoning us to make choices as well as answering an aching need for organisation. It is therefore in two that resides the realisation of ideas as two urges us out of indecision and forces the atelier to unite the team members that have similar spirits. In a way, the number two symbolises the creative process with its constant calling into question everything that is designed.

Good things come in pairs, therefore the beauty of two is symbolic of partnership and kinship, a number that strikes a balance between black and white, between man and woman, between the old and the new. A beautiful sign that has formed couples, governed partnerships, created sandwiches and more. Without the number two, the positive and negative couldn't exist; the power of equilibrium is needed as a constant reminder of new possibilities from which new visions and innovations are born. Sun and moon; the collection gets highlighted by metal foil printing. Light and dark; the collection tests ancient dying processes. Day and night; the collection is conceptualised to go out and dance. Life and death; these designs are meant to be sustainable and collectable, to become hand-me-down items that will survive into the future. These collections embrace the ideas of re-generation and re-creation, which are so important to Issey.

Coco Chanel already knew that much, the number five is close to perfection! The most dynamic and energetic of all single digit numbers; it is unpredictable, always in motion and constantly in need of change, therefore the five has to be versatile and ingenious, able to improvise change. All things five are independent in mind and soul, averse to routine and repetition; change is an absolute necessity and requests innovative processes rather than a finished product. Never fully satisfied by his success, Issey is the embodiment of five since he has constantly taken his curiosity one step further, driving his teams mad with his constant and challenging requests. The story of his life has been landscaped by creative encounters with people from all other disciplines such as artists, designers, choreographers and photographers, feeding his thirst for knowledge. Ahead of his time, the master has now turned to science as a domain from which to derive inspiration and insight, listening to computer nerds and textile experts, transforming mathematical material into wearable pieces of abstraction.

From Pythagoras to Miyake, the power of mathematical thinking has created the first contemporary fashion statement of the 21st century.

The number three is the first uneven number that contains an even one, since in the first three numbers all others are synthesized. From the union of oneness and duality proceed all other numbers, and from its triangular form all figures derive⋯ Length, breadth and height are necessary to form a cube, the simplest form of a solid figure. As three (the collection) is the symbol of the cube, two (the team) is the symbol of the square and one (the spirit) represents unity, while five (the designer) escapes all logic in a quest for innovation⋯

Like a contemporary shaman, Issey stands at the crossroads of all these symbolic figures, figuring out where to go next, what challenge to accept, which bone to throw at his venerated studio. What number to embrace next?

My guess is it could be zero.

Paris, November 2015

Lidewij Edelkoort

## 寄稿者プロフィール

リー・エデルコート
トレンド・フォーキャスター

オランダ、ワーゲニンゲン生まれ。アーネム美術大学でファッションデザインを学ぶ。1986年、パリにトレンドユニオン創立。国際的に活動するキュレーター、出版者、人道主義者、また教育者である。2003年にはアメリカ『タイム』誌で、ファッション界で最も影響力のある25人のうちのひとりに選ばれた。2015年にはニューヨーク、パーソンズ美術大学のハイブリッドデザイン学の代表に就任。

ディディエ・グランバック
フランス国立近代美術館友の会会長
フランス・プレタポルテ連盟名誉会長
オートクチュール組合名誉会長

フランス・プレタポルテ連盟とオートクチュール組合の会長を1988年より務め、2014年9月には名誉会長に就任。2014年よりポンピドゥー・センター国立近代美術館友の会会長。ティエリー・ミュグレー会長、C.メンデス グループ最高経営責任者、ピエール・ベルジェ氏と共にイヴ・サンローラン・リヴ・ゴーシュを設立、経営に携わり、イヴ・サンローラン・リヴ・ゴーシュ USA とイヴ・サンローラン・リヴ・ゴーシュ会長を歴任。クレアトゥール＆アンドゥストゥリエルとパリ・コレクションズの創立者であり最高責任者を務めた。2社はC.メンデスの系列会社であり、アメリカで初めて設立されたフランス・ファッションのエージェンシーであった。1985年にフランスモード学院で教鞭をとり、その後学部長に就任。著書『モードの物語』。

小林康夫
哲学者

1974年東京大学教養学部卒業後、同大学院人文科学研究科比較文学比較文化専攻修士修了。パリ第10大学テクスト記号学科博士号取得。東京大学教授を経て2015年より同学名誉教授、青山学院大学院総合文化政策学研究科特任教授。専門は、表象文化論、現代哲学。2002年フランス政府・学術教育功労賞シュヴァリエ受賞。著書は『表象の光学』（03年）、『知のオデュッセイア』（09年）、『光のオペラ』（13年）。ほか、編著、翻訳多数。

ツァイ・グオチャン
蔡國強
美術家

中国福建省生まれ。上海戯劇学院で舞台美術を学んだ後、筑波大学で学ぶ。日本滞在中に、大型のインスタレーションの制作に取り組みながら実験を重ねて火薬の爆発による絵画を発展させ、一躍、内外の注目を浴びるようになる。1999年、ヴェネチア・ビエンナーレ「国際金獅子賞」また、2008年の北京オリンピック・パラリンピック開会式・閉会式で視覚特効芸術監督を務める。2012年に高松宮殿下記念世界文化賞の5部門の中から絵画部門で受賞した。

ティエン
クリエイティヴ・ディレクター
フォトグラファー

フランス国立高等美術学校卒。パリ・オペラ座のメイキャップデザイナーとして、至高のバレエ作品のためのメイクをつくりだした。その後、パルファン・クリスチャン・ディオールのクリエイティヴ・ディレクターに就任。彼の写真は『VOGUE』誌や『ELLE』誌にたびたび掲載され、そしてさまざまな一流メゾンの広告を手がけている。モエ ヘネシー・ルイ・ヴィトンの顧問でもある。

アンジェロ・フラッカヴェント
インディペンデント・ファッション評論家
キュレーター

イタリア、シチリア島を拠点に、イタリアをはじめとする各国の出版社の仕事で世界中を旅している。『The Business of Fashion』及び『Il Sole 24 Ore』のコラムニストであり、『L'Officiel Italia』、『Flair』、『Fantastic Man』、『The Gentlewoman』、そして『Studio』に定期的に寄稿している。2015年には、フィレンツェのFondazione Pitti Discovery のために展覧会「Il signor Nino」のキュレーションを担当。Pitti Immagine の協力により、テレビ番組のシリーズ「Italie della Moda」を制作。このシリーズは2014年秋、Sky Arte HD で放映された。

森山明子
デザイン・ジャーナリスト
武蔵野美術大学教授

1975年東京藝術大学美術学部芸術学科卒業。特許庁意匠審査官、「日経デザイン」（日経BP社）編集長などを経て、1998年より現職、デザイン情報学科所属。NHKハート展詩選考委員、グッドデザイン賞審査副委員長、芸術工学会副会長・理事、公益財団法人 三宅一生デザイン文化財団理事、公益財産法人日本デザイン振興会理事・評議員などを務める。著書は『まっしぐらの花──中川幸夫』、『石元泰博──写真という思考』、『新井淳一──布・万華鏡』、『デザインジャーナリズム 取材と共謀 1987→2015』など。

（あいうえお順）

# PROFILES OF CONTRIBUTING AUTHORS

**Cai Guo-Qiang**
Artist

Cai Guo-Qiang was born in Quanzhou, China. He was trained in stage design at the Shanghai Theater Academy and later studied at the University of Tsukuba. While living in Japan, he worked on large-scale installations and explored properties of gunpowder in his drawings, an inquiry that eventually led to the development of his signature explosion events. Cai was awarded the Golden Lion at the Venice Biennale in 1999. He also served as Director of Visual and Special Effects for the Opening and Closing Ceremonies of the 2008 Summer Olympics in Beijing. In 2012, Cai was honored as one of five Laureates for the prestigious Praemium Imperiale, an award that recognizes lifetime achievement in the arts.

**Lidewij Edelkoort**
Trend Forecaster

Born in Wageningen, the Netherlands, Edelkoort studied fashion at the Arnhem Academy of Fine Arts. In 1986, she founded her consulting studio Trend Union in Paris. Edelkoort is also active internationally as a design authority, curator, publisher, humanitarian and educator. In 2003, *Time* magazine named her one of the 25 Most Influential People in Fashion and in 2015 she became Dean of Hybrid Studies at Parsons The New School, New York.

**Angelo Flaccavento**
Independent Fashion Critic
Curator

He works out of Sicily, constantly traveling on assignments for Italian and international publications. He is a columnist for *The Business of Fashion* and *Il Sole 24 Ore* and a regular contributor to *L'Officiel Italia*, *Flair*, *Fantastic Man*, *The Gentlewoman*, *Studio*. He curated the exhibition Il signor Nino for Fondazione Pitti Discovery in Florence in 2015 and with the mentoring of Pitti Immagine he created the tv series *Le Italie della Moda* broadcasted on Sky Arte HD in the autumn of 2014.

**Didier Grumbach**
President of the Société des Amis du Musée national d'Art Moderne Centre Pompidou, Honorary President of Fédération Française de la Couture and Chambre Syndicale de la Haute Couture

He had been President of the Fédération Française de la Couture and the Chambre Syndicale de la Haute Couture since 1998; he became Honorary President as of September 2014. President of the Société des Amis du Musée national d'Art Moderne Centre Pompidou since 2014. He was president of Thierry Mugler, CEO of Groupe C. Mendès. Founder & manager with Pierre Bergé of Yves St. Laurent Rive Gauche; president of Yves St. Laurent Rive Gauche USA and Inc.; founder & head of "Créateurs et Industriels", "Paris Collections, Inc.," both affiliate of C. Mendès, and the first French fashion agency established in the U.S. In 1985, he began his tenure at the Institut Français de la Mode and finally dean of Faculty. Publications: *Histoires de la Mode*

**Yasuo Kobayashi**
Philosopher

Graduated from the University of Tokyo College of Liberal Arts. Received a master's degree from the University of Tokyo Graduate School of Comparative Literature. Received his doctoral degree from University of Paris 10 in 1981. In 1993, he became a professor at the University of Tokyo Graduate School of Arts and Sciences. In 2015, he became a professor at Aoyama Gakuin University. He specializes in representational culture theory and modern philosophy. In 2002, the French government awarded him the Chevalier dans l'Ordre des Palmes Académiques. Publications: *Hyoushou no Kougaku [The Optics of Representation]*, *Chi no Odysseia [The Odyssey of Savoir]*, and *Hikari no Opera [The Opera of Light]*.

**Akiko Moriyama**
Design journalist, Professor at Musashino Art University

Graduated from Tokyo University of the Arts (Faculty of Fine Arts, Department of Aesthetics and Art History) in 1975. Worked as an examiner at the design department of the Japan Patent Office, she was editor-in-chief of *Nikkei Design* magazine published by Nikkei Business Publications. In 1998, became professor at Musashino Art University's Department of Design Informatics. Publications: *Yukio Nakagawa : An artist devoted his life to flowers*, *Yasuhiro Ishimoto : Beyond the eye that shapes* and *Jun-ichi Arai : The Dream Weaver, Design Journalism: Coverage and Resonance, from 1987 to 2015*.

**TYEN**
Creative Director
Photographer

After the École des Beaux Arts, TYEN becomes the Face Designer of the Opéra de Paris, where he creates the makeups for the most beautiful ballets. Parfums Christian Dior hires him as Créateur Couleur et Image (Color and Image Creator). His photographs are featured regularly in the *Vogue* and *ELLE* magazines, as well as the advertising campaigns of the most famous fashion houses. Now he also serves as consultant for LVMH.

(alphabetical order)

# 三宅一生

主な活動

1970　三宅デザイン事務所設立。

1971　ニューヨークで海外初のコレクション発表。

1973　秋冬よりパリコレクションに参加。

1975　ニューヨーク、メトロポリタン美術館主催「Inventive Clothes 1909-1939」を「現代衣服の源流展」として京都国立近代美術館にて企画・再現。

1976　ショウ「三宅一生と12人の黒い女たち」（東京・西武劇場、大阪府立体育館）

1977　1976年度毎日デザイン賞記念ショウ「Issey Miyake in Museum ― 三宅一生。一枚の布」（東京・西武美術館）ショウ「FLY WITH ISSEY MIYAKE」（東京・明治神宮外苑室内球技場、京都府立体育館）

1979　米アスペン国際デザイン会議に招聘され、ショウ「Issey Miyake East Meets West」発表。

1982　『ARTFORUM』誌（米）のカバーストーリーに紹介される。（執筆：Ingrid Sischy、Germano Celant）
退役した航空母艦を利用したイントレピッド海上航空宇宙博物館（ニューヨーク）にて1983年春夏コレクションを発表。オープニングにてブランド「Plantation（プランテーション）」を紹介。

1983　「ISSEY MIYAKE SPECTACLE: BODYWORKS」展（東京・ラフォーレ・ミュージアム飯倉800／500、ロサンゼルス・オーティス・パーソンズ・ギャラリー、サンフランシスコ近代美術館、1985年ロンドン・ヴィクトリア＆アルバート・ミュージアム）

1986　アーヴィング・ペンによる「ISSEY MIYAKE」コレクション撮影がスタート。
『TIME』誌（インターナショナル版）にカバーストーリーとして紹介される。（執筆：Jay Cocks）

1988　プリーツの仕事を始める。
「ISSEY MIYAKE A-ŪN」展（パリ・装飾美術館）

1989　「Issey Miyake Meets Lucie Rie」展を企画。（東京・草月ギャラリー、大阪市立東洋陶磁美術館）

1990　第1回ヒロシマ賞記念「三宅一生展 TEN SEN MEN」（広島市立現代美術館）
「Energieën（エナジーズ）」展に参加（アムステルダム・ステデリック・ミュージアム）
「三宅一生展 プリーツ・プリーズ」（東京・東高現代美術館）

1991　秋冬パリコレクションにて、のちの「PLEATS PLEASE ISSEY MIYAKE（プリーツ プリーズ）」の原型となるニット素材のプリーツ服を発表。ウィリアム・フォーサイス＆フランクフルト・バレエ団の公演「失われた委曲」のコスチュームデザイン・制作。

1992　第 25 回バルセロナ・オリンピック競技大会リトアニア代表選手団の公式ユニフォームをデザイン・制作。「三宅一生展 ツイスト」(香川・直島コンテンポラリーアートミュージアム)

1993　ブランド「PLEATS PLEASE ISSEY MIYAKE」スタート。

1997　「イサム・ノグチと三宅一生 アリゾナ」展(香川・丸亀市猪熊弦一郎現代美術館)

1998　A-POC（エイ・ポック）プロジェクトを始める。
　　　「ISSEY MIYAKE Making Things」展(パリ・カルティエ現代美術財団、1999 年ニューヨーク・エース・ギャラリー、2000年東京都現代美術館)

2001　「A-POC MAKING : ISSEY MIYAKE & DAI FUJIWARA」展
　　　(ヴィトラ・デザイン・ミュージアム・ベルリン)

2003　「なんなの? A-POC MIYAKE ISSEY + FUJIWARA DAI」展(東京 Axis ギャラリー)

2004　財団法人 三宅一生デザイン文化財団設立。(2011年に公益財団法人に移行)

2005　「ビッグバン20世紀の創造と破壊」展(パリ・ポンピドゥー・センター)に「PLEATS PLEASE ISSEY MIYAKE」を出展。横尾忠則とコラボレーション「横尾忠則が招待するイッセイ ミヤケ パリコレクション 1977→1999」展(富山県立近代美術館)

2006　ニューヨーク近代美術館(MoMA)の建築・デザイン部門に《A-POC QUEEN》が所蔵され、同館の新規コレクション展にて紹介。

2007　21_21 DESIGN SIGHT 開設。ディレクターに就任。
2008　21_21 DESIGN SIGHT 第3回企画展「XXI c. ― 21世紀人」をディレクション。

2009　21_21 DESIGN SIGHT「U-Tsu-Wa ／うつわ ― ルーシー・リィー、ジェニファー・リー、エルンスト・ガンペール」展をディレクション。

2010　21_21 DESIGN SIGHT「REALITY LAB ―再生・再創造」展をディレクション。

2012　青柳正規氏と共に「国立デザイン美術館をつくる会」を発足し、第1回パブリックシンポジウム開催。(11月27日)

2013　「青森大学男子新体操部」公演開催。企画およびコスチュームデザインを手がける。
　　　(クリエイション・ディレクション・コレオグラフィ：Daniel Ezralow／コスチューム：「HOMME PLISSÉ ISSEY MIYAKE（オムプリッセ）」)〈7月18日 国立代々木競技場第二体育館〉

2014　パリ・カルティエ現代美術財団美術館 30 周年記念展「Memoires Vives(生きた記憶)」へ「陰翳（インエイ） IN-EI ISSEY MIYAKE」を出品。

# MIYAKE ISSEY

SELECTED CHRONOLOGY

1970    Established Miyake Design Studio.

1971    First overseas collection is shown in New York.

1973    Participated in the Paris Autumn Winter 1973 Collections for the first time and, since then, has shown there twice a year.

1975    Instrumental in bringing *Inventive Clothes 1909–1939* exhibition of the Metropolitan Museum of Art, New York to National Museum of Modern Art, Kyoto with the full cooperation of Mr. Koichi Tsukamoto. After its success, the Kyoto Costume Institute (KCI) was established in 1978.

1976    Presented *Issey Miyake and Twelve Black Girls*, a show at the Seibu Theater, Tokyo and Osaka Municipal Gymnasium.

1977    Presented *A Piece of Cloth – Issey Miyake in Museum,* a show at the Seibu Museum of Art, Tokyo, to coincide with the 1976 Mainichi Design Award.
Presented *FLY WITH ISSEY MIYAKE*, a show at the Meiji Jingu Indoor Field, Tokyo and Kyoto Prefectural Gymnasium.

1979    Invited to present the show *Issey Miyake East Meets West*, as the closing event at the International Design Conference in Aspen, Colorado.

1982    A Miyake piece is featured on the cover of *ARTFORUM* magazine with an editorial by Ingrid Sischy and Germano Celant. It marked the first time fashion had been featured on the cover of the art magazine.
Presented Spring/Summer 1983 collection on the U.S.S. Intrepid aircraft carrier and museum in New York, with Plantation line worn by members of an amateur chorus.

1983    Presented *ISSEY MIYAKE SPECTACLE: BODYWORKS*, an exhibition at the Laforet Museum Iigura 800/500, Tokyo; the Otis/Parsons Gallery, Los Angeles; the San Francisco Museum of Modern Art; and in 1985 at the Victoria and Albert Museum, London.

1986    Started collaborating with Irving Penn on photographs of the collections that would become books, posters and ads. Featured in *TIME magazine*, International Edition: January 27, as its cover story written by Jay Cocks. (US Edition: October 21, 1985)

1988    Started experimenting with pleating.
Presented *ISSEY MIYAKE A-ŪN*, an exhibition at the Musée des Arts Décoratifs, Paris.

1989    Organized *Issey Miyake Meets Lucie Rie*, an exhibition of Dame Lucie Rie at Sogetsu Gallery, Tokyo; Museum of Oriental Ceramics, Osaka.

1990    Presented *TEN SEN MEN*, a commemorative exhibition of the Hiroshima Art Prize at the Hiroshima City Museum of Contemporary Art.
Participated in Energieën (Energies), an exhibition featuring RHYTHM PLEATS at the Stedelijk Museum, Amsterdam.
Presented *ISSEY MIYAKE PLEATS PLEASE*, an exhibition at the Toko Museum of Contemporary Art, Tokyo.

| | |
|---|---|
| 1991 | Presented pleated clothing made from a special jersey fabric, a prototype that would later become PLEATS PLEASE ISSEY MIYAKE; first shown in Paris in March. Designed the costumes for the Ballet Frankfurt's *The Loss of Small Detail* choreographed by William Forsythe. |
| 1992 | Designed and produced the official uniform for the Lithuanian team at the 25th Olympic Games in Barcelona. Presented *ISSEY MIYAKE '92 TWIST*, an exhibition at the Naoshima Contemporary Art Museum, Kagawa. |
| 1993 | Launched PLEATS PLEASE ISSEY MIYAKE. |
| 1997 | Presented *ISAMU NOGUCHI and ISSEY MIYAKE "ARIZONA"*, an exhibition at the Marugame Genichiro-Inokuma Museum of Contemporary Art, Kagawa. |
| 1998 | Embarked upon the A-POC project. Presented *ISSEY MIYAKE Making Things*, an exhibition at the Fondation Cartier pour l'art contemporain Paris that later traveled to the Ace Gallery, New York in 1999 and to the Museum of Contemporary Art Tokyo in 2000. |
| 2001 | Presented *A-POC MAKING: ISSEY MIYAKE AND DAI FUJIWARA*, an exhibition at the Vitra Design Museum, Berlin. |
| 2003 | Presented *Nannano? A-POC MIYAKE ISSEY + FUJIWARA DAI*, an exhibition at the Axis gallery, Tokyo. |
| 2004 | Established The Miyake Issey Foundation. |
| 2005 | Participated in *BIG BANG : DESTRUCTION ET CRÉATION DANS L'ART DU XXE SIÈCLE*, an exhibition featuring PLEATS PLEASE ISSEY MIYAKE at the Centre Pompidou, Paris. Collaborated with Tadanori Yokoo on *ISSEY MIYAKE Paris Collections 1977–1999: Invitations by Tadanori Yokoo*, an exhibition at The Museum of Modern Art, Toyama. |
| 2006 | *A-POC QUEEN* was selected to be included in the permanent collection of the Museum of Modern Art Architecture and Design Department, New York. Featured as part of the November *Digitally Mastered* Exhibition. |
| 2007 | Opened 21_21 DESIGN SIGHT in Tokyo Midtown. Appointed as one of its directors. |
| 2008 | Directed *XXIst Century Man*, third exhibition at the 21_21 DESIGN SIGHT. |
| 2009 | Directed *U-Tsu-Wa, うつわ – Lucie Rie, Jennifer Lee, Ernst Gamperl,* an exhibition at the 21_21 DESIGN SIGHT. |
| 2010 | Directed *REALITY LAB*, an exhibition at 21_21 DESIGN SIGHT. |
| 2012 | Established *Society for a Design Museum Japan* with Masanori Aoyagi and held the first public symposium, November 27. |
| 2013 | Organized the event *Aomori University Men's Rhythmic Gymnastics Team,* planning and costume-design by Issey Miyake, creation/direction/choreography by Daniel Ezralow, costume by HOMME PLISSÉ ISSEY MIYAKE, July 18, Yoyogi National Stadium 2nd Gymnasium |
| 2014 | Participated in Fondation Cartier pour l'Art Contemporain 30th Anniversary exhibition *Memorires Vives*, with IN-EI ISSEY MIYAKE. |

作品リスト
# List of Works

作品のデータは次の項目順に記載した：タイトル／テキスト／素材／制作年／コレクション・シーズン／ブランド名（ブランドの記入なし＝ISSEY MIYAKE）
素材：AR＝アクリル、C＝綿、W＝毛、L＝麻、N＝ナイロン、PE＝ポリエステル、PU＝ポリウレタン、R＝レーヨン、S＝絹
図版の上にある番号は出品番号

Information for each work is listed in the following order: Title/Text/Material/Creation Year/Collection Season SS=Spring/Summer, AW=Autumn/Winter/Brand Name (Without Brand Name=ISSEY MIYAKE)
Material: AR=Acrylic Fiber, C=Cotton, W=Wool, L=Linen, N=Nylon, PE=Polyester, PU=Polyurethane, R=Rayon, S=Silk
The numbers above the images are exhibit numbers.

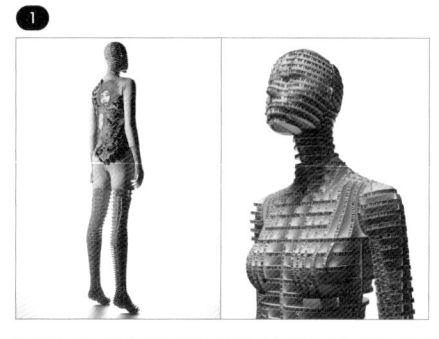

# A

**1**

左：**タトゥ** 1970年に相次いで死去したジミ・ヘンドリックスとジャニス・ジョプリンへのオマージュを込め、刺青の手法で描きプリントした綿ジャージーのジャンプスーツ。C：100％ 1970/1971 春夏
右：**グリッド・ボディ** 吉岡徳仁デザイン事務所

Left: **TATTOO** Jersey jumpsuit, printed with tattoo-like images in homage to Jimi Hendrix and Janis Joplin who past away one after another in 1970. C:100% 1970/SS 1971
Right: **GRID BODY** Tokujin Yoshioka Design

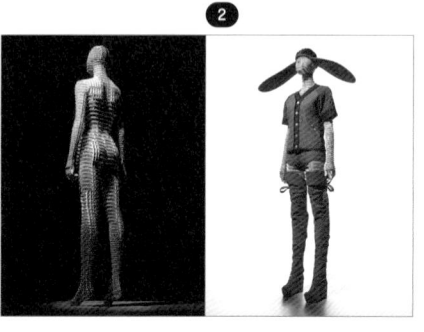

**2**

左：**グリッド・ボディ** 吉岡徳仁デザイン事務所
右：**刺し子** デニムに引けをとらない丈夫な素材である刺し子は、日本の柔道着や野良着に使われてきた。風通織という表裏異なる色を織ることのできる二重織に、太番手糸を織り込んで表現している。デザインは野球ユニフォームから発想。C：100％ V-1（合成皮革）のブーツ。1972/1972 秋冬

Left: **GRID BODY** Tokujin Yoshioka Design
Right: **SASHIKO** *Sashiko* is a fabric as strong as denim, used for the Japanese Judo uniforms and farmers' work clothes. It is created with a pocket weave, whose double-woven nature allows two different colors in front and back. The stitching pattern is woven into the fabric with a thicker yarn. Design inspired by a baseball uniform. C:100% Boots in synthetic leather V-1. 1972/AW 1972

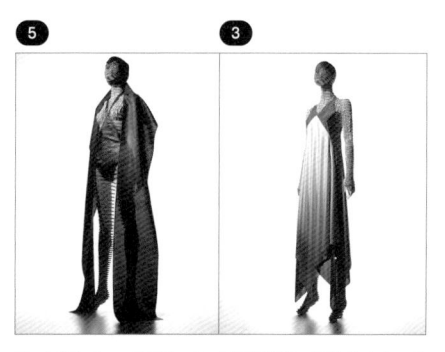

**5** **3**

左：**水着とキャップストール** 中国広東省の伝統的なシルク素材は、涼しく縮まずシワになりにくい。ソメモノイモを染料として用い、何度も染めと乾燥を繰り返し、光沢ある黒に仕上げている。S：100％ 1975/1976 春夏
右：**ハンカチーフ・ドレス** 3枚の正方形の布をバイヤス目で最小限の縫製で合わせ、背中でクロスさせたストラップはさまざまな体型が着用できるよう工夫されたドレス。素材はポリエステルジャージー「東レシルックレニエール」。PE：100％ 1970/1971 春夏

Left: **SWIMWEAR and CAP STOLE** Traditional silk from Guangdong, China. Cool to the touch and not easy to shrink. Repeated dying in potato dyestuff and dried, its finish is shiny black. S:100% 1975/SS 1976
Right: **HANDKERCHIEF DRESS** "One Size" dress made using three square pieces of fabric that hang on the bias, and with shoulder straps crisscrossed in back. Polyester jersey developed by Toray. PE:100% 1970/SS 1971

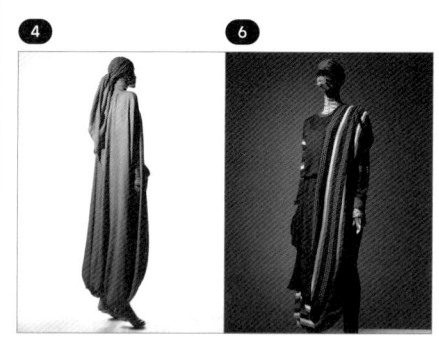

**4** **6**

左：**麻のジャンプスーツ** 絡み織り麻レーヨンの布幅をそのままに活かしたジャンプスーツとストール。R：70％, L：30％ 1975/1976 春夏
右：**ヌバ** ドイツの映画監督・写真家レニ・リーフェンシュタールの写真集『ヌバ』をテーマに制作されたシリーズ。アクリル長繊維「ピューロン」ジャージーのスパッツ付スカートとサイドスリットのチュニック。肩に掛けているストライプはスカートのヘムライン。AR：100％ 1976/1976 秋冬

Left: **LINEN JUMPSUIT** Oversized jumpsuit in rayon linen leno cloth, stole. R:70%, L:30% 1975/SS 1976
Right: **NUBA** Inspired by a book of photography *The Nuba*, by German film director/photographer Leni Riefenstahl. Skirt with leggings and tunic with side slits in acrylic long fiber Pewlon. The bottom of the skirt is pulled up over the shoulder. AR:100% 1976/AW 1976

**8** **9**

左：**丹前** 家庭や旅館で着用されてきた日本の防寒着「丹前」を表現した直線裁ちのコート。黄八丈の格子柄を表に、緋色の裏は緯糸に毛糸を用いて織られた緯二重織りの暖かなウール素材。W：100％ 1976/1976 秋冬
右：**正花木綿** 男物の着物の裏地に使われてきた木綿地を、太番手の糸を使い厚手の広幅に替えて使用している。シャツとボタンで留めた足の部分を外すとショーツになるパンツ。帽子、手甲、バッグ。C：100％ 1976/1977 春夏

Left: **TANZEN** Straight cut making use of the merit of *tanzen*, warm weather coat at home and hotels. The warm wool material with front surface in satin weave in the *Kihachijo* check pattern and in the red back with the weft double weave. W:100% 1976/AW 1976
Right: **SHOHANA-MOMEN** Heavier version of cotton used to line kimonos for men. Shirt and short pants with detachable three-quarters–length pants cap, gloves and bag. C:100% 1976/SS 1977

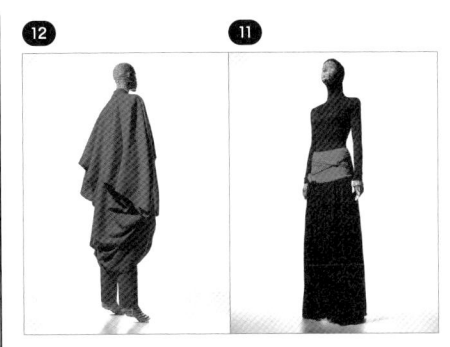

左: コクーン・コート 一枚の布から造形されたウール地のコート。W:100% 1977/1977 秋冬
右: 黒い生きもの フードつきシャツとスカート。長い紐ベルトで着る。素材はアクリル長繊維「ピューロン」ジャージー。AR:100% 1977/1977 秋冬

**Left: COCOON COAT** Wool coat form created using a piece of cloth. W:100% 1977/AW 1977
**Right: BLACK CREATURE** Shirt with hood and skirt ensemble with a long string belt in acrylic long fiber Pewlon jersey. AR:100% 1977/AW 1977

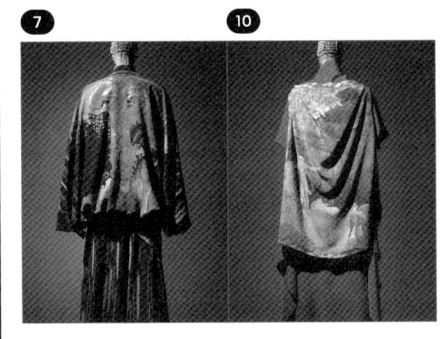

左: パラダイス（楽園）美術家・横尾忠則とのコラボレーションによる最初のデザイン。《パラダイス》と題したプリントを背中に配したシルクのブルゾンシャツとパンツ。S:100% 1976/1976 秋冬
右: パラダイス・ロスト（失楽園）「一枚の布」を代表する、腕を通すスリットを入れた四角形のシルクのコートとドレス。プリント・デザインは横尾忠則。布の地色を抜き別の色をのせる着抜プリントで色鮮やかに仕上げている。左右ともにプリントはイタリアのコモにあるレインボー社が手掛けた。S:100% 1976/1977 春夏

**Left: PARADISE** The first collaboration work with artist Tadanori Yokoo. The blouson shirt printed with the pattern titled *Paradise* on the back and pants. S:100% 1976/ AW 1976
**Right: PARADISE LOST** A square with slits for arms as a coat, one of the example of the "a piece of cloth" concept. Print design by Tadanori Yokoo. The brilliant hues are produced by discharging the colors in the base area of the pattern before dying. Both prints done by Rainbow, printing company at Como in Italy. S:100% 1976/SS 1977

# B

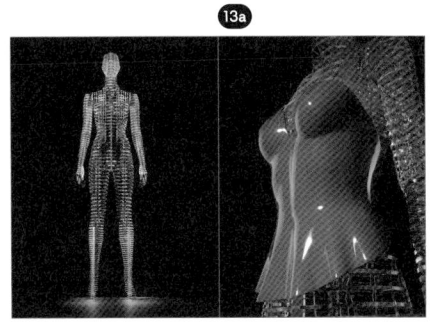

左: グリッド・ボディ 吉岡徳仁デザイン事務所
右: プラスティック・ボディ 繊維強化プラスティックを素材に用い成型で仕上げている。彫刻的なフォルムだが、量産も可能な製法で制作されている。1980/1980 秋冬

**Left: GRID BODY** Tokujin Yoshioka Design
**Right: PLASTIC BODY** Created using the fiberglass reinforced plastic. Sculptural shape but the piece can be mass produced. 1980/AW 1980

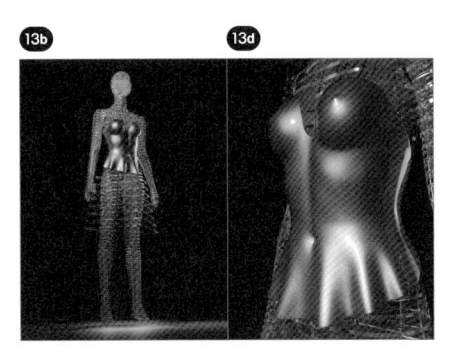

左右: プラスティック・ボディ 前ページに同じ。
**Both pages: PLASTIC BODY** same as the previous page

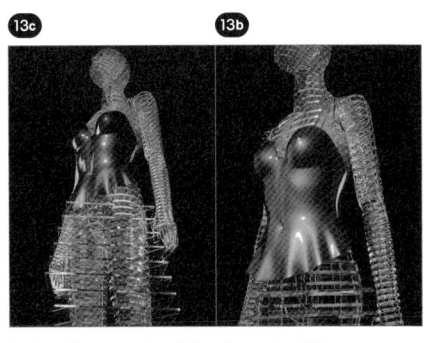

左右: プラスティック・ボディ 前ページに同じ。
**Both pages: PLASTIC BODY** same as the previous page

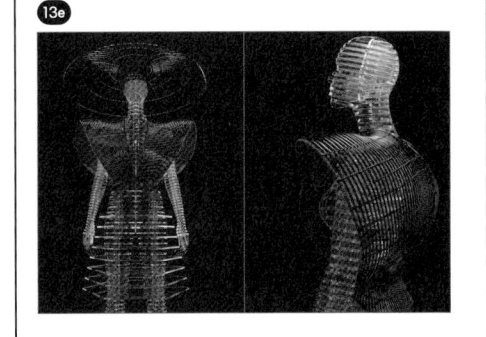

左右: ラタン・ボディ 籐と竹で編まれたボディ。制作は、工芸作家・小菅小竹堂。制作協力：アーティスト・福澤エミ 1981/1982 春夏

**Both pages: RATTAN BODY** A bodice woven with rattan and bamboo. Made by Shochikudo Kosuge in Collaboration with Emi Fukuzawa. 1981/SS 1982

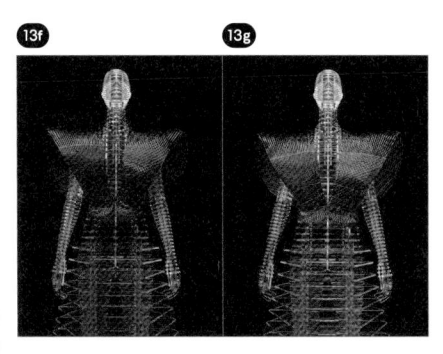

左右: ラタン・ボディ 前ページに同じ。
**Both pages: RATTAN BODY** same as the previous page

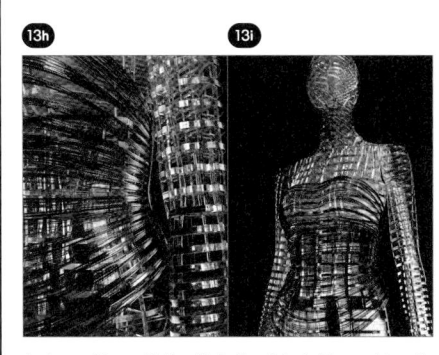

左右: ワイヤー・ボディ 数本ずつ束ねた細いワイヤーが、両サイドのパーツに取り付けられたボディ・ブレスレッド。1983/1983 秋冬

**Both pages: WIRE BODY** Wires are bundled and connected to the sides to create a bodice. 1983/AW 1983

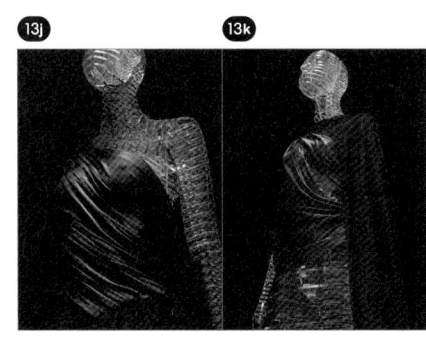

左右: ウォーターフォール・ボディ 部分的にシリコンを浸み込ませた「ピューロン」ジャージーをトルソーの上に置き、流れる水の形状を模して布地を手繰りフォルムを固めている。AR:100% 1984/1984 秋冬

**Both pages: WATERFALL BODY** A bodice is formed by draping Pewlon jersey partially soaked with silicon on mannequin bodice which then hardens in the shape of flowing water. AR:100% 1984/AW 1984

List of Works

235

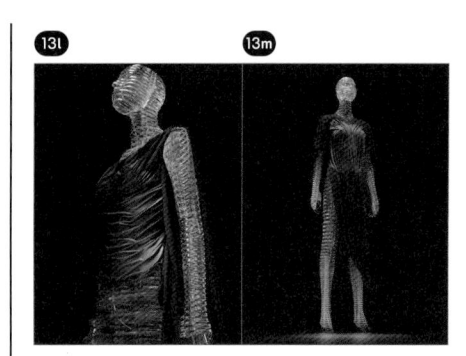

左右: ウォーターフォール・ボディ 前ページに同じ。
Both pages: **WATERFALL BODY** same as the previous page

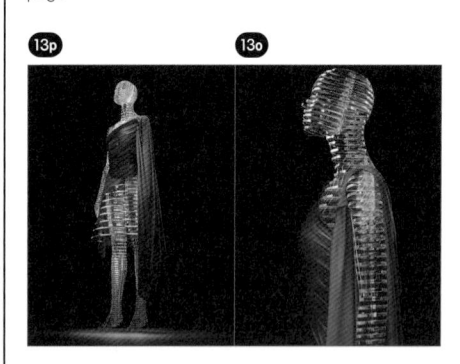

左右: ウォーターフォール・ボディ 前ページに同じ。
Both pages: **WATERFALL BODY** same as the previous page

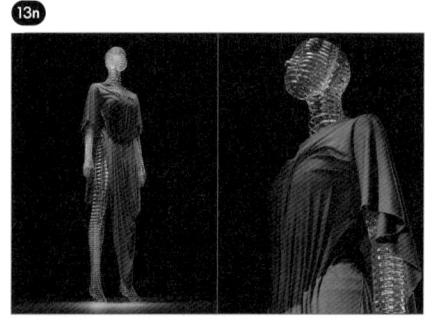

左右: ウォーターフォール・ボディ 前ページに同じ。
Both pages: **WATERFALL BODY** same as the previous page

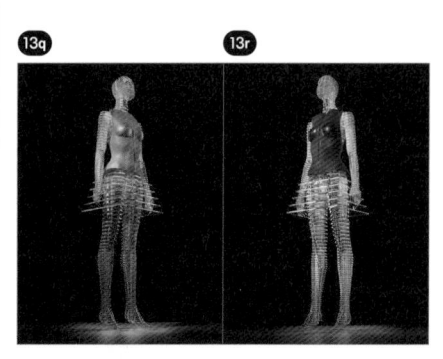

左右: シリコン・ボディ ジップアップで着用するシリコン製ボディ。1985/1985 秋冬
Both pages: **SILICON BODY** A bodice with a front zipper, in silicon. 1985/AW 1985

# C

MATERIAL

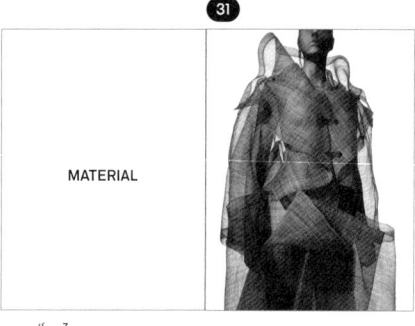

右: 馬尾毛 毛芯と呼ばれる伝統的な紳士服の芯地に織り込まれている馬の尾の毛のみで織った、張りのある素材感を生かしたジャケットとスカート。1990/1990 秋冬
**Right: HORSEHAIR** Jacket and skirt, in a stiff fabric woven with horsehair, normally used as an inner lining for mens traditional jacket. 1990/AW 1990

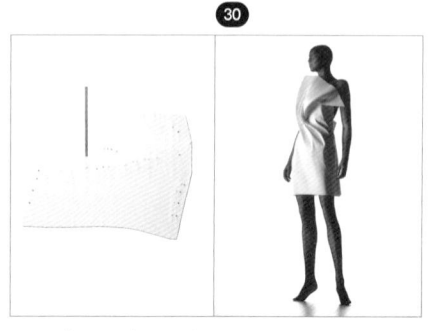

コロンブ 平和を象徴する「白い鳩」とフランス語で名づけられたドレス。モノフィラメント素材を用い、ハサミを使わずに熱で裁断し、針と糸の代わりにスナップ留めで造形する。左は、ヒートカットで裁断し、ドットボタンを打った造形前のパターン。PE:100% 1990/1991 春夏
**Both pages: COLOMBE** Named *Colombe* in French, or dove, after the symbol of peace, this dress of monofilament fiber is heat-cut rather than with scissors, and its shape is created by snaps rather than by needle and thread. PE:100% 1990/SS 1991

ダイナソー 「からむし」という苧麻（ラミー）を手紡ぎ、手織りにした韓国の伝統的な布を用い、恐竜のようなかたちを手で折りだしたジャケット。苧麻:100% プリーツの折山を金色にプリントしたシルク素材のスカート。S:100% 右はフラットに畳まれたジャケット。1990/1991 春夏
**Both pages: DINOSAUR** Each section of the *karamushi* (hand spun and woven ramie Korean linen) jacket bodice is folded by hand to resemble the spine of a dinosaur. Ramie 100% Skirt with the pleated edges painted in gold. S:100% Right: Dinosaur jacket, folded flat. 1990/SS 1991

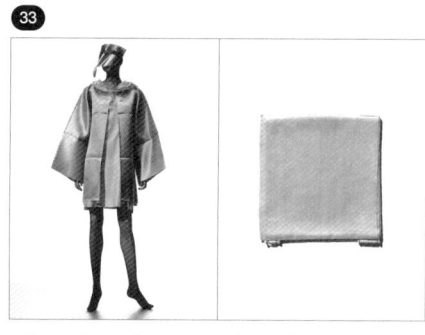

スクエア・オン・スクエアーズ 正方形で構成されたジャケット。四角形を折り重ね、プリーツ加工の方法で熱処理したことにより、簡単に折りたたむことができる。裾のメタルパーツは飾りであると同時に、軽いジャケットが浮くのを抑える。R:60%, S:40% 下は箔押しをしたシルクのシャツとドレス。S:100% ナイロン・ファイバーのウィッグ、いずれも 1991/1991 秋冬
**Both pages: SQUARE ON SQUARES** Jacket made with square elements. It can be easily folded because of the heat-press. Metal weights are attached to the hems to give them shape as well as ornaments. R:60%, S:40%. Silk shirt and dress pressed with metal foil. S:100% Wig made of transparent nylon fibers all 1991/AW 1991

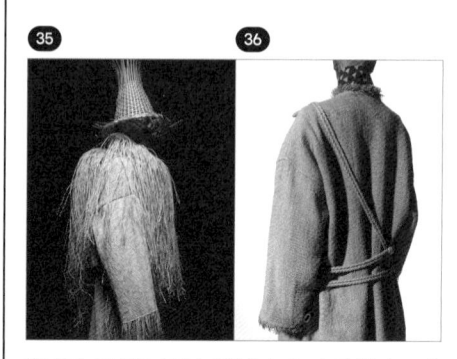

左: ラフィア ラフィアヤシの葉をメッシュに手刺したコートとリュック。メッシュ＝PE:100%、ラフィアヤシ100% 帽子、メガネ、いずれも 1993/1994 春夏
右: ムシロ テープ状のコットン糸を並べて接着した扁平糸を織ることで、荒々しいムシロの表情を表現したコート。裏にはシェトランドウールを使用して暖かさを加えている。C:70%, W:30% 1984/1984 秋冬
**Left: RAFFIA** Coat and backpack in mesh hand embroidered using raffia fiber. Mesh PE:100%, Raffia 100% Hat, glasses all 1993/SS 1994
**Right: MUSHIRO** A coat with the front woven using a flat cotton yarn to give it a rough straw mat look, and the back in Shetland wool to give warmth. C:70%, W:30% 1984/AW 1984

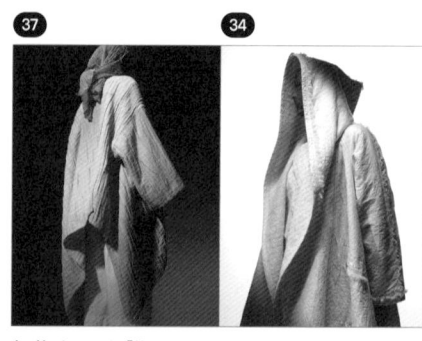

左: 乾パンコート 「乾パン」から発想したドライな質感を表現するジュートを表に、肌に触れる内側をコットンで二重織りにした鬼楊柳。ジュート80%, C:20% コート下は天日にさらした綿のジャケットとパンツ。C:100% いずれも1983/1984 春夏
右: 紙衣 長く柔らかな繊維を用いて宮城県の白石和紙工房が伝統的な技法で漉く和紙は、丈夫で暖か。なかでも縦横に繊維が絡み合うように漉いた、丈夫な紙を手揉みしたものを使用している。コートはさらにウールで裏打ちがされている。和紙、W:100% 1982/1982 秋冬

Left: **KANPAN COAT** Coat in a double woven fabric: on one side, woven in jute with a texture as dry as Kanpan (a hard backed biscuit): the other side is woven in a very wide cotton crepe fabric. Jute:80%. C:20% Worn over a jacket and pants in a sun-bleached flat-weave cotton. C:100% all 1983/SS 1984
Right: **KAMIKO** The *Shiroishi Washi* is made from the long and flexible fibers. Hand screened in the traditional methods by Shiroishi Washi Kobo in Miyagi Prefecture. It is strong and warm. The long fibers are screened horizontally and vertically so that they tangle in cross directions for strength. When dried, it is then crushed by hand. The coat is lined with wool. Washi, W:100% 1982/AW 1982

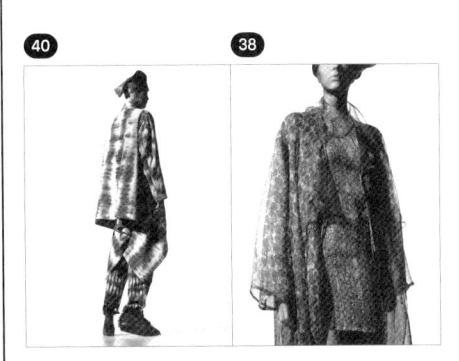

左: 組みがすり 三つ編みにしてむら染めにした、太く節のある糸を使って織られた厚手木綿の絣。前後の見頃は一続きの一枚の布。その後ろに一本のステッチを斜めにいれることでドレープがつくられたコート。共布のシャツ、パンツ、帽子。C:100% 1985/1985 秋冬
右: バティック ジャカード織りのシルクオーガンジーに本蝋を用いて2種類の柄をバティック・プリントしたシャツ、コート、パンツ。S:100% 1985/1986 春夏

Left: **KUMIGASURI** A heavy weight random space dyed cotton, woven with knotted thick threads which were first braided and dyed. The front and back bodice is one piece of cloth. A line of stitching on the back of the coat gives a draping effect. Coat, shirt, pants and cap. C:100% 1985/ AW 1985
Right: **BATIC** Coat, dress and pants in silk organdy jacquard, which is batik-printed using two different wax patterns. S:100% 1985/SS 1986

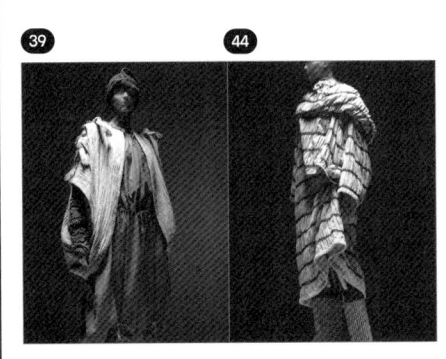

左: 象楊柳 リネンクレープを手絞りで荒々しい質感を出した楊柳のジャケット。L:100% 手染めコットンのジャンプスーツと手甲。いずれも紐使いで丈やフォルムを自在に変化させることができる。C:100% 帽子、いずれも 1982/1983 春夏
右: チューブ・ドレス 綿とウールで織られたボーダーのウールを縮絨させた筒織り。筒の形状をそのまま使い、服に仕上げている。W:65%, C:35% 筒織りウール・ジャカードのレッグ・ウォーマー、いずれも1983/1983 秋冬

Left: **ELEPHANT CREPE** Jacket in linen crepe hand twisted to give rough texture. L:100% Jumpsuits and gloves in hand dyed cotton. L:100% Both are adjustable in length and form by drawstrings. C:100% Cap, all 1982/SS 1983
Right: **TUBE DRESS** A dress is created using the tube itself from tube-weave. Cotton and wool are tube-woven in border and wool area is shrunk to give texture. W:65%, C:35% Leg warmers of jacquard tube-weave wool. Both 1983/AW 1983

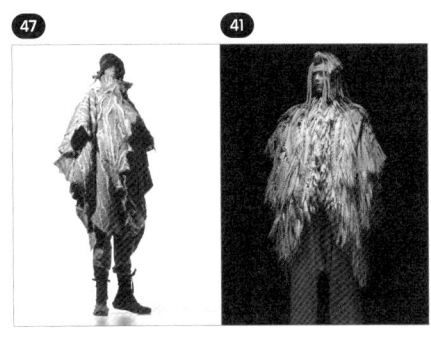

左: アニマル・ニット アルパカ混ウールの二重編みジャカードニット。表面に水溶性の糸を編み込み、縮絨加工により野性的な表情に仕上げたコート。W:67%, AR:27%, N:6% コート下は、溶岩をモティーフとしたプリントのジャンプスーツ。C:100% いずれも 1983/1983 秋冬 ツイスト帽 1993/1993 秋冬、テープシューズ 1996/1997 春夏
右: ゴボウ・フリンジ 綿の太い経糸に、緯糸のウール糸を幅広く飛ばして織り込んだ後、その間の糸をカットし、糸が絡み合いフェルト状のワイルドなフリンジになるまで強い縮絨加工で仕上げたコートと帽子。W:68%, C:32% 1985/1985 秋冬

Left: **ANIMAL KNIT** Coat in Alpaca wool; one side of a double-knitted jacquard fabric has dissolvable yarn knitted into the pattern. Then the yarn is dissolved and shrink-treated to created a rough surface. W:67%, AR:27%, N:6% Under the coat, jumpsuit with a lava-motif print. C:100% Both 1983/AW 1983 Twist cap 1993/AW1993, Tape shoes 1996/SS 1997
Right: **GOBO FRINGE** Coat and hat. The thick cotton-warp thread is woven wide-speaced with wool weft thread. The threads are cut and then shrunk until the wool yarn becomes wild felt fringes. W:68%, C:32% 1985/AW 1985

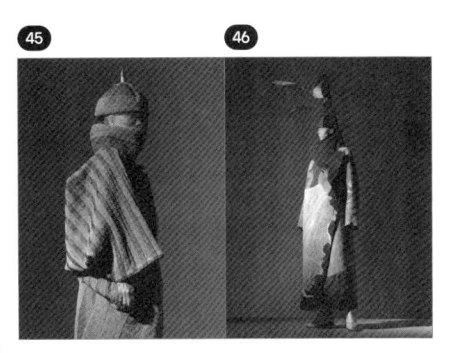

左: 葱坊主 ウールとナイロン・メッシュの二重編みストライプのコート。かぶりものは、片面のウール地をカットしている。W:65%, N:35% 1985/1985 秋冬
右: プリズム・コラージュ フリース地に、キャンバスに絵の具を置くように羊毛わたを置き、その上に真綿を配してから、ニードルパンチングの製法で仕上げたコート。PE:100% 帽子、シューズ、いずれも 1997/1997 秋冬

Left: **ONION HEAD** Coat in double-knit stripe made from wool and nylon mesh. Head covering is made with the wool side cut away. W:65%, N:35% 1985/AW1985
Right: **PRISM COLLAGE** Coat in wool fleece. Floss and chiffon are placed on the fleece and are needle-punched to attach them. PE:100%, Hat, shoes, all 1997/AW 1997

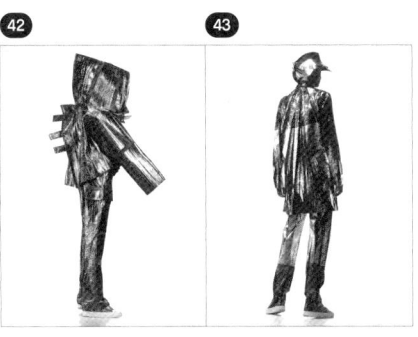

左右: スターバースト 再生・再利用の提案。既存の服に襞をよせ、その上から箔シートを熱圧着し、部分的に襞を開くことで服に新たな表情が生まれた。左はフリースのコート PE:100% とパンツ C:100%。右はチュニック丈のシャツとパンツ。C:100% 箔で仕上げたフェルト帽、シューズ、いずれも 1998/1998 秋冬

Both pages: **STARBURST** Proposal for re-birth/re-use. Existing clothes are first folded, then heat-pressed with foil; the folds are opened partially give to create a different appearance. Left: Fleece coat PE:100% pants C:100% Right: Tunic length shirt and pants in cotton. C:100% Felt hat is also folded and foil pressed. Shoes, all 1998/AW 1998

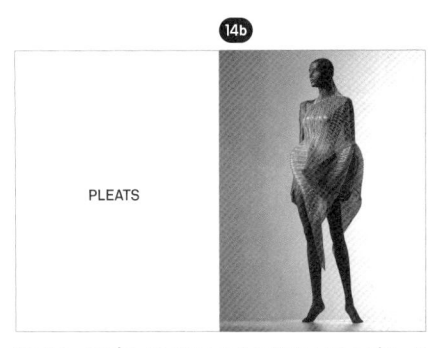

PLEATS

右: シカーダ・プリーツ 服のかたちに縫製してからプリーツをかけて仕上げる「製品プリーツ」のきっかけとなった蝉の羽のような透明感のあるオーガンジーのシャツ。一枚のスカーフを四角形に折り、斜めにランダム・プリーツをかけ、それを広げて三カ所を縫いあわせている。S:75%, PE:25% 1988/1989 春夏

Right: **CICADA PLEATS** Top which started using the "garment pleating" method whereby the clothing is first cut and sewn and then pleated. Organdy shirt, transparent as cicada's wings; scarf is folded several times and then random-pleated diagonally then secured by stitching three points. PE:100% 1988/SS 1989

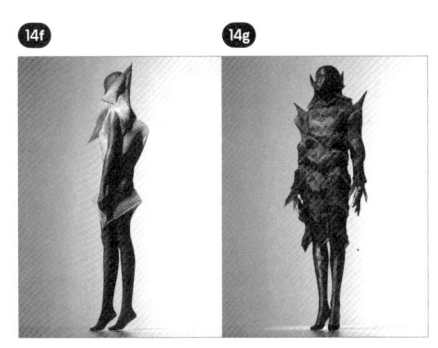

左右: ミュータント・プリーツ テープ状の布を縦に、さらにジグザグに折りプリーツをかけ、折りを開いて組み立てたドレス。PE:100% 右の下に着ているのは《タトゥ・ボディ》。PE:82%, N:18% いずれも 1989/1989 秋冬

Both pages: **MUTANT PLEATS** The tape fabric is pleated, folded vertically and in zig-zag and then opened to reveal the dress. PE:100% TATTOO BODY is worn under the pleats on right. PE:82%, N:18% Both 1989/AW 1989

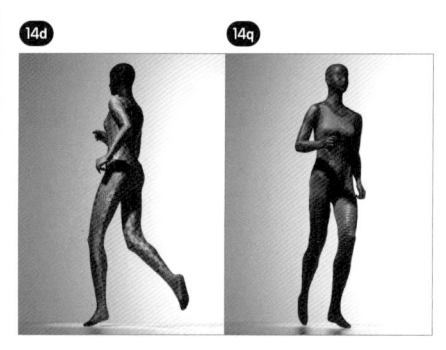

左: **タトゥ・ボディ** アマゾンの部族が施すタトゥのパターンをプリントにしたボディウエアと手袋。PU:82%, N:18% 1989/1989 秋冬

右: **タトゥ・ボディ** アフリカの部族に見られる立体的なタトゥを模してプリントで表現した水着。発泡プリントを施したのち、箔プリントをのせている。PE:90%, PU:10% 1991/1992 春夏

Left: **TATTOO BODY** Bodywear and gloves, printed with pattern of tattoo used by an Amazon tribe. PU:82%, N:18% 1989/AW 1989

Right: **TATTOO BODY** Swimwear with a pattern that imitates raised scarred skin used by African tribes made using two different techniques. First the pattern is applied using a "foam print" process; then foil is applied over it to achieve the final result. PE: 90%, PU: 10% 1991/SS 1992

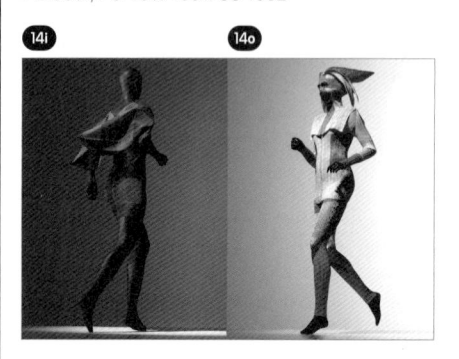

左: **ボーダー・プリーツ** アフリカで目にする色彩から発想した泥色ボーダーのシャツは、着用した時の立体的な形状と対照的にフラットになる。PE:100% 1989/1990 春夏

右: **ボディ・プリーツ** 薄地を二重に使ったランダム・プリーツのシャツ、パンツ、マスク。PE:100% 1990/1990 秋冬

Left: **BORDER PLEATS** Shirt with border printed in mud-dye color inspired by the colors one sees in Africa. Three dimensional when worn but becomes flat in contrast when not worn. PE: 100% 1989/SS 1990

Right: **BODY PLEATS** Shirt, pants and mask in thin polyester layered in double. PE: 100% 1990/AW 1990

左: **ウエーブ・プリーツ** ランダム・プリーツをかけたのち、型紙を使い熱処理で波形を加えたメタリック・シャンブレーのジャケット、パンツ、ヘッドピース。PE:100% 1993/1993 秋冬

右: **ステアケース・プリーツ** 長方形を横段に、袖は四角形を縦に、階段状に均等にずらして組み合わせ、プリーツをかけて仕上げたシャツとパンツ。PE:100% 1994/1994 秋冬

Left: **WAVE PLEATS** The metallic chambray fabric is first sewn into the shapes of a jacket and pants and head-piece, then random pleated; lastly it is sandwiched between wave-pattern molds and heat-pressed. PE: 100% 1993/AW 1993

Right: **STAIRCASE PLEATS** Shirt and pants: rectangular strips of fabrics are joined horizontally for the bodice and pants and square pieces are joined vertically for the sleeves;then all are pleated. The effect is like staircases. PE: 100% 1994/AW 1994

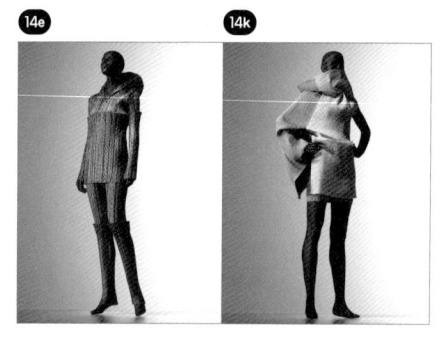

左: **バンブー・プリーツ** 竹の節目のように折りを加えプリーツ加工したシャツとパンツ。PE:100% 1989/1989 秋冬

右: **葉っぱプリーツ** アンリ・ルソーの絵画《夢》(1910年)からの発想。片袖と身頃のふたつの長方形によるチュニックとショートパンツ。PE:85%, L:15% 1989/1990 春夏

Left: **BAMBOO PLEATS** Shirt and pants pleated with bamboo-like sections. PE:100% 1989/AW 1989

Right: **BLADE OF GRASS PLEATS** Inspired by *Le Rêve*, 1910, by Henri Rousseau. Tunic and short pants, with one sleeve and body part made with two rectangular shapes. PE: 85%, L: 15% 1989/SS 1990

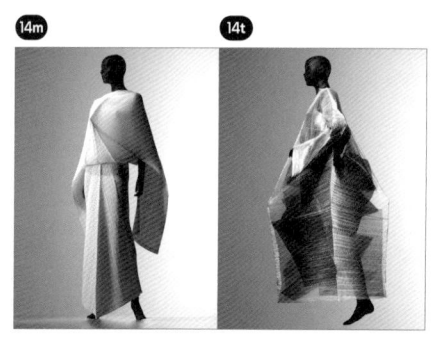

左: **ムーンライト** アンリ・ルソーの絵画《夢》(1910年)からの発想。胸元に折りを加えたストールがつけられたランダム・プリーツのドレス。PE:100% 1989/1990 春夏

右: **パオ** 遊牧民のテントを連想させるコート。モノフィラメント素材の裏から、柄をアップリケしたのちに横段にプリーツをかけて仕上げている。PE:100% 1994/1995 春夏

Left: **MOONLIGHT** Inspired by *Le Rêve*, 1910, by Henri Rousseau. Random pleated dress, with an attached long shawl. PE: 100% 1989/SS 1990

Right: **PAO** Coat inspired by the shape of a tent used by Central Asian nomads. The woven fabric made of monofilament fiber is appliqued with shapes in the back and then pleated horizontally. PE: 100% 1994/SS 1995

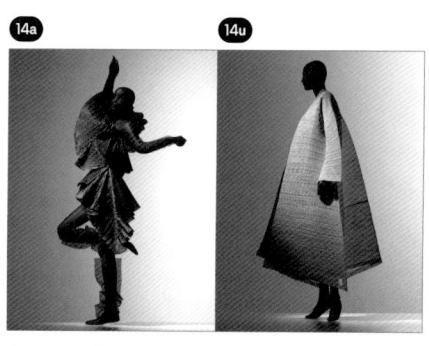

左: **ワカメ・ドレス** メタリック糸を織り込んだ地にプリーツを施したのち縫製で仕上げた「製品プリーツ」以前のプリーツ。PE:100% 1981/1982 春夏　チュールの手袋とブーツ 1982/1983 春夏

右: **クリスタル・プリーツ** マットとシースルーの2種類の材質を使い分けたコート。PE:100% 部分的に: アセテート70%, PE:30% 1994/1995 春夏

Left: **SEAWEED DRESS** Pleated dress, prior to garment pleating. The metallic thread is woven into the fabric, pleated and then sewn into the dress. PE:100% 1981/SS 1982 Gloves and boots in tulle1982/SS 1983

Right: **CRYSTAL PLEATS** Coat using both matte and see-through materials. PE: 100%, partially Acetate 70%, PE: 30% 1994/SS 1995

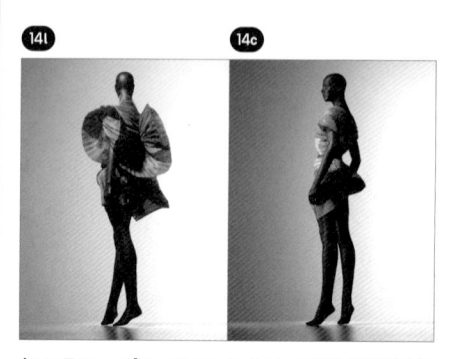

左: **フラワー・プリーツ** アンリ・ルソーの絵画《夢》(1910年)からの発想。二つ折りにしてプリーツをかけた帯状の布の扱いで花が開いたように仕上げたドレス。PE:100% 1989/1990 春夏

右: **ゴーギャン・プリーツ** ゴーギャンの絵画《タヒチの女たち》(1891年)からの発想。同じ柄をオーガンジーとタフタに転写プリントしている。一枚の布で造形されたトップとスカート。PE:100% 1988/1989 春夏

Left: **FLOWER PLEATS** Inspired by *Le Rêve*, 1910, by Henri Rousseau. Fabric is folded into two layers, then pleated and manipulated to form a dress looking like a blossoming flower. PE: 100% 1989/SS 1990

Right: **GAUGUIN PLEATS** Pattern inspired by the painting *Tahitian Women*, 1891, by Paul Gauguin. The same pattern is printed using sublistatic printing technique on organdy and taffeta. The top and skirt formed with a piece of cloth. PE: 100% 1988/SS 1989

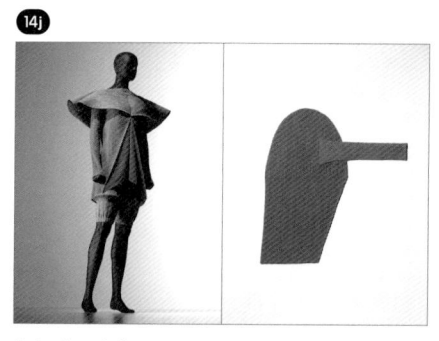

左右: **葉っぱプリーツ** アンリ・ルソーの絵画《夢》(1910年)からの発想。たたまれた平面と着用したときのかたちが大きく異なるシャツ。本展メインビジュアルに使用されている。オレンジ色のパーツはセンターに折り隠れている。PE:85%, L:15% 1989/1990 春夏

238

Both pages: **BLADE OF GRASS PLEATS** Inspired by *Le Rêve*, 1910, by Henri Rousseau. The shape when folded flat looks totally different when worn and shaped in three dimentions. The orange section is folded hidden at the center. PE: 85%, L:15% 1989/SS 1990

左右: ラッカー・プリーツ アンリ・ルソーの絵画《夢》(1910年)からの発想。均等な幅のプリーツをかけた紙のような風合いのシャツ。肩からまるく盛りあがったエッジを背中でボタン留めするとボリュームあるフォルムが生まれる。PE:100% 1989/1990 春夏

Both pages: **LACQUER PLEATS** Inspired by *Le Rêve*, 1910, by Henri Rousseau. Shirt with paper crisp texture, pleated in thin and even wale. The voluminous form is created when the edge, rounded from the shoulder, is buttoned at the back. PE: 100% 1989/SS 1990

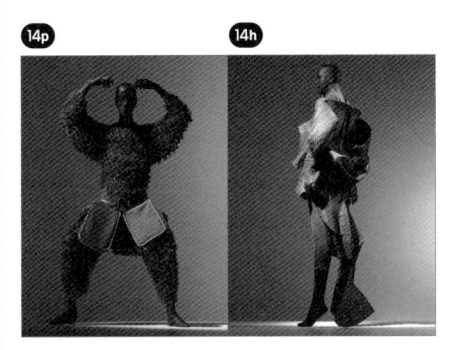

左: モンキー・プリーツ ジャカード織りの経糸をカットする加工で毛のように糸が現れた表面にプリーツがかかり、毛を縮らせたジャンプスーツ。PE:100% 5つの袋つきベルト・バッグ。いずれも 1990/1991 春夏
右: 鳥プリーツ アンリ・ルソーの絵画《夢》(1910年)からの発想。二つ折りにしてプリーツをかけた帯状の布の折山を立体的に活かしかたちづくられたドレス。PE:100%, 1989/1990 春夏 下は《タトゥ・ボディ》PE:90%, PU: 10% 1991/1992 春夏

Left: **MONKEY PLEATS** Jumpsuit with crinkled fringes. Warp threads of jacquard fabric are cut to make fringes, then pleated. PE:100% A belt with five bags. 1990/SS 1991
Right: **BIRD PLEATS** Inspired by *Le Rêve*, 1910, by Henri Rousseau. Dress: the fabric is first folded into two and pleated. The shape of the dress is manipulated by joining the folded edges three-dimensionally. PE:100%, 1989/SS 1990 Under the dress, TATTOO BODY PE:90%, PU:10% 1991/SS 1992

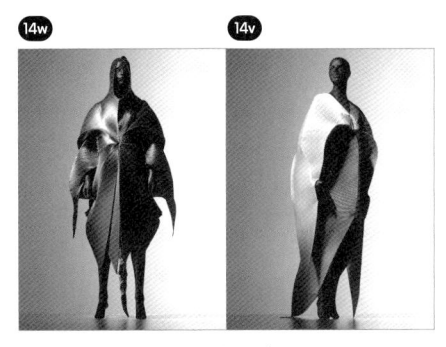

左: スターフィッシュ パーツごとにプリーツ加工し、星の形に組み立てたドレス。PE:100% 1999/1999 秋冬
右: スワロー・プリーツ パーツごとにプリーツ加工し、組み立てたドレス。PE:100% 1999/1999 秋冬

Left: **STARFISH** Each part is pleated separately and then constructed to a star shape. PE:100% 1999/AW 1999
Right: **SWALLOW PLEATS** Each part is pleated separately and then constructed. PE:100% 1999/AW 1999

服については、各ページを参照
左から、14g:メガネ 1986/1987 春夏、アクセサリー: ショルダー・ボディ・スカルプチャー 1991 制作: ジル・ジョンヌマン、14b: メガネ 1986/1987 春夏、14t: メガネ 1989/1990 春夏、14d: メガネ 1986/1987 春夏、14v: メガネ 1986/1987 春夏、14q:メガネ 1993/1994 春夏、アクセサリー: ショダー・ボディ・スカルプチャー 1991 制作: ジル・ジョンヌマン

For clothing, refer to the previous pages
From left: 14g/Glasses 1986/SS 1987, Accessory: Shoulder Body Sculpture 1991 by Gilles Jonemann, 14b/Glasses 1986/SS 1987, 14t/Glasses 1989/SS 1990, 14d/Glasses 1986/SS 1987, 14v/Gasses 1986/SS 1987, 14q/Glasses 1993/SS 1994, Accessory: Shoulder Body Sculpture 1991 by Gilles Jonemann

服については、各ページを参照
左から、14c:メガネ 1986/1987 春夏、14 l:メガネ 1986/1987 春夏、14a:メガネ 1989/1990 春夏、14m:メガネ 1989/1989 秋冬、14j:メガネ1986/1986 秋冬、14 k:メガネ 1983/1984 春夏、14u:メガネ1988/1989 春夏

For clothing, refer to the previous pages
From left: 14c/Glasses 1986/SS 1987, 14l/Glasses 1986/SS 1987, 14a/Glasses 1989/SS 1990, 14m/Glasses 1989/AW 1989, 14j/Glasses 1986/AW 1986, 14k/Glasses 1983/SS 1984, 14u/Glasses 1988/SS 1989

服については、各ページを参照
左から、14h: メガネ 1995/1996 春夏、14m: メガネ 1989/1989秋冬、14r:メガネ 1985/1986 春夏、14s: メガネ 1986/1987 春夏、14o,14i: メガネ 1986/1986 秋冬、帽子 1989/1990 春夏、ボディ・バッグ 1990/1990 秋冬

For clothing, refer to the previous pages
From left: 14h/Glasses 1995/SS 1996, 14m/Glasses 1989/AW 1989, 14r/Glasses 1985/SS 1986, 14s/Glasses 1986/SS 1987, 14o,14i/ Glasses 1986/AW 1986, Hat 1989/SS1990, Body Bag 1990/AW 1990

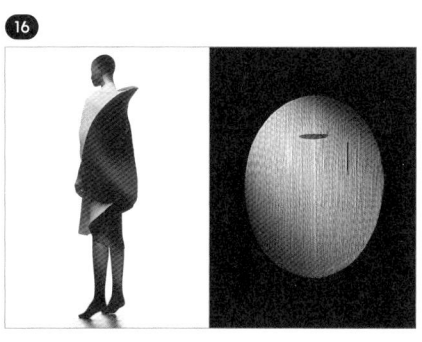

左右: リズム・プリーツ アンリ・ルソーの絵画《夢》(1910年)からの発想。楕円、丸、四角い平面のドレス。平面から立体への変化は、袖口や衿あきの位置がずれていることで3次元のフォルムが生まれる。置かれた平面の楕円形のもう一方の袖口は、後ろに開けられている。PE: 65%, L: 35% 1989/1990 春夏

Both pages: **RHYTHM PLEATS** Inspired by *Le Rêve*, 1910, by Henri Rousseau. Dresses in ovals, rounds and squares, with unusual placements of the neck and arm openings. Unexpected three-dimensional forms are created when worn. The other sleeve opening of the flat oval dress is placed on its back. PE:65% L:35% 1989/SS 1990

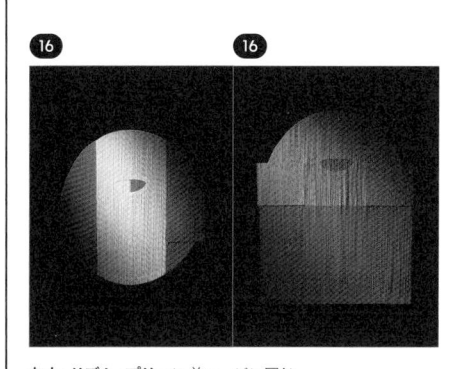

左右: リズム・プリーツ 前ページに同じ
Both pages: **RHYTHM PLEATS** same as the previous page

⓰

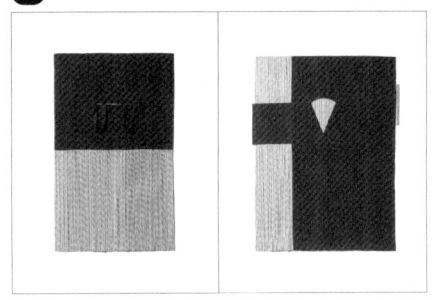

左右: リズム・プリーツ 前ページに同じ
Both pages: RHYTHM PLEATS same as the previous page

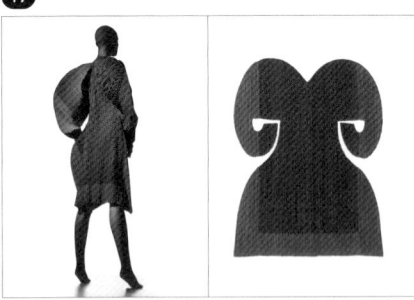

⓳

左右: ハロー・プリーツ PE:100% 1990/1991 春夏
Both pages: HELLO PLEATS PE:100% 1990/SS 1991

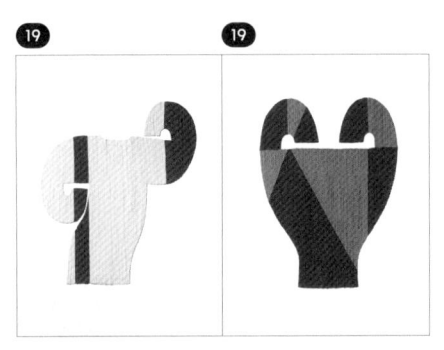

⓳  ⓳

左右: ハロー・プリーツ ハロー！と片方の腕を挙げたポーズからデザインされたバリエーション。PE:100% 1990/1991 春夏
Both pages: HELLO PLEATS Variation of dresses with one sleeve is up as if saying "Hello!" PE:100% 1990/SS 1991

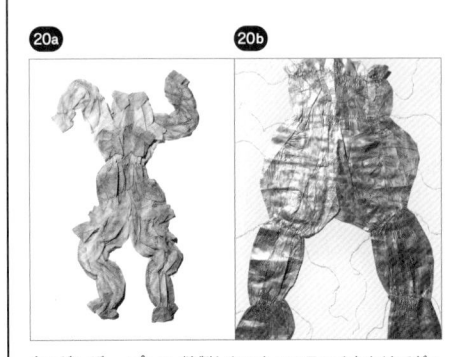

⓴a  ⓴b

左: ギャザー・プレス 縫製したのちにステッチをかけてギャザーを寄せ、プレス機でフラットに仕上げたジャンプスーツ。PE:100% 展覧会出展用制作/1996
右: パピエ・ド・ボンボン メタリック・オーガンジーのギャザー・プレスしたパンツ。PE:100% 1991/1992 春夏

**Left: GATHER PRESS** A jumpsuit, first cut and sewn, then stitched and gathered. Flattened by pressing. PE: 100% made for a exhibition display/1996
**Right: PAPIER DE BONBON** Metalic organdy pants, first cut and sewn into its shape, then stitched, gathered and then pressed. PE:100% 1991/SS 1992

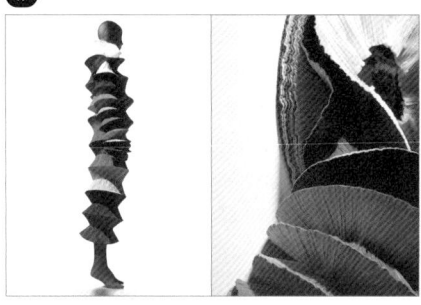

⓱

左右: フライング・ソーサー 身頃と袖の3つの筒を縦方向にプリーツをかけた後、ジグザグにたたむことで生まれたドレス。右: アコーディオン状に折りたたまれたドレス。PE:100% 1993/1994 春夏

**Both pages: FLYING SAUCER** A dress created by pleating three different-sized cylinders lengthwise for the body and sleeves; and then these sections were folded again, but in a zig-zag pattern. Right: A pleated dress that folds flat when not in use due to accordion pleating. PE:100% 1993/ SS 1994

⓲

ツイスト 直線的なマシーン・プリーツに対して手作業による、よりヒューマンなツイスト。二人がかりで服の端からねじりきる。それを釜にいれて熱加工でシワを定着させている。PE:100% プリーツ帽は紙。いずれも1991/1992 春夏

**TWIST** "Twist" added the human touch to straight-line machine pleats. Two people twist the ends of the clothing. It is then put into a vat and heat-treated to affix the wrinkles. PE:100% Pleated paper hat 1991/SS 1992

⓯a – ⓯u

仮想オリンピック バルセロナ・オリンピックに参加したリトアニア選手団の公式ユニフォーム。国旗、国名をアップリケした後プリーツ加工で仕上げたジャケット。1991年にソヴィエト連邦から独立後、単独国家として64年ぶりにオリンピックに参加した。三宅宛に一通の手紙が届き、石津謙介氏のアドバイスを受けながら、スポーツメーカーのミズノ、東レ (素材)、白石ポリテックス工業 (プリーツ加工) の協力をえて実現させた。この制作を発展させ、ISSEY MIYAKE MEN (1992/1993 春夏) で10カ国を発表。本展のために、新たに10カ国を制作し、日本のユニフォームはデザインを一新している。PE:100%
リトアニア、アメリカ、イギリス、イタリア、ギリシャ、スイス、スペイン、中国、ドイツ、フランス、1992/1993 春夏 ISSEY MIYAKE MEN。インド、エチオピア、オランダ、韓国、ケニア、ジャマイカ、日本、フィンランド、ブラジル、南アフリカ、ロシア 2016 パンツ PE:100% HOMME PLISSÉ ISSEY MIYAKE、シューズ 2015/2016 春夏 ISSEY MIYAKE MEN

**VIRTUAL OLYMPIC** The official uniform of the Lithuanian Team at the Barcelona Olympics. The jackets were finished with pleating after appliqueing the flag and country name. Lithuania gained its independence from the Soviet Union in 1991, and it was the first time in 64 years that it had participated in the Olympics as an independent state. The uniform came about because of a single letter addressed to Miyake. Kensuke Ishizu served as an advisor; and Miyake also collaborated with sporting goods manufacturer Mizuno, materials manufacturer Toray Industries, and pleat processor Polytex. The work was later developed and expanded for the ISSEY MIYAKE MEN 1993 Spring-Summer Paris Collection with 10 countries' flags. For this exhibition, Miyake has created uniforms for 10 additional countries and redesigned the Japanese uniform. PE:100% the United States, the United Kingdom, Italy, Greece, Switzerland, Spain, China, Germany, France, Lithuania 1992/SS 1993 "ISSEY MIYAKE MEN," India, Ethiopia, the Netherlands, Korea, Kenya, Jamaica, Japan, Finland, Brazil, South Africa, Russia 2016 The pants:PE:100% 2016 HOMME PLISSÉ ISSEY MIYAKE, Shoes:ISSEY MIYAKE MEN 2015/SS 2016

右: プリーツ・マシーン ランダムなプリーツを刻む。一点一点、丁寧に上下の紙の間に置かれた服は、人とマシーンとの息のあったコラボレーションでプリーツがかかり完成していく。

**Right: PLEATING MACHINE** This machine applies random pleats. Garments are pleated one at a time, carefully sandwiched between two layers of paper. Human operators control the process. The clothing on top of the paper becomes a collaboration between man and machine.

㉑b

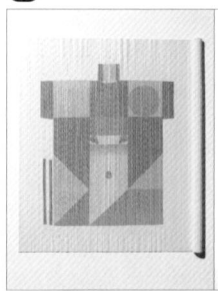

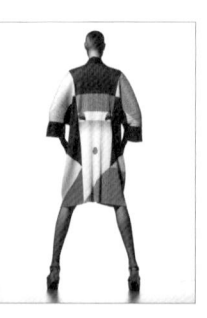

左右: NIHON BUYO グラフィック・デザイナー田中一光 (1930-2002) によるデザインをモティーフに制作されたシリーズの初回の作品から。モティーフにしたのはポスター《Nihon Buyo》(1981年)。オリジナル作品のサイズや色を忠実に再現するために、広幅の布地を特別に用意し制作されたコート。左は、プリーツがかかりマシーンから出されたままの状態。PE:100% 2015 IKKO TANAKA ISSEY MIYAKE

Both pages: **NIHON BUYO** From the first series made the poster *Nihon Buyo*,1981,Japanese dance designed by graphic designer Ikko Tanaka (1930-2002). Using a wide fabric that was specially made to be able to faithfully reproduce the size and coloring of Tanaka's original graphic. On the left is the pleated coat coming out of the machine. PE:100% 2015 IKKO TANAKA ISSEY MIYAKE

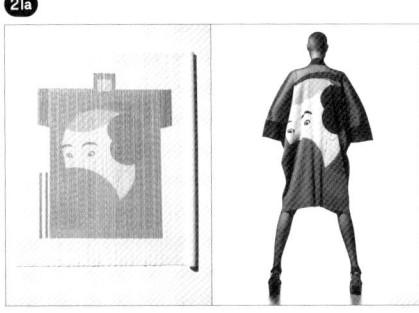

**㉑a**

左右: **SHARAKU** 田中一光によるデザインをモティーフに制作されたシリーズから。モティーフは、《写楽二百年》(1995年)。服についての説明は前ページに同じ。IKKO TANAKA ISSEY MIYAKE

Both pages: **SHARAKU** From the first series of IKKO TANAKA ISSEY MIYAKE, made from the motif, titled *The 200th anniversary of Sharaku*,1995, designed by Ikko Tanaka. Sharaku was a wood block print artist. The explanation of the clothing is the same as the previous page. IKKO TANAKA ISSEY MIYAKE

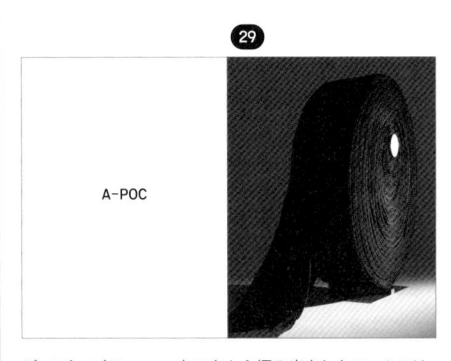

**㉙**

ジャスト・ビフォー 一本の糸から編み出されたロールには、すでに服が連続して編みこまれている。切り取り線にそってハサミをいれて完成した一着を切り取る。ほとんど無駄にする編み地がない環境にも優しい服づくりである。N:90%, PE:10% 1997/1998 春夏

**JUST BEFORE** The large roll contains dresses knitted sequentially, from a single thread.The dress can be extracted by cutting along lines of demarcation. There is almost no wasted cloth with this environmentally friendly process. N:90%, PE:10% 1997/SS 1998

**㉙**

ジャスト・ビフォー 数体ずつ間隔をあけて、マネキンに着け付けている。A-POCと命名される以前に、「誕生の一歩手前」「出来上がりの寸前」というネーミングで、一本の糸からのものづくりが発表された。N:90%, PE:10% 1997/1998 春夏

**JUST BEFORE** The photograph shows the dresses on mannequins spaced at intervals. Prior to the A-POC naming, "JUST BEFORE"—the name meaning just before finalized. N:90%, PE:10% 1997/SS 1998

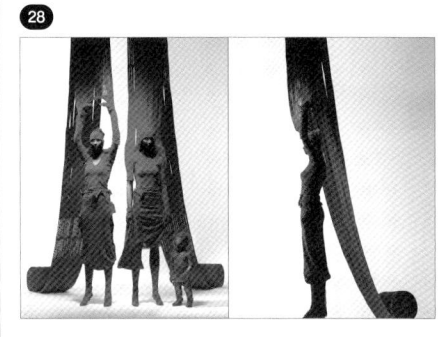

**㉘**

左右: **A-POC キング&クイーン** 服、帽子、バッグなどのかたちがコンピュータ・プログラミングによって、チューブ状の布の中に編み込まれたニット。編み地を変化させたガイドラインにそってハサミを入れてそれぞれを切り出す。1人分が約4メートルずつ連続して編み出される。1998/1999 春夏 A-POC エンジェル(ベイビー用): ドレス、帽子、靴下、手袋。2000 C:55%, N:42%, PU:3%

Both pages: **A-POC KING & QUEEN** Fully finished pieces: a shirt, skirt, hat, bag, and socks are digitally knitted into a tube. They can be extruded by cutting along the lines of demarcation. The tube is knitted continuously with sets appearing approximately every four meters. 1998/SS1999 A-POC ANGEL for baby, dress, cap, socks, and gloves. 2000 C:55%, N:42%, PU:3%

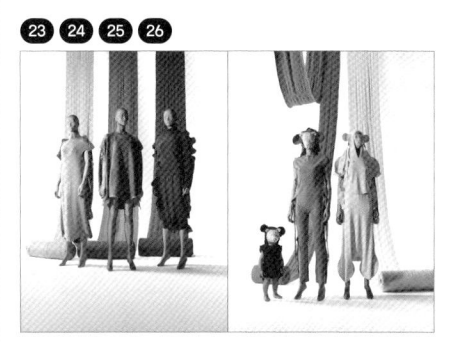

**㉓ ㉔ ㉕ ㉖**

左右: **ズー・シリーズ** 左ページから、《タートル》(縦)、《タートル》(横)、《オクトパス》、《キッズ・ベア》、《ベア》、《モンキー》。W:55%, N:43%, PU:2%《キッズ・ベア》、《ベア》はC:55%, N:42%, PU:3% 2001/2001 秋冬 A-POC
関口光太郎《動物マスク》2016年 素材: 新聞紙、ガムテープ

Both pages: **ZOO Series** From the left page: TURTLE (worn lengthwise), TURTLE (worn widthwise) OCTOPUS, KIDS BEAR, BEAR and MONKEY. W:55%, N:43%, PU:2%, except KIDS BEAR and BEAR C:55%, N:42%, PU:3% 2001/AW 2001 A-POC Koutaro Sekiguchi, *Animal Masks*, 2016 Material: newspaper, packing tape

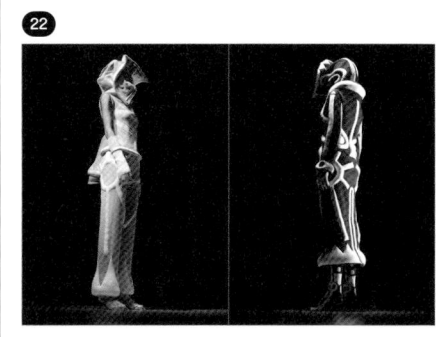

**㉒**

左右: **A-POC フェイス** 服のかたちを編み込みチューブ状のニットが編み出されるプロセスで、袋状になった柄の部分に糸状の綿を注入し、膨らみをだしている。左: トップ、パンツ、フード、バッグ、手袋、靴カバー、右: ドレス、フード、手袋、靴カバー。W:60%, N:40% 1999/1999 秋冬

Both pages: **A-POC FACE** This series was created using the A-POC process. They come out of the machine in a long tube with clothing embedded within, which can be extruded by cutting along lines of demarcation. Some areas are raised by injecting cotton threads into tube-like sections. Left: Top, pants, hood, bag, gloves, and shoes cover. Right: Dress, hood, gloves and shoes cover. W: 60%, N:40% 1999/AW1999

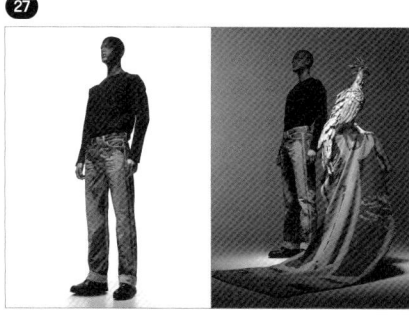

**㉗**

左右: **ジュピター** 履き込んだジーンズの様をジャカード織で表現したパンツ。一体成形の製法で一枚のパネルの中に、ジーンズをつくるために必要なすべてのパーツが柄として織り込まれている。縫製に必要な印や指示も織り込まれているため、プラモデルのようにパーツをカットし印にあわせて縫製するとジーンズを仕立てることができる。C:100% 2006/2006 秋冬 A-POC Tシャツ・シューズ ISSEY MIYAKE MEN 右: 関口光太郎《冒険》(部分)、2016年 素材: 新聞紙、ガムテープ

Both pages: **JUPITER** These pants use Jacquard weaving and are similar to a woven pair of jeans. The woven process of A-POC is similar to the knitted but here, the individual components of each garment lie within the woven panel and must be extruded by cutting along lines of demarcation and then sewn together. The final result is a pair of jeans. The sewing instructions and pattern parts are also built into the fabric much like a kit. C:100% 2006/AW 2006 A-POC, Right: Koutaro Sekiguchi, *Adventure* (part), 2016 Material: newspaper, packing tape

**No.10** 平面に折りたたまれたNo.10のスカート。たたんだ状態の表面を箔プリントで仕上げている。PE:100% 2010/vol.1-2, 2011 132 5. ISSEY MIYAKE

**No.10** The skirt folded flat. The surface that is visible when the skirt is folded has a foil print. PE:100% 2010/vol.1-2, 2011 132 5. ISSEY MIYAKE

List of Works

241

**54a**

左右: **No.1** アルゴリズムのプログラミングを使用した10の基本造形のうち最初に完成したデザイン。平面に折りたたんだ表面に施した箔プリントは、装飾であると同時に、折りたたむときのガイドにもなる。螺旋状に立ち上げるとドレスになる正方形と、同じかたちをふたつつなげたジャケット。右: フラットにたたまれた、ジャケット（上）、ドレス（下）。PE:100% 2010/vol.1-2, 2011 132 5. ISSEY MIYAKE

Both pages: **No.1** This was the first design completed from the ten original shapes of 132 5. ISSEY MIYAKE used to program with the algorithm. The foil print is both a decorative touch and a folding guide. The flat square becomes a dress, when unfolded spiraling upward, and the two connected square becomes a jacket. PE:100% 2010/vol.1-2, 2011 132 5. ISSEY MIYAKE

**54d 54e**

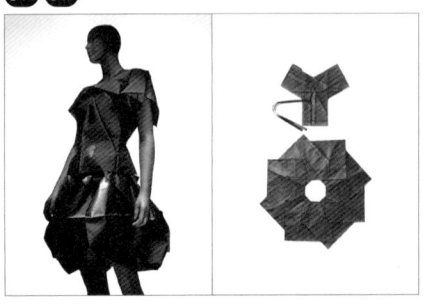

左右: **No.2 と No.6** No.2 のシャツ（右ページ上）と No.6 のスカート（右ページ下）。PE:100% 2010/vol.1-2, 2011 132 5. ISSEY MIYAKE

Both pages: **No.2 and No.6** The No.2 shirt (above on the right page) and No.6 skirt (below on the right page). PE:100% 2010/vol.1-2, 2011 132 5. ISSEY MIYAKE

**54c**

左右: **No.7** 同じ構造をもつ No.7 のシャツとパンツ。箔プリントされた面が、着用するといずれも体の脇にくる。右: フラットにたたまれた No.7 のシャツ（上）とパンツ（下）PE:100% 2010/vol.1-2, 2011 132 5. ISSEY MIYAKE

Both pages: **No.7** The shirt and pants have the same structure. In both cases, the surface with the foil print is at the side of the body when worn. Right:Folded No.7, shirt (above), pants (below) PE:100% 2010/vol.1-2, 2011 132 5. ISSEY MIYAKE

**54b**

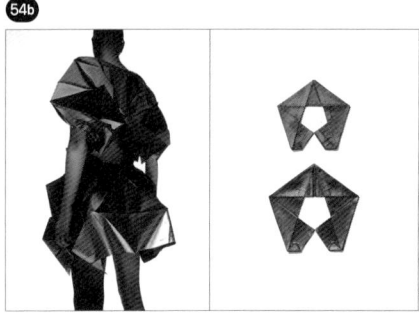

左右: **No. 4** 平面にたたまれた同じ五角形が、切り込み線の位置によって、シャツにもスカートにも応用される構造をもつ。右: フラットにたたまれた、No.4 のシャツ（上）とスカート（下）。PE:100% 2010/vol.1-2, 2011 132 5. ISSEY MIYAKE

Both pages: **No.4** The structure enables the same pentagonal shape when folded flat to become either a shirt or a skirt when worn, depending on where the cuts were made in the fabric. Right:Folded No.4, shirt (above), skirt (below) PE:100% 2010/vol.1-2, 2011 132 5. ISSEY MIYAKE

**54f 54g**

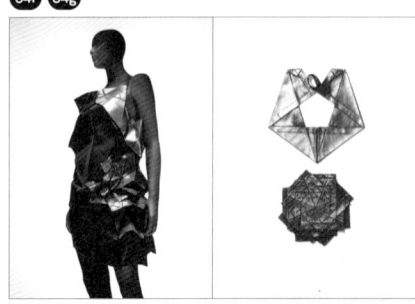

左右: **No.4 と No.10** No.4 のトップと No.10 のスカート。ストラップをつけることで、前出の No.4 とは異なるシャツが生まれた。右: フラットにたたまれた No.4 シャツ（上）、No.10 のスカート（下）。PE:100% 2010/vol.1-2, 2011 132 5. ISSEY MIYAKE

Both pages: **No.4 and No.10** The No.4 top (above on the right) and No.10 skirt (below on the right ). Adding a strap creates a different shirt from the No. 4 shown previously. PE:100% 2010/vol.1-2, 2011 132 5. ISSEY MIYAKE

**53**

左右: **IKKO シリーズ** 田中一光が手がけたポスターにみられる色彩や表現に使われた技法をモチーフに制作。日本の伝統的な染色技法である板締めや、色の境目に歪みやにじみを残して仕上げる転写プリントで表現している。PE:100% 2012/vol.3-4, 2012 132 5. ISSEY MIYAKE

Both pages: **IKKO Series** It is based on motifs derived from the coloring and expressive techniques that Ikko Tanaka used in the posters he created. You can see in them the traditional Japanese dyeing technique of *itajime*, that creates patterns by pressing objects between boards, and transfer printing. PE:100% 2012/vol.3-4, 2012 132 5. ISSEY MIYAKE

**55b**

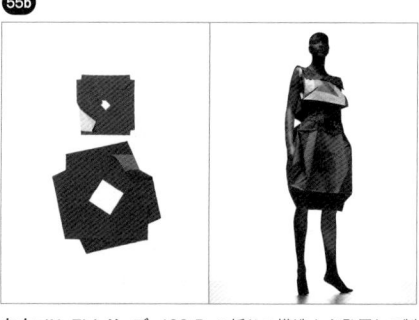

左右: **IN-EI シリーズ** 132 5. の折りの構造から発展して制作された照明器具、陰影 IN-EI ISSEY MIYAKE の折りのパターンと特徴を衣服に展開させている。折りたたんだ上から転写プリントを施すことで、「IN-EI」の折り構造がつくり出す光と影を表現している。《HAKOFUGU》をベースとしたシャツとスカート。左: フラットにたたまれたシャツ（上）、パンツ（下）。PE:100% 2013/vol.3-4, 2013 132 5. ISSEY MIYAKE

Both pages: **IN-EI Series** The folding structures created by 132 5. were used to create lighting fixtures; and then the folding patterns and characteristics from the IN-EI ISSEY MIYAKE line of lamps in turn inspired additional clothing designs. The folded material was transfer-printed to bring out the light and shadow created by the "IN-EI" folds. A shirt and skirt based on the HAKOFUGU. Left: Folded shirt(above) and pants(below). PE:100% 2013/vol.3-4, 2013 132 5. ISSEY MIYAKE

**55a**

左右: **IN-EI シリーズ**《FUKUROU》のシャツとパンツ。右: フラットにたたまれたシャツ（上）、パンツ（下）PE:100% 2013/vol.3-4, 2013 132 5. ISSEY MIYAKE

Both pages: **IN-EI Series** The FUKUROU shirt and pants. Right: Folded shirt (above) and pants (below). PE:100% 2013/vol.3-4, 2013 132 5. ISSEY MIYAKE

**55c**

左右: **IN-EI シリーズ**《MENDORI》のドレス。右: フラットにたたまれたドレス。PE:100% 2013/vol.3-4, 2013 132 5. ISSEY MIYAKE

Both pages: **IN-EI Series** The MENDORI dress. Right: Folded dress. PE:100% 2013/vol.3-4, 2013 132 5. ISSEY MIYAKE

**49**

左右: サーキュラー　円形を重ね、つなげ、足して構成された肩ストラップのドレス。右：フラットにたたまれたドレス。PE:100% 2014/vol.1-2, 2015 132 5. ISSEY MIYAKE

**Both pages: CIRCULAR** The shoulder straps on the dress are created by layering and connecting circular shapes. Right: Folded dress. PE:100% 2014/vol.1-2, 2015 132 5. ISSEY MIYAKE

**52**

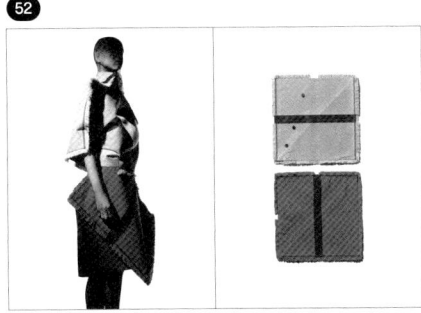

左右: スクエア・ウール　布に織り込まれた四角形をカットし、組み合わせてつくられたシャツとスカート。素材は、太番手のアクリルウール糸をつかい、カットしたときに周囲がフリンジになるよう四角形を升目状に織り込んだジャカード。AR:43%, PE:39%, W:18% 2015/vol.3-4, 2015 132 5. ISSEY MIYAKE

**Both pages: SQAURE WOOL** The shirt and skirt are created by cutting the rectangle and combining the pieces. The woven textile with course acryl wool thread used to create a rectangular shape that becomes fringed when cut. AR:43%, PE:39%, W:18% 2015/vol.3-4, 2015 132 5. ISSEY MIYAKE

**52**

左右: スクエア・ウール　ジャケットとパンツ。解説は前ページに同じ。AR:43%, PE:39%, W:18% 2015/vol.3-4, 2015 132 5. ISSEY MIYAKE

**Both pages: SQAURE WOOL** Jacket and Pants. Explanation the same as the previous page. AR:43%, PE:39%, W:18% 2015/vol.3-4, 2015 132 5. ISSEY MIYAKE

**48**

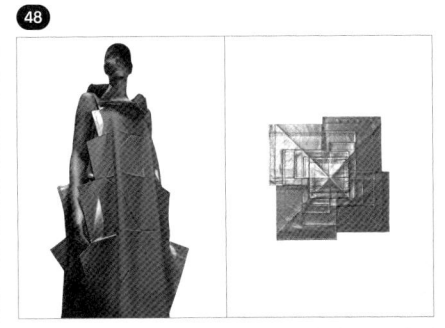

左右: No.13 フォイル　裾から順にサイズを変えた四角形を重ねて構成されたドレス。螺旋状に立ち上げると階段状のエッジのドレスになる。右:フラットにたたまれたドレス。PE:100% 2015/vol.3-4, 2015 132 5. ISSEY MIYAKE

**Both pages: No.13 FOIL** Dress created by putting different sizes of square folds one on top of the other, starting from the hemline. When spreading the dress in a circular motion, the dress takes on the appearance of the edges of a staircase. Right: Folded dress. PE:100% 2015/vol.3-4, 2015 132 5. ISSEY MIYAKE

**48**

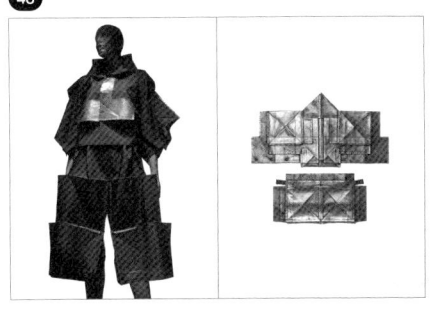

左右:No.13 フォイル　四角形で構成されたジャケットとパンツ。右：フラットにたたまれたジャケットとパンツ。PE:100% 2015/vol.3-4, 2015 132 5. ISSEY MIYAKE

**Both pages: No.13 FOIL** The rectangular structure to create a jacket and pants. Right: Folded jacket (above) and pants (below). PE:100% 2015/vol.3-4, 2015 132 5. ISSEY MIYAKE

**50**

左右: レクタングル　コンパクトにたためる構造を持つ、長方形で構成されたシリーズ。服を組みあわせると正方形になる。素材はストライプを織りだした再生素材と綿の交織に、さらに転写プリントでストライプを施している。右：たたまれた服を組み合わせた四角形／時計回りに、右上：ジャンプスーツ、中上：シャツ、中下: ボレロ、下：スカート、左：ドレス PE:92%, C:8% 2015/vol.3-4, 2015 132 5. ISSEY MIYAKE

**Both pages: RECTANGLE** The rectangular series is structured for compact folding. When folded, the clothing can be combined to create squares. Recycled material and cotton are alternated to create a striped pattern, with a transfer printing applied over the stripes. Right: The clothing folded into a square: On top, a brown jumpsuit with a shirt below it. left: a dress; on the bottom; a skirt with a bolero above it. PE:92%, C:8% 2015/vol.3-4, 2015 132 5. ISSEY MIYAKE

**56**

左右: 陰翳 IN-EI ISSEY MIYAKE 《HAKOFUGU》《FUKUROU》《MINOMUSHI sospensione》《TATSUNO-OTOSHIGO》《KATATSUMURI》のペンダントタイプ。素材はペットボトルからつくられる再生繊維 100％の不織布。2012

**Both pages: IN-EI ISSEY MIYAKE** The pendant type includes HAKOFUGU, FUKUROU, MINOMUSHI sospensione, and TATSUNOOTOSHIGO, KATATSUMURI. As material, non-woven fabric made entirely from recycled PET bottles. 2012

**56**　**56**

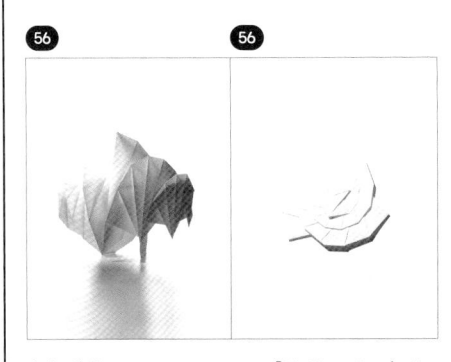

左右: 陰翳 IN-EI ISSEY MIYAKE 「IN-EI」シリーズのドレスに展開されている照明器具《MENDORI》。素材はペットボトルからつくられる再生繊維100％の不織布。2012

**Both pages: IN-EI ISSEY MIYAKE** The lighting fixture, pendant type included MENDORI applies its shape and structure to clothing. As material, non-woven fabric made entirely from recycled PET bottles. 2012

## MIYAKE ISSEY 展：三宅一生の仕事

| | |
|---|---|
| 総合ディレクション | 三宅一生／青木保（国立新美術館長） |
| プロデュース／クリエイティヴ・ディレクション | 北村みどり |
| キュレーター | 本橋弥生（国立新美術館主任研究員） |
| キュラトリアル・アシスタント | 日比野民蓉（国立新美術館研究補佐員）<br>西美弥子（国立新美術館研究補佐員） |
| アート・ディレクション | 佐藤卓 |
| 「グリッド・ボディ」インスタレーション | 吉岡徳仁 |
| 映像／音楽インスタレーション | 中村勇吾、Cornelius |
| グラフィック・デザイン | 野間真吾（佐藤卓デザイン事務所） |
| 照明デザイン | 海藤春樹 |
| 映像 | 高木由利子<br>中島信也<br>山中有（ブルードキュメンタリー）<br>パスカル・ルラン |
| A-POC コラボレーション作品制作 | 関口光太郎 |
| 展示 | 国立新美術館<br>株式会社 三宅デザイン事務所<br>公益財団法人 三宅一生デザイン文化財団<br>株式会社 イッセイ ミヤケ |

## MIYAKE ISSEY EXHIBITION: The Work of Miyake Issey

| | |
|---|---|
| General Direction | Issey Miyake, Tamotsu Aoki (Director General, The National Art Center, Tokyo) |
| Produce and Creative Direction | Midori Kitamura |
| Curator | Yayoi Motohashi (Curator, The National Art Center, Tokyo) |
| Curatorial Assistants | Miyon Hibino (Assistant Curator, The National Art Center, Tokyo)<br>Miyako Nishi (Assistant Curator, The National Art Center, Tokyo) |
| Art Direction | Taku Satoh |
| Grid Bodies Installation | Tokujin Yoshioka |
| Motion Graphic / Music Installation | Yugo Nakamura, Cornelius |
| Graphic Design | Shingo Noma (Taku Satoh Design Office Inc.) |
| Lighting design | Haruki Kaito |
| Video work | Shinya Nakajima<br>Pascal Roulin<br>Yuriko Takagi<br>Yu Yamanaka (BLUE DOCUMENTARY Inc.) |
| Collaboration with A-POC | Koutaro Sekiguchi |
| Installation | The National Art Center, Tokyo<br>Miyake Design Studio<br>The Miyake Issey Foundation<br>Issey Miyake Inc. |

MIYAKE ISSEY展: 三宅一生の仕事
展覧会カタログ

| | |
|---|---|
| 監修 | 三宅一生／青木保（国立新美術館長） |
| 企画 | 北村みどり |
| 編集 | 国立新美術館／公益財団法人 三宅一生デザイン文化財団／<br>株式会社 求龍堂 |
| アート・ディレクション | 佐藤卓 |
| 撮影 | 岩崎寛 |
| デザイン | 野間真吾（佐藤卓デザイン事務所） |
| 序文 | 青木保 |
| テキスト | 三宅一生 |
| | 本橋弥生（国立新美術館主任研究員） |
| | リー・エデルコート（トレンド・フォーキャスター）<br>ディディエ・グランバック（フランス国立近代美術館友の会会長、<br>　フランス・プレタポルテ連盟名誉会長、オートクチュール組合名誉会長）<br>小林康夫（哲学者）<br>蔡國強（美術家）<br>ティエン（クリエイティヴ・ディレクター、フォトグラファー）<br>アンジェロ・フラッカヴェント（インディペンデント・ファッション評論家、キュレーター）<br>森山明子（デザイン・ジャーナリスト、武蔵野美術大学教授） |
| 翻訳 | 木幡和枝／横田佳世子／アルトゥーロ・シルヴァ<br>中安真理<br>株式会社ブリッジ<br>山本知子（株式会社リベル） |

MIYAKE ISSEY EXHIBITION:
The Work of Miyake Issey Exhibition
Catalogue

| | |
|---|---|
| Directors | Issey Miyake,<br>Tamotsu Aoki（Director General, The National Art Center, Tokyo） |
| Producer | Midori Kitamura |
| Editorial Board | The National Art Center, Tokyo, The Miyake Issey Foundation,<br>Kyuryudo Art Publishing Co.,Ltd. |
| Art Director | Taku Satoh |
| Photographer | Hiroshi Iwasaki |
| Designer | Shingo Noma（Taku Satoh Design Office Inc.） |
| Forewords | Tamotsu Aoki |
| Texts | Issey Miyake |
| | Yayoi Motohashi（Curator, The National Art Center, Tokyo） |
| | Cai Guo-Qiang（Artist）<br>Lidewij Edelkoort（Trend Forecaster）<br>Angelo Flaccavento（Independent Fashion Critic, Curator）<br>Didier Grumbach（President of the Société des Amis du Musée national d'Art Moderne<br>　Centre Pompidou, Honorary President of Fédération Française de la Couture,<br>　Chambre Syndicale de la Haute Couture）<br>Yasuo Kobayashi（Philosopher）<br>Akiko Moriyama（Design Journalist, Professor at Musashino Art University）<br>TYEN（Creative Director, Photographer） |
| Translators | Kazue Kobata, Kayoko Yokota, Arturo Silva<br>Mari Nakayasu<br>bridge corporation<br>Tomoko Yamamoto（LIBER Ltd.） |

— 謝辞

本展覧会の開催にあたり、下記の関係諸機関、個人の方々に、
様々なかたちでご協力いただきました。
ここに記して深い感謝の意を表します。(敬称略・順不同)

前田 喜美子

森山 明子


— スペシャルサンクス

アーヴィング・ペン財団
アイティーエル
アマナ
ヴィトラ株式会社
株式会社 エスティファイブ
佐藤卓デザイン事務所
株式会社 三協
ソニー株式会社
tha ltd.
東北新社 Suudonn
トニー
pH スタジオ
株式会社 プリズム
吉岡徳仁デザイン事務所
株式会社 ライズ
ルフトツーク
株式会社 ワイ・イー・ブイ

五十嵐 瑠衣
市村 隼人
井上 みち子
内橋 和久
宇戸 浩二
遠藤 豊
岡野 令
梶内 昌史
金丸 義勝
榊原 敏
田村 孝史
野中 智司
樋口 佳克
宇禄
ピーター・バラカン
深沢 明
マーカス・トムリンソン
松村 真美子
三浦 節子
森 俊文
山田 遊
山崎 理恵子
吉田 悠

— Acknowledgements

We would like to express our deep appreciation to the following
institutions and individuals who have provided generous support
and cooperation for this exhibition.

Kimiko Maeda

Akiko Moriyama


— SPECIAL THANKS

The Irving Penn Foundation
ITL Corporation
amana inc.
Vitra Co.,Ltd.
ST FIVE CORP.
Taku Satoh Design Office Inc.
Sankyo Co.,Ltd.
Sony Corporation
tha ltd.
TOHOKUSHINSHA FILM CORPORATION, Suudonn
TONY Co.,Ltd
pH Studio Inc.
Prism Co.,Ltd.
TOKUJIN YOSHIOKA INC.
RISE Co.,Ltd.
Luftzug Co.,Ltd.
Yen electron Volt Co.,Ltd.

Lui Igarashi
Hayato Ichimura
Michiko Inoue
Kazuhisa Uchihashi
Koji Udo
Yutaka Endo
Satoshi Okano
Masashi Kajiuchi
Yoshikatsu Kanemaru
Satoshi Sakakibara
Takafumi Tamura
Satoshi Nonaka
Yoshikatsu Higuchi
Uroku
Peter Barakan
Akira Fukazawa
Marcus Tomlinson
Mamiko Matsumura
Setsuko Miura
Toshifumi Mori
Yu Yamada
Rieko Yamazaki
Haruka Yoshida

MIYAKE ISSEY展：
三宅一生の仕事

| 監修 | 三宅一生／青木保（国立新美術館長） |
|---|---|
| 企画 | 北村みどり |
| 編集 | 国立新美術館、公益財団法人 三宅一生デザイン文化財団、株式会社 求龍堂 |
| アート・ディレクション | 佐藤卓 |
| 撮影 | 岩崎寛 |
| デザイン | 野間真吾（佐藤卓デザイン事務所） |
| 発行日 | 2016年3月30日／初版 第1刷発行 |
| | 2016年4月22日／第2版 第1刷発行 |
| 発行者 | 足立欣也 |
| 発行所 | 株式会社 求龍堂 |
| | 〒102-0094 東京都千代田区紀尾井町 3-23 文藝春秋新館1階 |
| | 電話：03-3239-3381  Fax：03-3239-3376 |
| | http://www.kyuryudo.co.jp |
| 印刷製本 | 岡村印刷工業株式会社 |

本書は展覧会「MIYAKE ISSEY展：三宅一生の仕事」の公式カタログ兼書籍として刊行しました。
出品作品は、事情により変更になることがあります。
無断で本書の全体または一部の複写・複製を禁じます。


MIYAKE ISSEY EXHIBITION:
The Work of Miyake Issey

| Director | Issey Miyake, Tamotsu Aoki (Director General, The National Art Center, Tokyo) |
|---|---|
| Producer | Midori Kitamura |
| Editorial Board | The National Art Center, Tokyo, The Miyake Issey Foundation, Kyuryudo Art Publishing Co.,Ltd. |
| Art Director | Taku Satoh |
| Photographer | Hiroshi Iwasaki |
| Designer | Shingo Noma (Taku Satoh Design Office Inc.) |
| Date of Issue | First published in Japan, March 30, 2016 |
| | Second published in Japan, April 22, 2016 |
| Publisher | Kinya Adachi |
| Published by | Kyuryudo Art Publishing Co.,Ltd. |
| | Bungeishunju Shinkan bldg.1F, |
| | 3-23, Kioi-cho, Chiyoda-ku, Tokyo 1020094, Japan |
| | Phone: +81-3-3239-3381 Fax: +81-3-3239-3376 |
| | http://www.kyuryudo.co.jp |
| Printed and bound by | Okamura Printing Industries Co.,Ltd. |

This volume was published as the official catalogue of
the MIYAKE ISSEY EXHIBITION: The Work of Miyake Issey.
Works in the exhibition are subject to change due to unavoidable circumstances.
All rights reserved. No part of the contents of this book may be reproduced
without the permission of The National Art Center, Tokyo, The Miyake Issey Foundation,
Miyake Design Studio and the publisher.

Printed in Japan


©2016 The National Art Center, Tokyo, The Miyake Issey Foundation, Miyake Design Studio, Hiroshi Iwasaki
ISBN978-4-7630-1601-0 C0072